Principles and Practice of Management in the Hospitality Industry

Principles and Practice of Management in the Hospitality Industry

James R. Keiser
THE PENNSYLVANIA STATE UNIVERSITY

A CBI Book
Published by Van Nostrand Reinhold Company

A CBI Book
(CBI is an imprint of Van Nostrand Reinhold Company)

Copyright © 1979 by Van Nostrand Reinhold Company Inc.
Library of Congress Catalog Card Number 80-12866

ISBN 0-8436-2182-6

Published by Van Nostrand Reinhold Company Inc.
135 West 50th Street
New York, New York 10020

Van Nostrand Reinhold Company Limited
Molly Millars Lane
Wokingham, Berkshire RG11 2PY, England

Van Nostrand Reinhold
480 LaTrobe Street
Melbourne, Victoria 3000, Australia

Macmillan of Canada
Division of Gage Publishing Limited
164 Commander Boulevard
Agincourt, Ontario M1S 3C7, Canada

16 15 14 13 12 11 10 9 8 7 6 5 4 3

Library of Congress Cataloging in Publication Data

Keiser, James, 1928-
    Principles and practice of management in the
hospitality industry.

    Includes index.
    1. Hotel management.   2. Motel management.
3. Restaurant management.   4. Food service
management.
I. Title.
TX911.3.M27K45   647'.94'068   80-12866
ISBN 0-8436-2182-6

Contents

v

Preface

This book represents twelve years of experience teaching a mangement course for hospitality majors at The Pennsylvania State University. During those years, I never found a text that perfectly suited either my purposes or those of my students. I wanted a text that had strong conceptual underpinnings, yet addressed the needs of hospitality majors—a text, in other words, that combined discussions of management theory and processes with information directly relevant to the hospitality profession. I also sought a text that broached the hospitality "environment," characterized by precepts related to law, labor relations, finance, and marketing.

Of course, many excellent books written specifically for business administration students are on the market, but they tend to be too general and too theoretical for hospitality management students. Moreover, they generally assume and depend upon earlier course work not normally required in a hospitality curriculum. As I made do with these traditional texts, I (and no doubt my students as well) wondered whether the course might not be better taught under the auspices of the Business School. The lack of an appropriate text erased some of the advantages the hospitality management course can and should provide, principal among which is the ability to relate classroom material to the actual industry experience.

Broadly speaking, the basic principles of organization and management pertain to all industries, but their applications can vary considerably. Books for business students tend to concentrate on larger operations. Most hospitality operations, however, are relatively small. The factors encompassed in a feasibility study for a new steel plant, for example, differ substantially from those appropriate in a feasibility study for a new restaurant. Labor-management considerations appropriate to the steelworker hardly duplicate those appropriate to the cook or bartender.

Of course some specialized management and organization texts for the hospitality industry do exist. But they tend to be very elementary and very applied—they tend to adopt the "cookbook approach." In fact, some of them are more like training manuals than textbooks. As the student uses one of these texts, he escapes the conceptual background the general business student may acquire. He may learn one author's approach to some hospitality problem, but he loses the chance to confront management on an intellectual level and formulate alternative approaches and solutions.

Having enumerated the problems associated with teaching hospitality management and with the textbooks generally used in hospitality management courses, I hope that this book solves, or at least lessens, these problems. The book addresses the beginning hospitality student, and it requires no other courses as background. In fact, it is meant to be used in courses that are prerequisites for more advanced managerial courses. Moreover, the material here is applicable equally to students interested in commercial operations, where achieving profit is the main goal, and to students interested in an institutional operation, where providing the best products and services for the resources available is the goal.

Finally, I want those who use this book to note one editorial decision I have made. I have used the third person, singular, masculine pronoun (he, his, him) in its traditional neuter sense. When I say that "a student should profit from his hospitality lessons," I do not mean to imply that only males have a future in hospitality management. In fact, women have made and are making great strides in the profession. I do, however, want to avoid such awkwardness as "a student should profit from his or her hospitality lessons," however fashionable this kind of language may be.

University Park, PA
September, 1979

—James R. Keiser

Acknowledgments

Many of my friends, colleagues, and students have contributed to this book in a number of ways. I risk slighting some of them by undertaking to list any contributions at all. Nevertheless, I feel special obligation to Dr. Phil Becker, Assistant Professor of Fuel Science at Penn State, who criticized my chapter on energy; John Dombroski, Personnel Officer for Penn State's Housing and Food Service operations; and Jim Parker, Hiring Specialist for the Saga Food Service Corporation.

I am also indebted to Dr. Leo M. Renaghan, Professor in Charge of the Food Service and Housing Administration Program at Penn State and an expert in hospitality marketing; to Reed Phalan, Esquire, an attorney and a Professor of Business Law at Penn State; to Sara Clemen Parks, Associate Professor of Dietetics at Penn State; and to H. O. Triebold, Jr., Manager of Penn State's Safety Services.

John Swinton, Instructor and Editorial Specialist in Penn State's Food Service and Housing Administration Program, helped supervise the preparation of this book.

Most of all, I thank my wife Josephine and my children, who cheerfully suffered the inconveniences inherent in the lengthy preparaton of a book like this one.

1

The Hospitality Service Industries: An Overview

Foodservice Today

Types of Foodservice Operations

Inns, Hotels, and Motels

The overall purpose of this book is to help you explore managerial careers in the hospitality industry. Before considering management functions, techniques, and responsibilities, therefore, you should acquire a knowledge of the nature of the industry (the "environment") to which they apply. A manager in any one area of the hospitality industry should be familiar with the other areas as well. Moreover, a broad knowledge of the industry helps when it comes time to narrow career choices. Consequently, when you finish studying this first chapter, you should be able to

- *discuss briefly the various areas of the hospitality industry*
- *discuss briefly the scope of the hospitality industry and a sampling of the career opportunities it offers*
- *draw an outline of the hospitality management functions and techniques*
- *explain briefly how a knowledge of the various hospitality management functions can help a student narrow and refine career choices*

Foodservice Today

The foodservice industry in America today is immense in size. In 1979 it had 110 billion dollars of business for meals away from home and was, in fact, the third largest industry in the country in terms of gross retail sales. It employs about six million people, and still needs many additional employees every year. Various projections indicate great growth for the industry. Instead of the approximately one in three meals currently consumed away from home, this may increase to one out of two meals outside the home. Eating and drinking places are the largest retail employers in the country. It is projected that in the mid 1980s more food will be consumed away from home than in the home; and by 1987 the industry will employ more people and earn more money than any other segment of the American economy. But this foodservice industry of the future will not be merely an expanded version of the present industry. The foodservice industry has already modified itself many times in its relatively brief history. Today's fast moving society and sophisticated technology present to current operators a challenge unprecedented in the industry's past experience. Foodservice is in the process of changing from a craft or cottage industry to a manufacturing industry. Traditional manufacturing industries have felt the effect of the Industrial Revolution for more than a century, but the foodservice industry has, in many ways, just entered the Industrial Revolution. The scarcity, ineptitude, and cost of labor is, however, pulling the foodservice industry into the classic industrial pattern: the substitution of production line labor for craft labor; and the substitution of capital in the form of high investment and automation for hand labor processes.

For the purpose of analysis, the foodservice industry can be characterized in a number of ways. For example, one basic categorization of the types of operations labels them as either *captive* or *noncaptive*. Captive operations are those in which patrons are more or less forced to eat at the establishment. These include such places as schools, hospitals, institutions, prisons, industrial plants, and colleges. Patrons eat in the noncaptive operation by choice; they might just as easily eat in their homes or in other places of their choosing. The noncaptive operations can be further classified as luxury, convenience, and fast-food operations.

While many of the captive operations are nonprofit and institutional, the noncaptive operations are normally commercial and profit-making. Luxury operations supply far more than ordinary nourishment. They may feature exotic cuisine, entertainment, elaborate decor, deferential service, and other amenities to enhance the dining pleasure. Convenience restaurants may offer a complete foodservice, and they usually stress the food itself rather than the sort of attractions provided by the luxury operations. The fast-food operation typically offers a very limited number of items that can be prepared and served quickly. Likewise its dining room facilities tend to be small and sparse.

By far the largest number of operations are classified as independent restaurants, and they are the traditional backbone of the industry. Independent restaurants are mainly small businesses with average sales considerably under $100,000. Only a tiny percentage of them have more than one hundred employees. In the past, the typical restaurateur was most likely an independent businessman running an individualized establishment. But, beginning with the fast-food and franchise developments of the 1960s, the numbers and the influence of the group or chain operations increased dramatically. Although the entire food industry is flourishing, chains are growing now at twice the rate of independent operations.

Some of the reasons for this growth include the increasing complexity of food operations, which makes it difficult for an individual to be knowledgeable in all the areas. At one time a chef could open an operation and be successful on the strength of his fine food alone. Unfortunately, so many other factors are now involved that fine food itself does not guarantee success. The chains can provide specialized expertise in these various other factors. Chain operations also have other inherent advantages. The more units there are, the more readily these individual units are recognized. Moreover, the pooling of resources can provide promotion on a scale impossible for the individual operator. Savings result from the mass purchasing power of the chains, and their financial resources allow them to weather periods that would ruin an individual operator.

Although it has been prophesied that by the year 2000 up to 75 percent of the total volume of food eaten away from home will be controlled by no more than 50 giant corporations (presently about 40 percent of food-service volume is controlled by 400 large organizations including the military services), there will always be a place for the independent operator. Avoiding the standardization necessary in the chain, he can tailor his operation to local needs and develop local markets. An individual will, however, find it more difficult to start his own operation in the future, and the undertaking will require proportionately more capital and expertise.

To be successful, future operations will have to follow more of a designed and integrated system rather than a collection of components working randomly together, which is typical of most of today's foodservices. A list of the basic elements for any business includes: (1) customers, (2) products, (3) distribution, (4) equipment, and (5) personnel. To analyze the foodservice industry of today, let's analyze these elements one by one.

Customers The service industry is the fastest growing segment of the economy, and, with the possible exception of health care, foodservice is probably the fastest growing segment of this industry. A number of reasons account for the greatly increased patronage of foodservice enterprises. First, people have more leisure time and are thus more apt to be away from home or more inclined to eat out. Next, the average American is receiving greater amounts of disposable income and can thus afford to eat out more often. With the increased number of two-wage-earner families, where neither may feel like cooking after a full day's work, there is an even greater motivation to eat out. This benefits the away-from-home foodservice market. The increased number of foodservice establishments both answers and encourages an increase in total patronage.

Another very important factor has been the increased social acceptance of eating out. At one time large elements of the population did not think it proper to eat away from their homes. There was a certain stigma attached to being frivolous enough to spend money dining out. This stigma has now all but disappeared. Younger generations not only accept eating out, but look upon it as the natural state of affairs.

Our present demography (the statistical makeup of our population) also affects the market for food away from home. Younger people are inclined to eat out more than comparable numbers of older people, and this country has, at present, a relatively young population. Wealthier people also tend to eat out more, and there are growing numbers of these people. A high proportion of the population is away at college, and college students constitute a major captive market.

Certain geographic changes also encourage people to eat out. At one time a downtown location in a big city was considered most desirable for a restaurant. Now with the many urban problems in both large and small cities, a suburb or highway location is often more desirable. Shopping centers have become popular foodservice locations. Moreover, Howard Johnson, the "Host of the Highway," and other similar operations have prospered by catering to motorists. Operations also find that past formats do not necessarily attract today's customers. At one time Marriott's stressed carhop service at its Hot Shoppes. Today Marriott's stresses other types of foodservice. Stouffers first made its reputation with downtown restaurants. Today it is busy building other types.

Products The restaurant or foodservice operation really deals with two products—the product that it buys (the raw food) and the product it sells (the processed food together with service and decor). As the term implies, foodservice is in large part service. Part of this service is the preparation and provision of the food, but it also includes the serving of food to the customer as well as providing the decor, and creating an atmosphere of the dining experience. A dining experience is far more than just ingesting food.

At one time, raw food prices were relatively stable—unless some unusual climatic situations occurred raw food was always abundant in season. Lately, however, the cost of the raw foods used by foodservice enterprises has risen tremendously, and there have been supply interruptions, like the 1973 beef shortage. Few foods will ever return to their once low prices. In fact, a general economic boom encourages people to eat more and to seek more desirable foods. This helps to boost raw food prices. Moreover, wealth increases the eating standard, as evidenced by the fact that our beef-per-capita consumption almost doubled between 1950 and 1970. For a time large surpluses of once favored foods tended to hold prices down. But these surpluses have largely been used up and so can no longer restrain farm prices.

The form of the food purchased by foodservice operations has also changed dramatically in recent years. More and more, food is purchased in prepared or semi-prepared states rather than in raw form. These convenience foods (ready foods or fast foods) have many advantages. With some labor already "built into" these foods, less labor is needed on the job. An operation can offer greater variety, since food that would once have been too difficult to prepare can now be bought in convenience form. Convenience foods may also reduce waste because small quantities can be reconstituted to order. And, of course, these convenience foods may ease storage problems and improve cost control.

Some operations employ the assembly-line approach to food preparation by setting up their own mass production facilities rather than buying from purveyors. In the future the issue may not be small batch cooking versus quantity cooking but whether the system is *open* or *closed*. The open cooking system uses convenience foods purchased on the outside, while the restaurant with a closed system makes its own convenience foods. Operations with a number of outlets often set up their own commissaries to service these outlets, thus limiting the preparation at the individual outlet.

Coincident with the growth of convenience foods is a considerable change in standards of taste and acceptability. Soft ice cream has made strong inroads into the traditional ice cream business, and instant coffee has displaced freshly brewed coffee to quite a degree. Soft ice cream and instant coffee may, in fact, become the standards of comparison. Not too long ago most people considered chicken to be a special dish most suitable for the big meal of the week, Sunday dinner. Now, of course, there is nothing special about it. "Soul food" once disdained by much of the population, is now quite fashionable; and there is a noticeable trend toward finger foods that can be readily carried and consumed anywhere.

The public is also becoming more nutrition conscious. Public campaigns seek to limit the consumption of saturated fats—and these campaigns reverberate harshly in the meat and dairy industries. Certain segments of the population prefer organic foods. Articles with titles like "The American Diet is a Disaster" plead with us to change our eating habits. Prepared breakfast cereals are accused in a Senate committee hearing of containing "empty calories." And in response, most of the cereal manufacturers boost the nutritional content of their products.

It appears fairly certain that nutrition will soon be an increasing foodservice concern. Patrons will be ever more conscious of their nutritional needs, and the foodservice operator will have to respond. Unfortunately for many commercial foodservice operators, profitable foods such as fancy desserts are under heavy attack.

Another recent change in foodservice involves the new meal patterns. The customary three-meal pattern has not been the rule throughout history and in all places. But in the United States, the desire for meal variety is really quite recent. In times of short food supplies people often revert to limited food variety and the two-meal day. Even now in some areas people commonly have steak or pie for breakfast and cereal for dinner. Moreover, there appears to be a trend toward eating more food (some say too much), but eating it in smaller, more frequent meals. Coffee breaks and TV snacks are really mini-meals. Some hospitals now disregard the straight three-meal pattern and adopt the four- or five-snack feeding pattern.

These changing patterns can obviously affect the foodservice business. Fast-food restaurants benefit when people come in for an extra snack. But the more conventional operations find some customers complaining about large portions and wasted food, and consequently staying away.

A foodservice operation normally offers two products with its food. One is service and the other is decor or atmosphere. The level of conventional table service has changed—declined—in many areas in recent years, and shortages of well-trained and eager dining room personnel seem evident. Some prophets foresee considerable change in foodservice decor. Instead of merely fine (or appropriate) furnishings, the decor may someday encompass a "total environment." Lighting may be manipulated with different color combinations to engineer various moods. Synthetic aromas may enhance the olfactory senses. Background mood music is already common, but such mood sounds as waterfalls, winds, and rain may soon be added—all to comfort the harried, hassled, food-buying customer.

The distribution process involves moving food from the producer to the consumer. Like most other aspects of foodservice the distribution process has changed drastically. Fast-food operations, especially those featuring self-service, differ considerably from the courtly dining room service of traditional restaurants. Vending machines are another form of food distribution that eliminates dining room personnel. Take-out service is still another. To accommodate changing distribution demands and patterns, companies that formerly operated traditional restaurants are switching to new formats and new styles.

Not only do distribution changes occur within the foodservice industry itself, but there may also be major changes in the total away-from-home eating market. Certainly more people will eat meals prepared outside the home, but no one quite knows who will supply this food. In a relatively short time the deli has become standard in supermarkets; thus the supermarkets are making a serious bid for this away-from-home market. Will restaurants be able to compete with them? And even if people do not eat in the restaurant itself, will they be able to buy their food at the restaurant under a take-out arrangement? For certain, our traditional restaurants must find some better ways to market and service this take-out business. In many families, both the husband and wife work, and they do not relish the job of preparing food at home. The smarter local foodservices are making it easy for these families to secure prepared meals quickly and inexpensively.

Another new area of food distribution involves deliveries to elderly people who find it very difficult to prepare meals for themselves. At present these Meals on Wheels programs are administered largely by public agencies subsidized by public funds. Besides delivering the food, these programs also provide a measure of interest and companionship during the visitation. Commercial operators might find it difficult to supply the companionship, and they may be discouraged by the low economic levels of many of the patrons. But they may soon be contracting to supply the food to the public agency responsible for its distribution. It also seems logical that such existing facilities as school kitchens may be used for these programs. In some of the larger urban areas, food is served to the elderly in the preparation facility, to which the elderly transport themselves. Horn and Hardart have tried to do this in some of their New York operations, providing special inducements for elderly to come, to eat, and to linger for a while. This market is specialized now, but it might offer commercial possibilities in the future.

Off-premise distribution has been greatly aided by advances in hot and cold food packaging. Just as hot and cold vending machines (along with automatic coin changers) made the vending of complete meals feasible so future technological developments will probably offer new methods of food distribution. One method already in use combines the microwave oven and frozen foods. The patron selects food in the frozen state, carries it to a microwave oven (at the table), heats it, and is ready to eat. Adaptations of this approach are already used in some hospitals. The meal comes to the patient floors frozen and is placed in the oven and served only when the patient is ready. A patient can eat when he wants; he is not bound by the tray delivery schedule; and a hot meal is not kept waiting in case he cannot eat when the meal is first prepared.

The most marked change in food distribution has, once again, come more from the chain operations than the traditional restaurants. The chains promote standardization in food types and service from coast to coast (to the dismay of some who feel that eating should be an adventure). But the chains are molding our food tastes. Although they may not serve the same quality of food as the finer restaurants, overall food quality has probably gone up nationwide as chains crowd out the smaller operations, and in some cases the quality is superior.

Equipment   New equipment certainly affects foodservice. For example, in the 1920s commercial toasters made the sandwich shop and luncheonette possible. High-pressure steam cooking equipment introduced in the late 1940s allowed for the frequent preparation of small quantities of fresh vegetables. Fast heat recovery equipment, which came with the 1950s, permitted a kitchen to shut off cooking equipment not in use since it was no longer necessary to wait for the temperature to reach desirable levels. Though marketed as early as 1937, soft ice cream equipment was simplified in the 1950s and started a whole new eating trend.

The 1960s saw newer equipment and an entirely new approach to foodservice—the marriage of food and equipment into one system designed to produce food in the most integrated and efficient means possible. Instead of purchasing disparate pieces of equipment from different manufacturers, the operator could order a complete foodservice system, integrated from storage through waste disposal. Moreover he purchased only the equipment that fit into his system. In other words, the system determined the equipment rather than the equipment determining the system. Although perfectly sensible, this concept was revolutionary at the time and is not yet fully appreciated by the entire industry.

Chains and specialty operations obviously needed equipment to match their menus. Equipment was easily integrated into a system and was designed to increase productivity and reduce labor requirements through automation. The electronic or microwave oven was introduced back in 1943 but found its real home with convenience food operations in the late 1960s and the 1970s. The addition of conveyor machinery to move materials automatically has begun to appear, especially in the dishwashing areas. Great strides, too, have been made in food storage, which can now accommodate foods in all sorts of processing forms. In fact, new storage cabinets can thaw frozen foods and then maintain them in an appropriately refrigerated state.

Computers have, inevitably, entered the food production scene as automatic controls for foodservice equipment. Sensors in the cooking equipment can automatically "decide" when a product is done and remove it without human help. Conveyor-type "cooking streets" will soon replace conventional ovens or ranges. Instead of cooking on griddles, food can pass between heated steel bands that cook it on both sides, rather like a pants presser. Heat lamps now hold food at the proper temperatures. With all this emphasis on automation, the food preparation personnel of the future may resemble mechanics and repairmen more than chefs. Another application of computers has been in electronic cash registers. Besides keeping track of cash, new machines can keep records of item sales, inventories, and labor time, and point out when purchases are necessary. They can be connected to a home office to provide centralized control.

Personnel   In fact, food service is now really more of a labor business than a food business. Still in a "craft state," the business requires a large number of personnel compared to other industries. This presents many problems.

As you probably know, the industry has had a long history of personnel shortages, especially of skilled workers. Many people go into the field at the nonmanagement level when they cannot find work elsewhere. But they tend to view their job as a job of last resort rather than a career—something to do until better work comes along. It is unfortunate that the lower jobs in foodservice have such a stigma attached to them. The working conditions are, after all, better than those in many industrial jobs. And the jobs themselves are far more interesting than mechanized assembly line work.

Types of Foodservice Operations

Being, collectively, a huge industry, foodservice encompasses many different types of operations. Indeed, one of its attractions is that one can usually find an operation suited to one's particular personality and ability. We have already discussed the broadest breakdown of operations: the captive and the noncaptive operations. Captive food services, as you recall, occur in schools and institutions where the patrons can make no choice of an eating site. Noncaptive foodservices are commercial; people eat there voluntarily.

Restaurants   Restaurants constitute by far the largest number of commercial foodservice establishments. There are many different types of restaurants.

A *table service restaurant* is the conventional and traditional operation in which food is served on the premises in the dining room by a waitress or waiter. The atmosphere may be formal and the decor plush, as in exclusive restaurants and fine hotel dining rooms. Other table service restaurants are more simple in their service and decor, in the food they serve, and in the prices they charge.

The *drive-in* may or may not have take-out service. Here the patron may be served in his car or purchase food to eat elsewhere. The drive-in may also offer limited table facilities and limited service, notably the well-known car hop. In fact, a table service restaurant may be combined with a drive-in or take-out facility. The drive-in operation stresses fast service, relatively low prices, and finger foods like hamburgers, fried chicken, or pizza.

A *counter service restaurant* invites the customer to sit at a counter. It may be a snack shop, a luncheonette, a coffee shop, or a sandwich and soda fountain counter. The counter operation, too, may be combined with a table service or a drive-in operation.

Cafeteria and buffet service establishments display the food selection while their guests pick out the items they want, serve themselves, and carry the food to a table. With the increasing difficulty of finding dining room employees and with the rising cost of these employees, cafeteria and buffet service is becoming more popular. Patrons also enjoy collecting their own food this way.

Hotel Foodservice

Almost every major hotel, even today, has its foodservice facility. In fact, early English common law required the hotel to provide food for its patrons. As early as the year 1350 England had a legal statute that constrained *hostelers et herbergers* to sell food at reasonable prices. Before the advent of separate restaurants, the local or inn might be the only place in a community for a traveler to eat.

Today, hotel food operations expect little subsidy from lodging revenues and must operate on their own two feet, making their own profit. But hotel foodservice still differs markedly from other types of foodservices. For example, it often provides a considerable variety of settings. Food may be served in a relatively simple and economical hotel coffeeshop operation or in fancy, luxurious dining rooms serving gourmet food with continental service. Nevertheless, it is usually economical to serve all the operations from one main kitchen—and here is where economy presents certain operational problems

Many hotels do a great deal of luncheon, banquet, and reception business. In many locales, the hotel ballroom is the largest indoor facility available for such functions, and handling this business differs in many respects from routine restaurant operations. The hotel foodservice personnel must be able to cope with large numbers of people gathering at irregular intervals. Hotels that seek out convention business must offer superior service. Convention groups usually want some special, innovative touches to distinguish their affair, and in such cases the hotel food personnel enjoy real opportunities for creativity. Attracting banquet and convention business also requires different sales techniques from those employed by the ordinary restaurant. Much more work must be done to attract entire groups of people.

Since the hotel food operation is also a guest service, it may have to remain open on holidays or weekends or other times when restaurants find it feasible to close. This situation, together with the banquet and convention business hotels attract, may force management to schedule personnel over longer work periods.

Although not all hotels offer top quality foodservice, those that do have the opportunity to be creative and innovative. The volume of foodservice in a large hotel is considerable, and the size of operation offers some advantages as well as opportunities for advancement.

Hospital Foodservice

A most important foodservice centers on hospital patients and staff. Hospitals and their foodservices have had a long history. As early as the sixth century B.C., hospitals included foodservices. Hospital foodservice is unique in that its responsibilities go far beyond providing nourishment to the patients and staff of the hospital. Special diets must be prepared for patients in accordance with dietary prescriptions provided by the physicians. Dietary instruction must be provided not only for the patients but for student nurses, medical students, and interns as well. In fact, as nutrition becomes an increasingly important part of the medical process, the dietitian has become a full-fledged member of the medical team.

The importance of food to the patient beyond mere nourishment is obvious. At best, being hospitalized is an ordeal, and everything that can be done to make it easier should be done, so it helps if the patients enjoy the foodservice. This need has lead to a vastly expanded concept in hospital foodservice. In some institutions the food now equals that of fine restaurants and hotels.

Hospital foodservice normally has two divisions. One is the actual production and service of the food, and the other is the therapeutic aspect of the food. The therapeutic area addresses itself to patients with dietetic problems, to the preparation of the special foods they need, to instruction in how to handle their diets both in the hospital and when they return home, and to nutritional research. Some hospitals maintain outpatient clinics where people can consult with the therapeutic dietitians about dietetic problems.

Like other areas of the profession, hospital foodservice has changed radically in recent years. Upgrading the foodservice with, for example, selective menus is a common practice. New methods of hospital foodservice are designed to bring the food to the patient in the most palatable condition possible. Often these methods include a *total food delivery system* employing new convenience food concepts complete with automated handling. The therapeutic dietitian must also keep up with medical and nutritional developments and apply them to the hospital patients.

The skyrocketing costs of medical care are forcing hospital foodservice personnel to explore the most efficient types of operation so that they can control these costs. The government and other third parties that pay for so much of the hospital care are also demanding greater efficiency from hospital dietary departments (and demanding, as well, complex reports). The dietary department must accommodate large hospitals, thus dietary departments tend to become large organizations. In some areas, unions have organized hospital dietary employees, which adds a new dimension to hospital foodservice management.

A career in hospital foodservice offers a number of advantages. One is the fact that with over 7000 hospitals in the country, opportunities exist in almost every geographical area. Moreover, people who work in hospital foodservice have the satisfaction of helping their fellow man and sharing in the medical atmosphere. Hospitals have all the usual advantages of institutional foodservice plus some others. Generous public or governmental support allows some hospitals to spend more for equipment and facilities than other institutions. The skills of personnel tend to be higher than in many commercial or other institutional operations. And the therapeutic requirements add more variety to hospital foodservice operations than one finds in many other institutions. In addition, the hospital is usually a prestige organization in the community, which may add to the desirability of working there. And finally, hospital foodservice usually attracts service-minded people with outgoing personalities, which may be the best of all reasons for entering the field. Also in the health care foodservice field are institutions such as nursing homes, geriatric facilities, and extended care facilities. With an aging population, there will be increased need for these services in the future.

School Lunch Programs

One of the largest meals-away-from-home projects involves feeding the youngster in our country's primary and secondary schools. School foodservice had its real beginning during the latter half of the nineteenth century when large numbers of poor children began to attend schools. They obviously needed more than just education during the day, and various food programs were evolved to fill that need. The French writer Victor Hugo is given credit for founding school feeding programs in England in the 1860s. Some European countries instituted school feeding programs supposedly to improve the physique of potential military recruits. Also, the growing sense of social responsibility and developments in the field of nutrition contributed to the formation of school lunch programs.

The National School Lunch Act authorizes federal grants to the various states for school lunches. It provides cash reimbursement for a portion of the food costs and provides, as well, for the distribution of food acquired by the Department of Agriculture in price support and surplus removal operations. The act also stipulates that local school authorities not discriminate against any children who qualify for free lunches or lunches at a reduced price. One of the conditions for participation in the National School Lunch Program is the ability to serve a Type A Lunch. The Type A Lunch aims at furnishing at least one-third of the Recommended Daily Dietary Allowances established by the National Research Council for children of various age groups.

Besides providing students with food and nourishment, the school lunch program helps them develop good eating and health habits. It can also provide a social context for developing good manners and courteous behavior. And it affords an opportunity to supplement lessons on health, science, arithmetic, social studies, and consumer education—among other topics. In fact, the program is now recognized as one of the world's best examples of applied nutrition.

Originally the School Lunch Act served only a noon meal. But there has recently been a great incentive for it to go further. The school facilities can be used to provide food for preschoolers in Head-Start Programs and summer meals for children who may otherwise have little nourishment. The facilities may also be used to serve the poor and elderly, and for spreading nutrition education throughout the community. The expanding scope of the programs has encouraged satellite operations in which food is prepared in a central, "mother" kitchen and then sent out to other locations. This procedure obviously involves large-scale preparation and complex problems.

Not all schools that serve meals participate in the National School Lunch Program. Some schools in wealthy areas hold out because of paperwork and the federal restrictions. Others like more freedom than the Type A format permits. Still others object to serving children who cannot pay. But, on balance, school foodservice programs are becoming increasingly popular, and they provide attractive career possibilities. Once the programs were run by nonprofessional homemakers; today their size and complexity require the professionally trained manager.

College and University Foodservice

Although almost all areas of foodservice are in a period of rapid change, college and university feeding is experiencing more change than most. Common practices of a few years ago are unacceptable today, and in planning new facilities, college food administrators try to predict what the role of their foodservices will be in the years to come. College housing and feeding has developed into two systems. One is sometimes called the *German system,* in which the institution assumes responsibility only for academic instruction, providing no housing and no food. By contrast, the *English system,* developed from the early Oxford and Cambridge pattern, makes the university responsible both for academic instruction and for housing and feeding its students. The English system recognizes that a better living environment provides for better intellectual development.

The early American colleges like Harvard and Yale adopted the English system. But the "hands off" German system has also won its adherents. With the end of World War II, the nation's colleges and universities found themselves with drastically increased enrollments. Housing and feeding facilities were rapidly constructed to accommodate these large numbers of students. The facilities usually fell under university control, and administrators discovered that the foodservices could be operated efficiently with meal and dormitory contracts. But in many instances, these contracts led to social restriction and routine menus.

Beginning in the late 1960s students began to complain loudly about some aspects of university foodservice. They wanted, among other things, more variety. They also objected to the fixed meal contract, which required them to eat all their meals in the dining room or lose the value of that meal. (In calculating their food contract rates, the colleges tended to assume that not every student would eat every meal provided under the contract.) The institution found they could provide variety without the fantastic cost increases they had anticipated. The rigid codes of conduct in the college dining room were discarded with the introduction of more casual and informal schedules, and meal hours were expanded. Some institutions found they could lower costs by spreading their foodservice personnel over longer hours. College food managers also began to offer a variety of different food operations to cater to the various tastes of students. They opened snack bars, installed vending machines, and offered other, newer types of dining facilities. Some schools permitted students to keep refrigerators in their rooms, partly to counter the trend among students to rent apartments rather than use the dormitories.

The changes in attitudes toward college foodservices and economic pressures on them have focused more attention on the need for professional foodservice management. No longer can untrained people step in and run the large college food operation. In fact, many colleges and universities contract their foodservice program out to commercial caterers who then take responsibility for providing the food. This practice benefits workers in the field since they may advance through a variety of operations while still working for the same employer. The very size of the various foodservice contractors suggests many high-level management positions.

Airline Foodservice

One of the most challenging and exciting areas of foodservice management is in the sky—providing meals to airline passengers. But there are problems here, too. In fact, not only does airline foodservice have all the usual problems associated with restaurants but also has some unique problems. To begin with, you do not find the familiar three peaks of activity; planes have to be supplied with food at various times during the day, and there may be no time to "catch up." If something is forgotten, the plane cannot land to pick up the missing food or utensils. Many of the ground flight kitchens prepare meals for more than one airline. They sometimes have problems keeping each airline's china and silver separate and meeting the specifications of each. The location of the airports may make commutation difficult and thus create personnel problems. And there may be last minute changes in the number of passengers or flight cancellations, which can complicate foodservice scheduling. Additionally, if food is not ready on time, ground kitchens may have to pay the airline a penalty. And while much of the china and utensils airlines use are disposable, some supplies must be used over again. This occasions the familiar shortage problems. Most foodservice managers have some contact with their customers but not in airline service. And finally, planes fly day and night, weekends and holidays, and the flight kitchens must be continuously ready to serve them.

But these problems can all be conquered. In fact, they *must* be conquered if airlines are to use their flight meals as competitive tools. All airlines use generally the same equipment, their rates are set by a federal authority, and flight personnel are all about equally competent. So one of the few ways an airline can distinguish itself is by the excellence of its cuisine. Therefore, serving of food becomes more than just nourishment; it becomes part of an airline's prestige and part of the flying experience.

Because of the problems involved in feeding 350 people in one airplane in one hour, airline feeding has become one of the most innovative areas of foodservice. Airlines were pioneers in total system feeding and in designing equipment to fit that system. Meal preparation may be done by a subsidiary or division of the airline, or by outside food contractors. At certain airports, the airline may have its own facilities; at others it may employ contractors.

Club Management

Club management encompasses more than running a foodservice, but the foodservice is extremely important to the nation's eighty-five hundred total-facility clubs. These clubs include luncheon-city clubs, country clubs, yachting clubs, women's clubs, fraternal organizations, faculty clubs, and athletic clubs. We have also begun to see an increasing number of social clubs as parts of planned communities designed to supply both recreation and fine dining.

To attract members, a club must generally offer services superior to those available in the regular commercial establishments. It must also offer more personalized service. Although these requirements present certain challenges they can also provide great satisfaction to an energetic club manager. There is great pride in running "the finest foodservice operation in town," a boast many clubs can justifiably make.

Fast-Food Operations

The greatest expansion in the foodservice industry during the past few years has been in the fast-food chains. Although some of the chains began back in the 1950s, their growth really began in the 1960s and was, until 1969, nothing short of spectacular. At that time, however, overbuilding, underfinancing, and poor management led to a violent shake out. Since then, the stronger fast-food chains have improved their competitive position, and they are still growing. In fact, fast food is such a large part of the current foodservice scene that practically our entire chapter on franchising deals with it.

There are a number of reasons for this remarkable growth in the fast food industry. To begin with, fast food is aimed directly at the "youth market" that, because of the postwar baby boom, greatly increased during the 1960s. Second, the standard fast-food operations lend themselves to consolidation into chains and franchising. These chains use modern, effective marketing techniques so that their total promotion effort can be greater than the sum of the individual units. Many large companies have entered the fast-food field, including Borden, General Foods, Green Giant, Heinz, Pillsbury, and General Mills.

Fast-food operations have also been more profitable than other type of commercial foodservice establishments. Their limited menus and limited service formats allow them to keep the two major costs, food and labor, under control. Sales have been higher than for the usual restaurant, profits have been considerably higher, and return on investment has also been favorable. Between 1960 and 1970 the sales of multiunit eating places increased about 150 percent or about twice as fast as the foodservice industry as a whole.

The size of the chains allows for more managerial expertise and refinement of operating methods. The chains usually maintain their own staffs to supervise such matters as construction, finance, and supplies. As we make clear in a later chapter, a franchise in a fast-food company may currently be the most practical way for someone to run his own foodservice operation.

Although fast-food restaurants continue to proliferate, it is doubtful they will ever reach the 1960s rate again. The 1969–1970 shake out removed many of the weaker firms, and it will be harder for newcomers to compete against the entrenched and established firms now occupying strong financial and geographical positions. Of course, food tastes change, and the current favorites—hamburgers, fried chicken, pizza, fish and chips, and inexpensive steak—may not be the food fads of the future. At one time fast-food operations expanded partly because they created new markets and partly because they "took over" from such other operations as diners, lunch wagons, and coffeeshops. Today their market is more fully developed leaving less room for expansion. Instead of competing against old-fashioned, in-town operations, they now compete against each other. Basically each sells the same products—a cheap snack and cleanliness. Thus it becomes difficult for one to achieve a decisive advantage over another. Moreover, the median age of the country is growing older. Even though today's youth may have grown up with the fast-food concept, as they mature they may begin to patronize some other type of foodservice. Instead of finger foods and hasty service, they may want a more complete menu choice, more sophisticated food, and more genteel service.

Industrial Foodservice

During the early Industrial Revolution workers brought their lunch pails to work just as farm workers carried their lunches to the fields. Some early industries provided food for their employees. But the big boost in industrial feeding never really took place in this country until the period that spanned the two World Wars.

During these times, the government paid for many products on a cost-plus basis, reimbursing companies a certain percentage over the cost of production to compensate for normal profit. Foodservice could be one of the costs of production, and the higher the cost of production, the higher the "profit" returned to the company. Moreover, many of the new defense workers were women who were more insistent about having a hot meal while away from home than their male counterparts ever were. The companies that began serving nourishing hot food to their employees believed that it helped maintain morale and increased production, hungry workers never having been especially productive workers.

After World War II, management continued to seek the benefits derived from in-plant feeding facilities and often subsidized their operation. But generally speaking, except for the largest industries and plants, it became less and less feasible for companies to operate their own foodservices. Instead they began to ask specialized firms to run the operation for them. Vending at industrial plants was also a natural service, and many of the industrial catering companies merged with vending concerns. The Automatic Retailers of America (ARA) is one of the leading examples of this type of merger.

In-plant feeding may take many forms: dining rooms for management; cafeterias for workers; mobile units that tour the working areas; and canteens or lunch counters located around the plant.

Unless an unexpected increase in industrial facilities occurs, there appears to be little chance of a dramatic increase in industrial feeding beyond normal population and inflation growth rates. There is, however, a growing market in supplying food to white collar office workers. Industrial feeding is not limited to industrial plants. Many white-collar operations such as banks or office centers provide foodservice. In fact, one of the first employee feeding operations was a New York bank. Some of the white-collar operations are run by the owners themselves while others use outside caterers.

Prison Foodservice

Certainly one of the most captive of all audiences are the inmates of penal institutions. We do not intend, however, to belittle the importance of prison foodservices; someone once said that all prison riots to some degree reflect food quality. Besides, serving food to the prison population and staff personnel, it can help inmates train for jobs in the foodservice industry upon their release. Since many of these inmates have difficulty finding work and since the foodservice industry is eager to find trained, interested workers, prison would appear to be a natural place for foodservice training.

A career in prison foodservice does not depend merely on the desire to provide food. The atmosphere is crucial. Working in prisons may appeal to some people; others may find it depressing. But, the opportunities for public service and creativity in prisons occasionally rival those offered by hospital foodservices.

Inns, Hotels, and Motels

Since the beginning of recorded time people have traveled, and during their travels have needed shelter. Thus hospitality has been called the world's second oldest profession, and it probably deserves precedence over the oldest. In ancient times a traveler's safety was protected by the gods, and he could receive the three basics—food, drink, lodging—from the local people. But all the so-called civilized countries of the ancient world offered inns or their counterparts.

Inns   The invention of exchange mediums (money) brought trade expansion and an increased need for hospitality establishments. Pictures on Egyptian tombs show visitors being entertained in what we would probably call an inn. Hammurabi, the Babylonian who conceived the "eye for an eye, and a tooth for a tooth" dictum also concerned himself with the quality and control of the Babylonian inns. He even drew up regulations for them, including a proscription against the adulteration of beverages. Excavations at Pompeii reveal the remains of inns used thousands of years ago. And we know that slaves or war prisoners often ran the inns of ancient Greece.

Much of the trade of the ancient world was handled by caravans, and while on those trade routes people moved in huge *caravanserai* accommodating not only the travelers but also hundreds of animals. Through the Christmas Story most of us are familiar with the Biblical inns and how an overflow of guests might have to be lodged in the stables. In ancient Rome there were inns along the highways housing messengers of the Emperor. (The term *hospitium* meant an apartment beside a Roman mansion reserved for the guests.)

During early Middle Ages travel was infrequent, and trade virtually stood still. People stayed in isolated communities, and, if they did travel, they either camped in fields or lodged at the castles of nobles. Religious orders also offered hospitality—often for a fee. In the late Middle Ages travel and trade increased, and so did the need for inns. The Crusades stimulated travel and the accommodation business. The inns became social centers for the working and rising middle classes who did not have access to the castles of the nobility.

During the Middle Ages in England a surprising amount of travel went on. In fact, Geoffrey Chaucer's fourteenth century *Canterbury Tales* are told by a group of springtime English itinerants, and the Chaucerian classic offers a lively, accurate description of traveling and innkeeping practices at the time. Although there were few roads for wagons, there were paths for horses and walkers. The villages and towns were widely separated, and the forests and fields between them were infested by bandits—not all as gentlemanly as Robin Hood. Travelers would proceed in groups or "companies" for safety. At night, besides food and shelter, they had a genuine need for protection. This led local householders to open their homes to travelers, which led, in turn, to the development of inns.

The hospitality was not, however, all that might be desired. Far from home and unable to go elsewhere, travelers were often gouged by steep prices. An innkeeper might be capricious; he might even turn away a traveler he did not like. Or he might conspire with the local bandits to rob his guests. (It would be nice to quote Shakespeare's "I would take my ease at an inn" as a compliment for English Renaissance innkeepers, but unfortunately the next line is "and have my pockets picked.")

With the advent of the stagecoach, English and continental inns appeared every ten or fifteen miles at the stage stops. Meals and beer were usually included with the lodging. Typically the host carved, dished, and served the food. The early inns were usually large buildings with few rooms but perhaps a number of beds in one room. Trundle beds, or beds that pulled out from underneath one another, were often used. In some instances, mattresses spread on the floor passed for beds. Travelers often had to share beds, and an honored guest would get a place in the least crowded one.

Inns in America

After about 1750, the inns began to improve, adding such attractions as private brewhouses and bowling greens. The English inn was, of course, transported to the colonies in America. In 1656, Massachusetts enacted a law that required each community to provide an inn or pay a fine, and Samuel Cole who founded Harvard University was one of these early innkeepers. The inns were often called *ordinaries,* meaning that they were not reserved for the wealthy but welcomed ordinary people. Peter Stuyvesant authorized a tavern in New Amsterdam so he would not have to be host to all his visitors, and this building became (logically enough) the first New York City Hall. When William Penn landed at Philadelphia in 1682 he spent his first winter at the Blewe Anchor, the city's first inn. One year later, seven inns flourished in Philadelphia. In early Pennsylvania, inn prices were strictly regulated. A heavy penalty was imposed for diluting liquor and a light penalty for Sunday sales. It was also considered unethical innkeeping to sell liquor to the Indians.

In the latter part of the eighteenth century, American inns became by most accounts, the world's best. There were a number of reasons for this. First, many people actually took up residence in them. Many of the wealthier new immigrants did not have homes of their own, and inns became lodging places, sometimes for entire families. Second, Americans believed in the spirit of democracy and that all, regardless of social class, were entitled to whatever comfort and luxury the inns could provide. Third, inns had to accommodate social events since there were no local manors or castles. And fourth, there was considerably more travel in a sprawling, lightly populated America than in most other countries.

In 1794 the City Hotel was erected in New York City—the first building built strictly for hotel purposes. It had seventy-three rooms and was described, in its day, as an immense palace. Early America had its share of temperance houses whose operators forbade any sort of alcoholic beverages. But most establishments, like City Hall, mixed beverages and lodging from the first. The usual hotel had its own well-stocked bar.

In 1829 a truly memorable hotel, the Tremont, was built in Boston. It has been called the first modern hotel, and it definitely set the standard for a whole generation of new hospitality operations. It was also said to be the first hotel with a lobby so that guests did not have to register at the bar.

The Tremont had 170 guest rooms, an amazing number for its time. It boasted gas lights downstairs and a 200-seat dining room where a trained staff served a French cuisine. It had not only individual rooms but even locks on the doors. And to make sure that no one forgot his room key, a long iron bar was attached to each one. Instead of hiking to a backyard pump to perform ablutions, each guest had his own water bowl, pitcher, and bar of soap. Hence, the Tremont became known as the first of the bowl and pitcher hotels. The Tremont was, in short, a landmark that all America was proud of, and thus it encouraged a wave of similar hotels throughout the country including the famour Astor House in New York City, built in 1832.

A particularly interesting type of hotel of the era was the *spa*. Spas were probably the first American resorts, although the spa concept dates from Roman times, or before, and some still operate today. The spa usually has some special water that is thought either to act as a purgative or to provide some other therapeutic benefit. Notable early American spas were at Saratoga, New York (where the potato chip was invented) and the Greenbriar in West Virginia. At one time, Pennsylvania alone had thirty spas.

Hotels were built by the various railroad companies at their stops before the introduction of sleeping car service, allowing railroad passengers to stay at the hotel overnight before proceeding on their journey. In fact, a number of hotelkeepers were instrumental in starting local railroads.

During Reconstruction, hotels in general were heavily used by the Yankee peddlers or drummers, salesmen who spent most of their time on the road. Chain stores have since all but eliminated this colorful, typically American patron. Another prime source of hotel patronage was the traveling theatrical troupes that circulated among the various opera and vaudeville houses. Humorous tales are still told of their ability to sneak out without paying if their shows failed to earn a profit.

The Modern Hotel   In the late 1800s and the early twentieth century some magnificent hotels went up in this country. Some of them, like the Plaza in New York, are still first class operations. They stressed luxury and glamour, and they offered the finest cuisine and appointments. Caesar Ritz's hotels probably epitomized the luxury hotels of this time; from his operations we get the term *ritzy*, which the dictionary defines as "ostentatiously smart." For example, Ritz hired and patronized the great chef Escoffier; between them, the foodservice at Ritz hotels reached heights that have seldom been equaled. Dishes were named after the patrons or their lady friends—Peach Melba and Crepes Suzette, for example.

Caesar Ritz was supposed to have proclaimed, "The guest is always right." He had the resources to follow this maxim, and his hotels were always well staffed with carefully trained personnel. Working conditions in the luxurious establishments could, however, be very poor. The *vampire system* in which an employee "kicks back" a portion of his earnings to a headwaiter or head bellman for the privilege of working was often in force.

Shortly after the beginning of the twentieth century, Ellsworth M. Statler, perhaps the world's greatest hotel man, arrived on the scene. He had grown up as a poor working boy, a West Virginia miner's apprentice in fact. He became a night clerk in a hotel and soon acquired its bowling concession. He added food, including Mother Statler's homemade pie. The step into innkeeping was short.

Statler's hotels were designed for the traveling public. They featured baths in every room—somewhat of a novelty when he started his career. A popular ditty circulated far and wide about Statler: "Instead of a room and a path, you get a room and a bath for a buck and a half." He standardized his hotels so that whether you were in Boston, Cleveland, New York, or Buffalo, you could check into a Statler hotel and know what to expect. He also instituted such services as overnight laundry, circulating ice water, sterilized toilet seats, and newspaper delivery to the door.

Statler concerned himself with the operational aspects of his enterprises and greatly improved cost control recordkeeping. He also helped establish the American Hotel Association. In fact, he called a meeting at his Buffalo Statler for the purpose of starting a professional hotel association, and when the delegates could not agree, he reportedly boated them out on Lake Erie and threatened to keep them until they formed the association he had in mind.

The 1920s heralded a tremendous boom in the hotel industry, and a large number of hotels were built in New York City alone. In small towns, promoters would point that the town was without prestige unless it had modern hotel facilities. Next, he would organize a hotel company that sold bonds to the local people and erected the hotel. For his services, the promoter received a certain percentage of the funds raised or the bonds issued. For a time business was good, and occupancies in the 1920s averaged around 86 percent.

During the 1930s, however, the hotel industry suffered with everyone else through the Great Depression. People had little money and could not travel. Many hotels begun in the boom years of the 1920s failed completely in the early 1930s. Hoping for business, some hotelkeepers began to cut their rates. To remain competitive other hotelkeepers followed suit. The result was low cut rates that created little additional business— and even more failures. The occupancy rate in 1933 tumbled to 51 percent with a 65 percent breakeven point. Not surprisingly, some 80 percent of the country's hotels are said to have been in some sort of financial difficulty during the Depression. At one time, the Metropolitan Life Insurance Company was supposedly the largest hotel owner in the world because of the hotels it had financed, and later foreclosed on.

During the 1940s hotels, swamped with war and postwar activities, revived. Occupancy rates sometimes reached 94 percent, and in a few hotels it exceeded 100 percent. Reservations had to be made weeks ahead, and even with reservations, guests might have to wait hours for a room to become available. Some cities like New York limited the length of time a guest could stay in a hotel—three days being the typical limit.

But the hotels had real problems despite all this business. Workers were serving in the military forces or in defense industries, so hotels found themselves extremely short of help. Food was rationed, and it was difficult to buy such supplies as linen and tableware. The only thing the hotels had enough of was guests. The flood of business and the difficulty of serving it caused some hotels to condescend to their trade. To find a room, it often became necessary to grease the room clerk's palm. Some of this condescension paid bitter dividends later when large segments of the public remembered resentfully the treatment they had received in certain hotels. Also during the 1940s two of the major hotel chains, Hilton and Sheraton, started to expand, a trend that presaged nationwide hotel systems.

The end of the Second World War released a pent-up demand for travel. The prosperous war years had made money abundant, and automobiles and other forms of transportation carried people freely wherever they wanted to go. Not only did they stay at hotels but also at such other accommodations as tourist homes and motels. In the early 1950s, however, motels were not quite respectable. Some were known as "hot pillow joints," retreats for unsanctified couples in search of a temporary haven.

During the late 1950s and early 1960s trends developed that proved to be unfavorable for the conventional hotel. Many small hotels became unable to compete with the newer hotels and motor inns. Patterns of transportation reduced the need for hotels. People could fly from place to place and decrease their need for wayside hotels. In some urban areas the value of land became too high for hotel purposes, and it became more profitable to erect office buildings. Earlier hotels had often been built close to railroad or bus facilities. But as these locations became secondary to strategic highway or airport locations, the desirability of the hotel also decreased. And as urban areas deteriorated, the need for the fine hotels within them deteriorated as well. Perhaps an energy shortage will benefit downtown hotels because of their proximity to public transportation.

A Short History of Motels

With the automobile came accommodations catering to the motoring public. The first were, quite literally, tents in the fields. (Read John Steinbeck's novel *The Grapes of Wrath* for a vivid description of an automobile camping migration.) Local entrepreneurs then began to build very simple cabins—four walls with an iron bed. The traveler supplied his own linens and paid the owner a dollar a night. Some people opened their homes to highway travelers, and tourist homes became popular as stopovers. The simple cabins were soon supplanted by tourist cabins, groups of separate units, each with indoor plumbing.

The first use of the name *motel* reportedly dates to 1925 when the "Milestone Mo-tel" opened in San Luis Obispo, California. It failed four years later, but many more motels started around the country and some still flourish. These early motels were usually very utilitarian, not to say spartan. Their main virtue was, in fact, their economy. In 1940 the first formal group of motels, the Quality Courts, was established. These were individually owned, but all of them had to adhere to certain standards of service and management. This idea of uniformity, perhaps borrowed from Statler, became popular among travelers who wanted to know what to expect of a motel.

Between 1942 and 1945 the Second World War raged, and even though construction was difficult, many motels sprung up around military camps and defense plants. Hotels were too expensive for service-connected travel, but motels were not. Up to this time motels had remained small, and relatively few of them had restaurants. But the postwar travel boom caused an increase, first in the number of motels, and then, in their sizes and services. Many were "Mom and Pop" operations: an older couple would use their retirement savings to buy land and erect a few motel units. Pop would take care of the maintenance and the desk, while Mom did the housekeeping. A satisfactory retirement income might be the result of their investment.

Conventional hotels still sneered at motel competition, considering them only a weak challenge to the more traditional industry. But the hotels were wrong. Chains of motor inns developed, one of them the brainchild of Kemmons Wilson who, on a trip with his family, found the highway accommodations deplorable and expensive. He built his own motel in Memphis, offering large rooms, two double beds, restaurant facilities, and conveniences for the traveling family. He also increased the size of the typical operation, installing 100 units rather than the dozen or so prevalent at the time. Wilson was not an innkeeper; he was an entrepreneur who saw a need and filled it. His Holiday Inns have, of course, surpassed in number all of the hotel chains that dominated the industry when he started. In 1979 there were 2500 Holiday Inns worldwide, with sales of $3.1 billion.

Two developments in the 1950s encouraged the construction of motels or motor inns. One was a tax incentive—accelerated depreciation for new construction. Instead of taking normal depreciation on his building, a motel owner could accelerate depreciation and charge it against his profits. With such high depreciation charges, comparatively little taxable profit remained. And since depreciation is a noncash expense, the owner still had the depreciation money that he did not pay taxes on, at least at the beginning of the depreciation period.

The other important development, the Interstate Highway Act, came in May of 1956. This act established the Interstate Highway System, and at the same time eliminated one of the major motel problems. Heretofore, a motel, once built, might be bypassed by a new highway or a route change. The Interstate Highway System brought assurance that the highway route would not be changed. Motels built along the system could enjoy a long business life. Moreover, the highways themselves would generate large amounts of business. Motel companies began frantically to search for ideal locations along projected interstate routes so that they would have facilities ready when the highways came through.

In 1960 came the development of the *Grand Motel*. These motels out-lavished existing hotels. They offered the most modern facilities—tile baths, carpeting, air-conditioning, and swimming pools were all standard. Some of the early ones were garishly decorated, which nevertheless seemed to attract more patrons. The 1960s also saw a tremendous growth in motel chains and franchises. In many cases a motel's success depended (and still depends) on its referrals in which business is generated by one unit referring its travelers to other units in the chain.

And at last, motels that originated next to the highway have begun to move downtown and to spread vertically into high rises. It has, in fact, become difficult to distinguish them from conventional hotels.

Because of the depreciation advantage and other tax considerations, motels became a favorite investment for speculators with spare money to invest. Their main interest, of course, was a quick return on their investment, not necessarily the quality of service their motels provided.

The Hotel-Motel Industry Today

Innkeeping today is the country's seventh largest industry. As the number of hotels decreases, the number of motels or motor inns increases, but at a slower rate than during the 1960s. Up until the early 1960s, hotels and motels were thought to be different types of operations. But now that motels have added many hotel services and hotels have tried to incorporate motel convenience, the modern motor inn may as well be a hotel. Traditionally hotels were classified as transient or commercial (catering largely to the traveling business man); resort (catering to vacationing people); or residential (offering hotel services to permanent residents). There is a recent trend toward changing some commercial hotels into retirement hotels, which provide rooms and food at a relatively modest rate.

Although most people associate hotels with big buildings in large cities, most of them are actually quite small. Only about six percent have more than 300 rooms. Motels, on the other hand, are usually associated with highways, peripheral areas of town, or the airport. These associations are becoming increasingly inaccurate. The early appeal of motels centered on their convenience, recreation facilities, and economy. Parking was usually free, whereas hotels often charged for the privilege, and a guest at a hotel had to tip the bellboy to carry luggage from the car to the room. But motels became increasingly more elaborate and more expensive. In fact, a minority segment of the motel industry is returning to the economy scene by offering no-frills facilities at lower rates.

A hotel and motor inn are very important elements in the community. They can be the center of community life and provide facilities for such community functions as banquets, dinners, receptions, and dances. They also provide convenience for the travelers who want to do business in the community and need a place to stay. These travelers bring in out-of-town money, which can obviously help the economy of the area they visit. Moreover, hotels are traditionally located on expensive locations and pay, therefore, some of the highest real estate tax assessments.

The trend seems to be toward more and more chain operations for both hotels and motels. Building a motor inn is greatly simplified if it is part of a chain and the parent company can offer its counsel and assistance. Advertising and marketing programs are simplified when a number of operations chip in. The chains also facilitate reservation making; every unit becomes a reservation center for the others. The larger chains use computers to handle reservations, and computers are already linking hotel-motel reservations with travel arrangements and car rental services.

From a personal standpoint there are many advantages to working in a hotel or motor inn. To begin with, it is a service occupation, and many people derive real pleasure from serving others. Secondly, community leaders are usually well known to the managers of the local hotels and motor inns, and managers often help them plan functions held in their facility. Although no one knows precisely what the future of the hotel or motel industry will be, history tells us that a need for these types of hospitality establishments, and for people who can manage them, will continue.

SUMMARY

Throughout this chapter, we have discussed in general terms various aspects of the hospitality industry environment. From the managerial standpoint, you will find a knowledge of this external environment most useful because, to function effectively, a hospitality manager must be able to evaluate his business environment and predict changes in it. This managerial skill becomes especially important when the manager undertakes the planning function. You will learn a great deal more about external environments and the planning functions of management in future chapters.

IMPORTANT TERMS

Having studied this chapter, you should be able to define the following terms:

captive foodservice operation

fast-food operation

> **open system for convenience foods**
>
> **closed system for convenience foods**
>
> **finger foods**
>
> **Type A lunch**
>
> **German system of college foodservice**
>
> **English system of college foodservice**

REVIEW QUESTIONS

1-1. Compare the advantages of chain foodservice operations to those of independent operations.

1-2. Why is the foodservice business expected to grow in the future?

1-3. What are the probable changes regarding the raw food products that foodservice operations use?

1-4. What recent changes have occurred in distribution by foodservice operations?

1-5. Discuss the statement that "the foodservice system should determine the equipment rather than the equipment determining the system."

1-6. What recent changes have occurred in hospital foodservice?

1-7. Compare the advantages of a career in hospital foodservice to one in other types of foodservice operations.

1-8. What are the unusual problems of airline foodservice?

1-9. Explain the reasons for rapid growth in the fast-food industry. Do you think this growth will continue? Why? Why not?

1-10. Outline the history and development of motels.

1-11. Why are hotels and motor inns considered important elements of a community?

1-12. How might a current foodservice operation have to change its operation twenty years from now in terms of (a) customers? (b) products? (c) distribution? (d) equipment? (e) personnel?

1-13. Why might a college prefer either the English or German approach to student housing and feeding?

2 The Theory of Management and Its Development

Since you are studying hospitality management, you should quickly become familiar with the various approaches to management in general. After reading this chapter, you should be able to

- define briefly the term management
- discuss the four characteristics of management
- list the twelve functions of management
- describe briefly both the internal and the external environments in which hospitality managers must operate
- state the four management goals, as well as the processes that help a manager form these goals
- list the five approaches to management

Elements of Management

It is difficult to find two people who agree on a definition of management, mainly because it is such a broad term. On the one hand, management is in large part pragmatic and down to earth. On the other hand, it has a strong theoretical and conceptual basis. There are also a number of different approaches to management. As in religion where each faith feels it has the direct road to salvation, proponents of each management approach believe theirs is the one true way to manage—an attitude bitterly disputed by the others.

While much disagreement on the approach toward management exists, almost everyone would agree that management is vital to any human endeavor, and the larger the scope of the endeavor the more important management becomes. Management is important to business enterprises, but it is equally important in very diverse nonbusiness enterprises, such as churches, the armed forces, and schools and their PTA's.

Management can be conspicuous by its absence. If things are going smoothly and everyone is working toward the goals of the organization the management behind that effort may not be appreciated. But if troubles arise, the need for proper management can readily be seen. While we hear much discussion about whether management is an art, a science, or a process, it is probably a blend of all three. And management is interdisciplinary in that it draws principles from a number of sciences or disciplines besides being a recognized field of study on its own.

Definitions of Management

Management is a broad concept. Here is a sampling of definitions of management one might find in textbooks and business articles.

Getting things done through others. This behavioristic view of management assumes that since management can be accomplished only through people, the consideration of these people and their needs is all important.

Effective utilization of resources to achieve personal and organization goals. In this viewpoint the manager has a number of resources at his disposal. His job is to coordinate them for the best benefit of the organization. The usual resources are sometimes called the *six M's: men* (personnel), *materials, methods, machines, money,* and *markets.* These are what the manager and the organization have to work with. If there is no management, the goals of the operation may be missed, in spite of abundant resources.

Decision-making. This definition assumes that the primary job of the manager is making the decisions that will assure the continuation and success of the organization. The operations-research approach to management is heavily oriented toward decision-making.

The process by which cooperative groups direct their actions toward a common goal. Here management is seen as a process; common goals are assumed to have been formulated; and the cooperation or group effort to achieve these goals is emphasized.

Establishing and achieving objectives. This accents the goal-oriented nature of management where the success of management is determined by how well it achieves its goals.

Planning, organizing, controlling, staffing, directing, representing, and innovating. Not really a definition, this lists functions of management under the management-science approach. If a manager is able to perform these functions, the manager should, theoretically, be able to run any operation. The list of management functions varies among management theorists, but planning, organizing, and controlling are almost always included.

That process by which human and physical resources are guided into dynamic and viable organization units that obtain objectives to the satisfaction of those served with a high degree of morale and sense of attainment on the part of those providing the service. This long-winded definition includes both the idea of optimum utilization of the management resources and a behavioral consideration for both the customers of the operation and for its personnel.

A factor of production. This approach dates back to Adam Smith, who considered management along with land, labor, and capital to be a part of the production process.

There can be no doubt that, as intangible as management may be, it is also a very definite resource. Developing countries may find their development helped or hindered by the amount of management talent available. Thus management has also been considered as a class or an elite that can help fellow members of a society toward a better life through better utilization of the resources available to them.

Characteristics of Management

The preceding definitions suggest a number of different approaches to the study of management. In analyzing these various definitions, it may be easier to think of management's general characteristics. One of these is that it is *goal-oriented*. Good management must know where it is going and what it is trying to accomplish. Therefore it must have goals. The planning and decision-making functions are very important in formulating these goals, and the success of management can, in fact, be measured by how well it achieves its goals. Of course, this measurement assumes the goals were realistic and obtainable. If not, it may be necessary to change the goals for the best interests of the organization. The function of control, in particular, may indicate how well goals are being met. A hotel manager should know what he wants to achieve in terms of service, quality (an illusive word for hotels), new business, and profit, among other factors. Without goals he is just going with the tide, and this may mean heading on a downward slope. How well he achieves realistic goals is the measure of his success.

Especially in the industries where the product is service and tends to be handcrafted, *management concerns itself with people*. Quite often a manager's success is measured by how well he can motivate and stimulate the people he directs. There have been successful non-people-centered managers in the foodservice industry, but they usually have exceptional strengths in other areas, and they usually have somebody who can deal with "people problems" for them. And even though they have been successful, more of a people-orientation would probably have brought even more success. The hospitality industry is a "people" industry. In a factory, the management need deal only with its employees as people; in a retail establishment, the customers are the primary people concerned. The hospitality industry, however, must deal with both employees and customers as people at the same time. Love of people is, therefore, a prime reason to be attracted to the hospitality field.

Management usually requires the *coordination of effort*: a number of people working together rather than people working individually. Coordination of effort is very important since, despite individual motivation, an uncoordinated business may be weak and unfocused. Its approach would be hit-or-miss, and its success a matter of luck.

The need for coordination is in fact a need for management. Complicated service establishments such as hotels and restaurants require more coordination than many simpler nonservice ones.

Management is not passive. An organization, its resources, and its environment constantly change. If the organization is to survive and prosper, management must not only change but influence change as well. The success of motels over hotels was in the past due to the fact that many hotel managers did not realize changes in the environment. More concern for employees is another necessary change. The manager who has already expressed this increased concern helps to influence change in others.

A common fault among managers is that they like to do only the things that interest them, ignoring other equally important aspects. A manager of a foodservice operation may be fascinated by food production. But if he spends all his time with this one function, the operation is in for a hard time. One solution would be for the manager to delegate appropriate authority and responsibility for other concerns to someone qualified in those other areas.

Resources of Management

As we mentioned in our second definition, management resources or the six M's of management include men, materials, methods, machines, money, and markets. The *men* refers to the personnel, both men and women, in the organization. Involved are not only their selection, hiring, and training, but also their motivation and morale. Many theorists consider personnel the most essential resource of an operation; other theorists claim that the importance of personnel depends on the type of operation. *Materials* refers to the raw materials available to an operation. In foodservice operations we are talking about the food that is bought, prepared, and sold to the customers. *Methods* refers more specifically to production methods. In a foodservice operation these might include standard recipes or control procedures. *Machines* refers to the equipment necessary to produce a product. In a foodservice establishment the equipment tends to be the kitchen and dining equipment. *Money* refers, of course, to the capital necessary to start an operation and the working capital to keep it running. *Markets* refers to the customers for the products of the operation.

These are the six basic resources that any operation should have at its disposal to achieve its goals. To some extent these resources may be interchangeable; for example, money can be used to buy new equipment or hire more personnel, or approved methods can be used to decrease the amount of personnel. All resources exist for the sole purpose of serving and increasing the market resources. If market resources are not available, there is no need for the others.

Functions of Management

Certain functions or principles are common to all management, and if a manager is familiar with these functions and knows how to apply them, he should, ideally, be able to manage any type of organization. The first list of these functions was composed by French management theorist Henri Fayol in 1916.

Some Management Terms

At this point, we should define some of these functions of management so as to have a common vocabulary. Many of them will be discussed in greater detail in later chapters.

Planning. Planning is deciding what has to be done. It involves short- and long-range objectives (goals). An example of a short-range objective might be deciding production quantities for the day. A long-range objective might be deciding what general food costs and ratios to maintain. Planning involves forecasting the environment, determining objectives compatible with that forecast, and coordinating the available resources with the desired objectives.

Organizing. Organizing is determining what tasks and skills are necessary to achieve the chosen objectives, then allocating the human resources to achieve the goals. From a traditional management standpoint, organizing structures an enterprise; it creates the framework of jobs and activities. To a management behaviorist, organizing is more the sum of human relationships in any group activity.

Staffing. Staffing involves providing the people for the various positions that the organization has decided it needs to achieve its goals. This may entail recruiting people for the needs of the enterprise. Training responsibilities may also be included in the staffing function.

Directing. For management to succeed, the personnel must know what results are expected. *Directing*, therefore, involves explaining to others what needs to be done, then helping them to do it. Training employees, helping them improve their skills, and motivating them are all involved in directing. Without adequate direction, staff members tend to work at cross-purposes, inefficiently, and perhaps against the operation's interests. Direction includes supervision, and it is very personnel-related. It directly involves the staff. A competent, considerate director can usually achieve a higher level of production from his staff and have happier personnel than a manager who directs curtly or callously. However, some hardnosed managers are also effective, getting results even though disliked by subordinates.

Coordinating. Part of organizing, staffing, and directing, coordinating means matching the work of the staff to the goals of the enterprise. It involves eliminating duplication of effort and assuring that the various segments of the organization know what both they and other segments of the organization should be doing.

Controlling. From a traditional management standpoint, controlling means evaluating how well the work is being done. This requires that actual results be compared to desired or anticipated results (standards of performance). Food cost percentages and labor budgets are typical standards of control. Management behaviorists, however, argue that rigid control can be self-defeating. They hold that it forms a barrier between the employees and their organization. Behaviorists would prefer to base control on the assumption that employees are eager to do their best for the operation and that they therefore require little evaluation.

Innovation. Somewhat intangible, but very important, innovation means introducing and responding to change. Unless the organization innovates to meet the changes in its environment, it can fall behind. On the other hand, if the market will not accept changes, too much innovation can cause difficulty. Innovation, therefore, is especially involved with planning.

Communication. Communication is the two-way flow of information through the organization. Some theorists consider communication to be part of directing and reporting. Reporting, or the transfer of information for evaluation of planning or performance, is a type of control. One type of reporting currently enjoying considerable attention is management information services.

Budgeting. Though considered a separate management function, budgeting involves most of the other functions, especially planning, organizing, controlling, staffing, and directing. Budgeting requires that plans be drawn up, goals be expressed in a budget, and actual results be compared with desired ones recorded. A budget is usually expressed in dollars, but it can use different standards. A labor budget, for example, uses the number of hours necessary to perform certain work rather than the dollars required.

Decision-making. Decision-making means choosing the best course of action between possible alternatives. Sometimes thought to be a separate management function, it also involves the other functions. There are a number of processes by which decisions can be made, ranging from gut feelings to sophisticated quantitative (mathematical) analysis. Management has been described as largely decision-making, and some feel that the main job of the true manager is to make the proper decisions for the best interests of the enterprise.

Representing. Representing the organization to the various elements of its environment—the general public, the government, customers, unions, financial institutions—is also a management function. In a large part it consists of public relations. Many managers spend a great deal of their time in such work rather than actually running the enterprise.

The importance of the various management functions varies from one time context to the next. In periods of expansion, decision-making, planning, coordinating, and directing may be very important. When business is slow, control and budgeting may assume greater importance. And at certain times, public representation may be more important for the manager than any of the other functions. The relative importance of the various functions also changes with the level of management. A lower-line supervisor may be more concerned with directing, coordinating, and reporting. Middle management might be interested in control and budgeting. Upper management might be interested in decision-making, planning, organizing, controlling, and representation.

Environments of Management

No management operates in a vacuum. Management feels forces and stresses both within the organization and from the outside. The effective manager must understand these forces and be able to adapt to them. In some cases he must adapt them to his purposes. Forces from outside the operation are called the *external environment*. Forces within the operation can be part of the *internal environment*. (See Exhibit 2-1.)

External forces include the general economic level, political conditions, and cultural and social changes. If the economic climate deteriorates, management may not be able to proceed with its plans but, instead, may have to accommodate the changes. Many sociocultural changes in the last few years have led to widespread revisions on the part of foodservice management. Unionization and the sudden interest in labeling and nutrition are only some of them.

Internal environmental factors include time available, cost, geographical distances, and effort required for some purpose.

Both internal and external environmental factors can complicate the role of management. Management may desire to accomplish a definite project, but the external or internal environments may make it impossible. Thus, an effective manager must be well aware of his environments and the changes possible within them. The most effective managers are usually the best informed ones.

Goals of Management

What are the overall goals of management in an organization? For a profit-making operation the goal is usually the highest profit, the maximum increase of the owner's equity or both making a profit and increasing the value of the owner's investment. For a nonprofit operation, an overall goal might be to provide the highest level of service with the resources available. A nonprofit hospital dietary department, for example, would seek to provide the best food and service to its patients with the resources it can command.

Exhibit 2–1.
Environments of
Management

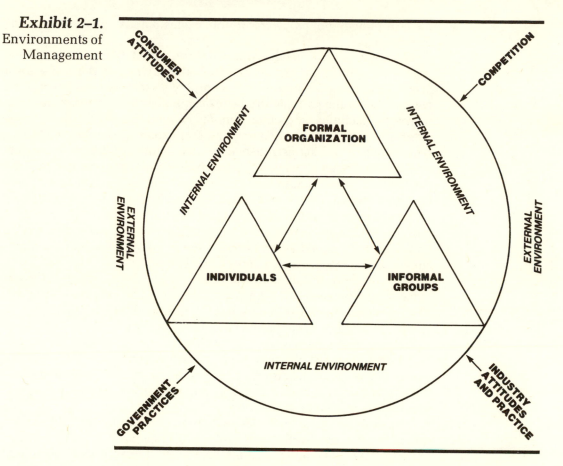

Subgoals collectively achieved accomplish the major goals. A chef may have a subgoal of maintaining a certain food cost percentage or creating a certain masterpiece. A head waiter may have the subgoal of achieving faster dining room service. These subgoals should augment the economic self-interest of the organization. Indeed, the job of management has been described as the consolidation and continuation of all these smaller successes.

While the job of the traditional manager was to see that the firm prospers, environmental changes (both internal and external) are interfering with this line of reasoning. Some now argue that an enterprise must not only provide money for the owners but also be responsible to certain other constituencies. One of these constituencies is the firm's employees. A firm, so goes the argument, has a responsibility to the people who work for it to provide not only comfortable wages but also pleasant working environments.

The argument is attractive and widely accepted, but it involves some irony. It summons up images of paternalism, wherein the owner of a firm takes a paternal interest in his employees that extends beyond the work place. In the past, paternalistic businesses often provided housing, recreation facilities, and other benefits beyond the paycheck. In these paternalistic situations, of course, the employees were expected to live according to a fashion established by their employer. Much to the surprise of those who applauded paternalism, employees resented overdependence on their employers, and wanted instead to feel free to live their own lives as they saw fit.

Another responsibility of an enterprise is to the local community. It must try to be a good citizen and neighbor, active in good works, paying its fair share of expenses, and making every effort not to mar the atmosphere with unaesthetic structures or pollution.

A third responsibility is to the customers of the enterprise. Honest value should be given, and the customers should be courteously served. The operation should feel that it has the responsibility to provide for its customers and not merely collect money from them.

It is obvious that this *social approach* to management has not yet been completely accepted. But it is a goal toward which all management can strive. Indeed, with the current changes in the external environment—the pressures of government and other exterior forces—the social approach may soon be mandatory.

Obviously, some tradeoffs between these various responsibilities must take place. An organization may feel strong responsibility for its employees, but if its actual need for them decreases, it cannot continue to pad the payroll. If a company encounters excess costs by trying to provide benefits it cannot afford, it not only will be forced to discontinue these excess benefits but may also be forced out of business—putting others out of work, too.

Service to the community may also present certain problems. For instance, chain operations with standard building designs commonly find that their structures may be praised in one community and banned in another as aesthetically undesirable. A manager must meet these issues with wisdom. Will acquiescence to a community's zoning ordinances make friends? Will it waste money? The best of public relations cannot help a failing enterprise.

This country has grown and generally prospered with its free enterprise system. Capitalism is supposed to have been a swear word coined by Karl Marx in 1854 to denote a system run by industrialists against workers. But capitalism involves two institutions, private property and the free market, and the incentives these two provide have helped people produce more than any other system—communal or otherwise. Social conciousness forces us now to question whether some of capitalism's rewards have come at the expense of others. Indeed, there have been many abuses in capitalism (many of them corrected by the publicity inherent in an open society). In this time of growing scarcity of resources, management now faces the problem of maintaining the capitalistic incentive—and assuring that both owners and employers share in its benefits—without exhausting the resources available for future generations.

Exhibit 2-2 offers a schematic view of one approach to management. The various resources available to the organization and its management appear at the left. Through the various functions of management, these resources are directed toward the achievement of the goals of the operation. Both the external and internal environments affect the whole procedure. This schematic viewpoint can be used both for the management of the whole organization and for different components of it. This

Exhibit 2–2.
Schematic
Diagram of
Management

EXTERNAL ENVIRONMENT
SOCIAL · POLITICAL · LEGAL · ECONOMIC · RELIGIOUS · INTERNATIONAL

INTERNAL ENVIRONMENT				
RESOURCES OF MANAGEMENT	*through*	**MANAGEMENT FUNCTIONS**	*produce*	**ORGANIZATIONAL GOALS**
Men (personnel)		Planning		**Return to investors (if a commercial organization)**
Machines		Organizing		
Money		Controlling		**Decent livelihood for employees**
Methods		Directing		**Good product or service for patrons**
Markets		Staffing		
Materials		Representing		**Good neighbor in the community**

approach could be considered more of a management process approach than a behavioral one.

To think of management as a system, add a feedback element to the drawing. This element would show, for example, that if desired goals are not met, the resources or management processes may need to be changed. If these cannot be changed, it would show whether a change in the goals would then be required.

Levels of Management

Management is a broad, much-encompassing term. In practice there are different levels of management; the functions performed at the different levels may vary.

Top management consists of presidents, vice presidents and chief executives. Normally they are most concerned with planning, organizing, decision-making, coordinating, innovation, and representation. Usually they do not directly supervise many subordinates.

Middle management consists of those who run segments of the enterprise under the plans and direction of top management. Included are department heads such as the chef, personnel director, sales manager, front office manager, and housekeeper. Middle management is often heavily involved in such functions as directing, controlling, staffing, communicating, budgeting, and decision-making.

First-line managers directly supervise the workers who provide the services or produce the product. Common titles for first-line managers include assistant department head and supervisor. Directing is their usual function, but they are also often involved in coordinating, communicating, controlling, and other functions.

Development of Modern Management Thought

The development of management thought and theory has followed a rather circuitous route; new developments have not always sprung from previous developments. Some of the approaches to management differ considerably from other approaches, and there is considerable dispute over the relative effectiveness of each. A hospitality manager should be aware of these often conflicting approaches and be able to draw from them what is best for his purposes. We suggest no one approach as the ultimate solution to management problems; each has its contributions, and each its drawbacks. Not only has management thought and theory been in a state of flux since 1900, but it will also probably be in a state of flux for the foreseeable future. That is why we emphasize that today's hospitality management student must be able to use the knowledge of past management development (see Exhibit 2-3) and at the same time be receptive to the new developments that come with the future.

Exhibit 2–3.
Continuum of
Management
Theory
Development

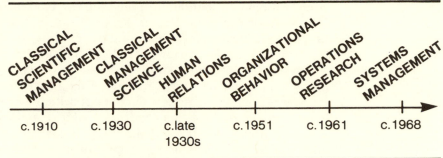

*Classical
Scientific
Management*

Classical scientific management and Frederick Winslow Taylor are virtually synonomous. Taylor's classical scientific management theories developed under industrial conditions, but they offer much that can still be used by foodservice and other service industries.

His first step was to analyze production methods and isolate the best and most efficient procedures. He taught these methods to the workers, but they had little effect since the workers still had little reason to improve their productivity. In fact, much hostility accompanied Taylor's introduction of new machines and equipment. Workers felt their jobs threatened or that they were being overworked, even though the work might actually be easier. Only by fining the workers could Taylor introduce new methods, but of course the hostility problem remained.

Taylor then realized that nobody knew what a fair day's work was. He began to analyze jobs to determine what a worker could logically be expected to produce. This analysis required him to time how long it should take to perform the jobs. (This timing led to the development of time-and-motion studies that systematically establish appropriate time periods for various operations.) Once work production standards had been developed, it became feasible to pay bonuses for production in excess of these standards.

Taylor had an analytical inquiring mind and he began to use the methods of analysis that helped him develop time-and-motion studies in such other areas as production planning, inventory control, cost accounting, and production methods. From this work came the idea of separating planning and doing. Instead of simply telling a worker what and how to produce, someone else planned how to do it and the worker strictly followed the production plan. Separating planning and doing is still relatively new in one area of foodservice. The chef was—and often still is—considered a craftsman. Many managers still shy away from giving the chef any instructions or advice. Traditionally the chef schedules the kitchen work, perhaps even secures the food and oversees kitchen administration, in addition to preparing the food to be served. Taylor also emphasized the importance of carefully selecting workers and continuing their development and training. Finding the right man for the right job, he thought, was far better than filling the job with just anybody.

Taylor often produced spectacular results typically characterized by increased production from a fraction of the former work force. But his innovations stirred up a great deal of opposition. Congress even investigated whether or not time study was ethical, and for a while it was excluded from federal operations. Taylor's goal was what he called "a mental revolution" in which management, using his methods of increasing productivity, would enjoy greater profits and would consequently pay its workers more. With the workers enjoying more of the fruits of their labor, there would be no industrial strife, and unions would not be necessary. (This idea helps explain why Taylor was thought to be antiunion.) With management and workers pulling together for each other's benefit there would be industrial harmony. Unfortunately, as we now know, neither management nor labor seemed willing to share with the other; each wanted as much of the pie as possible, and Taylor's goal of a mental revolution was never achieved.

Others who carried on Taylor's ideas included, notably, Henry Gantt, who concentrated on incentive plans and also on the *Gantt Scheduling Chart*, where progress is scheduled against time. Another leader in the field was Frank Gilbreth who, with his wife Lillian, made many contributions in motion economy. The term *therblig* which means a basic movement is "Gilbreth" spelled backwards. (Frank and Lillian Gilbreth and their twelve children were immortalized in the reminiscences written by their son Frank, Jr., and daughter Ernestine. Those stories became the book and motion picture *Cheaper by the Dozen*.)

The contributions of Taylor, Gantt, the Gilbreths, and others helped establish management as a science. Their primary area of interest is what we call *industrial engineering*, rather than the broader field of management. But they all focused attention on the fact that there were better ways of doing things than the prevailing traditional ways. They made significant contributions in scheduling, production methods, and time-and-motion study. The idea of a mental revolution failed because money was not the motivation Taylor thought it was. He reasoned that man would work harder only if he could improve his economic status. Later developments proved that stronger motivations could exist.

Taylor and his contemporaries worked in the environment of industrial plants, and much of their contribution was designed for large-scale industrial production, not the usual small batch-type activity found in foodservice operations. Time-and-motion study is more applicable to routine factory work featuring long, monotonous production runs of relatively few items. By contrast, a kitchen usually has short production runs of many different items. Despite this difference though, the foodservice and hospitality industry owes much to the early proponents of scientific management. As the term suggests, those studies of various production components used a precise, analytical approach. That scientific approach, that habit of applying the scientific method to management, has yet to be fully utilized in many foodservice operations.

Some industrial techniques are out of place in a kitchen, but the general approach and the accompanying idea that there is always a better way provide a constant goal for the hospitality manager. After all, labor-saving approaches can often be applied to foodservice operations. The idea of selecting the right person for a particular job and training him how best to do that job has brought significant changes to management in the hospitality industry. The separation of the planning and the actual work can still be fruitfully applied in the foodservice field.

Classical Management Science

Management science or the *Management Process Approach* is usually identified with Henri Fayol (1841–1925). Fayol had been head of a French iron and steel combine, and in 1916 he published a book on management based both on his observations as an industrialist and his training as an engineer. Although the book was translated into English as early as 1925, it was not widely circulated here until 1949. Fayol theorized that there are common "threads" or principles in the management of any endeavor, and if one knows these principles he can apply them to any type of business and be an effective manager. This theory is illustrated by the head of the business who successfully enters an entirely different type of business, or by the armed forces officer who successfully transfers into a civilian operation. Fayol was interested with *classical administration*, that is, the firm as a whole, not just a single segment like production or marketing.

Not only did Fayol theorize that management principles were applicable to any type of business, but he also felt they were applicable to the various levels in the business as well. Thus, a junior executive could use the same principles as the president. Fayol realized, though, that the higher one is in the level of management, the less technical knowledge and the more administrative knowledge one needs.

Fayol listed the functions of management as follows:

To plan

To organize

To command

To coordinate

To control

Fayol not only defined the functions of administration but also listed some of its important principles. These included the idea that *responsibility cannot be delegated without authority* or, phrased another way, that authority provided should be equal to the responsibility delegated. Another Fayol principle was *unity of command,* which said that one should take orders only from one's supervisor. A third principle was *unity of direction,* which suggested that activities having the same direction should have only one head and one plan.

Other management theorists have added to Fayol's principles, changed some of them, or fiddled with his list. But the basis of his approach to management remains: if an individual can understand these functions and how to cope with them, he can be an efficient manager.

Perhaps the importance of Fayol's contributions can be shown by the fact that many who have never heard of him utilize his principles. There has been some criticism that those principles may be too dogmatic, but Fayol himself always emphasized that they should be treated as rules of thumb rather than absolute laws.

The Human Relations Approach

The scientific management approach deals almost exclusively with ways to make a worker more productive. The management science approach is concerned with principles that lead toward a more effective management structure. Beginning in the late 1930s, a new approach to management developed that might be called the *human relations approach.* This approach focuses on the employees themselves. As such it is largely behavioristic. Using this approach, we recognize that an organization really consists of the people working in it and that management should be primarily concerned with working with these people.

Forerunners of the human relations approach were the famous Hawthorne Experiments conducted at the Hawthorne Plant of the Western Electric Company in Chicago between 1927 and 1932. There were a number of these experiments, but some of them involved changes in production due to changes in lighting and other environmental alterations. The researchers were, of course, eager to learn if production could be increased by changes in these factors to enable the company to sell more lighting equipment.

In one Hawthorne experiment, five workers with the job of assembling telephone relays by hand were taken from the general assembly floor. Their production was not paced by a machine but depended instead on the speed of the operators. One unit per minute was considered very satisfactory. In addition, there was a group financial incentive with extra pay given to the better groups. Unknown to the chosen five workers, careful records had been kept of their previous production—a standard to which future production could be compared.

The five workers were moved to a room by themselves with the same general environmental conditions as those on the main assembly floor. Changes were made in their routine. Rest periods were introduced. Production rose. Rest periods were increased. Production rose again. A coffee break was inaugurated. Production continued to rise. Hours were lopped off the working day. But still production increased. Saturday work was eliminated, and production continued to increase. At first these results suggested that the increases were due to the rest periods, the shorter hours, and the coffee breaks. To prove this hypothesis, all the new benefits were taken away to see if production would fall back to the original standards. But, even without these special benefits, the production of the five workers continued to increase. Benefits were reintroduced, and production rose higher than ever. Not only did production increase but the workers experienced only a fraction of the illness of those on the regular assembly line. And they appeared happy and eager to go to work.

Something akin to Taylor's mental revolution seemed to have occurred without the financial incentives that Taylor had thought necessary. Workers were producing at very high rates and working in the best interests of the company. What was the motivation? It could not be economic—they were receiving no more money incentive than the other workers. This tended to disprove the *rabble hypothesis* that industrial workers are a disorganized rabble of individuals each acting only in his own self-interest.

Atlhough the results and conclusions of the Hawthorne experiments have been interpreted differently by different people, it seemed certain that some psychological factors could cause higher production. One was the existence of an "informal work group," which might decide for itself whether to go "all out" for the enterprise on the one hand, or to sabotage it on the other. In the Hawthorne experiments, the five workers considered themselves a select group and believed that they were expected to produce. Thus they were eager to do so, and their production continued to rise. This higher production was not a response to management, but seemed to be due to a decision they had made among themselves.

Two other conclusions might be drawn from the Hawthorne experiments. One is the importance of a sense of belonging, or that people want to feel a part of something, especially their job. The importance of first-line supervision was also evident. No longer could just anybody be made a foreman. A title by itself could not be expected to motivate workers to produce. Perhaps the "Bull of the Woods" supervisor could be effective when people were worried about jobs and accepted more dominance. But even in the 1930s this style of supervision was being questioned (and many hotel managers and classic chefs were very domineering). With the work force today having even higher aspirations, the authoritarian foreman may be questioned even more. Perhaps most of all, the Hawthorne experiments showed that contributions could be made by acquiring an understanding of the dynamics of human behavior. It opened the way for the psychologists, sociologists, and other behaviorists who began to contribute to the science of management.

Throughout the rest of this book we will discuss various human relation approaches to management, and we will often compare these approaches to others. Remember always, though, that management involves working with people and (except in rare circumstances) management must be very aware of the needs of these people, how these needs may be satisfied, and consequently how the people can be motivated.

The hospitality field, in particular, is a "people industry." The hospitality operation is unique in that it is directly involved with both the people who buy the products or services and the people who produce them. Most other enterprises are either primarily retail or primarily manufacturing in nature. But since the foodservice industry is both, it encounters both sets of people. The current social trend suggests that relations with employees will become increasingly more important, and hospitality managers already know how important it is to keep their customers happy. It will be up to the successful manager to try to achieve Taylor's goal of a mental revolution—having employees voluntarily eager to give their best efforts for the business. We know for certain that financial benefits by themselves will not induce this enthusiasm.

Modern Management Theory

As the traditional theories of management stressing formal organization crystallized, they began to undergo attacks by social scientists, who felt that the traditional theories could create some undesirable conditions for workers. The traditional theories were, after all, based on the economic goals of profit maximization. Along with making a profit, the traditional theories were aimed at the efficient utilization of economic resources through the most efficient production and distribution of goods and services. (That economic success might, incidentally, bring economic growth, larger benefits for the workers, and greater employment for the community was an idea temporarily lost in the shuffle.) The traditional firm expected to achieve these goals through the hierarchies of authorities, through the division of labor and processes, and through specialization.

But the newer organization theorists challenged the assumption that man is purely or even primarily an economic being. They felt the common boss-subordinate relationship presented stresses that actually ran contrary to the goals of the operation. With specialization and division of labor, for example, workers would often resist a job and seemed to gain little satisfaction or feeling of craftsmanship in what they were doing. The new theorists saw that many of the specialized jobs were demeaning and socially unacceptable. In fact the same types of organization could create deep divisions and social problems within an operation. Bureaucratic control, rules, budgets, performance appraisals, and other such techniques stressed by the traditional management school were seen to be detrimental not only to the individual but also to the organization itself. Stronger authority and tight control were said to be not only antidemocratic but counterproductive.

Although the *organizational behavior approach* to management was certainly stimulated by the Hawthorne experiments, there had already been some discussion about the most humane ways to manage an organization and the people in it. Many different theorists contributed to that discussion over the years, and although there is not a unified organizational management approach, there is widespread agreement that organizations revolve around the people comprising it and not the work itself. Traditional organization, on the other hand, had always considered the work to be done first and then determined the jobs necessary to do it, rather than concentrating on the people themselves.

The organizational behavior theorists have pointed out that in accomplishing its goals, management should see to it that members of the organization accomplish their personal goals. Organizational theorists also believe that the informal organization of workers is surprisingly strong and that consideration must be accorded it. In the traditional organization chart, the informal organization would never even appear.

The newer organizational behavior theorists include *humanists* who are striving for a better world, of which the working world is obviously an important part. They include *participationists* who believe that participation by members of an organization in the organization's affairs has many positive advantages; they include *behaviorists* who feel that not enough attention has been given to the behavioral aspects of individuals in the field of management. On our continuum (Exhibit 2-3) the organizational behavior approach is shown as being introduced about 1950. Of course, there were many contributions before this, but there were a number of applications being made at that time. Progress is, in fact, still continuing rapidly.

The behavioral scientists would like to substitute a new theory of administration in which, instead of being primarily representative of the owners, the operation manager would also be the agent of all components of the organization at all levels. He would strive to provide an enlightened work force instead of forcing the workers into previously determined molds, and he would try to adapt individuals to the formal and informal organizations within the operation. By this means, the behavioral scientists hope to eliminate organizational conflicts and the dehumanization of workers.

In traditional organizations it is assumed that management knows what it wants to have done. It need only arrange for someone in the organization to do it and issue the necessary instructions through the formal chain of command. It can then assume that the job will be done and hold the people along the chain of command responsible if it is not. The behaviorists challenge this approach and say that the lack of scope and discretion make workers unhappy with their job. As they become unhappy, they tend to spend more time on breaks and in unproductive activity. Management notices the sluggishness and berates the supervisors for it. With this, the supervisors themselves grow disillusioned and apathetic, and management feels that to regain the control it must strengthen its operation with another level of supervision. Thus the whole vicious cycle begins to repeat itself.

Modern Organizational Behavior Theory

Many of the newer theorists have been persuasive and influential. Perhaps it would be worthwhile to consider some of the contributions made during the twentieth century. Chester Barnard decided that authority should flow also *upwards*, not primarily downwards. Orders, he saw, often are ignored unless they are *accepted* by subordinates. He also felt that an organization should be a system of cooperation encouraged by both financial and nonfinancial considerations. Barnard recognized that informal organizations usually exist within the formal ones, and that the relationships shown on the organization chart were not necessarily the most influential ones. Along with other contemporaries, Barnard stressed the idea of *equilibrium* wherein the survival of an organization depends on its ability to inspire cooperation in employees and to have everyone work together. Barnard had been president of the New Jersey Bell Telephone Company and wrote from the viewpoint of a practicing executive. His book, *The Functions of the Executive*, was published in 1938.

E. Wight Bakke, an academician, discussed organization as a fusion process in which the individual hopes to use the organization to achieve his goals while the organization hopes to use the individual to further its goals. In this fusion process, both must "remake" each other to some degree—the individual trying to *personalize* the organization and the organization trying to *socialize* the individual. In Bakke's view, for one to be a "benevolent supervisor" there must be a "grateful subordinate" and job descriptions and specifications should include both the needs of the organization and the personal goals of its participants.

Frederick Herzberg studied jobs as *satisfiers* and *dissatisfiers*. He found that satisfiers included achievement, recognition, the work itself, the responsibility, advancement, and growth. Factors that tend to cause dissatisfaction included supervision, working conditions, relationships with peers, and company policy and administration. From this pairing, one can draw the conclusion that jobs should be intrinsically satisfying or embody responsibility, interest, and opportunity. Herzberg's insights led to notions of *job enlargement* and *job enrichment:* when one is happy with his job, according to these notions, he should be contributing wholeheartedly to the goals of the organization.

Much management attention has focused on Abraham Maslow's famous *hierarchy of human needs.* Maslow recognized that an individual has a scale of needs and that the higher levels do not become pressing until the lower levels have been satisfied. Beginning at the lower level, Maslow's human needs are:

1. Physiological well-being
2. Safety
3. Belongingness and love
4. Esteem
5. Self-actualization

Satisfying these needs at whatever level they may arise, an organization makes an employee happier and, theoretically, eager to produce as much as possible.

Organizational Behavior and the Hospitality Field

Much of the organizational theorists' work has been done in large industries featuring routine production and assembly lines. It is easy to see why even a well-paid worker could become unhappy on an assembly line, where his only job is tightening one bolt as a product passed him. This extremely boring job presents little opportunity for craftsmanship and less opportunity of creativity. Specialization and division of labor encourages these arrangements, and tight control is usually necessary to enforce them.

By contrast, the hospitality industry is fortunate that it can avoid some of the behavioral problems of other more repetitive industries. Most hospitality establishments are relatively small with few levels of authority between a worker and the head of the operation. Knowing most of the people who are involved in an operation, an employee can more readily feel himself to be a part of it. Employees in most foodservice operations can also see the completed product as it goes to the customer. This can be more satisfying than seeing only the part that passes on an assembly line. Foodservice and other hospitality jobs are rarely machine paced, and although they may be demanding (at rush hours, for example) at times the work goes at a lighter pace. Many hospitality employees know or at least see their customers, which can be more satisfying than working on a product without knowing who will use it. There is definitely an element of craftsmanship in preparing fine food, and many foodservice workers take pride in their work. And finally, most foodservice facilities are not drastically affected by seasonal trends. The assurance of a definite work schedule adds an element of security.

These comments do not imply that the hospitality industry has arrived at the level most organizational theorists hope employees attain. The heads of many operations have never heard of organizational behavior, and if they had, many would be disinclined to practice its principles. Too many of our operations give too little consideration to their lower level employees. Nevertheless, the hospitality industry has inherent advantages over other industries in its ability to practice good organizational behavior principles. With growing independence and sophistication among its work force, the industry will undoubtedly begin to see these principles as more important than they have been in the past.

Other industries have begun to apply organizational behavior principles in human relations. Job rotation, for example, relieves boredom and increases production. It also allows a worker some feeling of craftsmanship and achievement. Instead of being ordered what to do, many workers have begun to decide for themselves the best way to do it. In these cases, the workers may schedule their own hours, perhaps working longer hours for a period with more time off later. Personal advancement and career paths are considered more frequently, and the employer may help subsidize further training needed for advancement. Supervisors are evaluated both on their technical skills and on their human relation skills, and training in human relations for supervisors is becoming very common. This approach has begun to pay off in American industry, and it will work as well in the hospitality field.

Operations Research

An approach to management called *operations research* became popular in the early 1960s. It is most appropriate where the definition of management becomes "the solving of problems in the enterprise." Operations research is largely quantitative; it often employs a mathematical basis for decision-making. It can also be interdisciplinary, utilizing specialists from different fields. Operations research is supposed to have had its first significant success in the Battle of Britain during the Second World War. Radar had been developed to provide advance warnings of air attacks and to plot the approach of German planes. But Britain did not have enough defending planes to defend the probable attack areas, so the problem was to find the best distribution system for the defending air force. To determine an optimal distribution of planes, the generals and air marshals called on a small number of scientists to work the problem out mathematically and scientifically. The deployment was of course successful; the German Luftwaffe went down to defeat.

Nonmilitary scientists were then called in to help plan a defense against submarine attacks. This defense included the determination of such things as the deposition of ships and optimum sea levels at which to deploy depth bombs. Factors involved in the mathematical calculations included the number of German submarines, their capabilities, where they would logically surface, and what antisubmarine defenses were available to the British. The United States Navy, too, successfully used operations research to provide a pattern for mining Japanese waters. The admirals asked the scientists what pattern of mine fields would most inhibit Japanese shipping, how many mines would be required, where they should be placed, and at what depths.

After the successful operations research track record in World War II, business began to adopt the technique for its purposes. Larger business organizations began to set up operations research sections. The approach was enhanced even more by the development of computers that could process mathematical calculations speedily and inexpensively.

A notable example of the use of operations research occurred when Robert McNamara was brought from the Ford Motor Company by President Kennedy to be Secretary of Defense. McNamara and his "whiz kids" applied quantitative techniques to handle decision-making problems in the Pentagon and were credited with introducing a great deal of logical efficiency to that sprawling department.

Operations research has been defined as "the application of the scientific method to management problems that can be expressed in quantitative terms." Another definition calls operations research "the scientific study of complex organizations aimed at identifying problems and giving executives a quantitative basis for decision-making that will increase effectiveness in achieving objectives." The analysts typically construct mathematical models that permit comparisons of alternative courses of action to determine which course will bring the best results. Its purpose is to aid an executive's decision-making. Operations research has also been called *quantitative common sense, mathematical decision-making,* and *the scientific method approach.*

As mentioned, operations research is primarily used in decision-making, and it is most useful when the decisions are of a recurring nature. The data bearing on the problem is assembled and processed. From this data, mathematical calculations can be made to determine the wisest course of action. But to use operations research, one must be able to state the problem in quantitative terms that can be used in mathematical calculations; and the results, too, must be measurable on a quantitative basis. Thus, operations research can readily help determine optimum inventory quantities, order sizes, and facility requirements. A typical operations research problem is to determine the best route to take to visit all forty-eight capitals in the continental United States with the least time and mileage.

Operations research employs a number of tools. Discussions of four of these tools follow.

Model Making

Model making is an attempt to represent the real world with a mathematical formula or model. The model is usually a simplification of the particular circumstances surrounding the problem. Model making is said to have been borrowed from the physical sciences when Einstein developed $E = mc^2$ (energy equals mass times the square of the speed of light), which is a conceptual model of the physical universe. A model can be either simple or complex. It can represent a complete organization or only part of the organization. It would be impossible, of course, to describe the real world completely in a mathematical model, but it is possible to include the most important variables so that accurate predictions can be developed.

Models can be used in a number of different foodservice situations. One obvious application would be to determine the feasibility of *establishing* a commercial foodservice operation. Foremost in such a feasibility study is the forecasting of sales. The amount of sales generated depends on a number of such factors as traffic density, average income in the area, competition, and pricing. It is possible to put these factors (and others as well) into a model and then insert predicted figures or values for the factors. The sales figure can then be determined, and from this figure, projected expenses can be subtracted to show profit.

Different models can be constructed for different types of operations. The factors for a luxury restaurant would obviously be different from those for a fast food shop. Not only can operations research help determine the feasibility of a particular type of operation, but the feasibility of different types of operations at the same location could also be calculated and the most appropriate operation chosen. Such a model can also be used to determine whether an actual operation is performing as well as the model indicates it should. And the model can be used in decision-making processes—for example, to determine whether to increase the advertising budget.

Game Theory

Game theory is a management technique used to determine which maximum-gain or minimum-loss strategy to employ under specified conditions. It derives from *war games* where simulation games allow players to explore situations and strategies. An attacker must consider not just his strategy but also what the defending forces are likely to do, what the chances are that they will adopt certain strategies, and what particular events are likely to occur. Conversely, the defender must anticipate what the attacker is likely to do, how his moves can be thwarted, and what the chances are that the attacker will make various moves in response to the defender's actions.

Now, imagine that instead of warring parties, two hospitality establishments in the same location are in competition with each other and serve basically the same clientele. One operation wants to increase its share of the market—presumably at the expense of the other operation. The strategies might include more promotion or price cuts. But if one operation were to adopt one of these strategies, it must also consider what the competition might do. Can it match any increase in promotion or decrease in selling prices? There may be little chance that one operation could determine with certainty what the counterstrategy might be. But the game plan approach would be to find the particular strategy that, assuming the opponent's most logical countermoves, would result in the greatest gain. There is a great deal of uncertainty involved in this approach, and many believe that gaming strategies should be used only as a decision-making aid rather than a primary tool.

Linear Programming

In linear programming, the manager takes a mathematical approach to determine the best use of limited resources. A planned kitchen should have the most efficient arrangement of equipment possible. If a definite menu has been planned, and especially if it includes a relatively small number of items, it is possible to determine the amount and arrangement of movement of people and materials needed in the kitchen to prepare the items under different equipment arrangements. Travel indices (the product of the frequency of movement of employees and materials times the distance moved) can be calculated. The layout with the lowest travel index should have the greatest efficiency. This is one mathematical approach to management.

Queuing Theory

Waiting line theory, as the queuing theory can be called, concerns the problem of insufficient facilities to handle personnel, machines, or materials, and the delays that result.

Let's say a restaurant has a long waiting line at mealtimes. What is the proper balance between this delay and the cost of correcting it? Conceivably it would be possible to provide enough tables and serving personnel to handle all the customers without any wait. But during slow periods a portion of these facilities and personnel would remain idle. Solving the problem would involve a determination of, among other things, the number of customers liable to be dissatisfied with varying waiting periods. Moreover, in planning a new facility, one must determine how many customers to expect during various periods, how long they can be expected to wait without dissatisfaction, and what facilities meet these requirements. The queuing theory can also be used to determine the number of people to have on duty in relation to the projected business.

Operations Research: Summary

As we have discussed, operations research requires the application of quantitative techniques in decision-making or problem-solving. Operations research has been greatly helped by modern computers that can handle the calculations both economically and rapidly. An overall operations technique should include the following steps:

1. Formulate the problem. The management must become aware of the real problem. (Sometimes, in the analysis and definition stage, the problem may be largely solved. Other times, the management may gradually become aware that the assumed problem is not the main difficulty.)

2. Form a hypothesis. A hypothesis is developed, most likely in the form of a mathematical model.

3. Develop an optimum solution to the problem using the model. This may require a number of alternative approaches.

4. Test the solution as far as possible.

5. Put the tested solution into effect.

Remember, operations research can be a most helpful tool, but it cannot be used indiscriminately or as the main source of decision-making. It is only as good as its data, and it usually involves a great deal of speculation. In short, it cannot take the place of management discretion or insight.

Closely allied to operations research is an approach sometimes called *management science.* This is not the management science of Fayol, but rather a quantitative approach that uses behavioral sciences besides the mathematical sciences found in operations research. Management scientists designing a kitchen, for example, would use quantitative approaches to determine the equipment layout, but they would also use behavioral approaches to determine the requirements of the employees using that equipment. Some of the behavior aspects could be determining color schemes that could promote efficiency, work locations of personnel that are pleasant but efficient, whether to have background music, and types of uniforms worn. All of these can have an effect on production.

The next development in the management continuum (see Exhibit 2-3) is *systems management.* Although it is usually dated around 1968, systems management has been around a long time, and progressive businessmen have been using it for years. We defer our systems management discussion to Chapter 3; but, briefly, systems management is a way of looking at the total enterprise, planning its organization, and providing the means for solving its problems.

Development of Management in Hospitality Operations

Conceptual and theoretical management in foodservice operations has generally lagged behind the other industries. Part of this is due to the fact that while the industry is large—the fourth largest in the country—it is composed of many small organizations. The smaller operations have had only limited access to conceptual management information or have been hesitant to apply it. (The larger the operation, the more time people can spend on strictly management development.) Many of the owners and executives in foodservice started in the field on a trade basis. Many started as cooks, for example, and worked to become chefs, then managers, and then owners of their own operations. This trade orientation leaves little time or opportunity to gain a theoretical management background. The fact that many foodservices operate at a relatively low level of management efficiency does not necessarily penalize these operations. Their competitors may be doing no better. On the other hand, a knowledge of management principles certainly gives an operation an edge.

The situation is, of course, rapidly changing in foodservice, as well as in other fields. Running an organization is becoming more complicated, and a foodservice operation can no longer feel that it will be successful just because it serves good food. Chain-type operations are becoming larger in importance, and their successful use of management techniques forces other operations to adopt them, to be at least competitive if not overwhelmingly successful. Professional management training, which up until recently had been a rarity, is now widespread. Academic programs in colleges, junior colleges, and technical high schools are graduating large numbers of qualified managerial people. Correspondence courses and other learning programs are now available to those who want to increase their technical proficiency but cannot take time away from work. There were once only a handful of specialized textbooks in hospitality management where now dozens are available. As people with management training prove themselves in the foodservice and hospitality field, the need for this training becomes more and more evident and vital.

Early hotel managers were often more interested in being a *Mine Host* type than an efficient manager. With labor and food relatively cheap, efficiency was not too important. Filling the "house" was important, since room sales were very profitable, and in the smaller establishments of earlier eras the manager's relationships with guests could be very important.

Ellsworth Statler was a pioneer in changing the concept that innkeeping was a business besides providing hospitality. The hard times of the depression years also forced a business outlook on the industry.

Hotels are a many faceted and sophisticated enterprise, and it is recognized that specialized business acumen is necessary in managing them.

SUMMARY

Though utterly indispensable to human endeavors, management may be approached differently by each manager. One can argue whether management is an art, a science, a resource, or an elite class of people. Management has, however, definite characteristics. It is goal-oriented; it strives for definite accomplishments. It is concerned with people, both as individuals and as groups. It is also flexible rather than static, changing with the changes in the external environment.

A manager commands certain resources for accomplishing his goals. These are sometimes known as "the six M's of management"; they comprise men (or personnel), materials, methods, machines, money, and markets. By using these resources—together with the management functions of planning, organizing, controlling, and directing—the manager works for the accomplishment of his enterprise's objectives. The broad goals of any profit-making enterprise include: producing a profit or return for the investors, providing a decent livelihood for employees, producing a worthwhile product or service for customers, and being a good neighbor in the community. Of course, a high return for investors may overshadow the other goals.

Management does not take place in a vacuum—internal and external environments affect all management decisions and procedures.

There are various approaches to, and philosophies of, management. Classical scientific management concentrates on increasing worker or plant efficiency. Classical management science (management process) assumes that there exist common principles in management, that these are applicable to any endeavor, and if the manager competently applies these principles he can be successful. The human relations approach to management focuses on employees. It holds that an organization consists of the people working in it, and that management should be concerned primarily about working with these people. The organizational behavior approach is concerned with how employees function in groups. It seeks to determine whether the manager can eliminate both organizational conflicts and the dehumanization of workers while he promotes the success of his enterprise.

Operations research is concerned largely with the managerial aspect of decision-making. The difference between a manager and other members of the organization is that the manager makes decisions. Operations Research provides tools, usually quantitative ones, to help the manager make decisions or solve problems. Another approach to management is systems management, discussed in detail in Chapter Three.

Different managers will use different managerial approaches, depending on their particular situations, needs, and characters. But even when a manager chooses one approach, he should be aware of other available approaches.

IMPORTANT TERMS

management

goal orientation

management resources

management functions

external management environment

internal management environment

capitalism

classical scientific management

classical management science

unity of direction

unity of command

mental revolution

organizational behavior

equilibrium

hierarchy of human needs

job rotation

operations research

model making

game theory

linear programming

queuing theory

REVIEW QUESTIONS

2–1. What are the characteristics of management?

2–2. State four definitions of management.

2–3. List and discuss management resources.

2–4. List and discuss three functions of management.

2–5. How does the importance of management functions change as one rises higher in management ranks?

2–6. What are the goals of management?

2–7. Discuss classical scientific management.

2–8. Discuss classical management science.

2–9. What is the human relations approach to management?

2–10. Describe the operations research approach to management.

3 Systems Approach to Hospitality Management

The systems approach to management had its beginnings in applied mathematics and computer science. Some managers use the systems approach practically by instinct, but all managers should be aware of its benefits, applicability, and usefulness. Therefore, after you finish studying this chapter, you should be able to

- *define the systems approach to management*
- *discuss the benefits of this approach as set forth in this chapter*
- *state the elements and draw a basic diagram of a system*
- *explain how to implement the systems approach to management in a hospitality establishment*
- *explain how a systems approach might be usefully applied to both a dietary operation and a fast-food restaurant*

An Introduction to the Systems Approach

At one time, if someone wanted to open a foodservice business, he would start by finding a suitable location. Then he would plan a structure, allowing space for dining, food preparation, and dishwashing. If the structure were already standing, he would designate space for these functions—and storage would probably fill any leftover crannies. Next, this hopeful operator would secure furnishings for the dining area that he considered both appropriate for the guests he expected and within his budget. While he would arrange for general preparation equipment in the kitchen, he would usually give more thought to dining room decor than to kitchen planning. Then he would hire personnel, write a menu, purchase food, and—possibly after some sales promotion—swing open his doors. With luck, the quality of his food and service, the location of his business, and perhaps his own personality would spell success.

As you can see, owners who started this way gave little consideration to the interaction of the various individual foodservice components or to whether they would work together smoothly. Similarly, the chef concentrated on food production and thought little of the dining room; and the headwaiter, in his turn, served the patrons with little thought about kitchen problems unless they interfered with customer satisfaction.

Eventually this owner might realize that the menu was crucial to the success of his operation instead of being almost an afterthought in the planning process. He might discover that customer acceptance, profitability, personnel morale, space, and equipment were all affected—and in large part determined—by the items on the menu. Thus, foodservice planning gradually came to start with the proposed menu. Instead of installing general kitchen equipment and hiring a general kitchen staff, an operator secured equipment and personnel appropriate for the specific type of menu he intended to serve. And, since his goal was now to serve a predetermined menu rather than to run a general foodservice, he began to look seriously at a new management idea called the *systems approach* that particularly suited his menu orientation.

Today's foodservice operator has many problems: high labor costs, a skilled labor shortage, intense competition, and decreasing profit margins, to name just four. To overcome these problems, he has to become as efficient as possible. This need for efficiency has led straight to the systems approach in which all foodservice components—ordering, storing, sanitation, and so forth—are coordinated to achieve the goals of the restaurant.

This systems approach requires an operator to determine in advance how each change in his facility will affect the whole business and its goals. The systems approach also requires the various subsystems to be integrated efficiently. The goals of a restaurant may be the highest profit consistent with patron satisfaction, while an institution might have the goal of providing the best foodservice that resources permit. Balanced nutrition, friendly service, thorough sanitation, and ample food variety might be some of the subgoals.

A modern foodservice operator no longer considers preparation and serving separately; rather he treats these elements as integrated subsystems of the operation. He must anticipate how, together with the other subsystems, these two elements can best accomplish the objectives of his entire business.

Technological progress has, of course, supplemented the systems approach. For example, convenience foods are being provided in more varieties and better qualities. Better methods for storing, holding, and reconstituting these foods have also come along. Data processing has lent new dimensions to food management. More efficient equipment and even some automation has been introduced. Such new service products as disposable utensils often streamline the foodservice system.

In its most basic form, a system meshes men, machines, material, methods, markets, and money so as to achieve the goals of an operation efficiently. In addition to these traditional six M's of management, a system includes a variety of subsystems which should be both interdependent and interrelated. For example, the dining room and kitchen should not be autonomous areas but should, instead, complement and support every other area in the restaurant. An owner may consider cutting costs in the dishroom by using more disposables, but he must also consider the subsequent effects of his decision in the dining room, in the kitchen, on the goal or profit maximization, and on patron satisfaction. Put more simply, the change to disposables will affect the dishroom, the kitchen, and the profits. A manager had better know what the effect will be in advance.

The Systems Approach in Perspective

The systems approach is not, of course, unique to the foodservice industry. It has not only been heralded as an answer to the knottier problems of business management, but it has also been advanced as virtually the only approach to such complex problems facing society as transportation, housing, education, and health care. Nevertheless, the systems approach is not really new. Various forms of the systems approach were advanced by Plato, St. Thomas Aquinas, and Machiavelli. In fact, at one time or another, most of us—whether or not we are philosophers or business managers—think systematically. All that the systems approach does is to take systematic thinking and formalize it into a step-by-step procedure so that a businessman like a restaurant owner can use it easily and to good advantage.

The word *system* means different things to different people, so it is usually easier to discuss than define it. To some people, system denotes a way of thinking about an organization. To others, it is a problem-solving tool. Someone interested in the organizational aspects of management may visualize a system as a set of components (or parts) to be coordinated and set in motion toward certain goals. We can, however, offer you this formal definition of a system: a grouping of separate components that work together toward a goal in the most efficient way possible. As you can see, an automobile, the human body, and a restaurant can all be grouped under this definition.

We have some trouble pinning down what we mean when we talk about systems because they have such broad applications. In management, a complete system encompasses all of the aspects of a business— its goals and objectives, its resources, its various interrelationships, and its processes. And all of these aspects are, in turn, affected by the environment in which the system functions.

It may be easier for us to talk, for the moment, about systems negatively—to ask what happens when a system is missing. Frankly, nothing at all may happen. It's possible that your restaurant has fallen into such a comfortable routine that it can "run itself." More likely, however, a business that runs itself has its various components working against each other toward narrow, self-serving goals. Rarely do such goals correspond to the overall goals of the restaurant. For example, your chef may want to express himself with some fancy gourmet dish. But his need for self-expression may conflict with your need to cut expenses. Here's another example: if the personnel in a certain area suddenly ask to have their jobs enlarged and made more important, meeting their request could erode the importance of other sections and employees elsewhere—to the detriment of everyone.

Some Systems Metaphors

The growth of the systems approach in modern business can be largely attributed, strangely enough, to a biologist: Ludwig von Bertalanffy, in the 1950s, was the first man to discuss living organisms in terms of the mutual interaction of related parts rather than as a conglomeration of separate elements. Borrowing von Bertalanffy's biological analogy, we can see that a system must have a definite organization and maintain a constant state despite changes in its environment. But a system is affected by environment and it affects environment.

The human body is, of course, a system: like most systems it has its various subsystems—for example, the circulatory, nervous, digestive, muscular, skeletal, and reproductive systems. Even these subsystems can, in turn, be broken down into "sub-subsystems." But the human body systematizes outward as well as inward. It tends to belong to a family system, to a community system, to a national system, to a world system, and yes, to a solar system.

You are probably beginning to get the idea now, even though the notion of a system must have sounded a little confusing at first. But we will abandon the human body as a systems metaphor and turn to the car as a systems metaphor, to reinforce our point. The importance of the components (or subsystems) can be shown by considering a hypothetical car equipped with a Volkswagen body, a Cadillac engine, a Buick transmission, a Ford braking system, and Chrysler parts and service. The vehicle might move—however, awkwardly. But the components, or parts, would hardly run in harmony with one another.

The Systems Approach and the Hospitality Manager

The systems approach can help a hospitality manager in several ways:

It helps a hospitality manager examine his operation, its goals, and its resources.

It helps organize the personnel and the work in an operation. It helps coordinate these people and their work to achieve the goals of the operation.

It suggests ways to solve problems, or at least puts problems in a perspective. It reveals the importance of such problems and, therefore, the effort that should be devoted to their solution.

Let us discuss these three advantages to the systems approach more thoroughly.

Goals and resources. As we have already pointed out, every system has its subsystems, and every system is, itself, a subsystem of some larger system. The food production system, for example, is quite obviously a subsystem of the entire restaurant. Thus, the goals of the food production system must coincide with those of the restaurant.

Just as the food production system is a subsystem of the entire operation, so it has its own subsystems—the bakery, the salad tables, or vegetable prep, for example—that must also help accomplish the operation's goals. Anyone who has the slightest doubt about the roles of these various subsystems can use the systems approach to put them all into perspective and see what they contribute to the restaurant's overall goals.

Organization and coordination. A manager or an owner can, as you know, get too close to his operation to see the faults a more objective person might notice right off. But the systems approach can help provide him with the objectivity he lacks. Are the subsystems pursuing complementary goals? Can some of these subsystems be combined? Has the right kind of equipment been installed? To answer questions like these, a manager must consider all the goals of the overall system. Then he can pinpoint the subsystems that are essential to reach these goals.

Organizing includes determining the exact labor skills required to achieve the goals. By tailoring the *input* of a system to the desired *output,* a manager uses the systems approach and, at the same time, accomplishes a great deal of organizing. Breaking the overall operation down into its subsystems, he can easily see what has to be done, and he can then assign employees to do it. By designing a system, in other words, he also designs his operation. The only difference is that each job in a system must help achieve the goals of the operation. Therefore, its relationship to every other job is clearly established—rather than being more or less separate.

Solutions and perspectives. Consider an example of the use of the systems approach to solve a hospitality feeding problem. The new 747 jets were both faster and larger than any previous commercial airliner. While they provided more passenger space, however, they allowed much less time for meal service. The procedures that had fed passengers on the smaller airplanes were, therefore, inappropriate on the 747s. Moreover, the 747 engineers had designed in no more food preparation space than the smaller planes had. Despite these constraints, the airlines wanted to maintain their dining standards in the 747s.

How did they solve their problem? They resorted to the systems approach. It allowed engineers to view airline foodservice as a system working with the other airline systems. Management listed the goals it wanted its foodservice to attain, and it prepared menus it thought appropriate. Meeting the menu goals required specific new equipment and the development of certain new feeding processes—or subsystems.

The new equipment included high-speed ovens, pressurized coffee makers, an elevator lift service, redesigned galley carts, aesthetically pleasing disposables, and special trash compactors. The new galley carts, for example, ensured straight-through service with no time-consuming backtracking; and they sacrificed none of the old efficiency.

Further analysis of the production objectives led to an alteration in the feeding procedures—specifically, changes in the ground commissary and the on-board preparation mix. In other words, the systems approach helped the airlines' analysts solve the problem of more meals in less time. Merely installing new equipment and urging the personnel to hustle would not have done it. The new procedures and the new equipment had to be integrated into an overall system.

Elements of a System

Analysts have traditionally diagrammed systems as three boxes (*input, process,* and *output*), connected by a backward running arrow (feedback), all surrounded by space labeled *environment.* As this is a useful way to describe a system, both the diagram (see Exhibit 3-1) and a discussion of each of these five elements follows.

Output. If you were asked what you were trying to accomplish with your restaurant, you might answer, "I'm trying to provide the best food I can with what I've got to work with." That statement is, of course, a *goal;* it is also the output you want from your system. But you've stated your goal far too vaguely. You must be more specific, perhaps this way: "I want to provide the same number of meals I provide now with fewer skilled employees; I want to improve the food around here; and I want to provide a wider menu choice." This is a more specific description of the "best food service I can," but you can make your goals even more specific.

It's time now for you to decide how many fewer skilled employees you need, how to measure food quality, and how many new menu items

Exhibit 3–1.
Systems Format

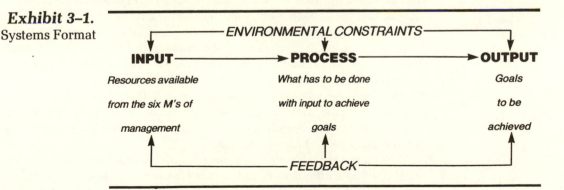

you want to incorporate. Moreover, these specifically stated goals must correspond to the *overall purpose* of your foodservice. Gourmet food, for example, would be out of place and out of the question in a corner luncheonette.

Process. Process refers to how a system's input is treated in order for it to achieve (or not to achieve) its goals or output. Actually there is usually more than one process in every system. And these processes, in most cases, correspond to the typical restaurant subsystems: administration, production, service, and sanitation, to name just four. (One such subsystem, usually called "assembling materials" by business analysts, involves purchasing, receiving, storing, and issuing.)

By changing processes (or subsystems) a restaurant owner can often utilize some of the new technical innovations that appear on the market. For example, the adoption of convenience foods might help an operator eliminate a good deal of other activity and some superfluous employees. Another innovation, disposable utensils, could certainly cut down on and simplify the sanitation subsystem.

Input. The resources available to a system are known collectively as input. Input is processed to achieve output, of one sort or another. Or, to put it another way, resources are treated in ways that contribute to attaining the goals of the restaurant. Input includes some or all of those six M's of management—men (or personnel); machines (or equipment); materials (largely food and cleaning supplies); markets (the customers); money (an operator's financial resources); and methods (such procedures as personnel policies, standard recipes, and operating instructions).

Once you have established goals for your restaurant, you must determine the best way to approach them. Then you collect the resources (or input) you need. We began with output, moved on to process, and saved input for last because this is the way managers actually proceed—even though input appears in the first position on our diagram. A manager will, of course, have to modify a process or a goal when he lacks certain resources. If, for example, he cannot find the skilled personnel he needs, he may be forced to change several processes and modify certain goals.

Resources are sometimes divided into two categories—human and material. Human resources, unlike material resources, are not static. People feel and sometimes express needs and desires; machines and food do not. Thus, the human resources—your personnel—require and deserve your consideration, particularly in view of the fact that their satisfaction can help achieve your goals.

One more critical resource is money. In fact, money can help overcome shortages among most of the other resources. It is a rare restaurant that has all the money it needs; but the systems approach to restaurant management can help a manager make effective use of whatever money he has available.

Feedback. "Feedback" is the term systems analysts use to describe the element of a system that signals a need for adjustments or changes in the processing of input. If your food is simply not good enough, or if your expenses exceed your budget, feedback rapidly alerts you to the need for an adjustment or a remedy. Another way to put it is to say that feedback compares actual output to desired or ideal output.

Feedback can, of course, take the form of various business reports. If you are an on-premises restaurant manager, you may not need formal written reports. But, if you are not directly involved in the running of your establishment, you may need this sort of regular information. In any case, you will constantly need informal reports from your various subsystems, even if you are on the scene. These informal reports may include, for example, charts that show the amount of food prepared, how it was used, the amount of leftovers, and how the leftovers were used. In practically all cases, restaurant owners need information about their costs, and they should devise some way to compare these costs with those that prevail in the area.

All this information is feedback. Each operation must decide what sort of feedback is essential for amending its processes and reaching its goals. In addition, the cost of the feedback must be compared to the benefits derived. Elaborate reports that detail every aspect of the business can themselves eat into profits. By contrast, quick, informal reports—even conversations and rumors—can straighten out a faltering process and turn a loss into profit. The idea is to be aware of the need for feedback and to act on feedback you have received.

Our talk about charts, formal business reports, and informal discussions suggests that feedback should be designed to supply the precise information you need to operate your restaurant. The typical routine financial statements supply some feedback, but their data may not be specific or complete enough to help with an immediate problem. For example, you may be interested in personnel shortages and requirements, food shortages, or food quality information; these are only three of many possible kinds of information often overlooked in routine financial statements.

Feedback should also be timely. A report on food spoilage delivered within the hour would obviously be ideal. Delivered much later, the specifics of the report may become hazy; and what is much worse, the time for corrective action would have passed. As you have perhaps already guessed, in certain situations computerized reporting can provide good, efficient, modern feedback. These machines process large quantities of input easily and rapidly, and their output can both reduce the cost and increase the effectiveness of feedback. Yes, computers are themselves systems and parts of larger systems.

Environment. All the elements of a system we have discussed so far interact with each other and with the environment that surrounds them. The restaurant that cannot adjust to changing conditions will have trouble meeting its goals; that is why you should learn to think of your restaurant system in the context of its environment.

Managers generally think in terms of two kinds of environments: *external* and *internal*. The external environment is made up of the conditions, circumstances, organizations, and individuals with which the system must interact and to which it must react. The internal environment includes such characteristics as employee morale, informal work groups, and working conditions. While a restaurant manager can do little to control the external environment, he can certainly do a great deal to control—and usually to improve—the internal environment.

Many managers, realistically enough, view external environment as a restriction or a constraint. Because of its environment, a particular restaurant may not be able to perform according to its preliminary planning. For example, zoning boards or codes may rule out a certain type of decor or restrict outdoor advertising. Moreover, where a commercial restaurant is concerned, the external environment usually centers on the customers and their needs. These needs are obviously influenced by such external factors as the general state of the economy and the local social mores, sociological attitudes, and cultural traditions. (To put it plainly, you can sell more shoofly pie in the Pennsylvania German regions of southcentral Pennsylvania, where people know and love that dessert, than you can in New York City, where most have never tasted it.) Environment and input are often related: a limited supply of money, for example, brings on an environmental constraint—reduced spending. The external environment may include such additional factors as the availability of food, governmental legislation affecting food services, and even international developments such as the Russian wheat deals.

Thus you can see that a system is not an entity unto itself. As we have pointed out, it is part of a larger system which may, in turn, be part of larger systems. The larger systems affect the external environment of the smaller systems; the smaller systems ultimately support the larger ones.

Processes, you will recall, usually correspond to the subsystems of a main system. Each of these subsystems has its own format, like our diagram in Exhibit 3-1. But notice that the goals of the subsystems, while contributing to the main goal of the system, become increasingly specific. The goal of the dishwashing subsystem is clean, sanitary plates, but, of course, clean, sanitary plates contribute to the overall goal of the larger system: the restaurant desire to please its customers.

The Systems Approach in a Restaurant

Now you know that the systems approach is

- a way of thinking about an operation
- a way of organizing an operation
- a device for solving management problems

Let's see how you can put this knowledge to work in your restaurant.

First, assume that you are a confident (perhaps even a smug) operator—you can see little room for improvement in your operation. Nevertheless, give the systems approach a try; it might help you provide even better service. It might, for example, help you reduce costs or raise productivity. It might also help you achieve greater employee satisfaction and motivation than you now enjoy. On the other hand, assume you have a problem or two. Perhaps recent changes in your restaurant—new equipment, perhaps, or an addition to your menu—have made some of your methods obsolete. Or perhaps you see a major repair job, alterations, or expansion looming on the horizon. In either case—a smooth operation or troubles around you—the systems approach can help.

You can begin by sitting down and composing a step-by-step analysis. Here is a sample:

1. Define the systems to be investigated (the dishwashing section).

2. List the goals of that system (abundant, clean, sanitized utensils in time for the peak service periods).

3. List all the subsystems and their respective goals (the food scraping, the rinsing, and the dishwashing machines, their operators, the drying procedures).

4. Suggest to yourself the best ways to accomplish the goals of the subsystems (higher pay? more encouragement? more automation? less automation? redesign the area to eliminate cross-traffic?).

5. Put your newly analyzed, streamlined system to work.

6. Evaluate your results (the goals of the main system are not being achieved, are being better achieved, are being completely achieved).

We will discuss this six-step list step by step a little further.

Definition of the System Defining the system may, at first, seem a little simple-minded to most restaurant owners. But sometimes when a manager defines a system, he discovers underutilized or overlooked elements. We recently heard of a dishwashing operation that used the open air to dry racks of plates but was having trouble getting the plates dry. Finally the manager remem-

Exhibit 3–2.
The Goal/Objective
Hierarchy

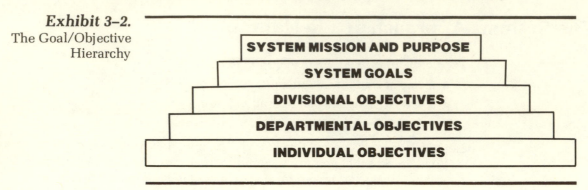

bered that his dishwashing machine had come equipped with a hot-air blower his employees had completely ignored. Whatever your operation, a hierarchy of goals exists (see Exhibit 3-2). Identifying and organizing these goals is the first step in the systems approach.

List of System Goals

The goals of the system can be listed in general terms at first. The goals depend, of course, upon which system you are analyzing. If you are examining your entire operation, you might jot down "a greater variety of food," "more ethnic dishes," "speedier service," or "more cheerful surroundings." If you're looking at a subsystem, you might include the specific goals for that subsystem.

In any case, you do not want to maintain the status quo. You want, wherever you can, to improve your operation. Improvement requires that you constantly review your goals. "To serve the best food possible" is not specific enough. You must define what you mean by best food—flavor? texture? aroma? appearance? price? cleanliness? service? what? Nor is "to provide more employee satisfaction" specific enough. Do you want to arrange an 8-to-5 schedule for more of your employees? Good! That is a specific goal, and the systems approach should help you toward it.

One goal that has become important lately is energy conservation. But *specifically* how can you save energy and energy costs? To achieve the general goal, you should collect a list of lesser goals. For energy conservation this list would include turning off extra lights, using shorter oven warm-ups, turning down the thermostat, insulating the roof, and keeping doors and windows closed. Individually, these steps will not accomplish much. Collectively they can help you reach the goal.

List of Subsystem Goals

You can list all of your subsystems and their respective goals by recalling the various processes that take place in the system or subsystem under examination. Ask yourself *why* they are present, *where* they are located, *what* they accomplish, *when* they accomplish it, *how* they accomplish it, and *who* does the work. Using this systematic approach, you may well formulate an entirely new way of approaching your goals. This systematic approach is sometimes called *brainstorming,* especially when several colleagues participate in it with you.

**Accomplishment
of
Subsystem
Goals**

Your list of subsystems and their respective goals (Step 3) leads naturally to Step 4: suggest to yourself the best ways to accomplish the goals of the subsystems. Having decided that the goals of your dishwasher subsystem, for example, include clean, sanitized plates, you can ask yourself what steps you should take to ensure that you reach this goal. Do you maintain the correct water temperatures? Do you use the right washing and sanitizing chemicals? Can you adopt a different, more reliable, or faster piece of machinery? Are your employees reliable and conscientious? Do they appreciate the essential nature of their work? Do you appreciate their work?

If one of the objectives of your systems approach is to solve a particular problem, the processes (the subsystems) are the places to solve it. In analyzing these subsystems, you may want to think of all the work in your establishment as forming a big pie. Subsystems represent the different slices; each slice stands for some task that contributes to the accomplishment of the restaurant's main goal. Or it may be helpful to prepare a hypothetical, ideal organization chart that illustrates what has to be done and who can do it best. All these ideas—and most particularly the setting of specific goals for each individual subsystem—embody the systems approach to foodservice management.

**Installation of
a New System**

Developing a new or an improved system on paper is not enough. You must put your newly analyzed, streamlined system to work. The installation of a system may, of course, be more difficult than its planning. Most employees hesitate to accept change. Therefore, you should thoroughly explain the new system before you install it. As you explain the reasons for the change, you should stress how it will make the work go easier, shorten the hours, or bring savings that could result in pay increases. In other words, stress the advantages to your employees— accentuate the positive.

Your new system may not run perfectly at first. And you may have to continue using some elements from your old system during the changeover. Depending on the circumstances, it may be best to make the changes all at once, or very gradually. That careful goal analysis you performed should suggest your timing. Those goals should also reassure you that your system probably will work eventually. Don't abandon hope just because of a few preliminary problems. You can expect both employee resentment and some early bugs, but do not be discouraged.

Evaluation of Results Actually employee resentment and those bugs are part of the last important step of evaluating the results of your system. Once a new system starts to work, a manager should continue to watch it carefully and to compare his goals to the output of that new system. This analysis is, of course, accomplished with feedback. Remember that feedback can come in many forms: financial reports, machinery breakdowns, missed schedules, employee grumbles, and frequently (for the manager who has followed these six steps conscientiously) praise, happiness, and profit.

Every now and then, however, a new system must be scrapped because its output does not match or surpass that of the previous operation. Obviously this retrenchment can be expensive, particularly if new equipment has been installed. But careful analysis in the preliminary stages should all but rule out these exceptional cases. In fact, the systems approach tends to eliminate extra equipment, since the design of the system specifies exactly what equipment is needed and discourages the introduction of attractive new machinery into an already smooth operation.

And this observation leads to one final point in this section: no change should be made simply for its own sake. A change should improve upon past performance. In fact, improvement is the only good excuse for change. But the systems approach, itself, is always and everywhere useful. It costs nothing for a manager to analyze his system constantly, and improvement in that system is routine once the habit of constant, objective analysis is established.

Systems and Subsystems in a Hospital

A hospital can use the systems concept in a number of interesting and particularly appropriate ways. The goals of a nonprofit teaching hospital would certainly include

- general care of the sick and injured
- medical research
- education of medical and paraprofessional personnel
- public health promotion and disease prevention

Hospitals also subscribe to the more general objectives of providing services, providing a decent living for their employees, and being good neighbors in the community.

Notice that a systems format can be drawn up for each of the four primary objectives mentioned in the first paragraph. Thus, the goal of caring for the sick and injured would have its own input, process, and output, together with its own feedback mechanisms. And it would be controlled by its own environment. Similarly, the education, research, and public health functions could each be "systematized," although in some cases there might be an overlapping of input.

In the area of caring for the sick and injured, for example, medical care, nursing care, foodservice, and housekeeping would appear as subsystems. The hospital foodservice subsystem could itself be broken down further into normal patient foodservice, hospital cafeteria, food production, therapeutic foodservice, and administrative functions that might include purchasing, receiving, storage, and sanitation. Each of these subsubsystems would have its own input, process, and output. Still, the stress would be on the fact that all "subgoals" should reflect and complement the overall goals of the hospital rather than merely representing the desires of a particular section.

Analyzing the Dietary Department

Exhibit 3-3 shows a typical organization chart for a hospital and Exhibit 3-4 shows a systems approach. It assumes, logically enough, that the dietary department is one of those components of the hospital that contributes to the care and treatment of patients. Because hospital staff personnel are also served in the hospital cafeteria, it assumes that the dietary department is involved in making the hospital a nicer place to work for its employees.

But more specifically, what does the hospital want the dietary department to contribute to the overall goal of patient care and treatment and to employee satisfaction? One contribution would be food that appeals to the patients and contributes to their recovery. And how can this be achieved? Obviously the food should be tasty, should be served at the proper temperatures, and should be attractively arranged and garnished. What else might a patient want? Well, now's the time to start thinking about selective menus, perhaps an occasional glass of wine, and a systematic study of patient food preferences.

Another goal the hospital expects the dietary department to achieve is to serve enjoyable food to the hospital personnel. How does the dietary department pursue this goal? This question leads to investigations of food preferences among those employees, of food affordability, and of food variety. Perhaps, for example, the employees would appreciate self-service, buffet items, the opportunity to make their own salads, or inexpensive snack foods.

Notice that I have addressed the patient foodservice and hospital cafeteria as though they were separate. It might be well to examine, at this point, the exact place of the hospital cafeteria within the dietary subsystem. Bearing in mind the need for all subgoals to complement the facility's overall goals, how would you analyze this issue?

It seems to me that the food for patients has to be not only attractive

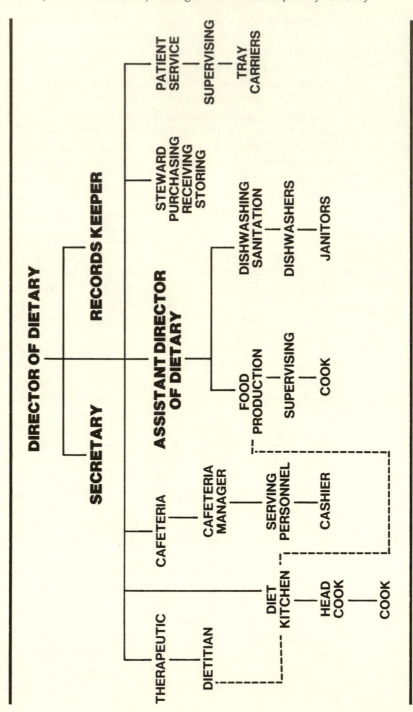

Exhibit 3–3. Typical Hospital Organization Chart

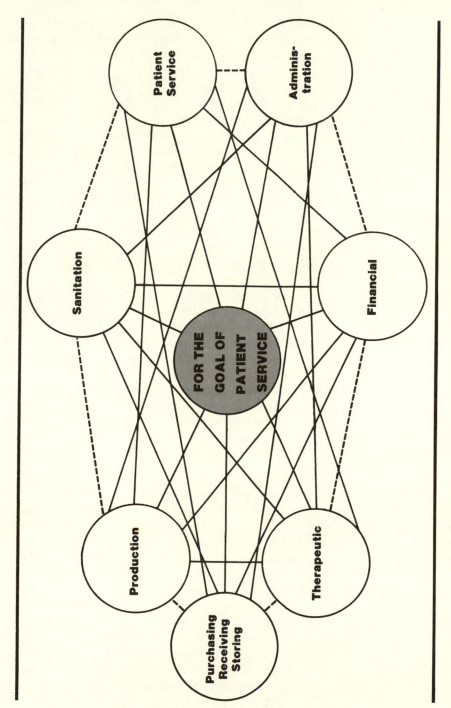

Exhibit 3–4. Systems Concept for a Hospital Dietary Organization

and palatable, but nutritious as well. The nutritional aspect is extremely important. Does the importance of the nutritional aspect set patient food-service and the cafeteria apart?

Remember, systems analysis should help determine the best way to accomplish work and the best people to accomplish it. Moreover, systems analysis should help bring problems into manageable proportions. Using systems analysis to answer the question we have raised, you might ask whether *menu planning* ought to be a separate subsystem. After all, the major difference in the patient foodservice and the employees' cafeteria lies in the menu planning function.

Other goals unique to the hospital dietary department include therapeutic counseling and nutrition instruction. In fact, these goals appear to suggest a separate subsystem, although certainly they have to be approached in a way that is harmonious with the other subsystems. In one hospital, special diets have to be prepared and a special diet kitchen established. This special diet kitchen, too, has all the earmarks of a separate subsystem.

The dietary department is only one system of the hospital working toward the care and treatment goals common to the rest of the units. Therefore a part of its activity involves cooperation with the other hospital departments: the physicians who order the special diets; the nurses in direct contact with the patients; and typically, the housekeeping department. But notice that care and treatment is only an incidental goal of the employees' cafeteria. Contented, well-fed employees are more likely to work hard toward the major hospital goals, and that is reason enough to provide a topnotch cafeteria. So, while both patient foodservice and the cafeteria involve the dietary department, they probably represent distinct subsystems—distinct subsystems, that is, with a good deal of overlapping input.

Dietary Department Input

Its goals established, a system or subsystem must work with the resources necessary and through the processes required to accomplish them. One must determine, for example, whether essential skills are already available in the dietary department. Perhaps some new people are needed; perhaps a position or two can be eliminated. Is the kitchen equipment well suited to the menu already chosen? Should you maintain a generally equipped kitchen that can produce practically any kind of food? Or are you trying to specialize, perhaps by adopting convenience foods?

Once you have determined how your food is to be processed, you will want to examine the utensils essential to the delivery and consumption of that food. What, in other words, is the best way to handle the problems associated with silverware and china? Are disposables the answer? Or do aesthetic considerations outweigh mere practicality? If computer capability is available to you—that is to say, if a computer supplies part of your input—how can you use it in such areas as processing, patient menu selection, cost control, and ordering and inventory maintenance?

When your goal becomes the actual delivery of food to patients, how do you go about it most efficiently and in greatest harmony with the hospital's other systems? Should you, for example, adopt a centralized or a decentralized food delivery system? In some hospitals, the dietary department employees deliver the meals only to the respective floors. Thereafter, the nursing personnel distributes the trays to the rooms. Perhaps this is the most efficient way to handle things; perhaps it is not. But in either case, there is need for close contact and mutual consideration between dietary and nursing.

Dietary Goals   Obviously some of our discussion of dietary input has touched upon some of the dietary processes—the use of the input to produce and distribute food, for example. Now let's look a little more closely at the food-service consumers—those patients on special diets, those patients on regular or "house" diets, and the hospital personnel themselves. Take one of these groups, the hospital personnel. Define them precisely: should your staff-oriented meals appeal mainly to middle-aged people? to people on diets? to hefty appetites? to those in a hurry? Do your patients need hot food? And if so, are you keeping it hot for them? Have you found a foolproof way of making sure the special diets reach those for whom they are intended? The nature and requirements of the food-service consumers obviously offer certain constraints on the dietary system.

Dietary Department Environment   Most hospitals remain open twenty-four hours a day. This means that foodservice must provide meals usually for three shifts of employees. Overcoming this environmental constraint, you may choose to install vending machines, or improve your food holding techniques, or adjust the actual shift hours.

With the constant change of patient population, and the constant change in the conditions of the patients, menu orders also change abruptly. Abrupt changes present constraints for any system. In this case, they make it more difficult to deliver the right food in the right quantity to the right patient.

Hospital layout—part of the general hospital environment—often presents certain difficulties for the dietary system to overcome. Hospitals are typically spread out over quite a wide area; wide areas to serve automatically result in distribution problems.

There is also a psychological constraint imposed by the peculiar environment of a hospital: patients (and to a certain extent, personnel too) represent a captive clientele. The mere fact that they *must* eat in the hospital tends to turn them into food critics. Moreover, anyone who has been removed from the security of his home and family does not tend to welcome the added insecurity of unfamiliar food. And finally, people tend to focus their general fears and annoyances on something tangible. Patients who are nervous about their doctor, their nurses, an upcoming operation, or their treatment often wind up complaining about the foodservice. It is, after all, one of the few things over which they continue to exercise some control.

In hospital foodservice, money represents both a resource (part of input) and an environmental constraint. All of a hospital's systems have their budgetary requirements, and the allotments they receive are rarely enough. The receipt of too little financial input (money) is an obvious constraint. But the force of the constraint can be lessened in a hospital—as it could be everywhere—by a little, old-fashioned honesty. Budgets should be prepared realistically. Common sense suggests that wasted funds are as big a sin in health care as insufficient funds. It makes as little sense to have too much money as it does to be forced to scrimp.

Feedback in the Dietary Department

Sooner or later, the dietary department is going to learn whether, in fact, it has been achieving its goals. Has the food been reaching the right consumers on time? Has it been appetizing? Answers to questions like these can (and often do) come in the form of rumors and complaints. Much better that the dietary department itself undertake to collect the information and make the necessary corrections before the grumbling grows too loud. Regular management inspections serve this purpose, and so do short questionnaire cards. Moreover, regular checks with nurses and doctors—in fact, with everyone involved with patient care and comfort—can correct mistakes and head off hard feelings.

Uncomplimentary reports (negative feedback, in managerial jargon) often reflect on the relative efficiency of the employees. These "people problems" can be analyzed and usually corrected. Personnel efficiency and productivity reports can be developed. Management should also watch its turnover rates and institute regular supervisor evaluations.

Feedback involving hospital costs are particularly essential. Without providing a lengthy analysis of hospital accounting techniques here, we want merely to point out that a dietary department ought to have some sort of a cost reporting system to be certain that it stays within its budgetary allotment.

The Systems Concept and Fast-Food Operations

The systems concept was initiated on a large scale in the foodservice industry in fast-food operations. Significantly, the originators of these operations were not primarily foodservice people but people who came to the industry from the outside with new managerial ideas including the systems concept. These early developers were primarily interested in making money. They realized that to make money, they would have to attract a well-defined market to serve. One such market, widely ignored by traditional foodservice operations was the families-with-children group. Cost was very important to this group, but on the other hand they did not need the traditional sit-down service and the formality of the traditional restaurants. The early developers of the 1950s also realized that mobility provided by automobiles increased the feasibility of bringing the family groups to the foodservice operation.

Establishing Goals

The primary goal of making money convinced the operators to offer a cheap snack. The snack might be hamburgers, chicken, pizza, or other types of food that could be eaten with the fingers. In essence, all of them were what the consumers regarded as cheap snack-type meals. The operators also desired minimum labor both in the number of personnel required and the level of skill required. They realized also that meager facilities made for a high turnover of guests. Moreover, this service would have to be speedy enough to satisfy impatient children. For marketing purposes a standardized image of quality, cleanliness, uniformity, and speedy service was desired. This could best be obtained by having a multiunit organization with each unit contributing to and reinforcing the general image. Economy was also a factor, although some maintain that for value received economy was only relative.

The need to achieve these goals led to systems analysis. After deciding on the goals (or the desired output) plans were formulated to determine what input to use, what processes would be necessary, and what the desirable choices between the various available alternatives would be. From the first, the traditional approach to food preparation (where the food was prepared and served at the same site) was questioned. Food operations are, of course, one of the few businesses conducted this way. In most industries, products are produced at one site and merchandised at another. Why couldn't the same approach work for food? (If the shoe industry operated as foodservice does, every shoe store would have a shoe manufacturing plant attached to it!)

It was established early that some food preparation labor traditionally done at the restaurant could be accomplished better elsewhere. All possible pre-preparation was performed before the product was delivered to the serving location. Hamburgers were mixed and preformed and, in some cases, even partially cooked before reaching the serving location. French fries were preprocessed up to the point of being blanched.

Refining the System

By concentrating this pre-preparation labor in one spot, new fast-food operations considerably reduced the labor requirements of the individual serving operation. Since a cheap snack was one of their desired outputs, they discarded elaborate menus. The simplified menu provided many ordering and storing economies. Pre-preparation allowed for many of the items to come in frozen form, which simplified storing and handling. With only a few items offered on an unchanging menu, much kitchen equipment could be eliminated. Simpler but specialized equipment could be installed for high production of the few items. The simplified menu and pre-preparation also eliminated the need for skilled chefs on the premises, fulfilling another of the desired outputs. The system could be refined for even more efficiency by using conveyor lines and lazy susan devices to bring the products from the preparation equipment to the serving personnel, product color coding, disposable paperware to eliminate dishwashing, and electronic devices that allow one person to take an order and transmit it to the kitchen.

With a relatively few number of items, cost control was enhanced and ordering meant simply the replenishing of the par stock level. Any items purchased by an individual unit had to meet preset standards and specifications, which eliminated complicated decisions on the local manager's part. Since none of the positions (with the possible exception of the manager) required any great skill, personnel could be readily interchanged. And when they were not actually waiting on a customer they could be preparing or wrapping some of the food items.

This general approach allowed a local food operation to attain a factory goal of long production runs of relatively few items compared to the traditional restaurant concept of short production runs with many different items. Moreover, with a standardized operation, it was relatively easy to install quality controls involving storage times and leftover usage.

Fast turnover resulted from the ability to provide speedy service with brief intervals between ordering and service. Limited or no seating facilities discouraged customers from dawdling on the premises. High light intensities used in the parking lots encouraged the younger customers to move on.

The success of the fast-food operations is well known. They developed and satisfied a new market; they also accomplished new breakthroughs in operating efficiency. By studying their goals, outputs, and processes, they achieved that definition of a system: an organization of personnel and machines to accomplish a designated purpose.

SUMMARY

The bulk of our discussion of the systems concept has focused on the commercial restaurant, but it should be clear that the systems approach is clearly just as applicable in health care foodservice. The systems approach helps refine and streamline the work, provides the best solu-

tions quickest to a variety of dilemmas, and prevents a piecemeal approach to problem-solving. A systems approach can be very helpful to the hospitality manager. It can, for example:

> help a manager examine his operation, goals, and resources
>
> help organize the personnel and their work
>
> coordinate these people and their work to achieve the goals of the operation
>
> serve as a problem-solving device

The systems diagram consists of: input, or the various resources available to an operation; processes, or the subsystems involved in the system; and the output, or goals of the system achieved by the input and the processes. Feedback refers to the information that tells a manager how well the output or goals are being met and whether adjustments or changes must be made. These elements obviously have to work within the internal and external environments, which can act as constraints on the system.

In foodservice, the systems approach has been supplemented by such technological developments as convenience foods, automation, data processing, disposables, and better methods of storing, holding, and reconstituting foods. Maximum benefits from utilizing these developments can be achieved by employing the systems perspective, which considers how such developments affect the whole operation, not just one segment. The six steps in implementing the systems approach are as follows:

1. Define the system to be investigated.
2. List the goals of that system.
3. List the subsystems and their respective goals.
4. Suggest the best ways to accomplish the goals of the subsystems.
5. Put the newly-designed system to work.
6. Evaluate the results.

A system is not an entity in itself; it is always a subsystem of another larger system. Thus, in trying to solve a problem, managers often experience difficulty in that they consider only immediate effects rather than the effects on the whole system.

IMPORTANT TERMS

Having studied this chapter, you should be able to define the following terms:

system

subsystem

input

output

feedback

internal environment

external environment

REVIEW QUESTIONS

3-1. How has technological progress supplemented the systems approach?

3-2. Briefly define the term *system*.

3-3. How can a system be used as a problem-solving tool?

3-4. Name and discuss the elements of a system.

3-5. Discuss the environment of a system.

3-6. What would be the ideal output of a hospital dietary system?

3-7. Discuss the internal environment of a hospital dietary subsystem.

3-8. Discuss feedback in a hospital dietary subsystem.

3-9. What steps are involved in putting a systems approach into effect?

SPECIAL PROBLEM: Systems Project

The systems concept is a way of thinking. It provides an organizational framework for visualizing an operation. It allows recognition of the proper place and functions of subsystems and allows consideration of the internal and external environments. It may be the vehicle of adapting to change and incorporating newer technological concepts. This assignment is intended to give practice in systems thinking and application.

Assignment   Develop a systems model for a foodservice operation, identifying the system elements (inputs, outputs, feedback mechanisms, and environments or constraints) for both the general system and appropriate subsystems.

Guidelines   1. The operation may be of any type in which you are interested. It may be a fabricated one or an existing one. If the latter, care should be taken not to simply describe present procedures but to analyze the operation in a systems-concept context and suggest changes for improvements.

2. The subsystems will be those necessary to support the main system. These may include, among others, service, production, administration, sanitation, procurement, storage, and issuing. Even the above may be broken down: administration may have a separate control subsystem; production may be divided into pre-prep and preparation subsystems; and procurement, storage and issuing could be separate subsystems. A hospital might also have menu-planning and therapeutic subsystems and a restaurant or beverage one. For most operations, promotion and feasibility planning will not be subsystems. Personnel is usually not a separate subsystem unless a separate personnel department is requested. If the main system is in itself a distinct subsystem such as the food delivery system in a hospital, mention should be made of this relationship.

3. The output or goals should be for your operation and not the general ones of return for investors (if profit-making), providing a needed product or service, being a good employer, and being a good neighbor. A school lunch program's goals, for example, would include an inexpensive but nutritious meal, fast turnover, nutrition education, and relatively low-skilled help. A fine restaurant might include gourmet food and a dining experience among its goals. Each subsystem will have its specific goals to support the main system. Often, after examination, original or past goals are found to be not really appropriate.

4. The processes include what has to be done in the system and subsystems to accomplish the desired output. Questions of why, what, when, where, who, and how should be asked. Through these, an entirely new way of achieving the goals may be developed. Technological developments such as convenience foods, ingredient rooms, automation, and satellite operations should be considered. A system approach can be considered a problem-solving device, and operating problems may be resolved in this phase.

5. Input consists of possible management resources (personnel, money, machines, methods, materials, and markets) that are appropriate. The primary system may not require all of them, and the subsystems will probably require fewer. Markets refer to patrons and not purveyors. Money refers to capital funding or income. Materials includes foods and supplies. For personnel, it may be desirable to indicate the level of skill required.

6. The environment, constraints, or limitations show those factors which affect capability. They may be of a time, cost, social, legal, union, or other nature and will vary for the different subsystems. OSHA regulations may be significant constraints.

7. Feedback will consider what should be known to allow the accomplishment of goals and what is feasible to use. For exam-

ple, the primary system may require a monthly operations report and the production subsystem a daily report of leftovers. It will be necessary to consider the extensiveness and timing of control points.

8. Normally, the goals are first determined, then the processes to attain the goals, and then the resources necessary for the processes. It may be necessary to redefine and goals or other elements of the system if resources, process capability, and constraints will not permit their attainment.

9. The results of the system analysis will be summarized in a report. Although the nature of the system analyzed will determine the organization content of the paper, possible sections could include:

   The goals of your operation (and system)

   A listing of subsystems necessary for your system, which may be similar to the processes in the primary system

   Overall resources needed along with feedback and constraints

   Development of each subsystem in a system format. It may be desirable to include a discussion of why your particular subsystems represent an improvement over existing practices. This is especially true if new concepts are employed.

10. It may be helpful in completing the project to consider the "Methodology of Systems":

    Define the system to be investigated.

    Define what the system should accomplish.

    Define the elements or processes (usually subsystems) that make up the system.

    Consider the resources necessary for the system. It may be necessary to change goals and processes to conform with available resources.

    Determine what feedback is necessary.

    Develop subsystems.

    Consider cost effectiveness.

4 Organization

Organization is the heart of management. A manager's success depends largely on how well he organizes his personnel and the other resources available to him. Consequently, after you study this chapter, you should be able to

- *explain in a brief paragraph the importance of organization to a hospitality enterprise*
- *discuss how you might apply the principles of classical organization to the work of a hospitality manager*
- *define in two paragraphs theory X and theory Y*
- *explain how informal work groups exercise power, convey status, and affect the organization of the workplace*
- *be able to define terms related to organization*

The Need for Organization

When two or more people combine their efforts toward a definite purpose, an organization exists. But there are usually certain accompanying problems: the division of labor within the organization (or, who does what); division of the resources the organization uses; and division of the gains from the enterprise.

Every enterprise has a reason for being. For a commercial operation like a hotel or restaurant, that reason may be primarily to make money for the owners. For an institution like a hospital, it should be to provide the highest quality service to the consumers that its resources allow. In fact, to satisfy the needs of the individuals involved, to coordinate their efforts, and to achieve the goal or goals of the enterprise, organization is essential. Enterprises engaged in furthering their goals often increase the number of their employees, and unless these people are organized, the trouble and expense may be far greater than the additional contribution they make.

Organization exists whenever individuals band together for a purpose. But the greater complexities and problems that face the modern hospitality manager (and managers in most other types of enterprises) have made organization an extremely important practice in today's environment. Nevertheless, organization cannot be considered apart from other aspects of the hospitality operation. In fact, the word *organization* is related to the word *organism*, an entity whose parts can scarcely exist separately. In a foodservice operation the work of the kitchen personnel, for example, must be geared to the goals of the whole enterprise; they cannot be geared merely to those of the serving personnel.

Organization fits directly into the systems approach to management in which the system is designed to satisfy a goal and the various subsystems are closely integrated to facilitate the overall goal. Organization arranges the human resources of an enterprise to achieve the subgoals, which in turn achieve the larger objectives of the enterprise.

Everyone knows of enterprises where disorganization exists—where some personnel are overworked while others are under utilized. Many do not seem to know what is going on or what they should be doing. Coordination among the various groups has disappeared, and they often work at cross-purposes. It may be that extra personnel and the problems involved in dealing with these extra personnel actually reduce production.

In contrast, the well-organized enterprise divides its work and its personnel into definite segments. The workloads are constructed so that the personnel will be fully utilized but not overworked. The various jobs are coordinated so that each contributes to the goals of the operation and not merely to the narrow goals of the segments.

The successful hospitality manager must be able to organize in this way, to break down the work necessary to his goals, to assign people to this work, and to coordinate their activities. Whether he does or not, there will always be some type of organization, be it desirable or the haphazard sort that evolves naturally among the employees. Since the latter informal organization may be counter-productive to the goals of the hospitality enterprise, a manager should have an effective organization that controls the situation. This does not imply forced domination: newer organizational approaches are very concerned with the motivation and human relations aspect as opposed to the more authoritarian themes of earlier organization theories. And organization is not an end in itself; it is, rather, a tool to help the hospitality manager achieve desired goals.

Traditional Organizational Theory

Approaches to the study of organization are sometimes divided into two general types: the *traditional* or *classical* theory of organization and the *modern* theory of organization. The traditional theory owes much to Henri Fayol who prescribed how jobs should be organized. This theory focuses more attention on the *structure* of the enterprise and on allocating work in the structure so that the objectives can be achieved. Fayol and others formulated rules which ideally provide optimum organization. These rules are universal in the sense that they apply to all organizations regardless of the nature or size of the enterprise. In other words, they are as applicable to a small corner restaurant as to a large metropolitan hotel.

The terms traditional or classical refer to the fact that these principles, though developed largely in this century, are nevertheless older and more established than the organizational behavior theories of some of the newer and more modern theorists. As we mentioned, the classical theorists are more concerned with *work goals* than with the workers themselves. The classical principles were obviously formulated during a much more authoritarian era than prevails now. But this does not mean they cannot be effective (although the validity has been questioned by some) or that they cannot be used to supplement the theories of modern organization theorists. Indeed, both the classical principles and the modern theories can be helpful to the hospitality manager. Depending on the particular circumstances of the enterprise and his own make-up, the hospitality manager may want to stress, in certain situations, one of the approaches over another.

Formal Organization

Before discussing some of the classical principles we should consider briefly what an organization is and which elements in it are affected by the organizing process. The formal organization is a group of people who have banded together to achieve definite goals. It might also be thought of as a hierarchy of positions or tasks formed to achieve certain goals.

The first component of the organization is *the work* which has to be done to achieve the goals of the organization. To achieve the goals, the work must be grouped into common tasks, then broken down into jobs appropriate for one individual. The work units must include all the work that has to be done and eliminate both job duplication and uncertainty about who does what. In a hotel the work is often divided into categories such as front office, housekeeping, sales, engineering, and catering.

Each of these five categories can be broken down. For example the kitchen or food production may include a range section, pre-prep, baking, and the various other tasks the production unit is expected to perform. (In large operations even the subunits may be subdivided.) Each of the work units has its own goals which, when coordinated, should achieve the overall goals of the enterprise.

Clearly, proper organization a realistic breaking down of the work into work units, each with its own goal, is very similar to the systems approach. The main difference is that the organization approach predates formal systems development and is less employee-oriented.

The second element in a formal organization is *the personnel* involved. They must fit into the jobs designated by the division of work. One of the problems with the classical theory is its assumption that rules applicable to everybody assume that all personnel are alike. Individual feelings or abilities tend to get lost in the shuffle.

The third element of an organization is *the internal environment* of the enterprise, or the particular section of the enterprise where the work is performed. For the personnel involved, internal kitchen environment may vary considerably from the internal environment of the dining room. In many cases, principles have to be modified for the particular environment or the environment itself may have to bend because of rigorous principles.

The last component of the organization is *the interpersonal relationships* among the personnel. A manager may delegate formal authority to a particular person; but if the subordinates do not accept that authority or recognize instead the natural leadership of a fellow subordinate, he will have a problem exerting his authority.

The formal organization, then, is based in a very definite *structure*. Everyone is expected to know where he stands in the structure and what position he holds in the hierarchy of importance. He should know who he is responsible for and to whom he is responsible. A direct chain of command should exist, and orders from a higher level are typically relayed to the appropriate lower ones. This hierarchy of authority implies a rather strict control since independence outside one's assigned area is not generally acceptable. The personnel are assigned a specific job so attention can be given to making them more productive in these jobs. This approach encourages specialization since one tends to be more productive doing one thing over and over again than doing a number of different tasks. With this type of organization it is relatively easy for managers to pinpoint areas of individual or sectional responsibility. And with each person or section having specific goals, responsibilities, or production quotas, it is easy to compare desired output with actual results. When every person or section has a specific job it is easier to coordinate the work of the individuals and sections. In this situation, the personnel should be adequately but not rigorously supervised, since the amount of supervision required has been thought out in advance when planning the actual work assignments.

Classical Principles of Organization

The more basic principles of classical organization appear in the following paragraphs. Although they are sometimes stated as almost laws, keep in mind that they are not always effective and that they often have to be modified or abandoned. The elements of organization—the work to be done, personnel, environment, and the relationship between the personnel—all have their effect on the usefulness of these principles, so think of them as useful guides to follow but not as inviolate laws to be strictly construed.

Objectives. Every enterprise, and every segment of an enterprise, should have carefully defined objectives. For example, the objectives of a hospital might include caring for the sick and wounded, promoting public health, training medical personnel, and investigating medical problems.

The dietary department of the hospital could have its own objectives: serving patients and staff food of the highest quality, or providing the finest service that resources permit. Other objectives might include providing dietary instructions and training personnel. In addition, subsections of the dietary department, like the kitchen or the therapeutic section, would have their own objectives.

Not only should every section of the hospital have its objectives, but every individual position in the hospital should also have its own specifications. In contrast, hospitals often hire people out of a vague feeling that they need more help without specifying what they expect.

If every individual segment of an organization meets its objectives or goals, the overall goals of the enterprise should be accomplished as well. But problems may arise in setting individual objectives. If for example objectives are too demanding, an employee may grow discouraged. If they are too easy, the employee may feel unchallenged, grow bored, and reduce his production. Objectives that are less quantitative than qualitative (such as providing a high level of service rather than any specific number of meals) produce results that are hard to measure.

Specialization. Specialization is considered in two ways. One involves having an employee perform only related jobs, which is sometimes called *homogenous assignment.* The other type of specialization is called *departmentation;* it involves having a segment of the enterprise specialize its activities. The purposes of specialization are to increase productivity, make supervision easier, and produce better control.

Specialization of the individual dates back at least to Adam Smith who found that workers could produce more when they worked only on a few specialized tasks rather than trying to produce a complete product. He saw that when a worker alternates tasks, he requires extra set-up time and clean-up time afterwards. Psychological adjustments may also have to be made. And different tasks may have to be completed in different areas, which causes delays.

Atlhough specialization of the individual can increase production and may make a worker particularly adept at performing a certain task, it can cause problems. Repetition produces boredom; and when work becomes routine, the worker gains little feeling of craftsmanship, achievement, or pride. The hospitality field is fortunate that most of its positions usually require several duties and interaction with other workers. This is not true of a strict assembly line, where special efforts have to be made to make the work enjoyable. These efforts include shifting workers to new and different jobs or increasing wages. The hospitality manager should be aware of the advantages of specialization and should try to keep personnel working at one job as much as feasible rather than spreading them over a number of jobs. But he should also try one shift of his employees to other tasks when the first task is completed.

Departmentation. An organization may also want to distinguish between activities and assign them to specialized groups. The division may be based on function or geography. Industry also employs commodity departmentation, or bands of employees producing a certain commodity. Departmentation can also be based on supervision and the size of the group. Geographical departmentation implies forming workers in one specific area into a group. Functional departmentation implies grouping workers who are all doing the same thing. Supervisory departmentation may include diverse segments in one group because it is logical for one supervisor to handle them and because the supervision does not stretch beyond his capabilities.

The hospitality manager must determine the appropriate specialization or departmentation for his enterprise. A segment that is too specialized may cause problems.

Authority. Every organization should have a top authority and a clear line of authority from the top to every person in the organization. This is sometimes called a *chain of command* or the *scalar principle*. Everyone should know who he or she is responsible to and who he or she is responsible for. The term *hierarchy of authority* is sometimes used. It refers to the fact that those of a lower position in the hierarchy are responsible to those in higher positions of hierarchy.

Efficient management uses as short a chain of command as possible. The fewer the number of supervisors instructions must pass through until they reach the person who will perform the work, the better the chain of command will be. A short chain of command, though, may conflict with another principle, *span of control,* which concerns the number of subordinates one person can effectively supervise. Also involved with the authority principle are two other principles, delegation and unity of command. A very important reflection of authority is responsibility. If one has the authority to do something one should be responsible for the results. Problems arise when someone is made responsible for a certain area but lacks the authority to obtain desired results.

Delegation. Delegation is the process by which authority gets distributed downward through an organization. In theory delegation is quite logical; in practice it may become garbled. Some managers find it difficult to delegate authority to others; either they feel that they can do the job better themselves, or they may unconsciously rebel at distributing any of their authority. Moreover, rivalries can be caused by a struggle for the authority being delegated. This struggling often occurs in an institutional environment where the nature of the institution does not incorporate such direct measures of one's achievement as profits made or quotas filled. In such a situation, advancement can be tied to politics or, sometimes, to winning the fight for delegated authority. Examples of this problem readily appear in governmental agencies, which routinely fight for authority delegated by Congress. Congress itself is rife with this problem with different committees fighting over areas of particular personal interest to the members of various committees.

At what level should authority be delegated? A pat answer might be at the lowest competent level to handle the situation. The lowest competent level may be further defined as the lowest level where the person making the decision can anticipate all the ramifications of his decision. The front office manager of a hotel might like to change the rate structure of the hotel, but he probably would not anticipate all the ramifications of this decision. Thus it should be made at a higher level.

The idea of delegation often includes the *exception principle*. Where recurring decisions are handled in a routine manner, but unusual ones are referred upward for appropriate action. To use the exception principle effectively, one must institute policies and standard operating procedures. Instead of having to go to supervisors for a decision each time an event occurs, the subordinate can confidently go ahead if the policies of the organization or supervisor are posted. Problems may arise when it is not clear whether a particular complication should be handled under the policy or referred upward for an individual higher decision. (The same problem may arise in the field of law where attorneys can argue over the governing precedent or ruling.) In any case, the exception principle can considerably reduce the workload of the busy executive and also save his subordinates time.

In delegation it is understood that even though authority and responsibility have been delegated, the higher level of authority is ultimately responsible for the acts of subordinates. Thus it is impossible for a senior to say he is absolved of blame just because one of his subordinates made a bad decision. Obviously, though, practical problems may arise when the managers have comparatively little say over the choice of subordinates yet are responsible for their actions (see Exhibit 4-1).

Unity of command. Unity of command requires that every person be accountable to a single superior and that a superior must not bypass a lower superior in dealing with a subordinate. The unity of command rule appears in the Bible: "No man can serve two masters: either he will hate the one and love the other; or else he will hold to the one and despise the other." (Matthew 6:24). Many managers have a tendency to correct mistakes of lower-level subordinates themselves rather than

Exhibit 4–1.
Delegation
Diagram

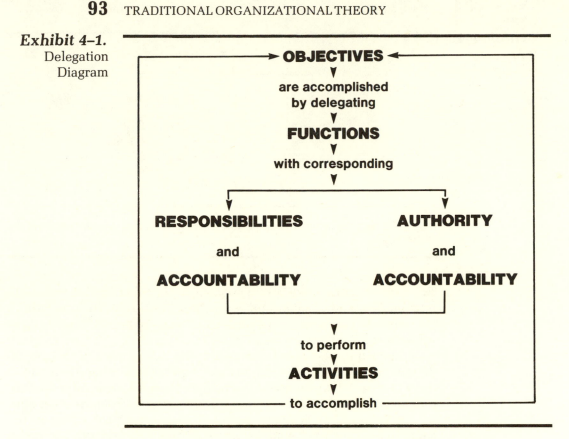

going through the immediate supervisor. This practice leaves the employees confused about who the real supervisor is and certainly detracts from the authority of the immediate supervisor. Hearing complaints about the food in his hotel the manager should not directly approach the chef. Instead he should proceed through the catering manager or whoever the chef's immediate supervisor happens to be.

Span of control. Span of control refers to the number of people that can effectively work under one supervisor. Early authorities suggested, rather arbitrarily, that supervisors should have no more than six immediate subordinates. Increasing the number of subordinates (an arithmetic increase) also increases the number of relationships between the subordinates (a geometric increase). This problem can be expressed mathematically by $C = N(2 + N - 1)$ where N equals the number of employees reporting to a superior and C equals the number of potential relationships. One supervisor with one subordinate has one relationship.

Exhibit 4–2.
Supervisory—
Subordinate
Relationships

$$X$$

A   B   C

X ⟷ A	X ⟷ (A + B)
X ⟷ B	X ⟷ (B + C)
X ⟷ C	X ⟷ (A + C)

X ⟷ (A + B + C)

N.B.: There are seven direct relationships; adding indirect relationships gives a total of eighteen relationships.

Two subordinates yields six relationships; six subordinates yields 222 relationships; and 12 subordinates provides 24,708 relationships. Exhibit 4-2 shows the direct relationship of one supervisor and three subordinates.

More modern theorists have been trying to discover the factors that determine how many subordinates one supervisor can handle. Some of these factors include the amount of contact required, the level of the subordinate's education and training, the supervisor's communication ability, similarity of function among employees, geographical proximity, the complexity of the work, and the amount of time a supervisor can spend with the subordinates. It is also obvious that the supervisor's own ability and energy will affect the number of subordinates that he can handle. If the subordinates are doing routine work with only casual contact necessary, the original six may be far too low a number. If, on the other hand, very involved work requiring much help is performed, the supervisor may be better off supervising fewer employees.

Though there have been many outstanding exceptions, the hospitality industry as a whole has been noted for its low level of supervision. Part of this reputation can be attributed to an industry affection for large spans of control. Another part may reflect the lack of supervisory training given to supervisors by the industry. In a practical situation the size of the work group necessary may affect the span of control. Eight people may be working in a kitchen, and the ideal number may be six to supervisor. But do you hire another supervisor because of the two extra employees? Or can you achieve the ideal with two groups of four?

Balance. The principle of balance involves such aspects as relationships between the size of various departments, standardization or flexibility of procedures, or flexibility between centralization and decentralization. Of course, balance is desirable, but establishing standards for balance can be difficult. Balance is often required in applying such other rules as span of control together with a short chain of command. The application of short span of control can work to the detriment of short chain of command. In other cases, there may have to be a balance struck in the application of standardized principles and procedures. Although principles and procedures can reduce decision-making and supervisory action, an organization may become too involved in going by the book to recognize the need for individualized decisions. Specialization may increase productivity, but overspecialization can be harmful. A balance must be struck between the two.

Centralization and decentralization. Involved with both balance and authority is the rule of centralization and decentralization. Fayol believed that in every business situation there is an optimal balance between centralization and decentralization. This optimal balance depends on the capabilities of the managers involved in the various departments. A manager must always decide, Fayol thought, to what extent he wants to centralize or decentralize the segments under his authority. Some argue that centralization provides better control and possibly better management since the top people can better keep informed and involved. But the very advantages of centralization can turn into disadvantages in some circumstances. Having to clear all decisions through a top, and perhaps somewhat distant, authority may be cumbersome. It can stifle initiative among employees. And top-heavy authority may not be truly aware of the individual facts and circumstances, and thus may not make the best decisions about them. An example of the centralization-decentralization issue in the hospitality industry might center on whether a hotel should maintain one central kitchen or maintain decentralized kitchens for some of the preparation.

Whether food production decisions should be made in the kitchen or at a higher level is another case in point. Fast-food operations, with their very standard procedures and centralized control, have proven to be very successful. Even though these operations have a standard format which does not vary with the locale, they seem to have universal appeal and seem to be able to compete with the varying conditions in different locales. But one factor that must not be overlooked in a decentralized organization is that the person in charge of the segment is receiving excellent management training and probably is more advanced in this area than if he were in a more specialized position in a centralized organization. This management training must also be balanced in that it may take away time that should be spent on the immediate goals of the enterprise.

Organizational Structure

Any operation that employs two or more people is, of course, an organization, and to be efficient it must have specified lines of authority and lines of responsibility. If these lines are lacking, informal organization will prevail, and much of the power and control of the organization will fall into the hands of those not designated as management. The employees, rather than management, may actually begin to run the business.

The organizational structure should provide that every employee know how he is involved in the total operation in terms of his authority, his responsibility and his communication with superiors. Each employee should know his position, the person or persons to whom he is responsible, and the employees who report to him. If this knowledge is lacking, an employee may have several conflicting supervisors directing him. His work may be left undone. Various other employees may begin blaming each other for the deficiencies. And management may begin to experience an inefficient—even a chaotic—situation.

Management cannot do everything itself; it must delegate work to other employees. But a common fault of management is holding an employee responsible for deficiencies beyond the purview of his responsibility and authority. A job analysis spells out the details of this authority and responsibility for each job and each worker, and it prevents this misunderstanding.

The Organization Chart

An *organization chart* shows in graphic form the relationship between jobs along with the lines of authority, responsibility, and communication. It is relatively easy to prepare, and every operation should have one. In fact, each department can draw up a suborganization chart of its personnel. The armed forces frequently prepare organization charts that include photographs of the people above their names, their titles, and their responsibilities. This practice allows new employees to learn the identity of personnel more easily. In preparing the organization chart, management frequently gains a better understanding of its own operation which can in turn suggest areas of improvement.

There can be a problem: some employees who are content as long as their status is not formally spelled out may object to the introduction of an organization chart. These employees may readily take directions from another but resent the other if he is placed on a higher level in the chart. Age and seniority may also aggravate this situation.

Exhibit 4-3, a typical organization chart, depicts the various components of a restaurant. The ownership has given the manager the responsibility and authority to run the operation. Under him are three major divisions: the dining room, the kitchen with its supporting units, and the

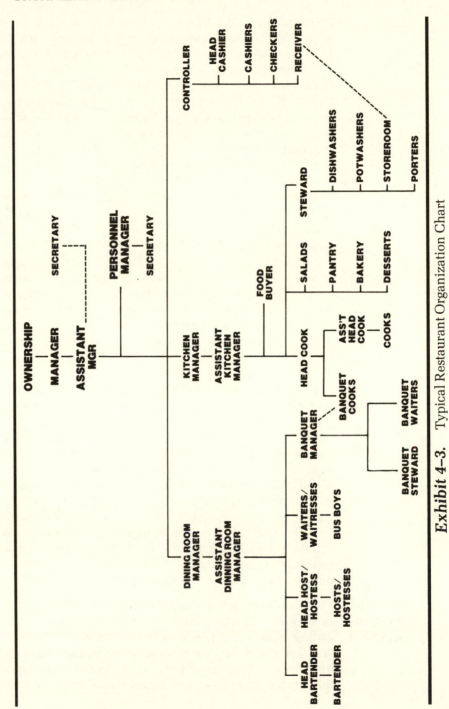

Exhibit 4–3. Typical Restaurant Organization Chart

cost controller. The dining room is subdivided into four categories: hostesses, banquet, waiters/waitresses, and beverage. In this restaurant, the hosts or hostesses do not direct the waiters and waitresses, and in case of difficulty between a hostess and a waiter, the chief host or hostess asks the dining room manager or the assistant (depending upon who is on duty) to settle the dispute. The bus boys work under the waiters and waitresses, with one bus boy assigned to every two servers. The banquet manager makes banquet arrangements and also directly supervises the banquet waiters and waitresses, most of whom are called in only when needed. Bartenders are under the direction of the head bartender, who is responsible to the dining room manager.

The kitchen manager and the assistant kitchen manager are responsible for all food production. The head cook works with the various other cooks, including the banquet cooks (who also enjoy a line of communication to the banquet manager). The other kitchen production units do not report to the head cook but to the kitchen manager or the assistant. A steward is responsible for the dishroom, the potwashers, the storeroom and the various cleaning and housekeeping functions. The food buyer works directly under the food manager. No one reports directly to the food buyer although he or she does have lines of communication with the food cost controller, the head cook, the storeroom, and the receivers. In this particular restaurant, the food buyer sometimes relieves the kitchen manager or the assistant.

In many operations, the cost controller is primarily a staff position with little direction over employees. The restaurant depicted in Exhibit 4-3, however, believes it best for control purposes that certain positions be under the cost controller's direction. So the cashiers, food checkers, and receiving clerks report to the cost controller, along with his or her own clerical assistance. (Many operations require these people to report directly to the manager.) The personnel manager appears directly under the manager and assists all sections in the screening of applicants, the training of employees, and the maintenance of employee records.

If the manager sees something wrong in the receiving department he should not approach the receiver directly but should contact the cost controller. Conversely, the receiver should not go directly to the manager but should go through the appropriate supervisor, the cost controller.

Types of Formal Organization

The traditional mode of organization requires a definite arrangement of positions within the hierarchy of the organization's management. The arrangement of the positions in a relative place in the hierarchy can, as we have noted, be shown on an organization chart. Places in the organization chart are usually shown as one of three types—line organization, staff organization, and functional organization.

Line organization. In line organization the personnel are primarily directed to carry out the functions needed to achieve the organization's goals. In a restaurant, for example, these goals would be the kitchen, dining room, and sanitation, where personnel are all engaged in carrying out the goal of producing and serving food for the customers. Each level of the hierarchy has authority over the level beneath it. Line organization is the simplest and most direct type organization. It resembles the military where the sergeants are in charge of the squads, above them, the lieutenants are in charge of the platoons, above them the captains are in charge of the companies, above them the majors are in charge of the battalions, and so forth to the President, who is Commander in Chief of the Armed Forces.

Staff organization. With staff organization, employees perform work which contributes indirectly to goal achievement by performing whatever services the line people do not encounter in their regular duties. A bookkeeper or secretary, for example, may not be involved with the direct food production goal of a restaurant. These would then be staff positions. Positions that provide advice and counsel are almost always staff positions.

Functional organization. The third type of organization is of a functional nature. In this category people are organized by the functional nature of their work. This can lead to mini-line (and staff) organizations with each function being so organized. In such a situation a high-level manager in one function would have little authority over those in other functions. A hotel, for example, may have an accounting department under a chief accountant one of whose responsibilities is cash control and to whom all the cashiers report. (This is actually a mini-line organization.) Accounting is a function that supports the primary mission of the hotel.

In the traditional theory of organization, the work to be done to meet the organization's goals is determined and then broken down into various segments, or components, or compartments. Each receives responsibilities that, together, accomplish the organization work. To make these individual components or departments as effective as possible is a goal of management. Functional organization or departmentalization may be helpful. This involves grouping personnel and activities according to the functions they perform. Typical groupings in a foodservice operation might include administration and general, production, sanitation, and dining room service. Groupings for a hotel can be front office, housekeeping, engineering, accounting, and foodservice.

The functional arrangement is probably the most commonly used type of organization. People performing similar tasks are organized together.

Thus, the kitchen or dining room are all organized in separate functions each with its own line of organization and necessary staff assistance. A problem can, however, arise in functional organization when employees see only their own goals and their own interests. If this happens, the overall organizational goals may be sacrificed for departmental or self-interest goals. The systems approach to management would, of course, try to break down these departmental barriers.

One organization chart can represent all three types of organization. The employees and supervisors primarily interested in the productive thrusts of the enterprise would be *line*. Those primarily involved in giving advice and providing related support are *staff*. *Functional staff* work for the organization in incidental capacities.

Line organization is the simplest form. Decisions from the top can be directly transmitted and acted upon more readily and speedily than if they were coming from a staff or functional position. But if staff support is absent, the line management must contend with nonproduction problems. Without staff support a chef, for instance, might be forced to do a considerable amount of paperwork rather than concentrating his efforts on food production. Moreover, few line managers have all of the knowledge they need to handle complex or different problems at their fingertips. For example, the typical manager cannot keep up with all the new environmental or safety legislation in the country and in his locality. Better to call on staff specialists for this information rather than attempt independent and hasty or limited research in these areas.

The staff organization, of course, allows specialized experts to handle the problems in their fields of expertise, thus freeing the line management from such work. Besides having sounder knowledge of the field, a staff person can also spend more time on the problem than the line executive who is primarily concerned with the production of his unit. Yet a manager must know where to draw the line between staff, line, and functional authority. Since the staff personnel do not have authority over line personnel their decisions or recommendations can be thwarted by line management. A tendency also exists for the staff personnel to approach the line personnel directly, bypassing line management and creating confusion in the minds of the line personnel. And with strong staff support there is a tendency toward strong centralization since all the experts can usually be found at the central headquarters. This can have its advantages, though, if the enterprise needs strong centralization, as the fast-food operations or some hotel chains do.

Functional organization, like staff organization, can relieve the line executives of routine specialized decisions since functional managers handle the decisions for their functions. But functional people may make organizational relationships more complex. They may pose a coordination problem over who has the authority to order what. And, like staff organization, functional organization tends to encourage centralization.

In planning organization, a manager can improve his understanding of the work by carefully considering the relationships between staff, line, and functional positions. Not only must they be thought out but they must also be spelled out so there is no mistake about responsibility. Problems arise when staff personnel enter areas that are the responsibility of line personnel or when functional personnel go beyond their functional responsibilities.

Informal Organization

When two or more people casually join together in an enterprise there may be an organization; but this is also an informal organization. The formal organization is preplanned to encourage employees to work toward the goals of the enterprise, but the informal organization develops without definite planning or effort. Management can encourage goal setting, but the drift is always toward informality. In some lower-level employee areas, informal organization may actually take over the formal one. The workers may look for work cues to one of their own (who thereby becomes an informal leader) rather than to the assigned supervisor. An extreme but dramatic case of informal organization is the prison riot.

Management and Informal Organizations

The assigned supervisor has the upper hand because besides his stated position, he also has the power to reward or punish. But many supervisors learn that they do not have complete control over their personnel when they find the personnel as a group circumventing directions and, in extreme cases, sabotaging production efforts. Problems often befall a new manager placed over an established group. He fails to gain the cooperation of the group and his chances for success narrow. Peer group pressure may even discourage those employees who would be inclined to cooperate. On the other hand, a supervisor's understanding of an informal group may encourage its members to produce beyond normal expectations.

Informal work groups sometimes compete. It is not unusual in a food-service establishment to find waitresses uniformly antagonistic to kitchen personnel. Both groups may be antagonistic to management.

A successful manager should be aware of the informal work groups operating within his operation and try to utilize them for his purposes. Remember, informal groups occur naturally in a work situation. They form because of the social needs of the people in them, because of location and working proximity, or because of shared jobs or duties: people who work at the same job feel a kinship even though they may be physically separated at work. Common interests may also promote natural associations: people of the same religious faith or national background may seek each other out. Sportsmen may naturally fall into an informal relationship with one another. The fact that special interests may cause informal groups often explains why in a particular location where everybody does the same work, several different informal work groups spring up. Informal groups may also form over a special issue or cause. Dissatisfaction with low wages, for example, may cause an informal group to form. Once the dissatisfaction is resolved the group often dissolves. The special interest informal group is therefore usually less permanent in nature than the others.

Characteristics of Informal Organizations

Informal organizations have several important characteristics to consider. First, they are an agency of social control and have a culture which requires conformity of all their members. This culture may be considerably more rigid than the supposed gray flannel suit culture of the business executive. Although the culture may start out in rebellion against the strictness or supposed limitations of more orthodox culture, the informal one may in itself be more restrictive. For example, the culture may call for decidedly anticonservative dress, which means that everybody in the informal group will dress in an "anti" way. Even though the culture may be a rebellion, it normally tolerates little dissension within the group.

The informal group may also have a status system all its own, though the status symbols may be opposed to that within a traditional group. For example, a person with the worst criminal record may have the highest status. A person who can goof-off constantly may achieve higher status than the faithful worker. Official status may have relatively little effect in the informal group compared to the unofficial or informal status. The informal leader, rather than the formal one, is the one who counts.

The informal group may also have a communication system of its own. Information travels rapidly through the grapevine. Management studies have shown that grapevines tend to be accurate. In fact, many managers are interested in knowing what is being communicated along the grapevine, since its messages may be considerably different from the formal announcements, or interpretations may differ from those expected.

Informal organizations also have a tendency to resist change. The informal organization must, in fact, have a certain stability to survive. Often during a change in environment, the informal organization dissolves since it cannot adapt to the change, and another informal organization usually rises in its stead. Changes in the informal group also affect the stability of the informal relationships. Sometimes, if management wants to break up a negative informal group, it transfers group members.

Leadership in Informal Organizations

Although its leadership is seldom planned, the informal organization inevitably produces that leadership. The leader may enjoy little effective position, authority, or status on the formal organization chart, but in actual practice he has a great deal of status, authority, and clout. Reasons for gaining informal leadership vary widely and may be unrelated to the work itself. For example, an informal leader may be a bully, an especially good bowler, or an old timer on the job. Dealing with the informal leader is one of the most difficult aspects of organization. Ignored, he can make a great deal of mischief. On the other hand, catering to him only expands his power and undercuts the person with the formal authority. An interesting situation sometimes occurs when management makes an informal leader part of the formal management or supervisory set-up. The new formal leader may suddenly change from "one of us" to "one of them," and may lose clout he had as an informal leader.

Management should be aware of the leadership in its informal groups. As much as possible, it should try to get the leaders to direct their groups to activities that work towards the goals of the organization. These informal leaders are a natural development; and if one leaves the slot, another informal leader will take his place.

Benefits and Drawbacks of Informal Organizations

Informal organization may be inevitable, but it can also be necessary and desirable. The informal organization can be very helpful in accomplishing the work of the group. It is impossible for the formal organization to plan or direct every activity. So, even when there is a void in formal organization the work can continue if the informal organization takes over despite the lack of formal direction. And even in situations where very detailed instructions exist, trouble can develop if they are carried out in an absolute manner. As a matter of fact, a tactic sometimes used by groups when they want to bargain without actually striking is to go by the letter of instructions. Air traffic controllers have slowed traffic in airports to an intolerable degree with this tactic.

With informal organization, individuals and small groups interact together quite effectively, which leads to a larger effective span of control. Because of the informal organization, the manager or supervisor has to spend less time directing and coordinating as people in the informal organization adjust to doing what has to be done.

The informal arrangements may be the best means of accomplishing the work of the enterprise. If it is necessary always to go through channels, the red tape expands, especially in larger organizations. On the other hand, members of the informal organization can trade favors needed to further the goals of the organization effectively. In many health care organizations, for example, the dietary department or food-service department is in a unique position to do favors for other departments and, consequently, to get things it wants. A mess sergeant or food-service officer in the armed services has a great deal he can trade when he needs resources from other areas. It is a problem when individuals use this particular power or resource for personal gain. But when they use it to advance organizational goals, it can make the wheels turn smoother.

While the informal organization is almost inevitable and it can be a positive force for organizational goals, it can also be a negative force. If the informal organization is against the enterprise, it may actually try to sabotage the work. Since it is a group, management may find it difficult to pinpoint and punish individuals. Moreover, the informal organization is made up of human elements, and the human element is difficult to predict. No one is ever quite sure what individuals in an informal group really want or what they will do. Certainly informal groups cannot be expected to follow the orders of a supervisor automatically.

One of the advantages of an informal group is that it provides employees with a means of social satisfaction. But the sociability aspects of the informal group can also cause a loss of productive time. Such informal group activity as gossiping, coffee breaks, and betting pools, to name only a few, drain productive time. For example, from a strict efficiency standpoint, it makes sense to have two chambermaids clean a hotel room together especially in making the beds. But despite the theoretical efficiency of a team approach to hotel cleaning, in practice it is more efficient to use one person because the pair tend to talk, take breaks together, and waste time.

Modern Organizational Theory

The traditional or classical theory of organization which stresses specialization, well-defined jobs, and narrow responsibility has come under attack from management theorists with behavioristic backgrounds. These theorists originally relied on the famous Hawthorne experiments and the Glacier Theory, which emerged from a research project begun in 1948 at the Glacier Metal Company in England.

The behavioral theorists cite a number of weaknesses in the classical approach. For example, the traditional theory stresses the "economic man" concept, in which money is the prime motivation. Moreover, it emphasizes exact rules on the assumption that employees will automatically conform to these exact rules. Behaviorists point out that the idea that employees (or any other humans) act in a rational manner at all times is doubtful. Yet the classical theory works on the assumption that people are rational and will respond to rational incentives or directions.

The classical theory often infers that employees will function independent of their environment. In other words, they will do what management requires without regard to outside events that might influence their performance. Behaviorists also feel that the strict lines of authority and responsibility stipulated by the classical theory are self-defeating. Strict reminders of exactly who is superior and who is inferior can lead to resentment and poor job performance.

The modern theory people would, however, agree with the classical people on a definition of management: the accomplishment of an organization's goals through people. The all-important aspect of this definition for both groups would be the various human relationships between the people in the organization. And the two groups would probably agree that the worker's environments have changed considerably since Fayol developed his principles of organization. Few managers can now operate completely in the authoritarian and unilateral style once available to them. This style has gone the way of monarchies and rule by divine right.

Precepts of Modern Organization Theory

No one approach has emerged from modern organization theory. But there are some general precepts that can be applied and are widely used:

Participation. Whenever possible all members of an enterprise should participate in the affairs of the enterprise. Participation can include both decision-making and information about the enterprise. In decision-making, members of the enterprise can help define their own goals, working conditions, and organizational goals. (In some European countries this type of participation is achieved by having worker-representation on boards of directors.) In any case if an employee is to feel close to an organization, he must know a lot about the organization and what is going on in it. Thus, management should report both to stockholders and to rank and file employees about the affairs of the enterprise.

Sociability. A sense of belonging for all members of an enterprise should be stressed. An adversary relationship between management and non-management or supervisory and nonsupervisory should be eliminated as much as possible. If an individual feels he *belongs*, he has a tendency to do everything he can to accomplish the organization's goals—a real improvement on the classical approach of assigning very narrow specialized goals.

Upward authority. In the traditional organization arrangement, authority flows from the top down; orders and instructions are passed by superiors to subordinates below them. Management assumes that the instructions will be accepted without dispute. The modern theory assumes that authority really has no meaning unless employees accept it. Thus in the modern theory, authority travels both downward and upward—and laterally and diagonally, too. In any case, the authoritarian one-way line of authority is no longer inviolable.

Personal consideration. Modern theory stresses the person over the job or goal he is to accomplish. Employees are not robots programmed to carry out tasks decreed from on high.

Group recognition. No man is an island; people naturally form groups. Some of these groups are difficult or impossible to place on an organization chart, and they may change or vary with the composition of the employees. Nevertheless, the modern theory recognizes these groups and considers how they may help accomplish the organization's goals.

Self-fulfillment. An employee's individual goals and problems should be considered. This precept can lead to such practices as "job enrichment," in which managers try to encourage job satisfaction. A job should not be just an income source. It should also provide satisfaction and feelings of accomplishment and comradeship. The foodservice field is particularly fortunate in that many of its jobs are creative and thus allow a feeling of satisfaction. A cook, for example, can derive pride from his culinary creations. A waitress can (in all honesty) be very proud if she provides conscientious service. This satisfaction is often missing in very specialized assembly line jobs.

Flat hierarchy. Flat hierarchy or flat organization refers to having few levels or hierarchies between lower employees and top management. Many different ranks can engender feelings of inferiority. They do not stimulate the feeling of "we're all in this together." The more ranks or levels of hierarchy, the more remote top people are from the lower people. Thus the modern theory encourages a blurring or elimination of the middle levels of the typical hierarchy.

Loose span of control. Few behaviorists approve of a tight span of control or a supervisor who constantly checks subordinates. With a loose span of control subordinates feel freer to achieve the goals in their own way without somebody constantly looking over their shoulder and checking. The tightness or looseness of control depends, of course, on the nature of the work involved. But from the behavioristic standpoint, an individual employee should be allowed as much self-determination or freedom as possible.

Theory X and Theory Y

Differences between the traditional and modern organizational precepts have been codified in the famous theory X and theory Y analyses developed by Douglas McGregor in the 1960s, a professor of management at MIT. A summary of the two theories follows.

The traditional theory—theory X—involves a number of assumptions:

1. For most, work is inherently distasteful. To perform work, people must be pushed.

2. Outside determination is preferred to self-determination. Most people prefer to be directed rather than act on their own. Tyranny is the natural state of man; thus people like to be bossed rather than make their own decisions.

3. Motivation is largely economic. Bread and butter issues and material incentives are the way to motivate people. Man is an economic creature and will respond to these material motivators.

4. Close control is required to achieve an organization's objectives. Management must keep things under control and observation. Without close control there is no accomplishment.

To begin with, the theory X assumptions imply unilateral authority. The boss gives the orders and the workers obey them without question. There is no doubt about who is in charge and where supervision and direction come from. Tight supervision is also necessary; without it, subordinates "goof off."

Accompanying tight supervision is a narrow span of control. To adequately supervise and direct them all, a supervisor should have relatively few subordinates.

Theory X also requires isolation of the individual in the sense that the individual employee remains unaffected by peer pressures or other group pressures. He will function as management desires if group feelings and pressures do not influence him.

The X theory limits creativity. It appears only at the top and permeates only in one direction—downwards. If problems arise, the supervisors or managers solve them.

The modern theory of organization—theory Y—makes some assumptions of its own:

1. Self-control is not only possible but desirable. Instead of keeping workers under tight supervision with a narrow span of control and limited responsibilities, they should be encouraged to work on their own with as little supervisory or managerial direction and control as possible.

2. Work is as natural as play. Instead of being pushed to work, most people like to work. No undue pressure is necessary.

3. Employees, too, can work creatively toward organizational goals. Each employee comes equipped with a mind at no extra cost. He can think for himself and can contribute insights that help the organization.

Under theory Y, efficiency rises when authority flows from all parts of the organization—up and across. The employees should exercise as much responsibility and authority as possible. They should be able to make their own decisions. And they should be able to handle their own direction.

Supervision should be as general as possible, permitting a wide span of control. As much as feasible, employees should be encouraged to "do it on their own" and in their own way.

An individual's social and psychological needs must be considered and every attempt made to let an employee find fulfillment and a sense of creativity in his work. Job enrichment techniques should be employed wherever possible.

Finally, the importance of a single job to the entire organization should be made clear. An employee should not feel like just a cog in the wheel, but the importance of his job should be stressed. For example, a dishwasher may be a low-status job according to some, but it is crucial to the overall foodservice operation. There is no reason why a dishwasher should not realize that fact and take pride in the work he does.

Organic and Mechanistic Approaches to Organization

The modern approach to organization is sometimes called *organic*, meaning that it exhibits a minimum of formal duty divisions. The traditional approach is sometimes called *mechanistic*, meaning that it relies strongly on rules, operating regulations, and formal procedures. The organic form of organization has few hierarchical levels, which leads naturally to a flat type organization with few apparent differences between the lower employees and top management. Most decisions are, in fact, at the lower levels. People do what they want in the way they want to do it as long as they accomplish the organization's goals. There is loose supervision with a wide span of control. Supervisors concentrate on providing advice, information, and consulting services rather than on giving hard and fast orders. Authority is largely based on the knowledge of the individual rather than on his position. A manager, for example, does not tell a trained chef how to proceed with his cooking unless the manager can do it delicately and happens to be a trained chef.

A mechanistic organization has a number of hierarchical levels that closely control operations. Thus there are a number of levels of control to accomplish. There is, as well, a narrow span of control. Decision-making occurs at the higher levels, and there is a high degree of decision-making centralization.

The mechanistic organization employs formal procedures and rules that show how each employee functions. These rules leave relatively little discretion to the employee. And instead of primarily giving advice and information, supervisors tend to instruct and direct.

Most people probably prefer to work under organic conditions which, theoretically at least, provide greater enjoyment and produce more and better work. But the mechanistic approach is necessary in some types of organizations. Large fast-food chains, for example, require uniformity and thus tend to adopt the mechanistic approach. (In fact, the structure is so limited they sometimes have trouble attracting good managers.) Everything is set up to operate within the system, and the jobs involve supervising personnel and ordering food according to a fixed menu using fixed procedures. The mechanistic approach allows for weaker management at the unit level with decisions and management functions being performed for everyone at the higher level.

Informal Relationships

In a formal operation the relationships between individuals in the organization are spelled out in terms of authority, appropriate responsibilities, and accountability. In the informal organization, the leadership is not formally spelled out or planned. But it is usually evident, and the power centers within it are usually known. Informal relationships affect both the formal organization and the informal organization. They are influenced by such factors as *status*, *power*, and *politics*. The status of any one individual employee may be quite different from that indicated on an organization chart, and the power of that individual may also vary considerably. These informal relationships may well rise above and be apart from those suggested by either the formal or informal organization.

Status   Status is one's position in the pecking order of the group. Formal status can be conferred by management, and informal status can flow from the regard accorded an employee by his peers. Status is probably inevitable in any organization; in even the most egalitarian groups, a sense of status arises. Some people, as the saying goes seem to be "more equal than others."

Management confers formal status according to the nature of the position filled. A manager has more status than a dishwasher in a food-service establishment. In older, traditional kitchens, the status of cooks is reflected in the height of their white caps. The highest caps are worn by the chef; the lower hats are worn by his successive underlings. Escoffier himself is supposed to have formulated these symbols of status.

Since status is very important to individual employees, it makes good sense for a manager to provide each job with as much status as possible. Status can appear in a job title: Instead of being called dishwasher or pearl diver, the employee might be referred to as a scrub steward, a machine operator, or a sanitation specialist. Uniforms can also affect status. The military has long recognized this principle and has provided different uniforms for different ranks. In the hospitality field, a trim uniform may provide its wearer with more status (at least to himself) than normal work clothes. A hotel had difficulty maintaining an esprit de corps among maids because their uniforms made them look like servants with aprons. When the uniforms were changed to a more professional type, there was a distinct improvement in the morale of the group.

Awards can also provide status. Pins for long periods of service may give the wearer a feeling of status. In a military hospital, status was used to motivate the hospital corpsmen to prepare for the weekly inspection. All that was required was a plaque saying "Honor Ward" with appropriate insignia that looked very impressive. This plaque was awarded to the group that in the opinion of the inspecting officer was best prepared for the inspection. The award implied a certain degree of status among the personnel in all the wards, and they competed vigorously to obtain it.

Status is sometimes assumed by implication. Dietary aides occasionally call themselves dietitians when away from the hospital because dietitians have more status. And occupations can by themselves, connote status. (A recent survey shows that Supreme Court Justices have the highest status in the country.) Many people who might earn far more money doing something else consider the high status of the position equal to more monetary rewards.

Status symbols. Status symbols can take many forms. In some operations, access to the executive lavatory is a high status symbol. In some organizations you can tell the status of the employee by the size and design of his desk. Top executives sit behind fancy desks; lower-echelon executives have more utilitarian desks. Perhaps you have heard the old water fountain analogy: top executives have their own silver water carafes; vice-presidents drink from ordinary water carafes; and the rank and file employees use the water fountain.

In some operations, status can be determined according to where the people eat. The top managers may eat together, and to be admitted to their table is a mark of status. The status here may be either formal or informal. It may be formal in the sense that only people of a certain rank are permitted to eat together or that certain tables are reserved for higher executives. It may be informal, as when the invitation from the group rather than the location of the table carries the status.

Many operations use an induction ceremony to provide status. Nurses, for example, have their capping ceremonies to designate a certain educational attainment. A hospitality operation can utilize the same concept with its employees by supplying some sort of acknowledgment when they have achieved a certain proficiency. One hospital developed a training program for its tray girls. It consisted of about six hours of instruction. At the end of the instruction there was a graduation ceremony and a tangible symbol of recognition—a certificate—was presented. Besides making the tray girls generally more proficient in their jobs, the fact that they had achieved a certain professional accomplishment proved to be important to them. The certificate was invariably framed and placed in a position of honor in their homes.

Uses of status. Status is not only inevitable, but it also has certain functions and uses. To begin with, it is obviously a motivational device. To achieve a certain status, employees often strive conscientiously to improve their work. The status is "the carrot" they try to reach. Status can also soothe one's ego, and may even compensate for lower salaries. It can also make employees far happier in their jobs and provide them with a sense of fulfillment.

A study of status among dining room and kitchen personnel revealed how much status means to hospitality employees. In the operation studied, the waitresses could give the orders to the chefs, who considered themselves "higher" than the waitresses. Thus a condition arose in which higher status people appeared to be serving and taking orders from lower-status employees. The conflict was resolved by installing a "buffer" device whereby the orders came to the cooks indirectly on a rotating spindle.

Power
Power is the ability to get someone else to do one's bidding. Power, of course, is inherent in formal organization where it takes the form of the authority needed to accomplish the organizational tasks. The informal organization, however, has the power to affect the formal organization, and the informal leaders have the power to affect their informal organization.

The desire for power is quite natural. Some psychologists feel that it rivals sex as a human motivator. Proponents of this theory believe that people with feelings of inferiority compensate for them with a drive to have power over others. The revelations from the Watergate investigations revealed that the drive for power was central to all those involved. As with status, power is inevitable in an organization. But if misdirected, its effects can work against the goals of the organization—and again, the Watergate tragedy is instructive here.

A position may have power simply because it carries the responsibility for achieving certain goals. This could be called *legitimate power* or *power of authority*. It usually appears on a formal organization chart. Thus, in a line organization a direct line of power can be shown from the top down to the lowest member in the organization. But just because a position, or an individual in a position, is supposed to have power, does not necessarily make that power effective. Informal leaders or groups may contravene legitimate power. Many a new college graduate in his first job in a position with some power finds he has a problem with subordinates who may be older and more experienced. They are often reluctant to accept him and effectively block his power even while paying lip service to it.

Power may be based on an ability to provide rewards, punishment, or otherwise coerce those around him. Someone in a position to bestow salary raises or promotions or provide other tangible benefits has a definite power. People will obey him in hopes of receiving the reward.

An individual may have power because of his particular expertise or knowledge. A cook's power may flow from his skill in producing fine dishes. If a person is the only one capable of a certain skill in an organization, he may have a certain power even over his nominal superiors.

The nature of one's position may also carry a certain type of power. In the armed forces, the supply sergeant wields more power than his rank might suggest because of his access to and control over resources. Moreover, a person may have power because of his personal qualities. If others want to identify with him, he will naturally have a certain amount of power over them. This phenomenon is sometimes called "basking in reflected glory." It is most evident in the retinues surrounding certain celebrities.

It must be stressed again that a superior position in a formal organization does not by itself convey power. Other factors contribute. But, if a person has to use punishment or coercion to maintain power, the impression on employees will be negative. There may, however, be no alternative.

Every organization of any size has power centers, and in analyzing the organization's effectiveness, one must locate these centers. Sometimes very direct means must be employed to dilute some of the power in these centers when they work against the goals of the organization. Moreover, personal power struggles that contravene the goals of the organization must be stifled. It may, unfortunately, be necessary to remove both sides from power and install a new power figure if neither of the original sides can accept the other. As the English historian, Lord Acton said, "Power corrupts and absolute power corrupts absolutely." Some people who gain a measure of power become obsessed with obtaining more. Sometimes they become unscrupulous in their methods. An individual who wants to obtain power for power's sake can be harmful to the organization and, at the very least, make others in the organization uncomfortable. Yet in all fairness, some people who are eager to acquire power for themselves also pull their organization along with them.

Politics   Probably the most overlooked subject in management textbooks is politics. Like status and power, politics are inherent in an organization. The you-rub-my-back-and-I'll-rub-yoursphilosophy is natural to practically all environments. Politics are beneficial when they allow an organization to work towards its goals. Tit-for-tat helps lubricate the organizational machine. If it were possible to write a book of standardized operating procedures to cover every eventuality, and everyone followed them to the absolute letter there might be no need for politics. But in the real world, trading favors can be helpful. As it is with power, when politics are exercised for their own sake rather than for the goals of the operation, trouble begins. The same occurs in our larger society when politicians work for their own political ends rather than for the goals of the country. Although politics are an important function of an organization, the informal political process is very difficult to teach. This is probably why it remains so widely overlooked. We do not propose to discuss business politics exhaustively, but here are some techniques you might consider:

1. Acquiring of favors that must be repaid. Someone who does favors for others normally expects them to do things for him in return when the occasion arises.

2. Alliances. A politician likes to effect appropriate alliances. If somebody supports you with the understanding that you will support him, both of you have increased your political power.

3. Conviviality. Friendliness can help a politician. A person who is well liked frequently gathers political strength because people like him and want to help him.

4. Building constituencies. Politicians often try to weld different blocs or groups together to provide a larger political base. The person who can get several different sections of an organization to unite behind him increases his influence.

5. Currying favor. Enjoying the approval of superiors can bring political advantages. Politicians sometimes "play up to" others or at least act as accommodating as they can. Of course, these people risk the disapproval of other employees.

Of course, the art of politics can facilitate the operation of an enterprise. But once the decisions have been made on the basis of office politics alone, the organization goals may suffer. Moreover, when an organization is rife with politics, people who do not like political games grow uncomfortable. They may be forced into political activity for their own protection if advancement and recognition stem more from politics than from achievement, and favoritism always discourages those who are not favored.

SUMMARY

When two or more people combine their efforts for a definite purpose, an organization comes into being. How to form an organization and then make the most effective use of it is the job of management.

There are two basic approaches to organization. The traditional or classical approach is concerned with the organizational structure of the enterprise. The work to be done is determined first. Individuals or components then receive the responsibility and authority to see that the work is performed. Principles of classical organization include objectives, specialization, authority, delegation, and unity of command. We call them principles, but they are really more like guides.

The formal organization arrangements can be considered as line, where the personnel are primarily concerned with the functions to achieve the organization's goals (such as serving hotel and restaurant patrons). Staff organization assists the line organization and consists of various support groups. Functional organization features personnel organized according to the function of their work. Each function normally has its own suborganization and hierarchy.

Modern Organization Theory, the second basic approach to organization, does not revolve around the work to be done or the structure of the organization. Instead it is primarily concerned with the individuals involved and how they act in groups. It assumes that employees will not necessarily act in a rational way, be motivated by economics, or function independent of their environment. Some precepts of modern organization theory are participation, sociability, upward authority, group recognition, personal consideration, self-fulfillment, flat hierarchy, and a loose span of control.

The difference in classical and modern theory is illustrated in theory X and theory Y. Theory X relates to the classical or mechanistic approach; theory Y relates to the modern or organic approach.

Very important in organization but not defined on an organization chart is the informal organization. It can drain power from the formal organization and reduce legitimate authority. However, if the informal organization cooperates with the formal organization's goals, it can be a potent force for the accomplishment of those goals. Also important in organization are informal relationships of status, power, and politics.

IMPORTANT TERMS

Having studied this chapter, you should be able to define the following terms:

traditional (or classical) theory of organization

modern theory of organziation

homogeneous assignment

supervisory departmentation

functional departmentation

commodity departmentation

specialization

unity of command

span of control

chain of command

scalar principle

delegation

exception principle

direct relationships

indirect relationships

organizational balance

centralization and decentralization

job analysis

organization chart

staff position

line organization

functional organization

economic man concept

flat hierarchy

theory X

> **theory Y**
>
> **organic approach to organization**
>
> **mechanistic approach to organization**
>
> **legitimate power**

REVIEW QUESTIONS

4-1. Discuss the various components involved in organization.

4-2. List and briefly define the principles of classical organization.

4-3. What is departmentalization? How may it be achieved?

4-4. How can you determine whether a specific responsibility can or should be delegated to a subordinate?

4-5. What are the advantages and disadvantages of centralization?

4-6. Differentiate between line, staff, and functional organization.

4-7. An informal organization develops within the formal organization. What are the characteristics of this informal organization?

4-8. Behaviorists are often critical of the classical approach to organization. What are some of their criticisms? Explain with as much detail as you can.

4-9. What are some general precepts that can be applied with the modern theory of organization?

4-10. Discuss the theory Y approach to organization.

4-11. Status is an important aspect of informal relationships. How can status be conferred on a dishwasher's job?

CASE PROBLEM: Hospitality Incorporated

A regional hospitality firm consists of a number of previously independent hotels and restaurants that have been merged together. The merger has proved neither happy nor successful. The operations remain largely autonomous, with little coordination or cooperation, even though all operations are owned and theoretically controlled by the parent company. Some of the operations compete primarily with each other. The duplication should be eliminated, but each unit wants to continue its own existence. Financing is a problem: some of the units urgently need more working capital or funds for expansion, but so far it has been impossible to get money from the financially stronger units—who would rather spend any money for rather dubious purposes for themselves. The chain has not been able to get any general financing; a limited amount, though, is a possibility if lenders see an improvement in organization and operations.

Labor relations are very unsatisfactory. A new, aggressive union has come on the scene. So far it has been able to overwhelm individual operations by dealing with each separately. One result has been that each operation has drawn up different contract and benefits, even though a more uniform one for all covered establishments would be beneficial. The individual managements do not seem to be able to deal with the more experienced union negotiators.

Sales efforts are mainly individual. Each sells only for itself, though a combined, coordinated sales effort could help all. Much money could, possibly, be saved through centralized purchasing of food and supplies, but none of the operations wants to give up former prerogatives.

The organizer of the chain is a flamboyant individual and a super salesman. His goal has been growth, even when some of the acquisitions were very questionable and should have never been considered. He can put together good acquisition deals and generate fine publicity, but he cannot handle operational details. Payment of acquisitions has been through transfer of stock. Most of the former heads still run their operations; some, though, are clearly disenchanted. There is no team effort for corporate purposes. Clearly it would be traumatic but possible to remove, transfer, or retire many of these people. Termination costs would be high, but these people now receive considerably higher compensations than others in the field with equivalent responsibilities. They are also generally older, easing off, and not receptive to new ideas. Little junior or middle management potential exists within the corporation. With the exception of the president, no central administration exists.

One of the most serious problems facing the chain is the almost exclusive focus of its efforts on acquisition growth; little thought has been given either to large immediate problems or to the long-run survival of the enterprise. The chain literally does not know where it is going, nor where it wants to go. The president supplies no leadership regarding this. The chain was organized on the assumption that the combined strength (synergy) of the chain would be greater than the sum of that of the individual operations, but there has been little to support this claim.

Financial and quality control is very uneven and generally weak, while the quality of service provided by the operations is generally acknowledged to be deteriorating rapidly. The accuracy of some of the limited financial reports from the individual operations are very suspect.

The chain now consists of six hotels. Two are large luxury prestige operations, one of which is making money. Three are medium-size commercial operations, one of which is doing very well. The other two could be competitive if renovated. An airport motor inn is dong very well and could readily expand. A resort operation is marginal and not geographically close to any of the other operations. Another old hotel is losing money but could be sold or used as a nursing home. Twelve general restaurants are in operation, with about half being profitable, although all were successful at one time. Several of the restaurants do extensive outside catering. There appears to be considerable potential for expansion here. A number of plants, schools, and hospitals in the area have catered foodservice; these could be a possible market. Six franchise fast-food operations also operate. They are profitable but, except for staffing, are largely supervised by the franchise company. All operations except the resort are within a circle with a 300-mile diameter.

Part of the reason for forming a chain was to provide a recognizable chain image. This has not developed. The board of directors now comprises owners or heads of the operations absorbed into the chain. Too large, the board has had much internal squabbling and is too narrow in perspective to be effective. Although personally owning only a small percentage of the stock, the president has enough control over additional shares to effect any change he wants in the board's composition.

The president of the chain is greatly concerned about the deteriorating prospects. Recognizing the need for more direction and control from headquarters, he asks you to produce a preliminary organization plan. This would include an organization chart with a listing of the responsibility of each job or section. It would also include a discussion about time, staff, and functional authority in the organization, as well as the relative place of centralization versus decentralization. The plan should consider organization in terms of function, geography, customers, and products. You are asked to give any other recommendations you can for the betterment of the firm. Specifically, you are asked to provide the following:

Goals of a new, basic organizational plan

Organization chart indicating divisions and key jobs (creating jobs as necessary)

Descriptions of key jobs

Recommended organization of the board of directors

5 Control

Control, like organization is a basic management function, and a hospitality manager should certainly be familiar with the principles applicable to and associated with control. Therefore, after you study this chapter, you should be able to

- *explain briefly how control interacts with the other management functions*
- *list six areas of control*
- *explain, in sequence, the approaches to and the steps involved in the traditional control pattern*
- *explain in some detail how you might combat the problems of patron and employee theft in a hospitality operation*
- *define in a short paragraph the behaviorist approach to control*

All management functions, such as planning, organizing, directing, coordinating, and controlling, interact with each other. The control function is somewhat unusual in that without the other functions there would be no need for it. In other words, control by its nature services the other functions and cannot operate independent of them.

What is control? The dictionary definitions are "to increase in authority or dominating influence over; direct; regulate;" "to hold in restraint; to check;" and "to verify and regulate." As a noun, control is "a standard of comparison." Control is supposed to have come from an old Latin word meaning a counter or register.

In hospitality management, control involves all of these definitions. And for our purpose, we might define it as "helping to assure performance conforming to plans, objectives, or goals." (In this definition we assume that there *are* plans, objectives, and goals.) Our special definition suggests the presence of an authority or dominating influence over direction, regulation, checking, clarification, and standards of comparison.

Control and Other Management Functions

According to one scheme of management, to secure control an organization must:

Define its objectives

Prepare plans and programs to achieve these objectives

Provide suitable organization to implement the plans or programs

Set policies and procedures to provide direction

Provide the necessary funds

Provide the necessary personnel

Inspect, regulate, verify, and compare performance with goals or objectives

The definition of long- and short-range objectives and goals is, of course, planning. If an organization really wants to accomplish something, it must know what that something is. Control, however, is vital to the actual movement toward that planned goal. Without control, planning would be merely an academic exercise; plans will have no validity there would be no way to measure progress toward a goal. Many pie-in-the-sky ideas issue forth as plans unsupported by control.

Plans get accomplished within organizations. An organization determines what has to be done and assigns responsibility to personnel or sections to accomplish this work. This is called *organizing*. Control sees to it that the organizing has been developed. It also sees to it that personnel sections pursue individual goals that, collectively, approach the organization's overall goals.

Establishing policy procedures is largely a function of direction. Like everything else, direction must submit to some control. Lord Acton's observation that "power corrupts and absolute power corrupts absolutely" is as true in the field of management as in politics. There must be control over the authority to direct not only to keep individuals from abusing power but also to keep the goals of the enterprise paramount.

An organization can accomplish very little without funds; to achieve its goals or plans, an organization must have financial resources. Control over funds is thus a vital aspect of overall control. An organization's cash and other fiscal assets must be jealously controlled.

Personnel are also necessary to practically every endeavor, and their activities, besides being directed and motivated, must be controlled. In the traditional view, controlling personnel involves both keeping an eye on everyone and comparing their activities. The more modern thoughts about control emphasize motivation and the feeling that, if people are motivated toward an enterprise, they will work on its behalf and need comparatively little on-the-spot supervision.

But some comparison is necessary. Besides being tools of planning and directing, policies and procedures are also tools of control. With definite policies and procedures, a manager can see whether performance matches them. And he can take appropriate action when it does not. Along with policies and procedures, periodic and special reports may be required to let management evaluate overall progress.

Some control is obviously essential to both the largest and the smallest of hospitality organization. But, it becomes increasingly important as the organization grows and involves more personnel. A hot dog pushcart operated by its owner requires comparatively little control since its owner is present and therefore needs no formal reports and few policies. He may also be highly motivated to achieve success since his rewards are more direct. But as an organization gets larger, its personnel acquire vested interests of their own. Moreover, the largeness brings more difficulties in communication, and the overall picture gets cloudier. When the goals of the enterprise are not necessarily intertwined with an employee's goals, the need for control becomes much greater.

Constant checking, rechecking, verifying, regulating, and comparing are the very essence of control. PPBE—planning, programming, budgeting, and evaluation—are the letters to remember. An enterprise must *plan* its goals. It must *program* how they can be accomplished and *budget* the necessary funds and personnel to accomplish them. And the results must be *evaluated* to see how they compare with the planned objectives or goals. Evaluation, of course, is the central control process.

Control involves communication. Managers must know what is going on. It has been said that almost all faulty decisions are due to faulty or insufficient information. Thus, proper control implies the necessary interchange of information for planning and decision-making.

Areas of Control

While control should permeate an entire organization, it is possible to identify some areas where it is unusually important. In the hospitality industry when one thinks of control one probably thinks first of controlling cost overruns—the major costs in the hospitality industry being food and labor. Many techniques have been developed to exercise control over these areas.

The traditional approach to control emphasizes *how to* control these costs. The traditional theory would impose rigid control that makes it difficult for employees to get away with actions that might increase costs. Behaviorists would say that if employees are really interested in the goals of the operation, there is no need for them to be rigidly controlled because the main control is their interest and desire to do the best job possible.

A commercial operation may have control over its sales or volume of activity. Even a noncommercial operation may have control over its volume. In the profit-making organization, which depends on sales volume to maintain or enhance profit levels, realistic sales goals are necessary. For example, what amount of business can be expected, and how can this business be secured? The control function involves studying such goals as these and seeing to their achievement. Various departments in the organization may have sales goals. Hotels, for example, may have room sales goals, food sales goals, bar sales goals, and other types of goals as well. But for effective control, these sales goals must be realistic. A hospital or nonprofit operation must also concern itself with its volume of activity or sales. In planning for the new facilities, one must estimate whether there will be sufficient volume to justify these facilities. This estimate is a form of control. When planning its budget expenses, an organization must estimate the volume of business it will do to justify these expenses. There may be control involved in trying to "space out" volume. A hospital, for example, may want some control over how its facilities are utilized in normally slow periods. It may want to avoid overcrowding. Thus, some hospitals ask surgeons to operate during summer months when they would rather vacation but when the hospital needs more activity.

The very goals of the organization are sometimes thought of as controls. What is the organization really trying to accomplish? Is a hospital, for example, really trying to provide the best possible service and care to its patients, or have subsidiary goals intruded? Pet projects of some staff members may be interferring with the overall goals. An open-heart surgery unit may not really be needed if others are available nearby. Yet it may be maintained more for prestige than for practical reasons. In commercial operations the goals may be more specific: a desired return on an investment, an increase in profit, or greater sales. But the goals and objectives must be constantly evaluated along with the progress towards achieving them.

It sometimes may be necessary to change the objectives, raising them in some cases and lowering them in others. But there should always be a control comparison. The saying goes that with every element of cost control there must be an equal element of quality control. Certainly maintaining the quality of the service and the products should be one of the objectives, and controls should evaluate this objective. As organizations become larger, they require more control over their goals and over the personnel working toward them.

Associated with the control of goals is control over the development of the potential of the enterprise. Both commercial and noncommercial operations must move with the times and the environment. They must decide what new services must be offered and what old services may be discontinued. A profit-making organization must ask whether it is putting its resources to the best profit-making use. Perhaps the leverage of borrowed money could extend an operation's own financial resources in order to increase profits. There must also be some development of staff potential and leadership. There is another management saying: every supervisor should have three jobs, doing his own job, training someone to take over his job, and training himself to take the job above him. The potential leadership personnel must be developed both to provide continued leadership for the enterprise and to encourage conscientiousness among the regular leadership personnel. Inevitably some of these potential leaders go on to other operations. This is a risk that must be taken to continue the development of leadership potential.

Probably more than any other industry, hospitality service is a "people" industry. There must be some control over the people who serve the people. Part of this control involves simply the cost of labor, a subject discussed earlier. Another part involves the growth of potential discussed in the preceding paragraph. Still another part of control over people involves such intangibles as providing personal satisfaction, direction for achievement, or morale and motivation. Recruiting, selection, hiring, and orientation are all involved. Control over people requires that everyone know what his job should be, that job descriptions be available. Job specifications, too, should list the special abilities necessary for the job, and an organization chart should show where the job fits into the total organization. Control over people also should involve regular evaluations that point up an employee's strengths, shortcomings, and areas for improvement. Individuals should be encouraged to formulate their own goals which work for the achievement of the organization's goals. Training programs should be tailored to increase efficiency on the job and also to provide a feeling of professionalism.

A manager must exercise control over the physical assets of his enterprise. Some managers milk these assets, diverting upkeep money to other pusposes so that the assets deteriorate. (Older hotels kept in first-class condition often remain quite competitive.) But, control over physical assets is not confined to those large fixed assets like buildings and major equipment. It includes control over supplies, furnishings, and even less significant assets. Management must ensure that all assets provide as much productivity as possible. Although the comparison process of control may not be directly applicable in this case, control in general applies because the assets are recorded and their condition and maintenance is checked. This comparison occurs when the planned life of an asset can be compared to its actual life and use.

Cash and negotiable instruments readily converted to cash are a specialized type of asset. Since these are so inherently attractive, some special control over them must be maintained. This control will be discussed in more detail in the section devoted to internal control.

Approaches to Control

As in many other areas of management there are different approaches to the process of control. The most traditional approach is the measurement of planned and actual performance. Those approaching control from a behavioristic, nontraditional slant believe management is the accomplishment of goals through the personnel involved. If these personnel do their best work and are highly motivated, there is little need for the formal or traditional approach to control. In fact, the traditional approach may be self-defeating in that it may cause conflicts and difficulties within the group necessary to obtain control. Both approaches have elements to recommend them to the hospitality service operator, and both will be discussed in some detail. The traditional approach, however, is by far the most widely utilized and thus will be emphasized here.

Traditional Control Theory

Traditional control theory depends upon someone having the responsibility and authority to achieve the goals of his part of the enterprise. It is a boss-subordinate relationship. The boss (or supervisor) is responsible for the activities of his subordinates and must take necessary action when results do not meet the standards.

The traditional theory of control usually has two aspects: the direction of personnel and their activities, and the measurement of performance. The first aspect is called "keeping an eye on things." If employees feel that a supervisor is constantly lurking around, they tend to be more inclined to stay busy and less inclined to be careless, negligent, or thievish. In this context, other means of formal and elaborate control become a substitute for absentee ownership or management. If the manager is constantly on the scene, knows completely what is going on, and is interested in the goals of his operation, there is less chance that resources will be used ineffectively and inefficiently.

The second aspect of traditional control is measurement, or the comparison of actual performance with planned performance, and the consideration of any discrepancy. In traditional control theory, the measurement aspect of control can be presented in four steps:

1. Establish standards or goals.
2. Measure performance.
3. Compare and analyze.
4. Take corrective action.

Establish standards or goals. Standards can be set according to many different terms. They may be financial, like budget costs. They may be time related, like the amount of time necessary to perform a certain task (often expressed in terms of production, or number of covers per workday or workhour). They may specify quality, as in manufacturing, where quality control inspectors are used, quality tolerances are developed, and rejects analyzed. Defining quality in a service industry can be difficult because it is inherently difficult to define the quality of food items and because it is hard to numerically measure the personal aspects of service—pleasantness, cooperation, and helpfulness—though quality standards like customer evaluations are used with some success. Standards can also specify quantities, which in a foodservice operation could involve portion control in the food served or receiving control in the food that is purchased.

Goals include such things as a desired return on investment, percentage of the market, increase in sales, or percentage of profit. These goals may be based on industry averages, on improving the past performance of the enterprise, or on any other desirable standard. Hospitals and nonprofit operations can aim to cut costs, upgrade their staffs, and increase their effectiveness.

Measurement of performance. Once your standards have been set, you can measure what is actually being performed. Sometimes the costs of the measurement must be weighed against the advantages it can deliver. Although control reports are generally desirable, the effort in writing the reports can outweigh the loss due to poor control that might occur without them. The supervisor's time spent keeping track of certain subordinate activities may be more than the loss through unobserved poor performance. Supervisors tend to spend more time on their own interests and less time on other activities. For example, a supervisor could spend most of his time implementing food cost control and completely neglect labor cost aspects even though the latter may amount to more of the total expenses in the operation.

Measuring performance can create problems. Dollars-and-cents measurement is relatively easy, but measurements of quality are more difficult. How would an operation measure its goal to improve the quality of its management? Part of the measurement would have to be subjective— a feeling that things are going better than before or a feeling that employees remain disorganized. In inflationary times increased costs may not really measure control accurately either.

To measure performance, standards should be set up at strategic points. These might include a daily food cost report, daily labor cost report, a yearly management audit, or even an evaluation of the total quality of the management. In establishing strategic points, remember to make certain that no employee controls himself. An outside auditor should audit the books, not the bookkeeper. Otherwise there would be no check on a bookkeeper who, for example was falsifying the records. To control the quality of a smaller or medium-sized operation, a manager might have all customer or patron comments referred directly to him, not to an assistant who prepares summary reports. With the direct information, there is less chance that reports will be "doctored."

Compare and analyze. Once the actual performance is measured, you can compare it with the standards that were previously set and note any discrepancies. But, about when or how often should this be done? Operations with control systems often do not have control problems since the systems act as preventive control measures. Without control, parts of the operation begin to act independently and can run wild. Thus, each manager must determine the best balance between overcontrol and undercontrol for the particular operation. Remember that comparison and analysis are easier when both the planned goals and the actual measurements are expressed in the same units (for example, dollars or manhours). A manager must decide how much tolerance to allow before taking corrective action. This obviously calls for individual decisions for each operation. For example, a manager may decide that for every cook-day-of-work there should be between 100 or 120 meals produced.

It is not always desirable for a manager personally to make the comparison and analysis. It may be better to bring in outside experts, or committees of experts to evaluate some control reports or projects. A manager may be so close to the operation that it becomes hard to compare and analyze objectively. This objective viewpoint is crucial to control. Some organizations are in the business of providing this viewpoint. For example, hospitals are accredited by a national commission organized by the members of the medical and hospital associations. These outside evaluators do a better job because not only are they skilled, but also they can be completely objective. In a sense, some government regulatory organizations are designed to provide an objective control viewpoint. Local health officers, for example, can effectively evaluate the sanitation standards of a foodservice operation. Some government agencies can effectively check and evaluate safety conditions in compliance with other government regulations. Unfortunately these governmental agencies do not always fulfill their role adequately. They may not understand a situation or rely blindly on certain policies or regulations, thus creating circumstances worse than the discrepancies.

A particular problem of evaluating one's own organization is the relationship maintained with the personnel. Personal friendliness can cause the manager-evaluator to be less critical than is warranted.

Take corrective action. A manager must reduce or eliminate the discrepancies between the predetermined standards and measurements of actual performance, as shown in his comparison and analysis. He must determine what types of preplanning, reorganizing, or new controls can correct these deficiencies. This may mean a change in personnel, different job assignments, more observation by management, or many other approaches. Hard choices are often involved, but that is management's responsibility—a manager has to act, however unpleasant the consequences. Another problem in the corrective action phase is overreaction—the manager may take drastic action to correct relatively insignificant problems; left alone, these small problems might have resolved themselves, causing far less trouble than the manager's "corrective" action.

The means of taking the corrective action can be important. Some managers can be effectively blunt and uncompromising in taking the corrective action. Others find this approach uncomfortable, preferring instead to take corrective action gradually and try to gain employee cooperation. In some cases a labor organization may agree to help correct faults, but this cooperation is not always forthcoming.

Behaviorist Approach to Control

The traditional theory of control has been attacked by behaviorists. They often feel that the authority-responsibility or superior-subordinate relationship limits and demeans employees. Management, after all, means the accomplishment of the organization's goals through people; these people should be eager to do their best. Behaviorists argue that the control ought to be a desirable goal formulated by the group itself. When the group achieves these goals, they reason, effective control exists, and the need for the external procedures of the traditional control systems disappears. Since the controls are, in effect, the individuals themselves there should be a greater degree of harmony, better coordination among the participants, and a resolution of conflict.

This approach does not involve merely providing control, it also seeks to make the work more meaningful and important. An example of the effectiveness of this type of control arose from the Hawthorne experiments during the late 1920s and early 1930s. Some of these experiments encouraged workers to pace themselves. Production soared without the usual controls or strong supervision, possibly because the workers had aligned themselves in an informal group and were determined to produce to their utmost without the usual formal controls or motivations.

Of course, aspects of the behavioral approach can be combined with aspects of the traditional approach: certainly the individual employees should be aware of their importance to the enterprise. (People like to have pride in their work, and being part of a service-producing institution can easily be a matter of pride.) As much as possible they should be included in the formulation of goals. Communication should travel not just from the top down, but also from the bottom up. The rank-and-file employees should be aware of how efficiently the overall operation is proceeding toward its goals.

There are a number of ways that management can implement the behavioristic approach to control. Much of the behavioristic approach involves motivation and morale. If people are motivated, so goes the theory, they need little control. If people feel favorably towards the organization they work for, they need little control. Obviously the personnel selection process can be very important. If employees have a personal need to produce quality goods, the need for quality control is to a large extent eliminated. The cook who will not serve something of inferior quality is certainly an asset to a fine foodservice operation. In fact, problems can arise when an employee has high standards but the operation just wants to push out ordinary food rather than desirable and creative items. In this case, the employee may well become unhappy. The hospitality field has unusual advantages in that it should stress products and service quality. Many manufacturers are more concerned with quantity and provide their employees with little incentive to produce quality work. A hotel, by contrast, must maintain clean rooms. Thus the maid has an incentive to do a good job of cleaning. A maid should therefore be a person who derives satisfaction from doing a competent job, and the operation should reinforce these goals and values. If it does, the maid will need little supervision on the job.

Socialization among employees can also reduce the need for control. If employees feel they are part of a group, they will be reluctant to let the group down by doing less than their best or by producing inferior work. In some of the food operations of yesteryear, food returned to the kitchen was an insult to the whole kitchen staff, not just the person who produced it.

Peer pressure may be the most effective of all controls if it supports the goals of the organization. But if it contravenes the goals (if, for example, there is pressure to hold production down, or not to do more than you have to) the results can be disastrous.

In hiring, orienting, training, and supervising new employees, management should strive to see that they fit in with the group. Federal laws must also be considered. If an employee is a misfit, he will probably be unhappy, the quality of work will suffer, and the need for control will increase. Management development itself can have an effect on behavioristic control. Managers adept at behavioristic techniques should have to rely less on traditional authoritarian methods.

Control may also be achieved through the use of symbols of prestige or importance. Everyone has a need for prestige, recognition, and acceptance. By fulfilling these needs, management can help produce a happy, willing employee motivated toward the goals of the organization and requiring little control. These needs may be fulfilled by such devices as euphemistic titles (scrub steward, instead of dishwasher); awards like "waitress of the week"; and by stimulating the acceptance of all employees with meetings, gatherings, and social events.

Top management should exert as little pressure or formal control as possible. Some behaviorists feel that when control comes from the top, workers become more apathetic and require even more control, which in turn may require another "layer" of supervision and cause the top to become more remote.

Positive results can be realized by encouraging an employee's participation in establishing his own objectives, and then asking how he expects to accomplish them. Of course, the supervisor should also participate in such an interview. The employee may then be rated on how well he achieves his own objectives.

Another less traditional management technique is the pyramid approach. The top or point of the pyramid represents management and the lower employees constitute the base. Instead of reports traveling immediately to the top, the people at the base have access to them first. They can make corrections before the higher authority becomes aware of any deviations from its standards. In other words, the employee is encouraged to correct his own mistakes before they come to the attention of top management.

Financial Control

Financial control is a major part of the control process. Chapter 9, "Financial Management," directly addresses financial control and shows many of the applications of financial management. Two special aspects of financial control are accounting and budgeting.

Accounting, a major part of the control process, can take several forms. One is *financial accounting,* or reporting financial information about an organization to the outside world. Financial accounting provides information about an enterprise not only to management but also to such outside parties as investors, lenders, and regulatory officials. This information is usually historical in that it may show profits or losses over a certain period; or it may show a balance sheet as of a certain date in the past.

Although financial accounting is definitely helpful, *management accounting* is more desirable for operational control. Management accounting produces information specifically to help management conduct the enterprise. It is not bound by the generally accepted principles of financial accounting, so it may alter these principles to provide more desirable information to management for control and planning. Types of management accounting that are helpful to the institutional foodservice operator include budgets, ratio analyses, and standard costs.

A budget is a plan that shows how the operation expects to perform during a specified period. It can coordinate volume, the income, and the expenses for this volume. Moreover, it can help a nonprofit organization provide the best foodservice its financial resources permit. Like accounting itself, budgets come in different forms.

An *operating budget* is concerned with activity and the cost of that activity during a specified period.

A *cash budget* records the inflow and outflow of cash and what the cash position is at a certain time during that exchange.

A *capital budget* forecasts the asset expenditures that will be devoted, over a long period, to equipment and facilities, for example

A *labor budget* shows the amount of personnel required during a certain period and can be expressed either in hours or in labor costs.

Other *specialized budgets* can accommodate such activities as maintenance, remodeling, or food purchases.

The operating budget especially useful in operational control, shows the level of activity as expressed in dollars, or the cost per meal times the number of meals in the food operation (see Exhibit 5-1). The operating budget also shows expenses for this activity and indicates whether the operation will break even, experience a loss, or show an overage of income to expenses for the period. One advantage to such a budget is that it provides a goal. Normally an institutional foodservice operation does not seek more business, but it can have a goal of controlling expenses, and this can be expressed in the budget.

The budget may also constitute a direct control device. Since expenses and needs are determined in advance in the budget, actual expenses which deviate from them may show the need for corrective action to be taken (see Exhibit 5-2). A budget may help coordinate an organization. In making up a budget, you must consider all the units that produce income or incur expenses, and then they must be combined. The budget can help with the combining and encourage the coordination. It may also make it easier to assign responsibility. Employees know what the goals in the budget are and should be motivated to achieve them.

Every manager should plan ahead, and the budget is his most basic plan. Instead of riding day by day with the waves, the operator should try to determine what his activity, and consequently, his income will be. By planning costs ahead of time the operator knows in advance where

Exhibit 5–1.
Restaurant
Operating Budget
Format

SEASHORE RESTAURANT BUDGETED PROFIT AND (LOSS)

	January	February	March	April	May	June
Sales						
Food	3,300	4,950	6,600	8,250	9,900	13,200
Beverage	1,105	1,658	2,210	2,763	3,315	4,420
Total sales	4,405	6,608	8,810	11,013	13,215	17,620
Cost of sales						
Food	1,320	1,980	2,640	3,300	3,960	5,280
Beverage	332	497	663	829	995	1,326
Total cost of sales	1,652	2,477	3,303	4,129	4,955	6,606
Gross profit	2,753	4,131	5,507	6,884	8,260	11,014
Controllable expenses						
Payroll	1,410	1,982	2,643	3,304	3,700	4,934
Direct	264	396	529	661	793	1,057
Utilities	250	250	250	250	250	250
Advertising	100	100	100	100	100	100
Repairs and maintenance	200	200	200	200	200	200
Administrative	200	200	200	200	200	200
Total controllable expenses	2,424	3,128	3,922	4,715	5,243	6,741
Operating profit	329	1,003	1,585	2,169	3,017	4,273
Noncontrollable expenses						
Occupation expenses	500	500	500	500	500	500
Interest expenses	32	43	54	54	54	54
Profit before depreciation	(203)	460	1,031	1,615	2,463	3,719
Depreciation	360	360	450	450	450	450
Amortization	200	200	200	200	200	200
Profit before taxes	(763)	(100)	381	965	1,813	3,069

Reprinted with permission from James Keiser and Elmer Kallio, *Controlling and Analyzing Costs in Foodservice Operations* (New York, John Wiley and Sons, Inc.. 1974). p. 238.

costs may be too high, and he can take appropriate action before any real trouble occurs.

Some institutions operate on appropriated funds that may not be too closely related to activity. For many operations, then, it is wise to have a fixed amount to cover fixed expenses. Thereafter, so much more for every meal served may be added. For example, if an operation has fixed expenses of $50,000, expects to serve 100,000 meals over a certain period,

Exhibit 5–2.
Restaurant Cash
Budget Format

SEASHORE RESTAURANT CASH BUDGET

	January	February	March	April	May
Opening balance	520	1,009	1,029	1,080	1,715
Sources of cash					
Sales	4,405	6,608	8,810	11,013	13,215
SBA loan	6,400	2,200	2,100	–	–
Total	11,325	9,817	11,939	12,093	14,930
Applications of cash					
Food	5,528	1,320	1,980	2,640	3,300
Liquor	332	497	663	829	995
Payroll	1,410	1,982	2,643	3,304	3,700
Direct	264	396	529	661	793
Repairs and maintenance	500	500	140	140	140
Other controllable	550	550	550	550	550
Other	–	–	–	–	–
Mortgage amortization	–	–	600	–	–
Mortgage interest and taxes	500	500	500	500	500
SBA interest	32	43	54	54	54
SBA principle	–	–	–	–	–
Equipment loan	–	–	2,000	500	500
To partners	1,200	1,200	1,200	1,200	1,200
Total	10,316	8,788	10,859	10,378	11,732
Closing balance	1,009	1,029	1,080	1,715	3,198

Ibid., pp. 133–240.

and considers $2.00 appropriate for each variable meal expense, it would need a $250,000 budget.

As we said, a budget can also provide a goal. Goals may be expressed in many ways: increasing sales (for a profit-making organization) or controlling costs (for a nonprofit organization). It also provides the enterprise with a yardstick and during the budget period so it can compare actual results with the desired budgeted results. Such a comparison can reveal potential difficulties before they become acute. Since a budget involves all of the revenues and all the expenses, and since they all must be coordinated, the coordination process requires a manager to examine closely the expenses of various operational segments of the organization. In a nonprofit institution the various programs are coordinated on the basis of funds available. In deciding how much money will be available, a manager must also decide what results to expect and how they can be best achieved. This involves the coordination of other sections. A hospital, for example, establishes a budget for its physical therapy program.

Not only may this budget depend on anticipated revenue, but it should also reflect the importance of physical therapy compared to the other departments. If too much or too little money is spent on physical therapy in comparison to other departments, there is a need for budgetary change.

Ratio Analysis

Ratio analysis involves taking figures from control reports and putting them in ratio or percentage forms. Expenses may be broken down as percentages in relation to sales, and these percentages may be compared with goals, budgets, or past histories.

In commercial operations, the *food cost percentage* is the ratio of food cost to sales, and it is often used as a food cost control. It is not feasible, however, in most institutional food operations where there are no direct sales figures. It is also conceptually unsound as it is not a positive control. The food cost percentage concentrates on the relationship between food cost and food sales. It should probably be used more as a menu pricing device than as a control device.

Another ratio sometimes used in food operations is *inventory turnover* where the closing inventory (the opening, closing, or average inventory value may be used, as long as one is consistent) is divided into the cost of goods sold. The result indicates how often the inventory turns over during the period. Good inventory management generally maintains as fast an inventory turnover as possible.

Standard costs are a management accounting procedure frequently used in food operations, both commercial and institutional. Although they require a great deal of paperwork, they can be quite effective. Standard costs will be increasingly used especially since automatic data processing can handle this paperwork quickly and economically. The principle behind standard costs is to cost every item served in advance. The number of each item served is multiplied by the cost, and the totals of all items are, in turn, totaled. This procedure provides a theoretical standard cost. The actual food costs for the period can then be calculated. (They will invariably be higher since the standard costs include no provision for waste, spoilage, or unused food.) The difference between total standard costs and total actual costs is the potential saving to be achieved with ideal food cost control.

Control Reports

Much of the control process involves reports that management can use for its evaluations and comparisons. The control report shows a measure of performance management can use to compare and analyze actual performance and take corrective action, if necessary. Exhibit 5-1 shows a format for a monthly control report developed for a hospital dietary department. Of course, each operation is unique and may require information different from that in Exhibit 5-3.

Exhibit 5–3.
Typical Monthly
Control Report

HOSPITAL DIETARY DEPARTMENT
For Month of_____

	THIS MONTH	SAME MONTH LAST YEAR	TO DATE	TO DATE LAST YEAR

Activity Analyses
Patient days
Regular diets
Special diets
Cafeteria meals
Consultations

Payroll Analyses
Total payroll costs
Professional payroll
  Administrative
  Therapeutic
Nonprofessional payroll
  Preparation
  Patient tray service
  Cafeteria service
Professional hours / Patient day
Nonprofessional hours / Patient day
Labor cost / Patient day
Vacation days
Separations (or turnover %)
Overtime hours
Overtime hours as % of payroll

Other Costs
Food costs
Food cost / Patient meal
Budget food cost / Patient meal
Revenue / Cafeteria meal
Supply costs
Supply costs / Patient meal

Dietary Budget
Total budgeted cost
Total actual cost
Over or under

Special Events

Personnel on Leave

Accidents

Other

In preparing the control report thought should be given to what the operating and supervising management actually should know: what information is necessary to control the activity and for planning and decision making? Also, what is the standard current information being compared to? The first part of Exhibit 5-3 shows an activity analysis that can inform a hospital administration how busy the dietary department was during the month. For comparison purposes, there are columns for "this month," "same month last year," "to date," and "to date last year." Different columns could be listed if other comparisons are desired, and a goal could be used instead of the historical figures.

The next section analyzes *payroll*. Not only does it show total payroll costs, but it also breaks them down into professional, nonprofessional, patient, and preparation costs. These figures can also be used as standards by showing the number of hours utilized per patient day for the various classifications. Moreover, they can show such other relevant information as the number of hours of vacation time, the number of hours of overtime, and the turnover as expressed in separations or a turnover percentage.

The other major cost in an institutional foodservice operation is the *food cost* itself. The next section in Exhibit 5-3 is devoted to this. Again, it not only shows total food cost but also breaks it down into cost per patient meal and compares it with the budgeted costs per patient meal.

A third cost in food operations involves *supplies*, and this cost is also entered on the report. The report shows whether the dietary department is over or under its planned budget. There is also space for special occurrences and space to accommodate any accidents. The purpose of this report is to provide management with insight into the operations of the dietary department, to indicate whether its costs and other activities are in line, and to allow for corrective action if necessary. The reports should be individualized for the needs of each operation.

Internal Control

Internal control is a specialized type of control defined as the plan of organization and of the coordinate methods and measures adopted within a business to safeguard its assets, check the accuracy and reliability of its accounting data, promote operational efficiency and encourage adherence to prescribed management policies. We have discussed many areas of internal control already without specifically identifying them as internal. As the definition indicates, internal control involves a plan of organization and we have said that control involves both planning and organizing. The definition also concerns the safeguarding of assets, which we have mentioned before. It is concerned with accounting data, which is discussed here and again in chapter 9. It concerns operational efficiency, a form of directing. It is also concerned with adherence to prescribed management policies which are also involved in planning and organizing. Just as control is a necessary subfunction of the other management functions, internal control is a specialized sub-function of control.

We have emphasized planning and organization and the need to have both showing long-range and short-range objectives and the necessary organization to carry it out. From a control standpoint it is wise to sep-arate the operating, custodial, and accounting duties. For example, the person who purchases the food ideally should not be the person who receives it or stores it. Nor should he be the person who keeps the rec-ords and makes up the food control cost reports. In smaller operations it may not, however, be possible to separate all these duties.

Assets to be safeguarded include the major physical assets and the actual cash. But, safeguarding also encompasses such things as inventory control and guest check control. Providing reliable financial records involves accounting, thus a good basic accounting system is important to the operation. The hospitality industry is fortunate to have uniform sys-tems of accounts for hotels, hospitals, restaurants, and clubs. These uni-form systems have been developed by committees of thoughtful experts who have provided not only a well-thought-out system for the individual operation, but have also saved the small operator accounting fees. More-over, with different operations using the same system, it is much easier to compare the industry's figures and percentages.

In internal control, a budget can be a very basic financial record. Profit or cost centers can be set up. These show, for a profit-making operation, the direct cost attributed to the respective income center, the direct income received, and resulting profit or loss. In a hotel, the cost centers might include the dining room, the bar, the rooms, telephones, store rentals, and valet services. Cost centers record all the cost incurred by certain departmental activity. Even if there is no direct income from this activity it is possible to compare the amount of service provided to the cost involved. In a hospital, for example, the clinical records section generates no income. But considered as a cost center, its cost can be com-pared to the quantity and quality of service it provides.

In promoting operational efficiency we might be concerned with such things as labor cost analysis or food cost accounting systems. These ana-lyze the appropriate costs, showing if they are higher than expected and if corrective action must be taken. We have already discussed how con-trolling and directing are directly involved and how much of operational efficiency depends on the directing function. If a manager has no idea of his costs, he can have little idea about how efficient his department or organization is. This cost information should be available in control records.

Adherence to management policies involves management concern. Too often management may post a policy without really bothering to consider its implementation. Control involves setting up some management policies (very much involved with planning). And control also involves setting up standards to see how these policies are followed. For example, an overtime policy may be established. The control function would be determined whether the accumulated overtime squares with the policy.

Theft Control

Two types of people steal: the employees of the organization (internal theft) and the customers (external theft). Certain management policies can be applied in both cases to encourage theft prevention. There should be internal and external auditing, for example. The records can, after all, show discrepancies. (An auditor can evaluate the effectiveness of other control measures.) Rewards can also be offered. Specific policies, however, can be applied to employee and patron theft control.

Internal Theft The control of internal theft involves enlightened personnel and behavioral procedures. Generally, if an employee feels close to management, he will not steal. Thus, theft and employee morale can be related. Behaviorists (to be discussed shortly) would consider the management environment an important element in theft: if a "good relationship" exists between management and employees the chances of theft are reduced.

But, even with the best of managerial intentions and the best behavioristic techniques, some employees will steal. By one estimate, 85 percent of all employees have stolen at least *something* from their employer. Another rule of thumb is that one quarter of all employees are generally honest, and another quarter is incorrigibly dishonest. The remaining 50 percent are about as honest as the system under which they work—if there is opportunity to steal, they may take it.

When managers worry about keeping employees honest, they usually think first of supervision. Employees who are rather closely supervised do not have as much opportunity to steal. The real problem, in fact, is that too often management really does not care whether employees steal. One survey indicates that 62 percent of *executives and supervisors* steal from their employers. (If management doesn't care, why should the employee?)

Another aspect of thievery is lack of communication. The behavioristic perspective is that the more communication or empathy an employee has with an employer the less liable he is to steal. But management should also make known the consequences of getting caught—a managerial practice known informally as the *fear technique*. Moreover, if one person is actually prosecuted or otherwise punished, employees realize that the same thing can happen to them.

A great deal of resentment can be started by inefficient employees receiving as much as efficient ones. Rewards for efficiency, therefore, may be useful. There may be limits to rewarding individual differences, but the value of an employee should certainly be recognized. Public compliments or praise on a job well done is one kind of reward. Some organizations issue awards like "waitress of the week" or "employee of the month." However, the performance expected by employees should be realistic. Workloads that are excessive may cause resentment and can increase the chances of the employee "squaring things" with his employer by stealing.

An effective but controversial tactic to control theft is the use of "company stool-pigeons"—employees who report the thefts of their fellow employees for compensation. Many managers have learned that the use of stool-pigeons creates so much resentment and suspicion among personnel that it erases any savings derived.

An elementary theft control practice is to check the packages and handbags of employees when they leave for the day. (This practice would of course have to be a condition of employment before searches can be made.) The checks do not have to be made daily; an occasional spot check should be sufficient. In fact, if employees do not know when to expect a check they may refrain from pilfering altogether.

External Theft Management must also contend with patron theft. Fortunately it is harder to steal food from a foodservice operation than to steal merchandise from a retail store, but opportunities still exist. Hotels experience substantial losses of room furnishings, and hospitals lose large amounts of linens. Patrons or guests steal for a variety of reasons. They may desire material possessions and some of the assets of the hospitality operation may appear desirable to them. They may intend to convert the article into cash. Many steal, however, to have a souvenir or momento of their visit or stay. Some people who would never steal from anyone else do not scruple about stealing from a large impersonal organization. They rationalize that the large hotel or hospital will never miss what little they steal.

There can be psychological reasons for stealing: kleptomania for example, or thrill seeking. It is a challenge to steal, and some people just like to see if they can get away with it. Peer pressure may also cause otherwise law-abiding people to steal if pilfering becomes a status symbol in their group. Urban teenagers often encounter this pressure.

Management can use a number of techniques to combat patron theft.

Observing and vigilance are, of course, prime methods. The less someone thinks he can get away with the theft, the less he will be inclined to attempt it. Making employees responsible for certain assets can also cut down on theft. Not only do the employees become more vigilant, but also people who steal from large impersonal hotels find it harder to steal from an individual waiter they can see and talk to.

Closed-circuit television has been used to try to detect thefts. Of course, the mere warning that it may be used may be just as important a deterrent as the instrument itself. (The same procedure is used by state police patrol to reduce speeding. If a state police car is readily visible, people will not speed, and that is the real goal of the state police rather than issuing tickets.) Hotels and motels can make theft more difficult by anchoring removable objects. Expensive television sets can be rigged so that an alarm rings if they are disconnected.

Despite all these suggestions, the hospitality and foodservice industries continue to suffer the almost incredible ingenuity of employees and patrons determined to steal. The reassuring aspect, of course, is the fact that notwithstanding all the temptations spread out in our affluent society, most people remain basically honest.

SUMMARY

There are different approaches to the process of control. The traditional theory of control has two aspects: a direction of personnel and their activities, and the measurement of performance. In the traditional control theory, the measurement of performance has four steps:

1. *Establish standards or goals.*
2. *Measure performance.*
3. *Compare and analyze.*
4. *Take corrective action.*

The other main approach is the behavioral theory of control. If people feel close to an operation, this theory argues, they will be less inclined to take advantage of it or cause it loss. Especially desirable in the behavioral aspect are group goals which control members of the group. In implementing the behavioral approach to control, every effort is made to draw the parties closer to the operation.

It is up to the individual foodservice manager to decide what is best for his or her own operation. For some, behavioristic control has proven effective. Other operations have experienced a distinct letdown in control with these approaches. The personalities of management and the employees will obviously be the principal determinants. There can, of course, be "over control" in the traditional sense. And when that happens, employees may feel hemmed in and have little inclination to do their best.

Financial control is very important. It can involve accounting—both financial and managerial. It can also involve budgets, of which there are many types such as an operating budget, a capital budget, a labor budget, and other specialized types. The budget is a direct control device. Expenses and needs are determined in advance by means of the budget; when there are deviations from these figures, corrective action may be taken.

Ratio analysis involves taking figures from control reports and putting them into ratio and percentage forms. These may then be compared with goals, budgets, and past histories. Food and labor cost ratios are the most commonly used in a hospitality field. Standard costs are a management accounting procedure to determine in advance what costs should be; actual costs are then compared to these expectations.

Cost control must be coordinated with quality control. It is possible to cut costs and also cut quality. If management intends to do this, it should be aware of the effects that reduced quality may have. The effort and time expended in cost control must also be weighed against the value it returns. Cost control usually minimizes loss but it may have the reverse effect. At one time the author worked in a hospital that thought it had very tight control over its pencils. To secure a pencil one had to turn in the stub of an old one. More time was lost exchanging the pencils than the money gained by conserving them. Also, certain costs, such as fixed costs or costs demanded by a union are not subject to management control. These should be recognized so that no undue effort is made to control them.

Internal control is defined as the plan of organization, the coordinating of methods and measures within a business to safeguard the enterprise's assets, checking the accuracy and reliability of its accounting data, promoting operational efficiency, and encouraging adherence to prescribed management policy.

Hospitality operations often have difficulty with employee and customer theft control. There are many reasons why people steal. In combating theft control, it is very helpful to understand some of these underlying reasons.

In general, control is too often ineffective in the hospitality industry. Many hospitality operations are relatively small and have grown rather haphazardly. The heads of foodservice operations often earned their job because of their culinary skills rather than their management talents. Thus, too few are familiar with the concept of systematic control and its importance. Nevertheless, the present economic situation and the attendant difficulties in securing funds will undoubtedly increase managerial interest in control. The more distant the manager is from the actual operation the more control techniques he must use: formal control techniques amount to substitutes for managerial presence. Theoretically, a one-man foodservice operation would have little need for external controls besides accounting because the one-man manager would always know exactly what was going on.

Managerial concern can have a great effect on all control procedures. If management does not want to be bothered, little control will result. But if management has an interest in control, it will be alert to the cost aspects of the operation, eager to check reports, visibly on the scene, and willing to take corrective action when necessary.

IMPORTANT TERMS

After studying this chapter, you should be able to define or identify the following terms:

> **job description**
>
> **job specification**
>
> **financial accounting**
>
> **management accounting**
>
> **budget**
>
> **operating budget**
>
> **cash budget**
>
> **capital budget**
>
> **labor budget**
>
> **ratio analysis**
>
> **standard costs**
>
> **internal control**
>
> **profit (or cost) center**
>
> **external theft**
>
> **internal theft**

REVIEW QUESTIONS

5-1. Why does a hospitality enterprise need the control function?

5-2. Discuss the traditional approach to control.

5-3. How does the concept of strategic points affect the control function?

5-4. How is managerial accounting part of the control process?

5-5. How can budgets be part of the control process?

5-6. Discuss the concept of standard costs.

5-7. Name and discuss the areas of internal control.

5-8. Discuss aspects of employee theft control.

5-9. Why do customers steal from a hospitality operation?

5-10. Discuss the behavioristic approach to control.

CASE PROBLEM: Mrs. M

Mrs. M. has worked in your restaurant for ten years, and you consider her an ideal, if underpaid, employee. But on a tip from a waitress, you compare Mrs. M's cash turn-ins with a total of the waitress checks and find shortages. You also slip an extra twenty dollars into the register while relieving her, but no overage is subsequently reported. When confronted, Mrs. M. tearfully admits to the situation and upon further questioning says that total withdrawals have been about two thousand dollars over a three-month period. She claims that she needed the money for her son's orthodontic work and she intended to repay it. You know that Mrs. M. is hard-pressed financially and would have difficulty getting another job in your small town if the facts of her dishonesty were known.

a) How should you proceed in this matter?

b) What might be managerial shortcomings on your part regarding this unfortunate situation?

c) Do you believe slipping the twenty dollars into the register to help establish her guilt is justified?

CASE PROBLEM: Labor Costs

John Sanford operates a restaurant. He believes his labor cost to be excessive but does not know where or why. No specific labor cost records are available. However, the last income statement indicated a total labor cost of $150,000 on sales of $400,000, or 37.5 percent. Wages paid do not seem excessive for similar jobs in the geographical area. All employees work full time. Although working conditions seem good, John says he has a lot of turnover. Some time ago John thought he would cut labor costs by not replacing people who left. But service, food quality, and sanitation all suffered, and the remaining workers claim there is too much for them to do properly. A good deal of friction also exists as to who is responsible for what work—a situation aggravated by the smaller number of workers. The dishroom is a particular problem. Four people seem to be required but another operation with the approximately same volume and equipment gets by with three. John's employees say they are really busy and, if anything, are overworked. Waitresses have conflicting complaints: either they have too few customers for decent tips, or they have too many customers to provide decent service. There is no union involved.

What recommendations would you make to John to improve this situation? Why? Detail your response as much as possible.

6 Planning and Decision-Making

In the field of management, *planning and decision-making are intangible and crucial concepts. Success often hinges on careful planning, and a manager must spend a considerable portion of his time engaged in this activity. In fact, one characteristic that separates managers from other employees is that managers have (or should have) access to all the data that go into deciding the means to plan for an operation's success. After studying this chapter devoted to the planning and decision-making functions, therefore, you should be able to*

- *explain briefly the importance of planning in a hospitality operation*
- *state the seven advantages and four disadvantages of planning*
- *name and discuss briefly the two main types of planning and the objectives of each*
- *explain briefly how forecasting the environment affects planning*
- *formulate actual planning objectives appropriate for a hospitality operation*
- *discuss, in at least a paragraph, how a hospitality manager might utilize the planning process in his work*
- *list the eight types of decisions*
- *list the six "personal typologies" that may affect decision-making*
- *explain briefly how a hospitality manager might undertake to improve his decision-making*

Planning is the most fundamental of all management functions. In fact, without planning there would be little need for the other functions. Without plans there is no operation and no need for such functions as organizing, controlling, directing, and communicating.

Moreover, planning gains increasing recognition as an important function of management in proportion to the increases in complexity and size among modern businesses. This growth generates a corresponding need to map out formally both the short- and the long-range future. Although organizations have always engaged in some sort of planning, most management theorists feel that formal planning developed after the Second World War when managers faced the problem of converting from wartime to peacetime production. How could this transition be accomplished? What products should be substituted? What should the market goals be? Should expansion be considered? Postwar questions like these raised planning to a near science.

The Importance of Planning

The importance of planning can be illustrated by the long-range survival and success of certain hospitality operations. Before the Second World War, the prime movers in the hospitality industry included, among others, the Statler Hotels (later to become part of Hilton), Childs Restaurants, Horn and Hardart Restaurants, and Milner Hotels. Such enterprises as Holiday Inns, Hilton Hotels, Marriott, Colonel Sanders, and Sheraton had either not yet established themselves or maintained a small profile in the industry. Mainly because of their superior planning (marketing strategy, to use the prevalent jargon), the latter organizations attained their present eminence while the former lost theirs. The same patterns hold in other industries: planning causes the list of leading organizations in any industry to change constantly. If one believes that the prime goal of management is the continued operation of one's organization, then planning for survival has to be a prime responsibility of management.

The success of such innovations as fast-food chains or motor inns is due to the fact that their originators were sensitive to the changing environment and produced operations to reflect the needs in this changing environment. The other operations, which might have been financially stronger, did little planning for these changes and thus decreased their importance and success.

Definitions of Planning

Like management itself, planning has accummulated a variety of definitions. Planning can:

Provide a predetermined choice of action

Provide the premises for decisions in the future

Help increase the probability that desired future events that are the firm's objectives will occur

Be the process by which a manager looks to the future and discovers the alternate courses of action open to him

Specify the goals and courses of action managers need to achieve goals

Provide the process of deciding what to do and how to do it before action is required

Provide a design for tomorrow's actions

Provide an outline of the steps to be taken during some future period

Determine the goals that must be adapted to internal and external environmental influences

Throughout this list of short definitions runs a common element: planning involves short-range and long-range goals. In fact, a larger part of planning is the determination of those goals that are feasible. Notice, too, that planning must adapt to both the internal and external environments. Beautifully drawn plans are worthless if they fail to conform to the realities of the environment.

The most common reason for business failure is (not surprisingly) managerial incompetence. A major reason for managerial incompetence is the failure to find a feasible course of action for the enterprise (the failure to plan). In analysing a business failure, one often concludes that the enterprise did not seem to know where it was going and what it wanted to achieve. Even if it had some vaguely formulated long-range goals there was often no formal thought given to how to achieve them. Thus, the enterprise found itself buffeted by changes in its environment, rather than trying to turn these changes to its benefit, or taking steps in advance to minimize their effects.

Occasionally during prosperous periods or little competition, an enterprise may experience unsought success because of simple good fortune. Many early motor hotels, for example, went up without benefit of adequate planning. Yet, the great surge in automobile travel allowed them to be successful. Now we see many motor hotels in business difficulties because there is no providential help on the horizon.

The Need for Planning

We have examined how some operations suffer from a lack of planning. What is it specifically that planning does for an operation? First, it provides the framework so that the work of the organization promotes a desired purpose and everyone works toward these objectives. Without planning and with everybody operating independently, hard, diligent work may easily fail to contribute to the goals of the enterprise. If an operation does not know in advance where it wants to go it will quite often muddle around without really achieving anything.

Second, along with providing purposeful goals, planning can help coordinate the work and reduce overlap. Without planning, employees may discover that their extra efforts cause considerable friction as different segments intrude on each other's areas of responsibility.

As we have frequently noted, an organization must adapt to environment. And since the environment is in a state of constant change, the organization should plan for these changes. What are possibilities for the future? Commercial hotels lost much of their business when they failed to anticipate that after the Second World War many of their guests would use the automobile instead of the train. Consequently, they lost out to the motor inns or motels, which had anticipated the changing environment. The successful enterprise is usually ahead of its competitors in adapting to change. When change is forced upon it especially by actions of competitors, it must quickly catch up. Planning can contribute to the flexibility required in these situations.

Of course, the main problem in planning is forecasting the future. None of us is a fortune teller. Some operations find trouble when they plan for a future that does not occur soon enough and when the target markets do not materialize. One large restaurant chain erected an enormous commissary. Unfortunately the business did not develop sufficiently to require the commissary, and the consequent carrying costs put the company in financial distress.

Thus, planning can take on contingency features. What should be done *if* certain events occur? Fire evacuation plans for a hospital are a good example of this type of planning. Instead of trying to figure out how to evacuate patients while the fire rages, a hospital can set up evacuation procedures in advance and instruct personnel in these plans. Hospitality operations that depend now on the motoring public should be planning what to do if gasoline continues to be scarce or very expensive. Should new facilities be developed for markets predicated on the automobile if the automobile promises to lose popularity? This presents a difficult problem that involves forecasting what our energy situation may be in the future.

In the traditional sense, control involves comparing actual performance with a desired standard, and the plan provides this standard. Measuring actual achievement against this stated goal shows how effective performance is. Without such a standard, an operator would be hard pressed to determine whether performance is satisfactory or not. A plan, therefore, provides a basis for control and encourages achievement. With a goal to strive for, the individual segments of an enterprise stop "putting in time" and strive toward what they know is expected.

Because people in different segments of the organization tend to work for their own partisan interest, they fail to see the whole picture without a broad plan to refer to. We see, then, that planning follows the systems concept: it organizes work toward the desired goals and thus helps an operation reach them. In making up plans, a manager is practically forced to look at the whole picture—to comprehend the entire operation.

Another problem in many organizations is the need to balance the deployment of personnel and facilities. The kitchen may be in trouble if a large part of the production takes place at the grill while the ovens and steamers remain idle. The grill section is overworked and the other sections are underutilized. Planning can produce a more balanced utilization leading to a more efficient use of both equipment and personnel.

Not the least of the advantages associated with planning is that it encourages strong leadership and direction. The manager who must constantly cope with unforeseen problems as they arise is at a disadvantage. His usual approach is to let people on the spot handle the situation, a decision which leads both to confusion and erosion of his authority. Planning, by contrast, enhances his authority because he remains in charge of the situation.

Disadvantages of Planning

Although planning is obviously desirable and useful, it presents some difficulty. To begin with, the effectiveness of long-range or strategic planning is directly related to the accuracy of the forecasts. Even the most careful forecasting sometimes goes astray; planning based on it tends likewise to be wrong. Even the most sophisticated management organizations that have developed planning to a high art occasionally make expensive mistakes. The Edsel, Ford's monumental flop, and Corfam by Du Pont are two examples of new products that underwent extensive planning but failed in the marketplace. But, it is almost always better to do some planning than just to roll with the tide of events, reacting to them as they occur.

There are, as well, definite monetary and time costs in planning. People who spend time in the planning function cannot do other desirable things at the same time. It is not unusual for planning to become an end in itself, so that meaningless sessions consume valuable company time futilely. Furthermore, plans may become too detailed, or may be of limited use if the original forcasting is not entirely accurate and changes must be made. People are creatures of habit; they would rather stay with the tried-and-true than accept changes in the routine. This fact of life works against the planning function. If an organization is hidebound and its employees resist change, planning may be useless. In such a situation, one skill a manager should have is to interest personnel in the planning process and to give them a stake in the change.

In some operations when higher management leaves or retires, it is wise to hire outside personnel rather than promote from within. Although the opposite course is generally recommended, some operations need fresh air, new ideas, and initiative and somebody who can plan. Employees who have been on the scene for a long time often do not have this flexibility.

Although a plan can be a goal to achieve, in some circumstances it can actually stifle initiative. Once the plan or goal is achieved, the personnel involved may feel entitled to slack off. But even though a plan may stifle initiative, generally the planned goals or achievement produces the better results. And, a careful plan has enough elasticity so that goals can be changed if the situation changes—and this means even when goals are met.

Finally, planning can cause delay. Someone who wants to go ahead with a project may be thwarted because the plans have yet to be developed or distributed. In many cases, the independent foodservice operator has an advantage over the chain-type or multiunit operators because his plans need not "make the rounds" before the necessary directives are given.

Planning and the Environment

If a manager or planner could definitely predict the environment in which his organization must operate, planning would be relatively easy. The uncertainty in the environment—the only unchanging fact being the assurance of change—certainly complicates planning. The traditional environmental factors in all enterprises have been land, labor, and capital. But not only have these traditional factors increased greatly in complexity during the recent past, but a number of new factors have appeared on the scene as well. At no time has planning been more difficult for the manager than it is now—except perhaps during periods of war, or social or natural upheaval.

The traditional labor factor, for example, became more involved in the last few years because of the growth of labor organizations, more stress on fair treatment for minorities, increased concern for the safety and well-being of workers, and in general more aggressiveness on the part of workers in asserting themselves and demanding their due.

The capital or financing situation has also changed greatly. A few years ago, for example, few could ever have imagined the interest rates charged in the 1970s. And the sudden increases in oil prices recently have changed the whole financial and economic picture. More government intervention in business has changed many of the ways of conducting that business. (What some consider interference others see as a necessary control, but the effect is still a considerably different business environment.) Concern for the environment has also affected business, which now must determine such problems as whether its outside decor is appropriate for a particular locality. Designs that receive awards in some areas are declared unsuitable in others. Even such mundane matters as garbage and trash disposal have presented new problems and consequently a planning need to the hospitality operator.

Social trends also change at an accelerated rate. What was socially acceptable only a few years ago may be now criticized or even made illegal; while the disgraceful may now be socially acceptable. The rapid rate of technological change also involves planning. New equipment and procedures must be incorporated if an operation is to prosper.

The energy shortage ushered in a whole new planning element for the hospitality industry. Higher costs and limited supplies of gasoline can change the patterns of the American motorists, which a large portion of the hospitality industry directly serves. Kitchens, too, require energy sources and unavailability or high costs of these are also an environmental change.

One only has to read a book such as *Future Shock* by Alvin Toffler to realize the changes that are in store for us even on the near horizon. The changes will affect the environment of every hospitality operation, and the successful ones will be those that can plan for and adapt to their ever-changing environment.

Types of Planning

Planning may be classified in various ways, but the most usual classifications are *long-range* and *short-range* planning. Sometimes, instead of those terms "long-" and "short-range," one hears *strategic* and *tactical* planning. Planning, both strategic and tactical, can be further subdivided into external and internal planning.

Strategic Planning

Strategic or long-range planning is concerned more with the overall objectives of the operation, its survival, how it fits in with its external environment, and its continued existence. A plan that fundamentally affects the future of an operation would be strategic. Definite time periods may be specified in strategic planning. For example, an organization may have a five-year plan, a ten-year plan, or a plan of any other specified period for that matter. In strategic planning, management must consider particularly the external environment and its possible changes. It must also consider the resources that it expects to have available to accomplish the desired plans.

Top management is usually more concerned with strategic planning than with tactical or short-range planning. In some large organizations, in fact, the top personnel may devote the bulk of their time to planning the future path of the organization and comparatively little to the actual direction of company activities or the supervision of personnel. Or, when management wants to spend more of its time directly with operations, it may hire personnel to attend strictly to planning with little other responsibility. Concerned with the long-range objectives of the enterprise, they convey their information to top management, which may then make the appropriate decisions. Since most hospitality operations are relatively small, however, management personnel must usually include strategic planning with their other responsibilities.

Strategic planning being more within the province of the manager or executive, he must determine how best to adapt his organization to its various environments. Strategic planning requires innovative thinking, and the planner must draw on his knowledge and experience. Very likely, too, he will have to locate new sources of information. By contrast, tactical planning can often be "programmed," with the routes already set out. The tactical planner thus adapts his plans through regions that have already been chartered by the strategic one.

Tactical Planning

Tactical planning is short-range, and plans that do not extend beyond a single year may arbitrarily be termed tactical. Tactical plans typically direct day-to-day operations.

Tactical plans also include a goal but they tend to aim toward a more immediate result. A supervisor might want to cut down turnover in a foodservice operation or maintain a certain budgeted food cost percentage. The employees themselves may harbor personal goals that cannot be so quantitatively expressed: providing friendly or more efficient service, for example.

Note that qualitative goals are harder to specify and measure than quantitative goals. For example, a goal of gourmet food or of superlative service is hard to specify or measure quantitatively.

External and Internal Planning

External planning focuses on forecasting environmental influences and adapting to them—in other words, how to cope with environmental changes that may be economic, legal, social, political, or scientific. The energy crisis, for example, created many changes in the hospitality environment and necessitated a great deal of planning revision. External planning, then, is usually strategic.

Internal planning concerns itself more with defining procedures that promote the operation's already established external plans. An operation may draw up some firm goals. But, if the personnel within the firm do not share these goals, they cannot be achieved even though they accurately reflect the external environment. A foodservice operation manager may strive for the qualitative goal of providing "the best food in town." If the rest of the organization fails to adopt this purpose, there is little chance of its achievement.

A duty of management, then, is to resolve the external and internal goals so that they augment one another. A manager usually wants a better (and often bigger) operation. To achieve this goal, he must match his physical and personnel resources to his plan. External planning, as you can see, would make little sense if the internal planning were not sufficient to achieve the manager's goals.

Planning and Goals

By this time you must realize that any plan must have certain objectives or goals to which it is directed. Moreover, the plan must outline the means of achieving these goals. For example, strategic plans might collect general goals like these: the survival of the enterprise, the provision of a useful service or product to customers, a return to investors, a worthwhile existence for employees, and being a good neighbor in the community. Strategic plans can be more specific: increasing sales by 20 percent per year or increasing profits by 10 percent to 54 thousand dollars. Some hospitality managers consider a certain percentage of market penetration very important. Thus, the operation might establish the goal of increasing the amount of the market that it enjoys by, say, 10 percent during the planned time span.

Setting desirable and feasible goals is obviously important. In fact, goals can be effective motivators. If the goals are overly demanding, employees may make little effort to achieve them, and, in effect, there will be no real plan. On the other hand, if the goals are too easily obtained, there may be a lack of incentive to improve upon them. Goal determination involves a number of interrelated factors. One is a reasonably accurate *forecast* of activity. Another is the *constraints* imposed by the resources and the environment. And the *motivation* of the personnel can affect the success of the plan.

Goal achievement is also affected by the character of the organization—its past history or heritage, for example. Future decisions are influenced by past decisions and the work attitudes and habits of the employees. A manager who sees that drastic changes are necessary may find it difficult to convince personnel of the need for that change. Some food operations find themselves in this exact situation when management decides that the operation would be best suited to convenience foods, while the kitchen personnel believe that traditional preparation methods are best. (They naturally have a vested interest in keeping their jobs.) As with political leadership, the success of a manager may be determined, in large part, by a judgment of how much the organization will accept change. Then, the manager matches the judgment with the change. A manager who makes too drastic a change too soon may encounter resistance. Of course, some managers make their reputations by seeing the need for change and accomplishing it successfully.

Forecasting the Environment

Since a prime part of planning involves adapting operations to the environment and the main problem here is the uncertainty of future external and internal environments, forecasting becomes an extremely important part of planning.

No time in modern business history has been as difficult for forecasters as the 1970s and 1980s. Environments can change suddenly, ruining even the most carefully considered plans. Food shortages, for example, appeared in the early 1970s that had no counterpart in peacetime. Food-service operations were hard put to adapt. And who could have foreseen the possibility of the Arab oil boycott and its effect on the hospitality industry (as well as most every other industry)? Forecasting is at best an inexact art, ranging (some say) from star gazing to detailed mathematical analysis. But, useful forecasting methods and techniques do exist and will be discussed in the following paragraphs.

One method of forecasting is to project past trends into the future, the technique known as *extrapolation*. A hospital has increased its number of patient days by about 5 percent for the past five years. It is reasonable to assume that this trend will continue for some time into the future. Therefore, the administrator projects the level of hospital activity for each year at 5 percent more than the year before. Although this extrapolation can be helpful as a guide, it obviously cannot be treated as infallible. If, for example, another new hospital were to open in the same area, the growth rate of the first would probably diminish. Environmental conditions might also have a serious effect. A change in the economic status of the patrons could be reflected in hospital use. New governmental health programs might also change any past trends. The 5 percent growth may have depended at least partially on a 5 percent population growth in the area. If this rate lessens, the hospital growth also lessens.

As another example consider that part of the tremendous increase in the growth of convenience fast-food operations can be attributed to the fact that, as they developed, they also attracted more business simply by being available and creating new markets. This condition, by itself, invalidated past projections.

Another tool used in forecasting is *market research,* which is broadly described as gathering, recording, and analyzing all the facts and problems related to the transfer and sale of goods and services from producers to consumers. In this situation, a manager tries to get all the information he can bearing on future consumption trends involving his service or product. Then he determines what his particular volume of activity might be. For example, in planning a new motor hotel, he might conduct a feasibility study to analyze a particular location and to pinpoint factors that would generate business for the proposed facility. The study would analyze existing and anticipated competition to determine how much of the potential business already being done might switch to the new facility. In addition, long-range traveling trends might be analyzed. From this information a manager could reasonably estimate the size facility he needed, the types and levels of services it should offer, and the rates it could charge. Once the dollar volume of business had been forecasted, a manager could estimate his expenses and, therefore, his profit. This profit could then be compared to the investment required, which would determine whether the investment is, in fact, economically feasible. This is covered in more detail in chapter 13.

A technique that has achieved some popularity in planning is the *Delphi technique,* named for the well-known oracle in ancient Greece. The Delphi technique requires a committee or panel with expertise in the matter being planned. Each of the experts is asked, separately, to forecast what he thinks will happen. For example, planning for a new hospital, an administrator might ask a number of experts to forecast the utilization of various hospital services for a certain period. The answers of each member might be compiled and presented to the entire panel, without however, any suggestion of which members supplied which forecasts. With the added perspective of the other anonymous forecasts, each panel member could make a new forecast. In situations like these a consensus usually surfaces, and this consensus serves as a general forecast. It should be stressed that the Delphi technique does not merely arrive at a consensus; it also provides considerations overlooked in the original planning process.

Game playing can also be utilized in planning. In operations research games, the approach is to maximize gain and minimize loss by anticipating the possible actions and counteractions of competitors. When playing such games, the operation's experts decide on a certain strategy. Then, they determine what competitors will do to match this strategy and what the operation will do to cancel the competitors' moves. Assume, for example, that a manager plans to raise the rates of a hotel. If competition does not follow suit, the hotel may be forced to lower the rates again. In the game playing technique experts would analyze the various possible countermoves of "the enemy," and advise whether or not the rates should be raised.

A *scenario approach* may also be used in forecasting. The planner who adopts this strategy lists what he thinks is most likely to happen in a certain situation, basing his opinions on factual information available as well as on his best guesses. His scenario can then be evaluated by experts and employees alike and contingency plans can be based upon it.

A subjective method of planning is *playing a hunch.* We mention it only because it is still (unfortunately) a widely-used method in the hospitality industry. Some people seem to have hunches that prove out over and over again. But most of us are not this lucky. In fact, successful hunches are usually based on solid information lurking in the manager's subconscious. The hunches of experts, then, tend really to be informed decisions.

There is, of course, no infallible forecasting method, even though we have seriously discussed an entire range of forecasting methods. Some of the most sophisticated companies utilizing sophisticated planning experience their full share of errors. And the number of hospitality establishments that have failed in spite of conscientious planning is legion.

Even though forecasting is difficult, however, it is still desirable. The only constant environment is change, and an enterprise should be prepared to deal with this change. A tentative plan for dealing with the future is better than no plan at all.

Objectives of Planning

Objectives represent a "desired future condition of the business," and planning is employed to bring this future to pass. A profit-making organization is supposed to have these four general objectives:

1. A financial return to the owners
2. A desirable livelihood for the employees
3. A needed service or product offered to the public
4. The status of a desirable community member

Theoretically, planning should be done towards the end of meeting these four objectives. Concern for the owners and stockholders will probably receive a higher preference than the other three—though all of the objectives are interrelated. A nonprofit organization such as a hospital or institution, on the other hand, is interested in providing the best service its resources permit besides being fair to employees and being a good neighbor.

An individual manager in the hospitality field tends to foster a number of personal objectives. Some of these (like making a profit, increasing the profit over prior operations, increasing the profit over comparable operations) fall within the first category. To increase the profit or provide a better service with the resources available, a manager might reasonably adopt the objectives of greater efficiency or better control of costs. The manager in a nonprofit organization might adopt the objectives of increasing services to his clientele. A manager might also point for more personal objectives like increasing the size of the operation, becoming a leader in the field, creating industry innovations. These more personal objectives should, of course, parallel the objectives of the organization and supplement them. Remember, personal objectives can have a detrimental effect. An executive who becomes a leader in the field may lend greater prestige to the organization, but the effort required to achieve that prestige might better have been spent on the operation.

Profit Objectives

While a nonprofit operation tries to provide the best services its resources permit, the profit-making operation tries to maximize its owner's interest. This profit maximization can take at least two forms:

1. The return to the stockholders in the form of earnings or dividends
2. An increase in the owner's equity

A restaurant may, of course, plow its earnings back into the business; and although the owners may take out little from current operations, the value of their equity in the business steadily increases. This type of reinvestment is sometimes found in the stock market where a stock which pays small dividends may nevertheless be considered very desirable because it can be sold for higher prices as its value increases.

If profit is considered to be the principal objective of a business, there must be some method of judging whether the profit is appropriate for the operation. A twenty-thousand-dollar profit may be appropriate for one restaurant but very inappropriate for another. One way to measure profit is to compare it with the profits during past periods. A profit figure that increases every year is a good sign, that is, if the profit increase exceeds the increases due strictly to inflation.

Some widely used ratios can also help analyze the objective of profit in planning. One such ratio is the *ROI* or *return on investment*. It is derived by dividing profit by the owner's investment. Assume a motor inn costs one million dollars to build and equip. Out of the million dollars the owners themselves put in two hundred thousand of their own money with the borrowed balance owed to others. If the profit from the operation was fifty thousand, the return on investment would be fifty thousand divided by two hundred thousand, or a very satisfactory 25 percent. Normally investors desire the highest return on their investments consistent with the safety or security of that investment. Funds can be put into government bonds, savings and loan associations, or bank savings accounts—all very secure and, in fact, guaranteed by the government. But the interest from these investments is usually quite low. An investor may be willing to forego some of this security to gain a higher return. (He may, for example, be willing to invest in a new hotel or restaurant.) Each individual investor must determine for himself the optimum combination of return and risk for his particular circumstances.

Another measurement of the planning objective is *ROAM* or *return on assets managed*. ROAM includes the total assets of the operation available to the manager for the purposes of making money. The larger number of assets available, the greater the amount of money that should be produced. A motel with total assets of a million dollars and a profit of fifty thousand dollars shows a ROAM return of 5 percent. ROAM is a measure, then, of the effectiveness of the manager in gleaning the profits from the resources entrusted to him.

An *operating ratio* compares profit to sales. If our million-dollar motel with a profit of fifty thousand dollars had a million dollars in sales the operating ratio would be 5 percent. This ratio permits one to compare the financial success among operations of varying sizes. The operating ratio of our motel doing a million dollars worth of business could be compared to one doing five hundred thousand, two million, or any other figure to determine if the profit was appropriate for the volume of sales.

One who plans with the objective of making money or profit will want to quantify what that profit should be. The ratios just discussed can help with this task.

Planning and Management Functions

Planning can take place in all the various functions of a business. *Marketing* or *selling plans* can increase the volume of business. In a hospitality operation these plans could include strategies like changing the menu, providing different types of service, expanding facilities, and launching new promotion campaigns. *Financial planning* addresses the problem of financing the enterprise and keeping it liquid (maintaining its ability to pay its obligations). *Expansion plans* focus on long-range expansion or on internal changes to cope with changes in the environment. *Product planning* involves the food production system and how the best results can be obtained there. This planning can, in turn, involve scheduling personnel and equipment or perhaps hiring new personnel or buying equipment—or even perhaps eliminating some of the work.

A Planning Process
We have discussed the need for and advantages of planning, but these discussions are futile unless one knows how to go about planning. Too often an individual with a bright idea immediately seeks to implement it. This may be a type of planning, but hardly an enlightened type. It is difficult to describe the planning process in terms of definite procedures; but there are general steps which, if followed, usually prove more satisfactory than haphazardly implementing brainstorms (see Exhibit 6-1).

Learn what is going on. What opportunities exist for the organization? What are the current hospitality trends? What are other similar organizations up to? Few organizations operate in a vacuum; most are affected by their environments. Management must know what is going on in the hospitality environment in order to take advantage of opportunities. Management must "exploit the breaks," to use sports parlance.

Set objectives. Objectives may be either quantitative (expressed in amounts or numbers) or qualitative (such subjective goals as better ser-

Exhibit 6–1.
Steps in Planning

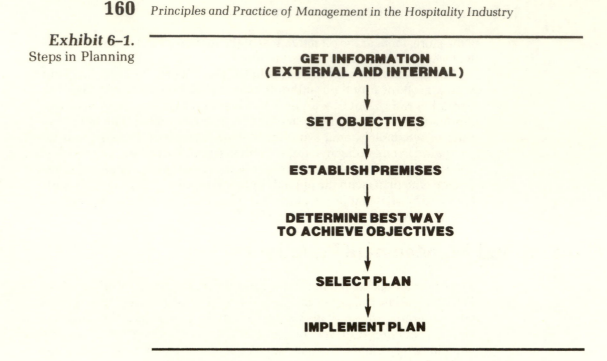

vice for patrons). Setting the objectives for an entire organization requires a manager to set subsidiary objectives for each of its segments.

Establish premises. Premises are planning assumptions, and they include forecasts of the factors important to the business and its environment. What will economic conditions be? What markets will open up for the organization's goods or services? What changes in the political and social environment will occur. If a plan is to succeed in a real world, the premises attempt to define what the real world will be during the life of the plan. After compiling the premises it may be desirable to change the objectives formulated in the second step.

Consider the best way to achieve objectives. Once a manager knows what his objectives are and is sure they can mesh with his premises, he should consider the best way of achieving the objectives. Objectives can be accomplished in a number of ways, and each should be considered. Quite often in the planning process only one method receives consideration; other, perhaps even better, possibilities never see the light of day. And when hasty, emergency planning occurs, the consideration of alternative methods usually suffers.

Select the best plan. After the various courses of action or plans have been developed it is necessary to select the best one. Here decision-making and planning become one and the same thing.

Implement the desired plan. The implementation of the desired plan can involve appropriate timing, setting policies, developing procedures, establishing methods, determining standards, and setting up a program to achieve the plan's objectives.

This planning process may appear to resemble many other aspects of management. It may also appear to be quite elementary. Yet it is surprising how many managers do not use a logical, commonsense approach when they confront a need for planning.

Especially important in effective planning is the accuracy of the premises (or forecasts). The uncertainty of the future is what makes planning so difficult but so important. The stronger, more definite the organizational structure of the operation, the easier it is both to plan and to implement the plans. Planning means setting objectives—objectives that must be implemented by the personnel in the organization. To implement the objectives a manager must establish clear lines of authority and responsibility.

Planning, like other management functions, is greatly enhanced if the organization projects a sense of purpose and progress. A sense of purpose and progress tends to raise the morale of a group. In a "can do" operation, planning is easier than when negative reactions arise in the face of any proposed change. Likewise, planning is most effective when a definite responsibility is assigned for it. Whether that responsibility stays with management or is delegated, someone should be responsible for planning and have the time and resources to accomplish it. Larger organizations often employ staff planners whose only job is planning. Regardless of who does the planning, all members should be actively committed to it, and this usually requires participation of some type.

Decision-Making

Business experts tend to treat decision-making as an esoteric, complicated subject. In fact, at one time it was treated not as a separate management function, but as part of the other management functions. But one who thinks about what differentiates a manager from other people in the organization is likely to notice that the manager makes the decisions. As a matter of fact, management itself has been defined as decision-making.

We now realize that the success of the manager may depend as much on his ability to make decisions as on any other managerial art. New quantitative methods have been developed for decision-making and much of modern operations research is devoted to it. As hospitality and other organizations become larger, many want to decentralize, and this means that increasingly more decisions are made at the decentralized levels than at the top—thus more decision-making.

Although many factors can cause an enterprise to fail, poor decision-making is one of the basic ones. In fact, faulty decision-making will doom an enterprise that has all the other ingredients of success. An enterprise headed by management that is afraid to make decisions destroys the confidence of the other members of the organization and usually invites unhappiness.

A manager may—and probably should—delegate many other management functions, but as Harry Truman's famous sign put it, "the buck stops here." A manager of a large operation may have specialists for planning, organizing, and control, but he must make the final decisions.

Decision-making is difficult because it is fraught with uncertainty. If the decision-maker knew all the consequences of the different courses of action open to him, he would certainly be more at ease making his decisions. But, if the future were clear and definite there would be little need for managers. Decision-making is difficult also because often the decisions themselves tend to be gray rather than black or white. A certain course of action may have its advantages, but it will also have its disadvantages. The net advantage (which is not often clear-cut) will probably dictate the course of action. Weighing advantages and disadvantages can be troublesome. For example, how much hostility will result when a hotel raises its room rates or a foodservice operation raises its menu prices? A manager must wait for the customer reactions and the balance sheet before he knows for sure.

Decision-making can be divided into two approaches: *quantitative* and *nonquantitative*. The quantitative approach focuses on reducing variables to numerical data which produces a mathematical figure that can, in turn, be compared to other mathematical figures. The anticipated investment payback period can be quantified in financial decision, or rating various elements of the job with points for job evaluation are two common examples of this approach. More sophisticated patterns of the quantitative approach often require mathematical models, mathematical simulation, and computer programming. In each case, the purpose is to evaluate various alternatives and reach a decision.

The other approach to decision-making is called nonquantitative. This approach includes such factors as intuition, judgment, experience, opinions, facts, and hunches. Of course, perhaps without even realizing it, hospitality managers always use some quantitative factors in their decision-making. His judgment may reflect a subconscious analysis of several alternatives. Some people appear to have a genuine knack for making decisions that appear nonlogical at first, but work out positively.

Decision-Making and Planning: The Difference

The difference between decision-making and planning can be confusing, because, even though decision-making is at the heart of planning, it is not necessarily the same thing. Planning involves an examination of the environment and the formation of long- and short-range goals suitable for this environment. Decision-making is the selection from among alternatives. For example, determining in advance what to do when a food item runs out would be planning, whereas quickly deciding what to substitute is decision-making.

Types of Decisions

Management experts talk about various types of decisions. Decisions, they say, can be categorized as *long-run* or *short-run*. Long-run decisions are like strategic planning; short-run decisions resemble tactical planning. Decisions may also be *recurring* or *nonrecurring*. Managers actually welcome recurring decisions because the job of management can be simplified by establishing standard operating procedures when the same circumstances continually arise.

A *policy decision* is a type of long-run decision for which a manager sets precedents or lays down general principles covering the conduct of the establishment. A policy decision for a hotel, for example, might govern the type of clientele it seeks to attract, the level of services it intends to offer, or the personnel policies and benefits it offers. *Administrative decisions* translate policies into general courses of action. Again, in the personnel area, administrative decisions would determine what specific benefits would be offered. *Executive* (or *ad hoc decisions*) are the day-to-day decisions made on the spot. Hiring applicants is normally an executive decision, at least in the smaller hospitality operations.

Who Makes Decisions

One problem with decision-making is assigning the actual duty. One traditional rule is that decisions should be made at the lowest possible level: where the incumbent has access to most of the pertinent information and (ideally) has no vested interest in the alternatives. Unfortunately, this role, though in wide use, has drawbacks. A front office manager of a hotel, for example, might notice that more sales could be generated by lower room rates. But, he might not have the whole picture. He might not see that lower room rates, while producing more sales, would also result in smaller profit than the lower occupancy percentage and the higher room rates. The sales manager might want to attract more business by lowering rates (especially if he works on a percentage basis of sales he produces). But he obviously has a vested interest in the situation; lower rates may not benefit the overall operation.

One approach to improve decision-making is through committees, a group of people working together on a situation that requires a decision. This approach has a number of theoretical advantages. For example, it draws on different viewpoints and varying expertise. More people become involved in making the decision, thus, they may be cooperative in carrying it out. With groups of people involved in the decision, there can be easier and more ready coordination between them in implementing the decision later. The number of people involved provides more creative talents focusing on the problems. Different, possibly antagonistic groups have their representation in the decision-making process, and so are not as liable to feel that they have been left out. Many hospitality managers have used group decision-making very successfully. These groups are typically composed of department heads; or a special committee might be assembled for a specific project and problem. The committee approach can also be used when an unpopular decision has to be made so that the blame for it can be spread over several people rather than placed on an individual. (This tactic sounds devious, but remember that an error in judgment is less likely when several people are involved.)

The committee approach has its disadvantages, however. To begin with, several people analyzing problems and making decisions consume a good deal of time. It keeps people from other work that might be more productive for the enterprise. It takes longer for several people to make decisions than for one. Assembling the committee might, by itself, delay the decision beyond what is considered desirable. When various viewpoints are represented in a decision, the result tends to be a compromise, which may not suit the needs of the organization. And, even though a committee structure is faithfully followed, some members of the committee may play up to their superiors, making the committee a facade with dominant individuals actually making the decisions.

Personal Factors Affecting Decision-Making

Decisions are made by people so personal characteristics will affect the decisions that are made. Those who study the decision-making process find it useful to analyze the types of people likely to make decisions. One commonly used typology was developed some years ago by Eduard Spranger. Although very few people are completely one type and most are a mixture of several, Spranger's basic typology can be helpful in understanding decision-making.

- The economic person. This individual is interested primarily in what is useful and practical. He is probably profit-oriented and not much interested in research or in theoretical matters.

- The aesthetic person. This individual is concerned with harmony, beauty, and individual expression. He is probably better suited to an artistic environment than to hard-driving business situations.

- The theoretical person. Here is an individual interested in knowledge for knowledge's sake. He is probably good at planning, especially strategic planning, but might have difficulty directing day-to-day operations.

- The social person. This individual enjoys other people. He may project a pleasant personality, and everyone likes his company, but he may find it hard to crack down on subordinates when necessary.

- The political person. This person is interested in power, particularly power for himself. As he advances himself and increases his power, he may also advance his organization. But, using the organization as a vehicle for personal power is not always the best way to advance the organization.

- The spiritual person. This type achieves satisfaction in self-denial and meditation. Although he may have strength of character, this person may not be an effective manager in the management of a mundane, pragmatic enterprise like a hospitality operation.

The Decision-Making Process

In referring to the formal decision-making process, analysts sometimes use the terms *scientific method* or *reflective thinking*. These two terms should warn a manager against making a decision too hastily—against jumping at the first solution that comes to mind. Decision-making is basically a choice among alternatives. When an idea is presented we should resist accepting the first solution without thinking of the broader picture or other possible approaches:

Understand the environment of the decision. The less we know about something, the more black and white things appear and the easier the decision-making seems. When the factors in internal and external environments appear, the picture becomes hazier. What seemed like a good idea may have to be discarded. A big problem managers face is decision-making in areas in which they are not completely qualified. The problem grows worse when they are unaware of their ignorance. But, a conscientious manager can almost always overcome this kind of shortcoming.

Recognize the right problem. Let's say a foodservice operation is not making the desired profit and it decides to reduce its staff or the size of its portions. It develops that the real problem was an underpriced menu for the available clientele. The manager was more *cost conscious* than *marketing conscious*. A little marketing knowhow in this case solves the right problem.

Search for possible alternatives. Brainstorming can be helpful here. A smart decision-maker opens his mind to others when he can think of only one acceptable solution. Collecting different viewpoints is one definition of brainstorming.

Evaluate the alternatives. Decision-making is, after all, choosing the best of the alternatives. Usually each alternative has its advantages and off-setting disadvantages. Quantitative approaches can be used in evaluating the alternatives, and there is also room for nonquantitative judgment. A computerized mathematical model can, for example, analyze a theoretical motor inn at two different sites. Even if this model shows that one site is preferable to the other, it would be foolhardy to use the computerized figures without injecting one's own experience and judgment.

Win the acceptance of the organization. The best decisions are often worthless if they are rejected by the organization; hence some perfectly reasonable decisions may have to be modified to gain acceptance. The way the decision is presented may also affect its acceptance. The committee approach may bring more acceptance than a message handed down from top management. Even if the manager decides firmly on a course, he may want to get others involved before he publicizes his final decision. Most people are happier with the status quo than with the unknown; most of us instinctively fear that a change will have ill consequences. The wise decision-maker will explain the reasons for his decision and try to educate the people affected by it. This approach can help still uneasiness about the consequences of the decision.

As we mentioned previously, the decision-making process can be quite logical and rational. A manager should follow the logical steps presented here to increase the chances for the success of his decision.

Reasons for Decision-Making

It is important for a decision-maker to be aware of the factors that may govern his decision. However logical the decision-making may appear, unless the decision is made by machine, the human element can always affect the decision. In making a decision and in trying to understand decisions made by others, a manager can consider the following discussion of motives.

Profit maximization. For a commercial enterprise the most logical reason for a decision is the hope that it will enhance profits. For a nonprofit organization like a hospital, the motive would be to achieve the best output from resources. These two examples illustrate the *bottomline approach,* also called *marginal theory.* A hotel considers adding another person to the sales department. It expects an additional profit from the sales generated by this person that more than covers the expense of paying him. If the profit seems certain, the answer would be to hire the extra person.

Should a hotel boost its room rates? Sooner or later higher prices will cut down on occupancy. Marginal theory would mean determining the room rate that provides high occupancy with the least customer resistance. This profit maximization (or bottomline) approach concentrates basically on dollars and cents or budgetary allotments. This approach is certainly helpful, but an overriding commitment to profits can eventually have undesirable consequences. Providing good service and producing high profits is fine, but cutting that service to increase the profits may threaten the future of the enterprise.

Psychological motives. A group of psychological theories can be grouped together to form a different approach to decision making. Psychologists know that we all have certain drives and that motivation represents attempts to satisfy these drives. If a drive is satisfied, the motivation will cease. For example, a hotel tells the sales manager that it wants to obtain a certain occupancy rate. There is placed in the sales manager a drive or motivation to achieve this rate. Success ends the drive or motivation. In this case, decisions are inspired not by the maximization of profits but by the need to achieve the desired percentage of occupancy.

Satisficing. The theorist, Herbert Simon, has coined the term, *satisficing*. He does not believe that managers are necessarily determined to maximize profits, but are instead generally satisfied to keep things on a satisfactory or a "good enough" level. Satisficing can also be interpreted to mean equilibrium or not rocking the boat. From an economic standpoint, a manager determines that a person in the organization can be released. But he knows, too, that this person is popular and that terminating him would cause friction within the organization. Instead of making the obvious economic decision, then, he maintains the equilibrium by keeping the person on. The wise decision-maker should be aware of those decisions he makes on a satisficing basis and those based on economics. Satisficing is not necessarily bad (in fact, it is often good). But there are times when a manager must rock the boat if his organization is to be effective.

Psychic income. Another psychological basis for decision-making is "psychic income" or "ego aggrandizement." To be blunt about it, decisions are often made for personal satisfaction. An executive decides upon an elaborate fancy office simply to gratify his ego. Restaurants frequently experience trouble when owners or managers try to make them fancier than the clientele desire. The owner psychologically wants a better restaurant than the economics can justify.

Improving Decision-Making

Every executive wants to improve his decision-making skills. But few know how to proceed. One way is to utilize the decision-making process we have been describing. Another way is to understand the reasons why decisions are made—a profit maximization or satisficing. The type of person making the decisions also affects the decisions he makes.

Beyond this knowledge, though, there are some additional ways for executives to make better decisions. One way is to have adequate information available. Information theorists believe that bad decisions are due to faulty information. Accordingly, management information systems (MIS) have become very popular. Wise managers have always examined company records and reports carefully before making major decisions. If these records and reports are unavailable, a manager should find out immediately how to get them.

Some poor decision-making results from a poor organizational structure. Are operational responsibilities clearcut, and has appropriate authority been established? The organization structure may not make it clear who should make the decisions in the operation's various segments, or it may pass decision-making to someone unfamiliar with the situation or with a partisan interest.

Centralization and decentralization also enter into decision-making. Remember, when possible and reasonable, decisions should be made at the lowest competence level. When decisions must always come from higher echelons, there is often a delay. Higher echelons may be swamped, and unable to devote adequate time to routine decisions. Also the higher echelons may not be familiar with the circumstances—circumstances perfectly clear to someone lower in the hierarchy and more directly involved.

Modern decision-makers have begun to develop a questioning attitude. This is especially true for steps 1 and 2 of the decision-making process—getting all the pertinent information and understanding the appropriate problem. These steps are crucial to developing possible alternatives before selecting the optimum one. The decision should not be made merely on the facts presented. Other factors are almost always consciously or unconsciously present, and a manager should learn to spot them and evaluate them. Inquisitiveness is one talent that should separate a manager from other employees in the organization. Managers should not see things only as they appear to be, but always inquire for facts beyond the first appearances.

SUMMARY

Planning is basic to all other management functions and to the enterprise itself. Planning can take place over both the long run (strategic planning) and the short run (tactical planning). Goals are basic to both, and a large part of planning involves deciding what goals are feasible. The advantages to planning include providing an operation with a framework and coordination. Planning also helps management specify what the enterprise expects—what its goals are.

The main problem with planning is forecasting the future environment. If one could be sure of the future, planning would naturally be easy. But it may be necessary to build contingency features into planning. The rapidly changing external environment makes long-range planning more difficult.

Although planning is necessary and vital, it has its disadvantages. The forecasts that govern the planning may be wrong. The time and effort required by planning is expensive. And the time managers spend on planning may come at the expense of other managerial duties. Planning may also become an end in itself rather than the accomplishment of the plan. Moreover, a plan can actually constrict an operation. People may not want to vary from the plan, or once the plan is accomplished they may not strive to exceed it. Formal planning may also cause delays if sudden needs cannot be met until the plan is changed.

Managers can select among several different approaches to forecasting, none of them entirely satisfactory. Extrapolation extends established trends into the future. Market research tries to gather all pertinent information and interpret the future of this data. The Delphi technique uses the opinions of a number of experts who revise their opinions as they learn of the opinions of others, eventually arriving at a consensus. Game playing and scenario approaches try to guess what will actually happen and how competitors will react.

For a profit-making organization, the objectives of planning theoretically are a financial return to owners, a desirable livelihood for employees, a service or product for customers, and good community relations. Profit-making enterprises probably concentrate more on the financial return, either in the form of dividends or as an increase in the value of the investment. Measures used to evaluate financial return include return on the investment (ROI), return on assets managed, and operating ratio or "profits compared to sales."

Too often, planning is a spur-of-the-moment process haphazardly undertaken. But a formal, well-considered planning process means

1. Learn what is going on.
2. Set objectives.
3. Establish premises.
4. Consider alternatives to achieving objectives.
5. Select the best course of action.
6. Implement the plan.

Decision-making resembles planning. All planning involves decision-making, but all decision-making is not planning, even when decision-making implements plans. Decision-making is what separates a manager from other personnel; in fact, decision-making is one definition of management.

Decision-making is divided into two approaches: quantitative and nonquantitative. The quantitative approach bases decisions on numbers. An example is making an investment decision on the highest ROI. The *nonquantitative approach is to make decisions on judgment, experience, and educated hunches.*

Decisions are sometimes separated into policy or long-run decisions, which translates policy into general courses of action, and ad hoc or administrative decisions, which are the routine, day-to-day decisions.

How to make decisions, and deciding who makes them, are important decisions in themselves. One pat answer is that decisions should be made at the lowest competent level, defined as the lowest level at which one can appreciate all the ramifications of the decisions. Decisions can be made by individuals or by committees. Each approach has its advantages and disadvantages.

The decision-making process comes after an understanding of the problem. It aims to develop alternative solutions to the problem. Then it involves selecting the best one. Finally, decisions are not always made on an economic basis. Psychological aspects such as satisfication and ego aggrandizement may enter in. An individual's psychological makeup affects his decision-making. This fact is well remembered when you make your own decisions or when you evaluate the decisions made by others.

IMPORTANT TERMS

Having studied this chapter, you should be able to define the following terms:

> **strategic planning**
>
> **tactical planning**
>
> **extrapolation**
>
> **Delphi technique**
>
> **game playing**
>
> **scenario approach**
>
> **policy decision**
>
> **administrative decision**
>
> **executive (ad hoc) decision**
>
> **satisficing**

REVIEW QUESTIONS

6-1. Some operations have been successful despite a lack of planning. How do you explain this fact? Why do we need planning anyway?

6-2. What are the differences between the purposes of long- and short-range planning?

6-3. Discuss various approaches to forecasting.

6-4. Profit is an objective of planning. How can profit be measured?

6-5. What are the steps in the planning process?

6-6. Differentiate between the various types of decisions.

6-7. Why might you want to use a committee for decision-making? Why not?

6-8. How do psychological motives enter into decision-making?

6-9. The president of your company believes a site of land owned by the firm would be ideal for a large motel. He assigns you to "look into it."

a) What would you investigate to determine if the project is feasible?
b) Describe the types of plans (either strategic or tactical in nature) you would have to prepare if the project is to be put into effect.
c) What might be the difficulties in implementing these plans?

6-10. You are presently operating a successful fast-food operation and want to try to ensure your continued success.

a) What are the probable changes in your environment ten years from now?
b) How can you plan to change to meet these changes?

6-11. The following decisions are typical of those a hospitality manager might make. Discuss the factors involved.

a) How much of various staple food products should be purchased?
b) Should you extend the hours of your restaurant?
c) Should you increase your room charges?
d) Should you go into a large-scale renovation program?

CASE PROBLEM: Choosing a Manager

You are the president of a multi-unit hotel chain and have to replace the manager of one of your larger hotels. For the unit to show an acceptable profit, you must terminate a number of the staff and also try to reduce some salaries and benefits. The unit will have to undergo extensive remodeling, which will involve aesthetic and design decisions. The present manager, with his gruff personality, has alienated both his staff (he tried to compensate for this with higher salaries) and his customers. The rebuilding of the business will require innovations in marketing to attract business.

You decide to replace this manager. You want to fill this position from within the organization. The following people are available for the job.

Wayne Ashenfelter, age 38, is presently in the controller's office. His background is largely financial. He is known as a hard-nosed individual who will brook no nonsense. He is very much of a nuts-and-bolts person who follows through and is good on detail. You know that if he is not promoted from the controller's office he will consider leaving the company. Dealing with people is not his forte.

Peter Miller, age 42, has been the assistant manager of another, similar hotel. He has had well-rounded experience but is not considered especially expert in any one area. In college he was a music major and is artistically oriented. He generally gets along well with people but can be tough with subordinates.

John Hake, age 34, is hard driving and eager to advance. He is the manager of a smaller hotel where he increased the profit considerably. However, he is self-serving, and lately there has been a great deal of resentment against him from the personnel who feel he has used them. Some good subordinates will probably leave or ask for a transfer to another unit if he remains. There appears to be no problem with his guest relationships, and he is technically competent in cost control and marketing.

William Forney, age 57, is an assistant to you. He has had managerial experience but his main forte is public relations. He has an ingratiating personality—everyone likes him. In his capacity as your assistant, he has worked on public relations and special projects. The latter he does in a competent manner, but he is not a conceptual person and requires some direction.

Evaluate these people in terms of desirability. You may first want to establish the factors necessary for success and give each of the individuals a quantitative ranking for that factor to help in your evaluations.

7 Productivity Management

The productivity of employees directly concerns a hospitality manager and, to a great extent, controls his chances for success. An increase in this productivity may result in greater profits—and more benefits for the employees themselves. This chapter, which discusses these aspects of productivity among several others, should help you

- *discuss from a managerial viewpoint the problems caused by low productivity*
- *list three basic elements of productivity*
- *explain in some detail the interaction between labor and productivity*
- *list ten environmental factors that affect productivity*
- *define work simplification and motion economy, and explain how they can increase productivity*
- *describe, in at least one paragraph, the role automation plays in hospitality productivity*
- *define productivity motivation, and explain how it can be applied in the hospitality industry*

An increasing area of importance to the nation in general and to the hospitality industry in particular is the need for greater employee productivity. The productivity of the American economy and the American employee has enabled us as a nation to enjoy for ourselves and share with others the greatest prosperity ever known to mankind.

Productivity is the key to an improved standard of living. Traditionally, our national productivity has constantly risen. The measurement of output per man-hour increased 3.3 percent annually between 1948 and 1957 and 3.5 percent annually between 1957 and 1966. But productivity slumped to an average increase of only 2 percent between 1966 and 1971, fell by 1.6 percent in 1977 and by 0.4 percent in 1978. In 1950 seven Japanese or three German workers were needed to match the industrial output of one American. By 1979 two Japanese or about 1.3 German workers could equal a single U.S. worker's output. The United States still leads the world in productivity, but it now ranks only eleventh in productivity gains among the world's eleven most industrialized nations. Our productivity growth rate has been the poorest of the industrialized nations competing in the modern world marketplace.

The slowdown in productivity increase has been at least partially responsible for some of our economic and social ills including inflation, recession, budget deficits, and deficits in our balance of payments. We must have greater productivity if we want to retain economic preeminence, work toward goals of greater economic benefits for all, and increase our living standards. A National Commission on Productivity was established in 1970. The challenge to the commission was outlined by the president as follows: "In order to achieve price stability, healthy growth, and a rising standard of living, we must find ways of restoring growth of productivity. The task of this commission is to point the way towards this growth in 1970 and the years ahead."

Productivity Defined

Productivity has been interpreted as the efficiency with which output is produced by the resources utilized. It is an expression of the physical or real volume of goods and services related to the physical real quantity of input. This input might be in the form of labor, capital, energy, or materials. Another way of defining productivity is "the efficiency with which output is produced by the resources utilized."

The most important input of productivity is labor; thus the most common definition of productivity is "the real output for the manpower or labor expended." Although helpful, this definition still presents some difficulty. It does not consider the quality of the output but only its quantity. It might well be possible for a hospitality establishment to serve more meals to fewer people but the meals or service might be far less desirable.

Government figures show that fast-food operations will serve a hundred guests with only 10.5 man-hours of labor input, while a luxury restaurant requires 72.3 hours of labor input to serve 100 guests. (The figure for a family restaurant is 20.7 hours per hundred guests; for a cafeteria 18.3.) A hotel maid could take care of more guests rooms but give less attention to each. The output would be increased but the results would probably be undesirable. If, however, a maid is given new tools and the room and its furnishings are designed so that less work is required, the standard of cleanliness may be maintained and productivity increased. Although the most important resource is labor, the amount of labor can be reduced by using more machinery or capital investment. This leads to the definition of productivity as "the output from the input of labor and capital investment combined."

The hospitality industry has an unusual stake in increasing its productivity. It is a service industry that is labor intensive, which is to say it employs a large number of people rather than utilizing machines to produce the services. But, many of the people in lower hospitality job classifications are underpaid in comparison to industrial workers. To increase benefits for these hospitality employees, management must somehow increase productivity. Much of the hospitality industry provides services of a discretionary nature: people usually do not have to eat out or patronize hospitality establishments. If the prices for these services become too high, they will, in fact, stay home and thus curtail hospitality productivity and profit. So increasing the employee salaries and benefits is almost like a chicken-egg conundrum.

Basics of Productivity

The basics of productivity are:

- the people doing the work
- the equipment they use
- their work methods

Of these, the most important is, of course, the people, and this is doubly true in the hospitality service industries.

Great productivity increases occurred in manufacturing and agriculture when machines were substituted for hand labor. But the hospitality field is somewhat restricted in the amount of machinery it can adopt. Hospitality, in fact, reveals many instances in which the productivity of an individual job is about the same as it was many years ago. A baker cannot produce any more pies than he did a decade ago, nor can a desk clerk serve any more customers than he did years ago.

But changes are coming. More efficient machinery may soon make personnel more productive, even in hospitality. Mechanical dishwashers, for example, are far more efficient and require less labor for the amount of dishes cleaned than they did only a few years ago. Cooking equipment with automatic timers requires less manual attention, and fast-recovery fryers also require less personnel time. Convenience products like powdered mashed potatoes eliminate much labor. Mass production and fast-food kitchens permit greater production—although they cut down on product variety. In the hotel front office, computerized billing systems eliminate the laborious old transcript. Electronic room racks can streamline the room clerk's job and eliminate the chance that available rooms are not marked as such.

Work methods are also changing in the hospitality operation. More use is being made of convenience food, which can, of course, be produced on the assembly line rather than in individual batches. This utilizes the factory approach (long production runs of comparatively few items) instead of the kitchen approach (short production runs of many items). Operations that do not buy convenience foods may have their own commissary to produce food in large batches. The individual baker is being replaced by commercially prepared baked goods of high quality produced by the thousands.

Merely reorganizing the work may improve productivity. One large food commissary operation was able nearly to double its productivity by rescheduling its employees and adopting a couple of simple industrial engineering techniques. The equipment they used was the same, and if anything, the food quality rose.

Larger operations that do not use a commissary have found an ingredient room to be a very productive addition. Here all the food preparation is done except for the actual cooking which is completed in separate kitchens. The food, prepared and weighed, is wheeled into the kitchen at the desired time, and all the trained cooks and chefs have to do is place it in the appropriate cooking apparatus. The ingredient room permits closer supervision over the preparation, employs less expensive personnel rather than several highly paid cooks, and permits 9-to-5 scheduling by eliminating the peaks and valleys of activity found in most kitchens. Operations with ingredient rooms often report substantial savings not only in labor costs but, because waste is reduced, in food cost as well.

Altering the service you offer can also increase productivity. Hotels have largely eliminated the need for bell boys, for example, by providing ice and drink mixers on each floor in vending and ice machines. In fact, some machines now dispense alcoholic drinks right in the room, adding the cost automatically to the guest's bill.

Fast-food operations practically eliminated the need for waiters and waitresses with their streamlined self-service concepts. Disposable utensils in the hospitals have eliminated the need for personnel required to clean and store china and silverware.

Despite improvements in machinery and work methods, however, the key to productivity in the hospitality service industry remains people. Improving productivity involves almost every aspect of good management and most of the chapters in this book suggest tactics for increasing personnel productivity. Planning, organizing, controlling, and directing are all necessary to high productivity.

Labor Relations and Productivity

The climate of labor-management relations has an important bearing on productivity. *Productivity bargaining,* a term sometimes heard, is a process that treats production as a central collective bargaining issue and explicitly recognizes the tradeoff between measures to increase labor productivity and the sharing of the resulting benefits. What will employers get out of changes that lead to increased productivity? And what will the union members get out of these changes? These are the questions central to productivity bargaining. By eliminating restricted work practices and allowing more flexibility in staffing, lower unit labor cost can result. In return, the workers receive higher earnings, more fringe benefits, and increased job security. The costs of restricted union work practices can be enormous both in dollars and in efficiency.

In some major manufacturing industries, maintenance costs are 10 to 25 percent higher than necessary because employees of certain crafts refuse to do work covered by the job definitions of other crafts. In the construction industry, some analysts have estimated that as much as 40 percent of the payroll dollar is spent for superfluous labor. Labor organizations and their members have a natural desire for job security. Restricted practices bring about increased employment for them. But the natural desire for job security can conflict with attempts to increase productivity. Labor-saving equipment may be available but the workers resist it because it could limit future employment or income. Thus, concessions on labor-saving devices may be incorporated in a labor contract. This may force management to make certain concessions, like promising not to discharge any workers supplanted by the new equipment. Subjects normally included in this type of productivity bargaining are work rules, training and upgrading workers, group incentives, job design and enrichment, work place participation and communication, safety, and work scheduling. All of these subjects concern both management and labor. They must somehow work both to increase productivity and to provide security and economic benefits to the worker. It is, at best, a ticklish problem.

There are definite human costs when workers are displaced. Ways should be found to lessen the psychological and financial costs of displacement. Thus both manager and employee should realize that productivity bargaining seeks to increase productivity as a basis for justifying larger wage increases. In a number of industries where worker restricting or featherbedding practices have been common, the health of the industry and the overall welfare of the workers have declined dramatically. Railroads offer the obvious example. Their sad state is also ironic. Partly because of this featherbedding, they can no longer provide the service the public clamors for and thus can no longer employ as many people as they rightfully should. In the construction field, many building trade union members remain unemployed while nonunion firms win business contracts. Although in the short run it may appear that restricted practices benefit the union or union member, in the long run it is probably unhealthy for both.

This country ranks at the bottom of all eleven major industrial countries in percentage of gross national product which is reinvested in fixed assets or which provides the equipment asset of new productivity. Much of our factory equipment is now obsolete compared to other parts of the world, and we must find investment incentives for new facilities—investment not only in machinery but also in the training and retraining of people. We are living in an era of rapid change and human beings must be "updated" to match current developments in technology. Although a lot of attention has been paid to obsolescence of machinery, the obsolescence of workers and executives detract far more from the success of an organization. Manpower planning, which involves projecting labor requirements and the labor supply, increasingly is being used as a tool to improve the development and utilization of the labor force. Suppose you realize that you will need fewer employees two years in the future. It would be better for you to now use attrition to produce the short fall than it would be to terminate people summarily when you put your labor-saving methods into effect. One good example of manpower planning occurred in the telephone industry with the conversion from operators to direct dialing. Telephone companies anticipated the reduced need for operators, but by using manpower planning they were able to avoid laying off operators. In some cases, they transferred workers. In others, they encouraged early retirement. Some employees left or retired in the normal course of events.

An example of upgrading of hospital employees is provided in a union program in New York City. In 1967, registered and practical nurses were extremely in short supply there, and the union trained nurses aides to become licensed practical nurses with training allowances paid by the federal government. Although many of the aids were disadvantaged minority workers with limited education, 91 percent of those who originally enrolled in the program passed the final licensing examination.

Another program in New York between the national union of hospital and nursing home employees and 17 private institutions has a jointly administered fund of about one million dollars for training and upgrading unionized workers. The fund is based on one percent of gross payroll and has no governmental contributions. Over twenty thousand workers are involved, and the benefits should come both to the workers who receive training and upgrade their status and to the hospitals who should experience greater efficiency due to these more highly trained paramedical personnel.

Almost any good management or personnel approach can help productivity. The remaining part of this chapter addresses some of the specific approaches available to you.

The Worker: Factors in Productivity

How much a person produces on the job is determined by a number of interrelated factors. These factors include, but are not restricted to, a worker's proficiency in doing the job, the psychological factors affecting him, the environmental and physiological characteristics surrounding his work, time factor pressures, and the facilities and equipment he needs to perform the job.

Job proficiency depends in large part on proper training, having the appropriate mental and physical dexterity for the job, and the degree of experience in the job.

Psychological factors include motivation, morale, relationship with other workers, and the nature of supervision. Boredom is also a psychological factor. No job, however, is intrinsically boring; what some consider boring can be challenging to others.

Physiology refers, of course, to the function of organs, tissues, cells, nerves, and bones—in fact, to the study of the whole human anatomy. A person's health, the climate he works in, and such other environmental conditions as light, odors, noise, sanitation, and cleanliness, all affect his productivity. In short, how comfortable a person is physiologically influences the amount that he can produce.

Time factors include scheduling, shifts, hours of work and rest periods. These can have a direct effect on production.

These factors are all concerned primarily with the individual. But no matter how highly motivated, carefully trained, and comfortable a person is at his job, his production will suffer unless he has the proper equipment and work arrangement to do the job efficiently, and this section explores the effects of the work place and the work method on productivity. The concept of human engineering (the adaptation of the work environment and facilities to the psychological and physical needs of the worker) as it affects productivity also receives attention in this section, since its stated goals entail improving the worker's welfare and comfort and making it easier for him both to do a better job and to improve his efficiency.

Environmental Factors

It is almost a truism that individuals can do their best work when they are comfortable. Yet the foodservice industry has generally thought of comfort largely in terms of patrons while devoting comparatively little thought to the comfort of its employees. When labor was cheap and plentiful, this management oversight held no adverse economic implications. Today, however, the shortage of skilled employees and the need to retain those available, along with the necessity of increasing productivity, have made employers conscious of human engineering. The science of human engineering has drawn its tenets from such diverse fields as psychology, anthropology, physiology, and biology. The concern with our astronauts' comfort in space has also stimulated human engineering. An only half-facetious analogy is sometimes drawn between contented cows who give more milk, pampered hens who lay more eggs, and comfortable workers who produce more products.

Environmental factors considered by human engineers include temperature, ventilation, humidity, lighting, noise, odors, contact surfaces, aesthetics, and colors.

Temperature. Many commercial kitchens become far too hot. Not only do workers produce less while they work under hot conditions, but they tend to require more rest periods more frequently as well. Tempers are more likely to flare in an excessively hot work area. According to some estimates it costs nearly three times as much to cool air as to heat it, but the resultant savings and increased production can more than make up for the cost of providing for the workers' comfort. Many commercial kitchens have long since installed air conditioning, more do it every day, and many more will in the future; in almost all cases it results in increased productivity.

If air conditioning or simple ventilation is not practical, much can be done to reduce the amount of heat which flows into the kitchen instead of into the food. Ventilating hoods can remove the particularly objectionable latent heat given off by cooking appliances. Steam and hot water lines can be insulated to prevent them from heating the kitchen. Covers should be used on pots and pans to keep heat where it is needed. Bains-marie should be covered. Faster heating units can be installed that allow appliances to be turned down or off during inactive periods; the appliances themselves can be insulated. (The practice of leaving cooking equipment running all day was necessitated by the old slow-recovery units.) A ventilating system can be used to remove heat. Generally, one fan should be used to bring cool air into the kitchen and another fan used to exhaust the hot kitchen air. Some operations exhaust their cooler and relatively clean dining room air into the kitchen. The ideal temperature range is 65°F. to 70°F. in the winter and 69°F. to 73°F. in the summer. A problem sometimes arises in air-conditioned dining rooms when active serving personnel set the temperature for their own comfort. This setting is frequently too low for the patrons.

Humidity. Humidity refers, of course, to the amount of moisture in the air; relative humidity is the percentage of moisture in the air compared to the amount of moisture the air could hold at a given temperature before being saturated. Excessive humidity, caused at least in part by evaporating liquids, is very common in commercial kitchens. Humidity control can utilize the same methods used to curtail excess heat: venting equipment, the elimination of open kettle cooking, and proper ventilation. The relative humidity should range between 30 and 50 percent.

Ventilation. Ventilation is the movement of air and is necessary in kitchens to remove excessive heat and humidity, unpleasant odors, stagnant air, smoke, and steam. It is best to exhaust the entire air volume of a commercial kitchen every two or three minutes—that is, 20 to 30 air changes per hour. As mentioned, ventilation can be accomplished by having both an intake and an exhaust fan installed. Excessive ventilation may cause such cooking difficulties as heat loss between an appliance and a pot or pan, too rapid cooling of prepared foods, and discomfort to individuals.

Air purification. Associated with ventilation is the practice of air filtration. The filtering process can remove such impurities as dust, dirt, odor, and smoke. It is especially useful in kitchens where the air may be grease laden as well. Filters come usually in one or two types: mechanical and electronic. An interception or mechanical air filter collects the impurities on a filtration medium such as paper, glass, fiberglass, and charcoal. They may be "throwaway" filters which eliminate cleaning. Electronic air cleaners (electrostatic precipitators) ionize dust particles with an electric charge and then attract them to an oppositely charged collection plate. Electronic air cleaners are considerably more expensive than mechanical air filters, but the new self-cleaning types can be very efficient and can, in fact, remove particles as small as $\frac{1}{25,000}$ of an inch.

Chemically treated mops, dust cloths and sweeping compounds control dust effectively. Air purification, generally, helps a restaurant save on cleaning, fabric and carpet wear, redecoration, and mopping. Of course it also promotes employee and patron comfort.

Temperature control, humidity control, air movement and air purification are all included in an air conditioning system. An air conditioning expert can often provide a great deal of help in controlling these factors.

Odors. Odor control usually consists of two separate practices. The first consists of preventing odors through proper cleaning, sanitation, and storage procedure. The second consists of removing the cooking odors through appropriate ventilation and air-filtering procedures. Garbage, a prime source of odor, can be controlled by refrigerated garbage storage, frequent removal, tight-fitting lids on containers, and heavy-duty plastic bags.

Lighting. Food production workers too often find themselves working in inadequately lighted kitchens. Not only does a food worker need adequate lighting to do his work properly, but he could also suffer serious visual impairment as a result of working too long in a poorly lighted kitchen. Straining the eyes constantly causes fatigue and poorer quality of work. In fact, health authorities assert that physical fatigue can be caused more quickly by eye strain than by muscular or physical strain. Accidents can increase if the work area is not properly illuminated. Proper lighting includes a number of considerations.

1. *Brightness.* Can the worker see adequately while performing his job? Following standards for kitchens such as 30 foot-candles throughout the kitchen, 70 foot-candles at critical areas, and 15 foot-candles in safety areas is suggested.

2. *Distribution.* Lighting fixtures and lighting intensities should be arranged to eliminate shadows, excessive brightness, and variations of brightness. Both brightness and distribution are helped by light-colored ceilings.

3. *Glare.* The shiny surfaces of much kitchen equipment often contribute to or create glare. The use of light diffusers or indirect lighting can help.

4. *Maintenance.* Lighting fixtures in a kitchen require careful and frequent maintenance. Ease of cleaning should be considered in selecting fixtures. Some operations prefer to change all bulbs at one time feeling that any life remaining in the bulbs is not worth the continual trouble of replacing them individually.

Noise. Excessive noise may interfere with the quality and quantity of work. Certainly, it is pleasanter to work in quiet surroundings without jarring or shrilling noises. Noise control includes two procedures. The first is eliminating as much of the source of the noise as possible. The second is reducing the intensity of the noise by using acoustical materials designed to absorb noise much as a sponge absorbs water. The source of noise can be reduced by such means as:

- placing rubber tires on carts or movable equipment
- coating dishwasher racks with plastic or rubber
- eliminating as much metal to metal contact as possible
- deflecting sounds by screens and walls

Sounds may be muffled or absorbed by acoustical ceiling treatments, dropped ceiling portions, for example. These ceilings can be very effective. Sound-absorbing materials on the floors also help. Sound-absorbing material can be used around noisy equipment and work tables.

Sometimes, a masking sound like music is added to an operation. Some claim that music increases the quantity of work; however, it appears more effective in increasing the output of young inexperienced workers doing repetitive tasks than in increasing the output of experienced workers doing complex tasks. Factory workers generally prefer music, although as many as ten percent of them may be annoyed by it. While its use as a production incentive may be debatable, background music is generally pleasant for workers and will hide the ordinary sounds of production.

Contact surfaces. Carpeting provides the feel of luxury, noise control, and comfort in a restaurant's dining room, but in the kitchen, the durability, ease of cleaning, and cost of the flooring is usually considered first. Concrete or quarry tile is durable and easy to clean but can be very hard on an employee's feet. In the past, wooden duckboards were used in front of the ranges. Today, a great many floor coverings have been developed which are durable and sanitary, yet provide resiliency and walking comfort. Carpeting that is easy to clean, is easy to walk on, and absorbs sound has been developed especially for kitchen areas. With these new products, much can be done to eliminate hard, reverberating floors. Similarly, many older kitchens retain their rough plaster walls. They are, of course, impractical; they not only collect dirt on their ridges but can also scratch an employee who comes in contact with them. Like hard floors, they reverberate with harsh noises.

Colors and aesthetics. Light and color are the primary visual aspects of man's environment. Traditionally, work areas in a foodservice establishment have been either very drab or sterile white: monotonous colors that workers unconsciously or consciously resent. Slowly management is realizing that colors can promote productivity. Some colors, notably green, make the premises appear cooler and produce a calmer atmosphere. Yellows and reds can be used to denote danger areas. Flat paints rather than enamels should be used in work areas to cut down on glare; contrasts between light and dark colors should not be extreme.

Sanitation and cleanliness. Washrooms and locker rooms too often appear unclean and unsanitary. A well-lighted, clean, orderly lockerroom attracts the conscientious employee. Kitchen uniforms must be kept clean and changed as often as necessary. In fact, management should supply clean uniforms on demand rather than limiting the supply or burdening its employees with the responsibility of cleaning their own uniforms. These factors are very important to the productivity of the employee and the production of good food. Efficient employees are usually neat and orderly in their work habits, and cleanliness encourages better work. Good employees resent a dirty and unsanitary kitchen atmosphere as well as unkempt locker rooms.

The less desirable employee is careless about dress and personal cleanliness. This attitude not only reflects in his work but can easily discourage the better workers as well. Experience in the food industry has shown that all too often management fails to emphasize cleanliness sufficiently during the training period.

Work Simplification and Motion Economy

How would you like to increase the production of your staff and, in addition, find them refreshed at the end of their work day because their jobs required less physical effort? Work simplification may help you approach this ideal condition. Almost any job or operation can be simplified after careful, objective study, and this applies not only to your job but to the dishwasher's as well. Adherence to work simplification helps management achieve the highest output for the energy and time input. By teaching people to work "smarter" instead of harder management can increase productivity with less physical effort required of its personnel.

The process of work simplification in heavy industry can be paradoxically very complex, involving among other sophisticated techniques, time studies, micromotion films, flow process charts, man and machine charts, and left-hand/right-hand charts. These sophisticated studies are extremely useful in analyzing repetitive jobs found in mass production factories. Though their use is somewhat limited in the foodservice field, the phases of work simplification that can be utilized by the average food operator include motion economy, methods improvement, and layout and design. This section is concerned more with the steps the average foodservice manager can take to improve his operation and facilitate the individual jobs. There may never be a single best way to perform a task, but there is always a *better* way.

Work Simplification   Work simplification is the general term applied to any systematic attempt to find the most economical, or a more economical, way of performing a task. Work simplification provides an organized, step-by-step application of old-fashioned common sense to the problem of finding more efficient ways of doing things. Work simplification does not stress working harder or faster, its emphasis is on eliminating unnecessary steps that neither add value to the product nor facilitate its production. Work simplification may involve changes in equipment, in the kitchen layout, and in work procedures, each or all of these changes could make it possible to do better, and usually more, work with a minimum of effort. Work effort wastefully expended by kitchen employees can be directed into effective channels. Because there is a tremendous amount of wasted effort in the average food preparation center (due primarily to the notoriously erratic peak and low periods) great possibilities exist there for the application of work simplification. Extensive programs of work simplification have reduced workloads as much as 50 percent.

Increased production with less human effort has been an industry-wide objective for years. Making the job easier is an effective aid to good management which has been accorded wide recognition and attention by both managers and workers in foodservice institutions. Getting the job done the easiest way is sure to appeal to workers, especially when they realize that some studies of foodservice worker performance show that workers are productive only 50 percent of their time on the job.

Employee (and union, if one exists) interest, understanding, and cooperation are essential to the successful operation of a work simplification program. Careful analysis and planning preliminary to starting any task is necessary if the task is to be accomplished efficiently and in the simplest manner possible. The elimination of wasted effort is easy once the worker becomes "motion conscious," learns to apply the simple principles which are appropriate for him, and sees objectively the benefits of the changed procedures. Such benefits may be evidenced by lessened fatigue of workers, safer and better working conditions, better and more uniform quality production, and, possibly, higher wages through increased production. Understanding of and agreement with the objectives, together with the realization that benefits will be shared mutually by workers and management, are factors helping to ensure success. The solicitation and incorporation of suggestions for job-improvement methods among the workers, and the implementation of these suggestions, can lead to interest and participation among employees. Any employee and union resistance to change in established work routines can often be overcome by the proper management attitude before and after the initiation of a work simplification program. People naturally resist changes that seem to threaten their complacency, habits, feelings of familiarity, and confidence. Management must explain why changes are being planned and make employees feel that it needs their ideas by asking for suggestions. Get everyone involved and participating, and change will be easier.

Implementing Work Simplification

Successful work simplification can result only if the complete job processs is examined in detail—only if each step is carefully analyzed by itself. To analyze a complete process, write down in careful detail the entire routine with which the process is carried out. When this is done, it is possible to see what part of the work is contributing to actual production and what part is waste. When the job is "rebuilt," the wasteful parts can be eliminated and only the productive parts retained.

One procedure for streamlining jobs was developed originally by the armed services. It is sometimes known as the *scientific method,* or the *creative thinking approach;* it has seven basic steps:

1. Select the area or job to be improved.
2. Break down the present method of doing the job in detail.
3. Question every detail about the job or present procedure.
4. Develop and record alternative methods.

5. Choose the best method.

6. Refine the chosen method.

7. Sell the new procedure and see that it is employed correctly.

Select the area or job to be improved. It is best to take one area or job at a time, rather than try to improve many jobs simultaneously. Select the job that has high costs, the job where present methods are obviously not efficient, or the job that involves too much labor and time. (Likely places for improvement are the dishwashing area, the serving line, the range area, and the waiters' stations.)

Break down the present method of doing the job to be improved in detail. Study the job. The time required to do the various functions of the job, along with the equipment used, the distances moved, the procedures used and the qualifications of the employees should all be recorded.

Question every detail about the job's present procedure. Kipling wrote:

> *I had six honest servingmen*
> *(They taught me all I knew);*
> *Their names are What and Why and When*
> *And How and Where and Who.*

What is being done? Does it acutally contribute to efficiency and productivity? Is it necessary, for example, to scrape, stack, prerinse, restack, and load dishes? *Where* is the job being done? Is it necessary to move all slicing food to the slicer, or might the slicer be more easily brought to the items? *When* is the best time to do the job? Do all the dishes have to be washed within two hours after serving? Could the dishwashing be done all afternoon at a more even and efficient production rate? *Why* is it being done? Examination may reveal that some job scheduling, for example, is being done strictly on the basis of habit. *How* is the job being done, and how could it be made easier and more efficient? Perhaps a new piece of equipment, or some modification of old equipment, could accomplish this task. (In one operation, cutting a hole in the dish table reduced scraping time by one-third.) *Who* is doing the job? Is the trained chef dicing vegetables? Would it be better for the waitress to spend all her time in the dining room servicing customers while bus boys or conveyors bring the food to her and intercoms transmit the orders to the kitchen? If a porter or chore boy can do the work, the manager or chef should not be doing it; this is the *subsidiary function* principle.

Develop and record alternative methods. If we get one bright idea, most of us are prone to spend all of our energies on that one idea without thinking of other possibilities. But there are usually a number of different ways to accomplish a goal. Think of other ways, rather than adhering to the first that comes to mind. Many of the alternatives may seem unorthodox, but often enough, unorthodox thinking produces better solutions. A consideration of alternative procedures may also refine the first one. Write down the alternative methods so they can be evaluated and studied. New ideas often come as you record the details. In developing alternatives, a manager should ask such questions as:

Have unnecessary details been eliminated?

Can any steps be combined?

Are there any unnecessary delays?

Is the right person doing the job?

Do the details of the job flow in the best sequence?

Is the work spread evenly among my staff and my equipment?

Choose the best method. The problem has been surveyed from every angle. Various solutions have been developed. Now it is necessary to choose the best solution or procedure.

Refine the chosen method. While there may be no best way of doing anything, there is always a better way. After you have chosen the general procedure you want to use, try to improve the details. Further study may show ways of saving even more time, space, or energy.

Sell the new procedure and see that it is employed correctly. One of the hardest parts of changing a procedure may be selling people on the idea of using the new procedure; and if it is not utilized, all the effort used to develop the new procedure is wasted. People are opposed to change. (You may have to sell the boss first on the new procedure, obtain his approval, and then enforce its use.) The worker who has been designated to utilize the procedure often feels that change means a speed-up and more work for him to do, even when the new procedure may actually be far easier for him. He may even consider the new procedure a threat to his job. It is important to gain his cooperation before the new procedure is introduced: ask if he has any further ideas or suggestions to improve the new procedure; and ask what potential faults he sees or why it may not work. Even though you may meet resistance, stress that the procedure has been designed to make his job easier and pleasanter.

Perhaps because the process of work simplification relies on a manager's common sense, many feel that they use the procedure automatically. But it requires a definite procedure which, if followed, can produce precision and efficiency. Too many managers get a bright idea and then rush helter-skelter to implement it without taking time to think out and write out their proposed procedure. Thus the bright idea often fizzles out. So, follow the listed procedures for maximum effectiveness. Many operations give work simplification instruction both to supervisors and to all regular employees to motivate them to improve their jobs and productivity. Especially in these cases, but probably in all cases, some reward or recognition should be given for the savings gained.

One of the greatest enemies of efficiency is habit. Humans are, of course, largely creatures of habit, and to a degree we all resist change. Management must continue to infuse new ideas and to stimulate its employees to improve their individual jobs, despite this natural reliance upon habit.

Motion Economy Efficient work and a minimum of fatigue may be abetted by the principles of motion economy. Here are some motion economy principles that relate to work simplification.

1. *Hands should begin and complete motions at the same time.* It has been shown that work goes easier and quicker if both hands are in operation at the same time. A worker dishing out soup should reach for the bowl with one hand and at the same time put the ladle into the soup with the other

2. *Hands should move in opposite and symmetrical directions.* It is much easier and more natural for hands to be working in opposite directions than in the same direction.

3. *Use curved, rather than straight-line movements.* In wiping a tabletop, for example, curved motions are more natural and faster than straight back-and-forth ones.

4. *Movements should be made by the smallest possible body member.* It is faster and easier to push a button with a finger than move a dial with a hand or push a lever with an arm. If possible, install equipment that can be manipulated by the touch of a finger rather than by the exertion of the whole hand, arm, or body.

5. *Relieve the hands of work that can be done by the feet, if the hands can be profitably employed elsewhere.* If a coffee urn has a pedal control, the server can use his hands exclusively for the cups and saucers. He need not set them down to turn the spigot on and off.

6. *Have the working area supplies within easy reach of the operator.* Do not make a worker stretch or move awkardly out of his normal position to reach something. Storing dishes within easy reach of the server is, for example, essential for peak volume service.

7. *Use gravity whenever possible.* Let gravity rather than the worker move material. A receptacle below the cutting block makes for easier disposal than lifting the cuttings into a container. A dish scraping operation should allow the garbage to fall by gravity into the can.

8. *Provide definite stations for tools and supplies.* A specific storage spot should be designated to eliminate confusion and

searches. Inventories can also be made more easily if utensils are not scattered haphazardly about. It is often helpful to duplicate some items and keep them at different stations of the kitchen to eliminate trips to and fro between a single station.

9. *Dual purpose tools should be used whenever possible.* A spatula with a cutting edge can often expedite the job faster than a spatula and a knife used together.

10. *Preposition items.* Utensils extending toward the worker at an angle of about 30 degrees are easier to grasp than utensils strewn carelessly about the kitchen. Racks for silverware and kitchen knives illustrate this principle.

Planning the Work Area

The goals in planning a work area should be to limit labor time and provide fast service. They should also aim at securing the highest rate of productivity while making the worker comfortable and eliminating as much physical and psychological fatigue as possible. (And to review, such physical environment factors as temperature and humidity control, noise reduction, ventilation, sanitation, cleanliness, and aesthetics should also be considered.)

One important factor in planning a kitchen is the centralization of all production areas so that the distance to the dining room is held to a minimum. Long distances increase the waitress and bus boy payroll and delay service.

The production methods of a kitchen usually differ vastly from those of a manufacturer. Production and sales occur within hours, or minutes, of each other, and small quantities of many items must be prepared. Food preparation does not readily lend itself to production-line methods. Therefore, the usual work standards of industry cannot always be applied to commercial kitchen work.

Wherever possible, work should be done in a sitting position, rather than standing. Adjustable stools are best and are frequently used in the salad and vegetable preparation departments.

The height of the work surface is important. Although work tables are standardized at around 36 inches, individual workers perform best at individual heights. Platforms, cutting blocks, and stools can all be used to bring within easy reach the work surface of the worker.

Gauges, timers, and thermostats should be placed at eye level whenever possible. (One chain of foodservice operations strictly specifies an eye-level recipe holder on its pieces of cooking equipment.)

Cooking equipment should be planned to eliminate improper handling and added work. In many kitchens, the cooking equipment is installed in a long line which requires many steps, wastes time, and adds to expenses. It has been found that a rectangular arrangement with a center aisle has a great labor-saving potential. Correct aisle widths are vital to controlling payroll. Too wide an aisle means excessive walking and increased payroll. Too narrow an aisle means confusion, interference and, again, increased payroll.

Equipment planners should also consider ease of cleaning and kitchen sanitation. Equipment can be built flush with the floor or wall, hung from the wall with no base, or installed on wheels. All these installations methods facilitate steam hosing of floors and germicidal washes, preferable to inefficient mopping.

A primary principle of production is the proper placement of tools, equipment, supplies, and materials in the production areas. Mixing bowls should be near the mixer. Overhead racks near the ranges should keep all cooking utensils plainly in sight. Drawers at appropriate stations containing the needed knives, ladles, and spoons, will reduce the frustration of hunting for a proper tool at a critical time. Ranges for cook-to-order items should have proper storage refrigeration close by. If dishing is done at the range, the dishes should be stored at the range, preferably in warmers. More and more kitchens are being planned around the menu especially with the increased use of convenience foods. Thus more equipment and kitchen layouts are being fitted to fast preparation and service. The traditional kitchen equipment is being replaced by microwave ovens, special pressure steamers, one-purpose fryers, and circulating heat ovens. Kitchens without partitions appear to be more efficient and allow for better lighting, more air circulation, easier transfer of materials, and unobstructed observation by supervisors.

As we have already suggested, ingredient rooms have been found to be very helpful in increasing productivity. Instead of just issuing quantities of food to the kitchen, the ingredient room issues the exact quantity needed for the recipe ready for cooking. Fewer cooks are needed, and they can concentrate exclusively on cooking since the pre-preparation tasks have already been accomplished.

The principles of work simplification and motion economy must be considered in all phases of the food preparation. Study a work area and find a better arrangement; payroll savings will likely follow.

Mechanization and Automation

Mechanization is the substitution of mechanical devices for manual labor. Automation is the use of electronic control systems to operate the producing machines, thereby making production, or work, as completely automatic as possible. Mechanization has allowed industrial operations to achieve better employee efficiency and higher output at lower costs. Automation will allow an employee to undertake workloads that have previously been impossible and to expand production beyond all previous limits.

Although mechanization is routine in most industrial operations, the foodservice field has, for the most part, continued to use manual production methods. And with some exceptions, the food field is still innocent of automation. Because of the nature of foodservice, with its short production periods and its wide variety of items (as opposed to industry's long production runs of comparatively few items), it will probably never utilize the high level of mechanization and automation found in most industries. But the average foodservice operation can do much in relatively simple ways to mechanize. In the future, large automated feeding operations may reduce much of the labor cost and labor and quality control problems in food processing. We already have automated plants producing such foods as baked goods, ice cream, and prepared frozen entrees.

To improve mechanization in existing foodservice operations, managers can concentrate profitably on the movement of goods, their equipment, and materials handling. They can put wheels on equipment so it can be pushed to the point of use, rather than having to bring materials to it. For example, a large toaster placed on a portable table at the range during breakfast can be moved to the sandwich station for lunch and stored there. Shelving and storage racks themselves should be on wheels.

Many operations now have their produce delivered to the receiving entrance. Here it is reloaded on a cart, delivered, and unloaded in the walk-in refrigerator. When it is needed, it may be wheeled or carried to where its preparation (its unpacking, cleaning, leafing, or husking) is performed. It is then transported to the preparation area. To save handling labor, the produce could be cleaned and unpacked in the receiving area, placed in containers of a size suitable for easy handling and issue, and finally put on a shelf cart which is wheeled to the walk-in. When the food is ready to be used, the whole cart, or the required number of containers, could be wheeled to the place of preparation. Less total work is required, the merchandise handling is cut down, the garbage is disposed of immediately, and refrigeration space is saved. In the future, food purveyors will probably prepare more fresh produce and sell it ready to use, which will reduce labor and shipping costs. Frozen vegetables, for example, have reduced bulk handling and storage immensely.

Improvements can almost always be made in garbage handling. Ideally, it is best to have garbage disposal units wherever garbage may accumulate, so that most of the refuse problem can be solved by washing the garbage down the drain. If garbage disposals are not used, plastic liners or other water-tight containers may be used for the garbage cans. This makes the garbage collection easier, allows it to be kept longer on the premises, and eliminates much of the time-consuming, messy job of cleaning the garbage cans.

Another area for improvement in materials handling lies in the use of conveyor belts. It makes little sense to have serving personnel carry food items from the kitchen and carry the dirty dishes back when conveyor belts can do much of the work. Portable conveyor belts on roller sections which can be moved where they are needed are now available.

TelAutographs and other intercommunication systems can save the trek into the preparation area to present an order. A TelAutograph has two basic components. As information is written on the sending unit, it is reproduced on the receiving unit. The reproduced information appears on a paper tape that can be used as a check or check duplicate.

Although mechanical dishwashers have been steadily improved, the future should see dishes removed be conveyor belt to the dish area where they will be automatically scraped and flushed. Mechanical sorters may than load them into a machine that will clean them by sound waves. Once clean, they will automatically be returned to the storage or use area.

In the meantime, much can be done to make the traditional dishwashing operation more efficient. Areas for improvement can usually be found at the dirty dish table. Is it the right height for unloaders? Often it is easier for the worker returning the dirty dishes to sort them, rather than to dump his tray and have dishroom personnel do the sorting. Overhead glass racks installed at a 30-degree angle make unloading easier and, at the same time, keep the glass racks filled. Planned garbage drops and containers for linens and paper waste make the waste disposal easier. Some operations have racks in the serving area where the dirty dishes, china, and silver can be sorted and kept out of sight until the end of the serving period. This practice saves having to move the dirty items during the busiest time of the day. Proper water temperature and rinsing procedures, together with the use of a drying agent, should eliminate any need for drying. The clean dishes can be placed in lowerators (if they are available) and moved directly to the point of use.

Materials handling is also expedited by using one container for more than one purpose, which saves loading and unloading. For example, silverware may be washed in the container in which it is stored. This saves on handling and also provides better sanitation since the individual items are not touched after being loaded until they are removed by the customer from the dispenser. Food items are stored in containers in which they can be cooked or served. Disposable pans or liners can eliminate the washing procedure altogether. Cooking pans that fit in the steam table can eliminate rehandling. Preparing the items in the very dishes in which they are served promotes efficiency. Such items as individual casseroles or custard cups can be served directly to customers— and the item is usually hotter (or cooler) than it would be if it had to be dished. Moreover, portion control is increased this way.

Refrigeration can certainly be made more efficient. The use of shelving racks on wheels simplifies handling, moving, and cleaning. Refrigerators with front and back doors can both receive food from the kitchen and then present it, when it is needed, on the opposite or serving-line side. Placing smaller refrigeration units by individual production operations can likewise save many steps.

Much more use can be made of automatic timing and control devices. There is no reason why French fryers, for example, should not have timers, or heat sensors, designed to cause the baskets to rise out of the fat when the fries are cooked. This development eliminates the need for someone to watch the product, to guess when it is finished, and then to stop doing something else to lift the basket. (The egg boiler is a perfect example of time cooking in the kitchen.) Many operations have devised their own timing devices for their cooking equipment, coffee makers, mixers, and dishwashing equipment. All restauranteurs hope that manufacturers will install more of these controls on their equipment in the future.

Also in the future, we can certainly expect to see more mechanization and automation among the larger operations. Food preparation facilities will be designed as integrated mechanized systems with machines doing much of the work now done by people. This will benefit the larger operations that can afford the expensive equipment. Limited menus present fewer problems for equipment and commissaries will allow centralization of equipment. With more mechanization, there should be better quality in preparation deriving from more precise measurements of temperature, portions, and pre-prepared food quality. The human effort may be largely reduced to button pushing, servicing the machines, and solving unusual problems. And a cook may become more of a kitchen technician.

Data processing will effect new concepts in cost control by absorbing and evaluating data that could not be utilized in manually kept records. Computers will indicate what to purchase, when to purchase, and reasonable prices. They will automatically determine proper issues and specify production amounts. Requisitioning and maintaining perpetual inventories will also be computerized. With mechanization, automation, and computerization, the foodservice operator of the future will have many more tools at his command than he has yet dreamed of.

Productivity Motivation

Vital to the success of any organization are its employees and staff. This is especially true in foodservice where the patron is served face to face, automation is still limited, and much of the service is personal. But these vital employees present problems. Their turnover is often high, and their productivity can be low. Many seem to have a distinct lack of interest in their job and in taking responsibility. And their attitude toward their job can be incompatible with the need to provide patrons with food service.

How can these problems be dealt with? Increased wages may simply be throwing good money after bad if no incentive for improvement accompanies them. Moreover, the average operation has very limited resources; it can rarely increase its employee's benefits beyond inflation compensation unless these increases are offset by a corresponding increase in productivity.

All employers want loyal employees who will produce a satisfactory quality and quantity of work and will subordinate themselves to the operation. Employees, for their part, look for a satisfactory standard of living, job security, recognition of their efforts, and either a challenge or the motivation to improve their work and themselves.

What can satisfy the desires of both employees and employers? Certainly, the more an operation produces through the dedication of its employees, the more it can and should reward these employees. Therefore, more operations are turning to *productivity motivation,* sometimes called *savings sharing, profit sharing,* or *total incentive systems,* to implement this approach. What are the advantages of productivity motivation?

1. It automatically gears remuneration over and above regular benefits to the capacity of the company to pay if the workers have increased that capacity.

2. It motivates the employee to reduce costs and increase productivity, and it gets him to encourage other employees to do likewise.

3. It draws the employee closer to the operation for his own self-interest.

4. It can provide a fund for retirement or disability and provide the employee with both psychological and financial security. This can be especially helpful in smaller operations without a regular pension plan.

5. Since employees may build an equity interest in a productivity motivation fund that they lose if they leave, a decrease in voluntary turnover results.

6. Especially in a deferred-type plan, the actual cost to the owner of the operation is considerably less than the benefits received by the employees because of tax and interest considerations.

Productivity motivation can be used in both profit and nonprofit operations. A profit-making opertion like a restaurant usually bases its contributions on a percentage of pretax profit. Savings are often increased by giving instruction in work simplification, which helps employees work out better ways of doing their job. The operation provides benefits only in proportion to earnings. Employees know that if earnings increase, so will their benefits.

For a nonprofit organization like a hospital, an operating budget is prepared that includes only those items in which employees can provide savings. This procedure eliminates many fixed costs. The employees are told that any savings over the proposed budget will be shared. Since the budgeted amount is what the organization would normally expect to pay, the contributions distributed cost it nothing. The savings distributed to each employee would depend on his annual earnings, seniority, and any special efforts he may have made.

Generally, productivity motivation plans follow one of three formats:

1. *Cash.* Employees receive cash payments at definite intervals based on the savings accomplished. This system pleases those who want cash in hand, but it does not provide security or retirement benefits. Nor should it be a substitute for an adequate wage. It also requires the employee to pay current income tax on his share of the profit.

2. *Deferred.* The most popular plan is a trust fund whereby contributions are credited to an employee's account. Payments from the fund are deferred until retirement, disability, or death, but provisions can be made for loans. A vested interest provision can also be included whereby the employee receives a portion of his interest in this fund if he leaves the organization for other reasons. Without a vested interest provision, the contributions of a terminated employee are divided among the remaining employees.

3. *Combination.* This plan has features of both the cash and deferred plan. Current benefits can be given, as in the cash plan, and other contributions can be set aside for future distribution, as in the deferred plan. Because of its combined features, this plan usually requires a larger contribution.

Productivity Motivation is presently used by a number of hospitals, individual foodservices, and foodservice chains. Before installing a plan, you ought to obtain additional information from either a specialist or a more detailed reference work.

Hours of Work and Productivity

The foodservice industry is notorious for the long and demanding hours it requires of its employees. These long hours often erode both employee satisfaction and productivity. Legislation, union pressure, and competition with other industries will, no doubt, shorten the foodservice work week substantially in the near future; they have, in fact, already begun to do so.

Research has indicated that productivity decreases and absenteeism increases when hours increase to over eight per day or forty per week. Injuries also increase at a greater rate as working hours increase. And like physical proficiency, mental efficiency decreases after longer periods of continuous performance. Perhaps the ten-hour day, four-day week will eventually be used in the food industry with the fewer days worked providing an adequate time break to compensate for the longer working day. But it is, of course, hard to suggest optimum work periods since the severity of the work, motivation, incentives, and pacing by machine are such diverse variables affecting the length and pace of the work. Although they may result in overall increased production, excessive hours generally decrease production per hour—which is to say, they reduce productivity *potential*.

Rest periods are fairly standard, and even if they are not scheduled, employees will usually "take five" or "knock off for a smoke" when they can. Research in this area indicates that besides being enjoyable, rest periods can result in higher rates of production. The often maligned coffee break can actually serve a function in the production process since production may decrease if there is no rest during a sustained work period. The timing and length of rest breaks depends upon the individual situation and management preference. Should rest breaks be scheduled or taken at the convenience and discretion of the employee? Some authorities feel that the best results are obtained if frequent breaks occur at times decided by the employee himself, especially if the work is hard and working conditions are very hot, as in a kitchen. These breaks can be rather short, since a pause of only a few minutes can help eliminate fatigue. For maximum effect, the break should be taken before the build up of excessive fatigue when recovery may take longer.

Fatigue takes two forms: psychological (sometimes called subjective) fatigue; and physical (physiological) fatigue. The former results largely from boredom and is often caused by mismatching an employee with the job. If the job offers no challenge and is monotonous, or if the employee simply dislikes it, the chances are that he will become bored with it. The same job, however, may appeal to another worker if it corresponds to his level of achievement. Much can be done in the hiring process and through the use of job specifications and job descriptions to match the worker with the job. Stressing the importance of a job to the total operation may also make it more acceptable to the worker.

Physical fatigue is the result of physiological processes. The operation's surroundings and its working conditions are important. These include such physical environment factors as proper temperature, sufficient lighting, and noise and humidity control. The work area should be designed to eliminate as much physical effort as possible. Rest pauses should be allowed, and overly long hours eliminated. Employees should be taught the proper procedures for lifting and moving materials.

One technique that is sometimes used to help alleviate fatigue is to have workers trade jobs. This adds a certain novelty and lets employees share both the monotonous and the more pleasant work. But it may also present some problems in employee relations.

SUMMARY

Increased productivity is necessary to provide increased profits to the owners of a hospitality enterprise and increased benefits to the workers themselves. The lack of productivity is a problem not only for the hospitality industry but also for the United States as a whole.

The three basics of productivity are:

1. *The people doing the work*
2. *The equipment they use*
3. *Their work methods*

People are, of course, the most important of these. Manufacturing and agriculture increased productivity by substituting machinery for human labor. This is now being done to an increased extent in the hospitality industry with specialized equipment and automation. A factory-like approach is being used with convenience foods, ingredient rooms, and commissaries. Another approach is limiting services or utilizing self-service.

Productivity bargaining can have an important bearing on productivity itself. Increasingly workers want to know how the benefits of productivity are to be shared. If workers give up rights for greater productivity, how much should they be compensated? Some might question whether management should have allowed the rights to accrue in the first place, but human costs are involved when workers are manipulated or displaced. Ways must be found to alleviate these costs. There also have been encouraging examples of labor management cooperation in the hospitality industry that increased productivity and spread the rewards.

How much a worker produces may depend on the workplace environment and its physical facilities. Such environmental factors as temperature, humidity, ventilation, air purification, odor control, lighting, noise, contact surfaces, aesthetics, and sanitation should all be studied and improved. Not only can they increase productivity, but they can also provide a more satisifed work force.

Besides the physical environment of the workplace, productivity can be increased through work simplification. There is never a single best way to perform a task, but there is always a better way. Work simplification seeks to find this better way. Nevertheless, we are all creatures of habit, and the introduction of work simplification is often met with suspicion or downright resistance from those involved.

The creative thinking approach or scientific method may be used to streamline jobs. Its seven basic steps follow:

1. Select the area or job to be improved.
2. Break down the present method in every detail.
3. Question every detail of the job.
4. Develop and record alternative methods.
5. Choose the best method from alternatives.
6. Refine the chosen method.
7. Sell the new procedure and see it is employed correctly.

Principles of motion economy can also be used with the scientific method.

Productivity motivation is not primarily concerned with providing an employee with the means of increasing productivity, but to motivate him to want to work more productively. It is based on the "carrot approach" in which at least some of the gains of the increased productivity go to the worker in the form of immediate cash payments, deferred payments, or a combination. The deferred plan can also be helpful in cutting down turnover and providing retirement benefits.

Workers are not equally productive every hour of the day, and the number of hours they work can affect productivity. Extra-long periods result in low productivity per hour. Rest periods need not reduce productivity; they can actually increase it.

IMPORTANT TERMS

Having studied this chapter, you should be familiar with these terms:

ingredient room

productivity bargaining

scientific method

productivity motivation

total incentive system

deferred productivity motivation plan

REVIEW QUESTIONS

7-1. Discuss the concept of productivity bargaining.

7-2. You are about to install some labor-saving equipment. How would you present this news to your employees?

7-3. List the steps of the scientific method.

7-4. How can the use of hands be made more efficient through motion economy?

7-5. Why would you want to install a formal productivity motivation system?

7-6. How would a defined productivity motivation plan work in a non-profit hospital?

7-7. How can you cut down on fatigue in a kitchen job?

7-8. Why hasn't productivity increased more in the hospitality industry?

7-9. Select a particular job, preferably in the hospitality industry. Using the scientific method, motion economy, and work simplification techniques, develop a more productive way to perform the job.

8 Labor Relations and Safety Management

*H*uman resource management *is concerned with personnel. Personnel are vital to any endeavor but especially to a people service industry such as hospitality. Human resource management covers many different areas and it would be difficult to cover most of them in a book of this type. Since most of our readers will take specialized work in various aspects of human relations we will limit ourselves in this chapter to union-management relations and safety, areas of increasing importance to the hospitality industries. This chapter addresses the various issues, problems, and opportunities this trend has created. In addition, this chapter discusses the area of employee relations included under the rubric "occupational safety." When you finish studying this chapter, you should be able to*

- *recount briefly the history of American trade unionism*
- *list the principal pieces of labor legislation*
- *explain, step-by-step, the typical union organizing process*
- *list and briefly explain the principal clauses in the typical union contract*
- *explain briefly the attractions unions have for some employees*
- *explain briefly the advantages and disadvantages of unions*
- *explain briefly what a manager faced with union organization activity can and cannot do to affect the outcome of this activity*

You should also be able to

- *discuss the importance of a conscientious accident prevention program in a hospitality operation*
- *list the three major causes of accidents*
- *describe a formal safety program*
- *list and discuss the provisions of the Williams-Steiger Occupational Safety and Health Act of 1974*
- *calculate an accident incidence rate, using the procedure provided in this chapter*

Union-Management Relations

An increasingly important part of hospitality human resource management centers on union management relations. Some 13 percent of all foodservice employees are unionized, and the Hotel and Restaurant Employees and Bartenders International Union is the fourteenth largest union in the country. In short, the opportunities for labor-management disagreement seem to be increasing.

Any management-employee relationship presents certain areas of potential conflict. The mere fact that someone must manage and someone must be managed tends to create friction. Managers may abuse their otherwise legitimate authority, or an employee may not understand its use. Like almost every one else, hospitality employees want more, so conflicts arise over how to slice the pie. While some say the only constant in life is change, many people have trouble adjusting to change. They resist it, and they seek to maintain the status quo. Each of us is an individual with individual hopes, aspirations, feelings, and boiling points. We react differently to different situations and may readily be upset at something that would not bother someone else. A major reason for unionization are these inherent conflicts. A union can be an avenue that can erase or at least lessen these conflicts, though some might point out that unions also can aggravate the situation.

Unionization began as an organized rebellion against domination by management and unfair management practices. Unions were begun by employees who felt they needed a change in the work situation. Pure unionization appears originally to have been a defensive strategy on the part of workers to protect themselves from management abuse. Following this line of reasoning, one can say that management failure gave birth to unionism. Management could not understand or chose to ignore employee needs and wants. If early management had sought conscientiously to accommodate its employees, there would have been little need for unionization and the resulting labor-management strife. This idea has been expressed in the slogan: "management organizes, unions don't."

Although increasingly important, union-management relations in the hospitality field have not advanced nearly as far and are not nearly as sophisticated as they are in some manufacturing areas. Some believe that labor relations in the hospitality field are ten to twenty years behind those in general industry; others put the lag at a full fifty years.

History of Unionization

Labor-management difficulties have existed since the dawn of civilization, but unions are traced to the craft guilds that flourished in Europe at the end of the Middle Ages and during the Renaissance. In this country societies of working people appeared before the Revolution, but they were primarily for mutual assistance, local in scope, and often did not include all the members of a specific craft. In the 1790s, American craft unions (whose members all performed the same craft or job) were first organized. We have records of printers' strikes in 1786 and a union of shoe workers in Philadelphia in 1799. Although these unions were legal, their strikes and boycotts probably were not. Strikes and boycotts were traditionally seen as restraints of trade and, as such, were struck down by the equity courts.

The nineteenth century saw increased union activity. Property owning qualifications for voting had been eliminated and rank-and-file workers could express themselves via the ballot. The conspiracy and the restraint of trade cases that grew out of unionization attempts brought workers together. Moreover, the Industrial Revolution saw to it that large groups of workers came to work in large, focused masses. The change from an agrarian to an industrial economy brought many labor problems. For example, should an industrial worker be expected to work sun up to sun down as people did on farms but only during certain seasons? Also, such special measures as the banning of child labor, the enactment of free education, the abolition of sweatshops, the abolition of convict labor, the abolition of imprisonment for debt all helped legitimatize unionization as a means of social change.

During the nineteenth century union membership would increase until a financial panic or economic hard times caused members to fall out. This tendency is still referred to as the "ebb and flow of unionization." But there was open labor warfare: the Homestead Steel strike, the mine raids of the Molly Maguires, and the Pullman car strike are examples.

The modern labor movement traditionally dates with the Noble Order of Knights of Labor, which was organized in 1869 but kept secret until 1878. The secrecy protected its members from blacklisting. The Knights of Labor sought to replace a competitive society with one that would let workers share the wealth they created. The Knights hated the money power of the banks and the unscrupulous manipulations of some of the financiers of the day. They also advocated such radical notions as the eight-hour day, equal pay for women, public ownership of utilities, and the establishment of cooperatives. Their emphasis was more on education and political action than on strikes.

The Knights of Labor were superseded by the American Federation of Labor founded in 1881 (as the Federation of Organized Trades and Laborers). The AFL was pure and simple—unionization for higher wages and improved working conditions. The Federation's long-time president was a former cigar maker, Samuel Gompers, who when asked what his goals were, said "More, more, now."

The First World War brought a rapid expansion of unions. A National War Labor Board, formed with union-management cooperation, marked the first time that a federal agency set forth the rights of workers. Nevertheless considerable industrial strife followed World War I. The Depression, with its loss of jobs, exacerbated the situation. New legislation limited the use of conspiracy and restraint of trade rulings against unions. This and other legislation encouraged union organizing activity.

As unions established themselves, they accumulated political and economic influence. They also began to organize industrial workers (an industrial union aims for all the workers in the industry regardless of the type work they perform) as well as craft workers (a craft union aims for all the workers plying the same craft). The major labor organizations became Gompers' American Federation of Labor (AFL) and the Congress of Industrial Organizations (CIO). In the 1950s, they joined to become the combined AFL-CIO.

It is significant that American labor, in contrast to the labor movements of many other Western countries, chose unionization and collective bargaining as a means of achieving their goals rather than trying to organize their own political party. (There is really no influential labor party or workers' socialist party, as such, in this country.) It is also helpful to note that unionization can aim simply for worker benefits (Samuel Gompers made clear), or it can aim for improved social status and benefit.

Labor Legislation

The first really significant piece of labor legislation was the Norris-La Guardia Act passed in 1932. Among other things, this Act prohibited "yellow dog" contracts, which forced an employee to agree not to join a union as a condition of employment. It also exempted a union from liability for antitrust activity and forbade courts from issuing injunctions during some kinds of labor-management disputes.

In 1935 the famous National Labor Relations Act became law. This act (sometimes called the Wagner Act) guarantees the right of workers to organize and to bargain collectively with their employers, or to refrain from all such activity. It also seeks to prevent labor disputes that may impede interstate commerce, and it imposes certain limits on the activities of both employers and labor organizations.

To understand the act, one must understand the environment in which it was passed. In the early part of the 1930s, the country found itself in the midst of the Great Depression. Economic activity had slowed, and widespread unemployment existed. This unemployment (at that time there were fewer benefits available to the unemployed than at present) gravely threatened the American political and social system. Desperate people can do desperate things.

One tactic to help the country out of its difficulties would be to give its citizens greater purchasing power. With more money, they could purchase more goods which would create more jobs. But how, the legislators asked, can we create this greater purchasing power? Well, if workers had greater bargaining power with their employers, they could demand higher wages which would then give them more money to spend. The Wagner Act encouraged unionization for this purpose; so it was, in part, a piece of economic legislation. By giving workers more power the legislators also sought to provide an escape valve for the tensions that were building up in the population. The Wagner Act was, then, a piece of legislation designed purposely to assist the organization and unionization of workers.

The Wagner Act underlies all our current labor legislation. Section VIII of the act lists the unfair labor practices in which employers are forbidden by law to engage. Although, the law was passed in 1935, these "thou shalt nots" remain in effect today. There are five major unfair employer labor practices:

1. *Interference, restraint, or coercion.* An employer cannot interfere with, restrain, or coerce employees in the exercise of rights guaranteed under the act. Examples of illegal conduct include threatening employees with loss of jobs or benefits if they should join the union, threatening to close down a plant if a union should be organized in it, or questioning employees about their union activity or membership. Employers cannot spy on union gatherings or grant wage increases deliberately timed to defeat organization among employees.

2. *Interference with or contributions to the administration of a labor organization.* An employer violates the act if he dominates or interferes with the formation or administration of any labor organization or contributes financial or other support to it. This prohibition is designed to prevent employers from establishing captive or token labor organizations that could forestall activity by a bona fide labor organization. Thus an employer cannot take part in organizing a union, bring pressure upon employees to join the union, or play favorites among the unions competing to represent his employees.

3. *Discrimination in employment on account of union activity.* An employer cannot refuse to hire, refuse tenure, refuse unemployment benefits, or discharge an employee because of his involvement in union activity. This kind of discrimination is a common unfair labor practice. An employer must be careful, when he discharges an employee who has engaged in union activity, that there are substantial grounds for the discharge. A potential employee can also sue under the law if he believes that he did not get a job because the employer thought he might encourage union activity.

4. *Discrimination against an employee who participated against him in a NLRB proceeding.* An employer cannot discharge an employee who has testified against him in a National Labor Relations Board hearing. This participation can include filing

charges against the employer or giving testimony under the act. This provision guards the right of employees who seek protection of the law by using the process of NLRB.

5. *Refusal to bargain in good faith.* An employer cannot refuse to bargain in good faith concerning wages, hours, and other conditions of employment with a representative chosen by a majority of employees in a group appropriate for collective bargaining and certified by the NLRB. Examples of violations here include making a wage increase without consulting the representative of employees when they have legally chosen such a representative, issuing a wage increase larger than the one offered to the employees' representative in bargaining, refusing to put into writing an agreement with the employees' representative, and refusing to deal with the representative of the employees because the employees are out on a lawful strike. It is illegal to refuse to negotiate with the employees' agent concerning subjects over which the employer and employee representative must bargain in good faith.

The Wagner Act also prohibits practices that are considered unfair labor practices *by unions.* These include:

- restraining or coercing an employee's right to join or not to join a labor organization
- mass picketing in such numbers that nonstriking employees are physically barred from entering the employer's premises
- exercising force or violence on the picket line or in connection with strikes
- threatening bodily injury to nonstriking employees
- threatening employees with job loss unless they support the union activity

The Wagner Act has been amended through the years. For example, in 1947 the Taft-Hartley Act became part of the National Labor Relations Act. It banned the closed shop (where a worker has to be a member of a union before applying for a job); it provided some procedures for dealing with strikes that imperil the national welfare; and it provided for an independent federal conciliation service. Taft-Hartley also dealt with jurisdictional strikes (strikes caused by unions disagreeing over which has jurisdiction over the workers). The original Wagner Act was pro-labor; the Taft-Hartley Act represented an attempt to redress some faults and return some power to employers.

In 1959, the Labor-Management Reporting and Disclosure Act became law. This act was designed to eliminate certain improper activities by both labor and management. While it protects the rights of union members, it also provides for the filing of reports describing the organizational, financial, and business dealings of labor unions, their officers and employees, certain employers, labor relations consultants, and unions in trusteeships. It also safeguards union election procedures, and sets definite standards for the handling of union funds.

The Organization Process

Under the National Labor Relations Act it is an unfair practice for any employer to refuse to bargain in good faith with representatives of duly certified labor organizations. But how does a labor organization become certified as the bargaining agent? To begin with, employees of an establishment can ask a union to help organize them, or the union itself may try to organize the establishment if they see the opportunity. Regular "organizers" are sometimes assigned to an establishment precisely for this purpose.

The second step is to get employees to sign cards requesting that a union representation election be held. If 30 percent of the employees within a bargaining unit sign cards, the National Labor Relations Board can be petitioned to hold a representation election. At this point it becomes the board's duty to define the bargaining unit. A fast-food chain has a number of individual operations in a certain area: Is the appropriate bargaining unit each restaurant? Or is it all the units together? Who are regular employees of an establishment? Are temporary and part-time employees eligible to vote? If the National Labor Relations Board agrees that 30 percent of the appropriate employees desire an election, it will hold one under its auspices. Both management and labor will almost certainly try to convince the workers that it would be in their best interest to join or not to join. If, however, the election produces a vote of 50 percent of the workers plus one in favor of a union, the union can be certified by the NRLB. If several unions are involved and none of them gets a majority but if more than 50 percent of the workers want a union, a runoff election between the two highest vote-getting unions takes place. Once the union is certified as the bargaining agent, the employer, by law, must bargain with it in good faith.

Collective Bargaining Potential areas of conflict in labor-management relations always exist. Resolving them is the aim of the labor-management negotiations. Before the Industrial Revolution, employers used a system of individual wage determination wherein each worker bargained individually with his employer. That employer often worked alongside his workers, or he at least knew them, knew their needs, and (generally speaking) took adequate care of them.

As businesses grew, however, the workers became more remote from their employer and received less consideration. This tendency led to an era of sweatshops and labor exploitation. It led, as well, to a unilateral (a one-sided) wage determination with individual workers often unable to stand up to their employers during salary bargaining. To resolve this inequity, this country's labor force eventually spawned the system of *collective bargaining,* in at least the larger industries. The term collective bargaining, is broad and a little vague. But some definitions of it follow here:

> A method or process by which an agreement is sought or reached between an employer and a group of employees who have banded together
>
> A substitute for industrial conflict, or sometimes merely a truce with the loser eager to "get even"
>
> A process by which parties work in common to solve their problems

Besides *group* collective bargaining, other types of labor-management determinations appear. One is the unilateral management decision, as in the pre-collective-bargaining era. Management says "Take the job on our terms or not at all." Some economists feel that this approach leads to the *iron law of wages* where wages rise only slightly above the subsistence level. It is certainly frustrating, to say the least, for the workers. The Wagner Act, which encouraged collective bargaining, was in part designed to prevent management from imposing wages unilaterally.

But wages may be determined unilaterally by a strong union. In effect, the union says, "Our workers will work only on these terms, and we represent enough of them to insist on these terms." If the union controls the supply of manpower, it may dictate the wages earned. But, if they push too far, the overall demand for workers may decline and the union may be forced to make concessions. In a socialistic environment, there may be little choice regarding working conditions and wages since the government can determine both, and industry and labor must abide by its decisions. In socialistic countries, workers may seek to gain benefits by having them dispensed through law. The government can legislate minimum wages and working conditions and prescribe the benefits that employers must offer. In socialistic countries the government may also take over ownership of the enterprise so that, in effect, the workers in a hotel may actually be working for the government under working conditions determined by the government.

The Union Contract   If the majority of the workers elect a union as their bargaining representative, management is required by law to bargain in good faith with that union. This compulsion, however, does not mean that either party must agree to the other's proposal or make concessions. Negotiating a contract is a most important and serious business, and both parties will examine and argue thoroughly. The principal difference between a labor contract and other types of business contracts is that a business contract does not usually require management to give up something unless management gets something of equal or greater value in return. By contrast, a labor contract amounts to a statement of what has been granted by an employer to the labor union and consequently to the employee the union represents. This being so, the contract itself should be simple, brief, and as clear as possible in specifying what has been granted. If management does not concede, the union does not gain the benefits.

Few hospitality managers have extensive experience in negotiating a labor contract. Union leaders, on the other hand, negotiate contracts constantly. They can be quite skillful at it, and they become very familiar with the applicable laws. Unless he has special expertise, therefore, a hospitality operator should call on a labor-management consultant or a lawyer who specializes in labor affairs to help negotiate. The consulting expert should be called in before the actual election or, in some cases, even before there is a hint of an election.

Labor bargaining can become an art, and some people are definitely more experienced and adept at it than others. Contract negotiations, to be candid, sometimes fail to proceed in a sane and logical way. They may involve histrionics, threats, and bluffs. Physical stamina may be required as one side may seek to wear the other down with drawn-out meetings. While some general rules for contract negotiations exist, the negotiation procedures themselves may, as you can see, vary considerably. Here are some of these general rules:

1. Management should be well prepared for negotiations. It should know how other operations of its size and type proceed. It should know what its labor shortcomings have been and what its strong points are.

2. Management should never settle on a contract without determining what its overall cost will be. Can it afford to live with the negotiated contract?

3. Management should always reinforce its arguments with facts and data. These may be illustrated with charts and graphs.

4. A potential strike is a traumautic situation, but, buying short-term industrial peace with unfair terms can be expensive and may even compromise the organization's future in the long run.

The product of the negotiation is the contract. This contract must usually be ratified by the rank-and-file workers. At this point, the union leaders side with management trying to persuade the workers that the contract is the best that could be achieved from them under the circumstances and that it is fair.

Clauses of Union Contracts

A union contract can be a page and a half long or a book-length document. It may contain special clauses for special situations, but the usual contract contains these standard clauses:

Conditions of recognition. The conditions of recognition typically becomes the first clause of the contract. It specifies the name of the employer and the name of the union the employer recognizes as the bargaining representative for his employees. That union might be a local hospitality union, or the local affiliate of an international union, or the international union itself. The employer could be an individual or a group of employers. In some areas, the local hotel association negotiates a master agreement that covers all of their members. Several unions may negotiate with an employer group, and these groups are often known as a *trades council*. A union may try to include the words "heirs, successors, or assigns" in the introductory recognition clause, but small hospitality operators should be wary of these words. They make it difficult to sell the property since the owners commit the new owners to the union contract.

Coverage. This clause describes the job categories included in the contract. It is better to be specific here than to be general; for instance, the words "all employees of a housekeeping department" covers everyone, while "maids, housemen, and linen room seamstresses" is a specific phrase, and those who are not named are excluded. It may even be desirable to list specifically the excluded positions, such as supervisory personnel; confidential employees; and clerical, temporary, and part-time help among other possible categories.

Duration of the agreement. The *exact time* and *date* the contract goes into effect should be stated. The length or duration of the contract should also be included. A clause should be included that contains the number of days, prior to the expiration date, that notice must be given by one of the parties to the other that he wishes either to reopen or terminate the agreement. The method of sending notice should be specified in the contract (such as, "by registered mail"). Some contracts are automatically renewable from year to year if notice of the desire to reopen is not given and received as specified in the contract.

Management rights. This clause states the rights, responsibilities, and areas of action management retains free from union questioning and interference. A union contract usually means that management surrenders or waters down some of its existing rights. Such management rights as the right to hire, promote, lay off, or discharge employees should be spelled out specifically. Making these things clear in the contract can avoid later argument or litigation. A good management rights clause can prevent multitudinous filings of grievances since management's rights are spelled specifically rather than being merely assumed by management.

Union security. Union security clauses are crucial to the union. The strongest kind of security clause would specify a *closed shop,* in which no one could be hired unless or he or she already is a member in good standing of the union; and workers would have to remain in the union to keep their jobs. A closed shop, however, is outlawed by the Taft-Hartley Act.

A *union shop,* by contrast, allows nonunion employees to be hired, but they must join the union within a specified time, often 15 or 30 days. Within the contract, employers should try to spell out their rights in accepting or rejecting union members for open jobs. A union shop would usually mean that a maid, for example, would not have to be a member of the union to get a job but would have to join the union to keep it.

An *open shop* gives the right to hire anyone and does not require an employee either to join the union or to maintain his membership if he is already a member. This arrangement is, of course, anathema to the unions. Some states have right-to-work laws, which prohibit employers from entering into any agreement that requires a worker to join a union in order to hold or to get a job. A state with this law would allow an employer to insert an open shop clause in a union contract. Unions argue that under the right-to-work laws nonunion members could be viewed as parasites, effortlessly enjoying benefits fought for and won by union members. Others take the view that any worker should have a right to work without joining a union and that right-to-work laws protect this right.

An *agency shop* permits a labor union to compel workers to pay the equivalent of union dues, whether they are union members or not. This arrangement alleviates some of the free-loading stigma when nonunion members receive benefits achieved by unions.

A system known as the *check-off* adds to union security. It requires the employer to deduct union dues (and sometimes assessments or initiation fees) from the employees' wages and to turn the deductions over to the union. In this case, the employer bears the cost of bookkeeping, relieves the union from a task of collecting dues, and helps avoid the problem of delinquent dues. There may also be an advantage for the employer in that the check-off eliminates the need for a union business agent to remain on the premises pressuring union members for dues while they work. (A union that has trouble collecting its dues often tends to become more militant in its dealings with employers.)

Working conditions. Working conditions represent an area in collective bargaining that directly affects employees. A clause that covers working conditions typically includes such matters as hours of work, overtime payment, specified holidays, seniority provisions, employee meals, employee uniforms, and shift rotations. Uniforms tend to be a greater concern in the hospitality industry than in others. Who has to supply them? What uniform is required? Who maintains and cleans them? These issues should all be specified in this clause of the contract. The long and odd hours that hospitality employees must sometimes work present problems related to overtime. Wages themselves may be covered in a supplementary agreement or in an appendix, especially if the contract provides for an annual or semiannual review.

Grievances. The most important clause of all is the one that specifies how grievances must be handled. Exactly what a grievance is (and wages are not usually included) should be specified, along with exactly how a grievance should be filed. The handling itself should also be specified. A typical grievance procedure follows:

1. Discussions between the department head or supervisor and the aggrieved employee take place.
2. If these parties reach no agreement or settlement, the union official and department head or supervisor attempt to reach a satisfactory settlement.
3. If an agreement still cannot be made, the employee, the union official, the personnel manager, and a representative of top management discuss the problem.
4. If the problem still cannot be settled, the grievance goes to arbitration.

A manager should keep written records of all that was said and done during and as a result of the various grievance steps. A contract should also stipulate time limits as to how much time can elapse before a grievance is filed and how much time can elapse between each step. This precaution elminates drawn-out disputes. As you can see, carefully specified grievance procedures can be very helpful to management when it comes to settling small problems that threaten to erupt into bigger ones.

Arbitration Arbitration is the term used to describe the situation in which a neutral third party decides issues that labor and management cannot between themselves. Arbitration may be undertaken by a single arbitrator or a multimember panel. Or each side may place representatives on the arbitration panel, with the deciding vote belonging to a neutral party. The neutral arbitrator may be a representative of the American Arbitration Association, a local person like a clergyman, a professor, or judge, or lawyer who has the respect of both sides. An arbitrator cannot alter an existing contract; he can rule only on the interpretation of the contract. The expense of arbitration is usually borne equally by management and the union.

Outside parties can exercise additional roles in trying to solve labor-management difficulties. While in *arbitration*, they make the final decision, in conciliation, they try simply to bring the parties together so that they may work out their difficulties. In mediation they take a more active role, suggesting various courses of action.

We have discussed some of the basic labor-management clauses. These are not the only clauses; individual situations, and even the type of labor-management relationship involved, can dictate the inclusion of many more clauses.

Unions in the Hospitality Field

Many hospitality employers express surprise and take offense when they learn that their employees seek union representation. These employers may honestly feel that they have always treated their employees fairly. Moreover some of the smaller, owner-managed hospitality operations are characterized by almost paternalistic feelings toward the employees. A rapidly growing industry, hospitality has become an increasingly desirable target for unions. A number of unions are involved in the field, and at this writing they have become far more aggressive organizers than they were a mere decade ago. The first widely known hospitality union in this country was the "Bartenders and Waiters Union, in Chicago," formed in 1866. Its members were Germans who brought ideas of German unionism with them to this country. Following the Bartenders and Waiters, various societies of foodservice employees organized, usually for purposes of mutual benefit.

Many of these workers were recent immigrants who found their working conditions stacked against them. The infamous, widely practiced *vampire system* forced foodservice workers to turn a percentage of their tips over to the headwaiter or to management. They might be charged excessive amounts for any breakage. A fourteen-hour day was common, and there was no job security. In the latter part of the nineteenth century, the loose unions that resulted from these inequities began to affiliate with the American Federation of Labor (AFL). It was a time of much friction with employers. For example, in 1893 the United States Hotel Association and Saloon Keepers were condemned for blacklisting employees thought to have union tendencies. Out of this blacklisting developed the Hotel and Restaurant Employees and Bartenders International Union, now the fourteenth largest union in the country. Since 1973, the HREBIU has struck and severely curtailed hospitality operations in Las Vegas and Miami Beach. The union presently has about 500,000 members. Its locals are concentrated in the larger cities, in the North, and on the seacoasts. The international headquarters is in Cincinnati, and there is strong representation in Chicago.

Local 1199 (National Union of Hospital and Nursing Home Employees) originally organized to help professionals at work in pharmacies back in the 1930s. In the 1950s in response to demand, 1199 began organizing in hospitals; and in 1969, it became a national union. The union received a big impetus in 1974 when the National Labor Relations Board ruled that health facilities are not exempt from the National Labor Relations Act. At this writing the union has approximately 100,000 workers in 19 states, located mainly in the eastern part of the country. The union has aggressively organized health care employees in hospitals and nursing homes.

Apart from these two unions, no other major unions currently exist in the hospitality or foodservice fields. But in many areas, the local union can be remarkably strong. In some areas, moreover, unions for governmental workers include those involved in hospitality work. The building service employees also include some hospitality workers.

Why Employees Join a Union

One of the reasons an employee considers union representation is, of course, economic. He or she may believe that the wages will be higher, the fringe benefits will be better, and more consideration will be given to such areas as overtime and holiday pay if a union negotiates the contract. The hospitality industry is, after all, one of the lower paying industries for the rank-and-file workers, and union promises of economic benefits often find fertile ground in hospitality operations.

But there are also psychological reasons for workers to consider unions. One of these is job security. Without somebody to stand up to them, employers can unilaterally fire employees (assuming such laws as those regarding discrimination are not broken). Through his union, however, a worker can back up claims he might have against the hospitality organization and his supervisors, and he may even become a factor in planning the future policies of the employer. A union can provide a channel for releasing frustrations and provide an outlet for personal action. The union can also give an employee the recognition that may not be forthcoming from the employer. It also gives the workers a voice in their work and the conditions under which it is performed. A union can impact a sense of dignity. It can also be a social vehicle and a framework for ethnic groups to join together.

Benefits of Unionization to Management

Although the great majority of hospitality managers would prefer not to have a union enter their establishments, a number of at least theoretical advantages for unionization appear from the management viewpoint. The union can, for example, keep wages out of competition. If all of the similar hospitality establishments in the area are unionized, each will be paying the same union wages. One operation will not gain a competitive advantage by paying substandard wages.

A union can also provide those training programs that many small hospitality operators cannot afford. In certain areas of the country, for example, unions have established training programs for foodservice workers and have also set standards of proficiency for those workers.

A union can also act as a supplier of personnel. It is much easier to telephone the union hall when you need several waitresses than to place advertisements in the papers, wait for responses, and then interview. This is especially true when you need temporary part-time help. Moreover, such benefits as hospitalization, insurance, and legal care may be handled more efficiently through a union than by individual employers. In fact, not only may it be cheaper to dispense benefits this way, but the union may also have developed specialized expertise in the field.

Notice too that if all the hospitality establishments in an area are unionized, the union can exercise greater discipline over its membership. Consequently if someone is drummed out of the union for work-related problem making, he will not be able to get work in the area. Without the union, this person might go from operation to operation causing trouble. Conversely, because of their ability to secure higher wages, unions can force management to use its personnel more efficiently. (The grievance procedure is widely regarded as a progressive policy, but few of them would have been put into effect without union urging.) Workers may also gain psychological advantages from their union: they feel they are a part of something; they may even feel more professional. This pride, which a union can instill, has been known to carry over into better on-the-job performance.

Disadvantages of Unionization

Unionization does, however, pose some potential disadvantages. For example, a strong union may have the power to enforce unfair wage demands. It may also block the firing of incompetent workers. A union may impose a distinct inflexibility in assigning workers to different jobs, and some unions have encouraged featherbedding (wasteful job duplication). Also, perfectly satisfied workers may be forced to stay away from work if their union calls for a strike.

A union is a political organization, and its priorities tend to reveal this orientation. In establishing goals and settling conflicts, a union may operate to preserve the following priorities for itself: First it may attempt to keep union leaders in power; then it might seek what is best for the overall union; then it might seek what is best for the union member; and then it might seek what is best for the employer. To protect his own position or to protect his union, a union leader may take actions not necessarily in the best interests of the union members and certainly not in the best interest of the employer. A strike might have been called against hotels even when the union leader knows full well that the strike will not produce economic benefits for the workers and may even cause some of them to lose their jobs. That strike may, however, cement the union leader's position with the union and perhaps strengthen the union.

Management Do's and Don'ts During the Union Election Campaign

Management must be extremely cautious during union election campaigns because many unions have been able to appeal election results to the NRLB because of management interference during the campaign. And if the board agrees that interference has occurred, it can order a new election or change the results of an election favorable to management. Some activities that management *may* engage in during an election campaign follow. Management may:

1. Inform the employees what its negotiating position will be if unionization occurs

2. Inform the employees that signing union authorization cards does not automatically mean that they must vote for the union. The voting is secret and quite often people sign authorization cards but do not subsequently vote for the union

3. Stress the disadvantages of belonging to the union, which include the possibilities of strikes, cost of dues, and fines and assessments

4. Relate any prior experience it might have had with unions and their policies

5. Inform its employees of what it knows about the union officials that are trying to organize the operation

6. Compare wages and benefits between union or nonunion shops

7. Stress that a local union may be dominated by an international and that individual members would have relatively little influence in such a case

An employer may correct statements made by an organizer, may express his opinions of the union or union leaders (even if they are phrased derogatorily), and may reply to union attacks on company policies or practices. Employees may be advised of their legal rights, but an employer cannot encourage or help finance an employee's suit or proceedings against the union.

Employers can, in short, campaign against the union that is seeking to represent its employees. And management can insist that any solicitation of membership or discussion of union affairs be conducted outside of working time. But there are many things management cannot do. Some of these management "don'ts" follow. Management may not:

1. Promise special raises or other benefits if workers would vote against the union

2. Threaten to close an operation if employees choose union representation

3. Indicate that employees "are being watched" to determine whether or not they participate in the union campaign

4. Take an action that would adversely affect an employee's job because of his union activity

5. Ask employees about their thoughts regarding a union or its officers

6. Ask employees how they intend to vote in an election

7. Ask potential employees whether they have belonged to a union in the past or have signed a union authorization card

8. Threaten to discipline employees if they are active in behalf of the union

9. Try to get employees to urge other employees to oppose the union

10. Prevent employees from soliciting others for union membership during their free time and when it does not interfere with work or work performed by others. (This solicitation may be done on the company premises.)

11. Give financial support or assistance to a union or its representatives

12. Visit the homes of employees with the purpose of urging them to reject the union (Union officials, however, can visit the homes of potential members.)

13. Make a speech to groups of employees on company time twenty-four hours before the polls open for a representational election

14. Help employees try to withdraw from union membership

Decertification of Labor Unions

Winning a representation election does not entitle the union to remain the employee's bargaining agent as long as the operation remains in business. Decertification of a union has been possible since 1936 and has seen greatly increased use in recent years. For many years the National

Labor Relations Board conducted only a handful of decertification elections a year. In 1978, however, it conducted over 800.

An employer has to be very careful regarding the decertification process, as only the employees themselves can initiate decertification. An employer may not suggest to his employees that they file a decertification petition. The impetus for the petition must come from the employees themselves. However, the employer can legally inform employees that a decertification process is available and give information on the details. Giving information about decertification procedures is one thing, but getting directly involved is another. The NLRB would probably dismiss a petition that was the product of the employer's sponsorship. A decertification movement can occur only when the employees are unhappy with the union and no longer seek either to be represented by it or to support it.

Safety

History of Safety in the Hospitality Fields

Sad to say, hospitality operations have traditionally devoted little consideration to employee safety. Of course, before the Industrial Revolution there were far fewer job-related hazards than there are today. Much of labor, throughout much of history, was thought to be a commodity owners and managers exchanged for productivity. This attitude was especially true where slaves or serfs did most of the dangerous work. But this attitude prevailed as well where an aristocracy directed the work of poor, nominally free people.

Thus, the early industrial safety record in this country was not especially good. Such industries as mining and iron making were especially hazardous. Immigrant workers were often employed there; and if they were injured, maimed, or killed, other immigrants could readily be brought in. Thousands of Chinese and Irish died building our western railroads.

It took a long time for employers to become aware of the need for safety. But gradually they realized that besides its humane implications, safety also produced an economic saving. The employee safety movement started in Europe with some of the early socialistic programs. It started in this country early in the twentieth century with the activities of the National Safety Council. This council coincided with the growing bargaining power of workers, often expressed in the formation of labor unions, and such federal legislation as the abolition of sweatshops and limitations on child labor. For its part, management realized it was cheaper not to have accidents and began to stress caution with the new, sophisticated machinery that could cause accidents. One would like to think that general humaneness was the basic consideration.

An economic factor that increased safety consciousness was work-men's compensation legislation. These laws are based on the assumption that accidental injury is a cost of production to be borne by the employer, and to be reflected in his selling price. Before these laws, if a person were injured on the job, he had little recourse if the employer were not inclined to be generous. The infamous "Fellow Servant Doctrine" stated that if someone was injured because of the actions of another worker, the suit should lie against the other worker. In practice, then, an injured employee might have little chance to collect for his on-the-job damages since fellow employees might have few assets. Suits against the employer could be drawn out and expensive and generate relatively little gain.

Workmen's compensation laws rectified these problems. It is a type of insurance that guarantees a worker a specified amount for his injuries without having to sue his employer or fellow employees. Although nationally applied, workmen's compensation is operated by the individual state; compensation paid for various accidents varies from state to state. A reduction of accidents would normally reduce the amount of insurance costs an employer would have to pay.

The Need for Safety and Accident Prevention

During 1976, approximately 590,000 recorded injuries and illnesses, including 550 deaths, occurred in the services industries alone. Nearly 220,000 lost work days resulted in a loss of some 17,000 employee-years of work. Moreover, the accident frequency rate in foodservice establishments approximately trebled the national average for all industries. The cost of pain, suffering, and low morale, and the loss of customer good will from these accidents are hard to measure. Some dollar costs can, however, be determined. These are the direct costs like compensation payments and medical expenses, and indirect costs which include the time lost by injured employees, the time lost by fellow workers whose work is interrupted, the time lost by management in assisting the injured, the paperwork, the increase in worker's compensation costs, and the cost of equipment damage or lost materials occasioned by the accident. These indirect costs probably exceed four times the amount of the direct costs, though this ratio has been challenged. Some studies put the ratio as high as 20 to 1; others as low as 1 to 1.

The terminology of *direct* and *indirect* costs have changed recently to *insured* and *uninsured* costs, because this is a more definite description of the cost and it also encourages management to regard those costs with more interest.

However one defines the costs of an accident, the result is that they substantially affect profit. In fact, a $100 accident can wipe out the profit from $5500 worth of hotel service sales.

Causes of Accidents

A large hotel chain recently analyzed its accident rate. Its analysis revealed that 60 percent of its accidents were caused by unsafe employee practices. These practices included lifting heavy objects improperly, short cuts, unattentiveness, unnecessary haste, and poor housekeeping. Overexertion caused about 14 percent of the accidents. The most frequent accident was the simple fall, which caused about one-third of the reported disabilities. As might be expected, more accidents occurred among inexperienced personnel and during very busy times.

Another study has shown that a large percentage of accidents is caused by a small percentage of workers. But this tendency toward accident proneness can usually be traced to some other factors. Most susceptible to accidents is the daydreamer, the social misfit, the uninterested student, the emotionally unstable person, and the slow learner. With 60 percent of accidents caused by unsafe employee practices, it is obvious that employees need to be motivated toward safety, and this motivation should form a large part of any safety management program.

Thirty percent are caused by hazardous conditions. These hazardous conditions could include wet, greasy, uneven floors; depressions in sidewalks; poor lighting; and a lack of safeguards on the equipment.

The final ten percent of the hazards were due to conditions or hazards from outside of the operation over which little control could be exercised.

A Safety Program for Hospitality Operations

Every hospitality operation should institute a safety program designed to eliminate and control accidents and to deal with those accidents that occur. The basic provisions of a safety program follow:

Draw up a management policy statement.

Establish a safety committee.

Prepare for emergencies.

Provide safety education instruction.

Establish safety inspection procedures.

Develop safe working procedures.

Reinforce accident investigation and report procedures.

Comply with state and federal safety codes.

Audit your safety program.

The management policy statement. Executive management must participate by reviewing the program, checking that both the mangement's and the program's objectives are being met. The management should also issue a policy statement covering management's intentions and expectations for the safety program. All employees should be alerted to these expectations and encouraged to participate in the safety program once it is instituted.

The safety committee. The heart of a safety program is a safety committee, headed by the manager or the safety officer. Committee membership could include supervisors, a union representative, a personnel representative, and such technical people as the chief engineer or maintenance supervisor. A safety committee can help maintain positive employee and public relations. It should involve employee participation in the safety program and encourage a close contact between management and the workers as they pursue their common desire for safer working conditions.

The safety committee handles many additional aspects of a safety program: it advises management on safety issues and keeps it informed on the condition of the premises, the equipment, and the grounds. The safety committee should hold regular meetings and follow a definite procedure for handling suggestions from personnel in the organization. The minutes of the safety committee meetings should be written down.

Preparing for emergencies. Employees should be taught how to respond to fire, medical problems, and other emergencies. Employees should, for example, learn how to use fire exhinguishers, how to call the fire department, how to evacuate the premises, and what kinds of firefighting activities the staff should undertake. Some members of the staff should be able to administer CPR (cardio-pulmonary resuscitation) and the Heimlich Maneuver for choking victims.

Providing safety education. To cope with emergencies successfully, employees must undergo a certain amount of safety education. This education does not address emergencies alone; employees should be trained to spot potential accident-inviting conditions and to report them. They should also be trained how to handle equipment and supplies so as to avoid accidents. This training should proceed continuously even though the subject has already been covered. The procedures should be repeated both for the benefit of new employees and to reinforce prior instruction given to older employees. Some operations use a checksheet to see that the various employees have received the appropriate safety training.

Safety education requires cooperation, teamwork, and the interest and enthusiasm of all employees. Most people like to be parts of organizations or groups, and a group that is interested in safety spreads that interest among all the people who join. One of the motivating factors that can be used in safety education is the healthy desire to avoid personal injury. No one wants to be injured, and employees are usually glad to be told about potential hazards on the job. The economic loss occasioned by an injury even can be another incentive. Insurance can cover all medical cost, but it rarely covers all of the other expenses associated with injury. The desire to excel, the desire to be outstanding, can be harnessed to prevent accidents. Not only do people want to protect themselves but they also want to prevent injuries to their fellow employees and to be known as safe, skillful workers.

Safety education programs can use films supplied by such different sources as equipment manufacturers, insurance companies and state agencies. Invited speakers are often available from government agencies, insurance companies, or other interested groups.

Contests can also help promote safety. A contest could award bonuses or prizes for accident-free records. And everyone wins in contests like these.

Establishing safety inspections. An operation should institute regular safety inspections conducted both by the safety committee and the supervisors and workers in their own work area. A checksheet can provide numerical ratings. Discrepancies should be noted, along with a means for following through on their correction. Sometimes outside experts conduct these inspections. These people are often available from the insurance companies who provide accident insurance.

Developing safety work procedures. This should flow naturally from safety education. Every job and job station should post a safety list of standard work procedures that must be developed for it. Every employee in that job should be given these procedures and should sign them to indicate that he has reviewed them. Procedures could cover such hazardous equipment as slicers, mixers, and ranges. They should be trained how to lift and move the products and how to handle slippery surfaces and spilled contents. Before starting to use a piece of equipment, every employee should be instructed not only in its operation but also in its *safe* operation. Workers should be aware of the safe operation of equipment, and they should also be aware that they must not interrupt the concentration of other workers using the equipment.

Accident investigation reporting and follow-up procedures. Every accident should be investigated. This investigation is usually a legal requirement; but even if it were not, it could help prevent similar accidents in the future. It is crucial that the accident be investigated as soon as possible after it has occurred. Even a short delay could dissipate useful information. An accident report form helps ensure that all facets of the accident are investigated. As in any investigative effort, eight basic questions should be asked:

Where did it happen?

Who was injured?

When did it occur?

What was the employee doing immediately before the accident and at the time of the accident?

What materials, machines, equipment, or conditions were involved?

What happened?

Why did it happen?

What can be done to prevent recurrence?

Along with these questions, some very specific information should be gathered. What exactly was the employee doing when the accident occurred? The exact time of an accident should be noted along with its specific location. You should note the type of accident (a fall, struck by, caught in, a burn). Note too the material or machines involved. Ask any witnesses to give a description of the accident; then ask the person involved to give his account. The supervisor's account may also be helpful. If there were any unsafe conditions, they should be noted; and the reasons for their existence should be included. Along with the unsafe conditions, unsafe activities should be listed together with the reasons for their occurrence: lack of skill, poor attitude, disregarding of instructions, inadequate instructions, misunderstanding, or whatever. By all means show, if possible, what can be done to prevent the recurrence of the accident.

Ensuring compliance with federal and state safety codes. Conscientious compliance with safety laws becomes increasingly important as new laws are constantly enacted and enforced. Some of these laws carry severe penalties for lack of compliance. Some state laws also require documentation of periodic safety inspections and safety training for employees. With increased governmental interest in safety, one can expect that additional requirements for compliance will appear. And besides the governmental requirements, owners and managers must protect themselves against personal liability actions. And above all, they should have a natural desire to prevent accidents among their employees.

Auditing the safety program. The safety program does not run itself. Safety committee meetings do not ensure, by themselves, an effective safety program. Management should continually audit its safety program and occasionally motivate the safety committee and all the other employees toward greater efforts. Management can ask questions like these: is the latest information and techniques in safety management available throughout the operation? Is the safety record low compared to similar establishments? The injury rate can be determined by the following frequency rate formula:

$$\text{Frequency of Injuries} = \frac{\text{Number of Injuries} \times 1{,}000{,}000}{\text{Number of Man Hours of Exposure}}$$

After finding that the injury rate among its full-time employees was about two and a half times that of the hospitality industry as a whole, one firm immediately overhauled its safety program and achieved an injury rate far below the national average.

The Williams-Steiger Occupational Safety and Health Act of 1970

Signed by the President in 1970 and implemented in April, 1971, the Williams-Steiger Occupational Safety and Health Act (OSHA) has had a greater impact on business and industry than almost any other piece of legislation in recent years. Its passage was hailed by some as "an all-out effort to achieve safer and healthier work places." The act culminated several decades of work by those who believe it would promote industrial safety. The act was also denounced by many as "the toughest piece of legislation business has ever had to cope with." The law certainly has a lofty purpose and was passed by a Congress hoping "to assure so far as possible every working man and woman in the Nation safe and healthful working conditions and to preserve our human resources."

The 1970 Safety and Health Act provides a number of means for the accomplishment of this lofty purpose. It encourages employers and employees to reduce the number of occupational safety and health hazards in the work place. It authorizes the Secretary of Labor to set mandatory occupational safety and health standards. It provides for research in the field of occupational safety and health, and also establishes medical criteria to assure, insofar as practical, that no employee will suffer diminished health, functional capacity, or life expectancy as a result of any work experience. Training programs and effective enforcement programs are also stipulated, and the development and promulgation of occupational safety and health standards is encouraged. The act also encourages the states to assume fullest responsibility and provides for appropriate reporting procedures. Joint labor and management efforts to reduce injury and disease arising out of employment are also supported by the act. As you can see, few governmental programs have made larger or more sweeping waves than this federal drive to improve health and working conditions.

Despite its lofty goals, the Occupational Safety and Health Act

(OSHA) has received much criticism. There have been frequent complaints of lax enforcement. There has yet to be a noticeable reduction in accidents or measurable increase in occupational safety that can be attributed to the law. Some have complained that enforcement has been capricious and arbitrary.

Some of these complaints are almost inevitable with a new program that has not had the time to develop a trained staff. But from industry's standpoint a number of OSHA horror stories can be told. An employer whose wife was his only employee had to install a separate restroom for her. Some safety railings required by an OSHA inspector at a meat packing plant were proscribed as unsanitary by sanitation inspectors. Farmers have been required to provide portable toilet facilities for employees plowing the fields. One case can even be cited where no ice water was allowed workers in hot surroundings—a remnant of the idea that ice can contaminate drinking water. At one point, the OSHA regulations occupied a shelf seventeen feet long. (By comparison the Harvard Classics take up only five feet.)

Administrative enforcement of the act rests primarily with the Secretary of Labor and the agency created for the act, The Occupational Safety and Health Review Commission, a quasi-judicial board of three members appointed by the President. Research and related functions are vested in the Secretary of Health, Education and Welfare (HEW) whose functions are, for the most part, carried out by the new National Institute for Occupational Safety and Health (NIOSH) established within HEW.

The Secretary of Labor is responsible for both promulgating and enforcing job safety and health standards. Occupational safety and health inspections are conducted by compliance officers located in offices throughout the country. Provisions of the law apply to every employer engaged in a business affecting commerce. Federal, state, and local government employees are specifically excluded from coverage, but they may be covered by other equally effective requirements.

Under the act, an employer has the general duty to furnish each of his employee's employment and places of employment free from recognized hazards causing or likely to cause death or serious physical harm; and the employer has the specific duty to comply with safety and health standards promulgated under the act. Each employee shares the duty to comply with these safety and health standards and all those rules, regulations, and orders issued pursuant to the act that are applicable to his own actions and conduct.

Complaints Centering on Violations and Enforcement

Under the Williams-Steiger Occupational Safety and Health Act of 1970, any employee or his representative who believes that a violation of a job safety or health standard exists and threatens physical harm, or that imminent danger exists, may request an inspection of the work place by sending a signed notice to the Department of Labor. This notice should include the grounds for the complaint. A copy must be sent to the employer, but the name of the complainant need not be furnished to the employer. Some management people feel that this provision can allow disgruntled employees to make baseless trouble, at no risk to themselves.

Where the investigation shows that a violation has occurred, the employer receives a written citation describing the specific nature of the violation. All citations allow a reasonable time for abating the violation, and copies of the citation must be prominently posted at or near each place where a violation occurred. Notices may also be issued for violations that have no direct or immediate effect on safety or health. No citation may be issued after the expiration of six months following the occurrence of any violation. The visit of a compliance officer because of a complaint can lead to a full safety and health inspection; it is not limited strictly to investigating the specific complaint. Also, there need be no advance notification; most inspections so far have, in fact, taken place without advance notice.

Penalties under OSHA The act provides for different types of violations and also for penalties: A Type I violation constitutes a violation that could cause death or serious physical harm. A Type II violation is not quite so serious, but could have a direct or immediate effect on the safety or health of an employee. Type III (*deminimus*) violations are situations that have no direct effect on safety and health.

A blatant disregard of a violation can result in a fine of from $501 to $1,000 for each violation. A serious violation can involve an immediate fine of from $201 to $500. A less serious violation can involve a penalty of from $100 to $200. *Deminimus* violations occasion no fines. In cases of willful or repeated violations the penalty can go to $10,000. (Some willful violations can, in fact, bring imprisonment.) An additional penalty can be levied if abatement or corrective action is not taken.

An OSHA official can reduce the penalties for various reasons: a reduction of 20 percent can follow an employer's good faith, as evidenced by effective safety programs, the identification and elimination of hazards, and the motivation and training of employees. Reductions of up to 20 percent can come from a safety history. An abatement credit for the correction of a cited deficiency within the specified period can produce a reduction of up to 50 percent.

An employer has fifteen working days to file protests if, in his opinion, (a) the citation is in error, (b) the time limit for abatement (corrective action) is unrealistic and cannot be met, or (c) the amount of the penalty is excessive.

An accident must be recorded within six working days of the occurrence. Within one month after the end of the calendar year, a summary of occupational injury and illness experienced must be prepared and posted in a place accessible to employees. (The posting must remain for thirty days). Fatalities or incidents involving the hospitalization of five or more persons must be reported to the OSHA within forty-eight hours.

Recordkeeping The regulations issued under the Occupational Safety and Health Act of 1970 requires that careful records be kept of recordable occupational injuries. These records consist of a log of occupational injuries and illnesses (OSHA Form 101), a supplementary record of each occupational injury and illness (OSHA Form 101), and an annual summary of occupational illness and injuries (OSHA Form 102). Minor injuries requiring only first aid treatment need not be recorded; but a record must be made if the injury involves medical treatment, loss of consciousness, restriction of worker motion, or transfer to another job. A company typically maintains these records for five years.

Another record that must be kept is a poster regarding OSHA laws that must be displayed in a prominent place in the establishment where employees normally report to work.

Incidence Rate With data from the OSHA forms, one can calculate an operation's accident incidence rate and compare that rate to rates in similar establishments. These figures are published by the government. To calculate the rate accurately, however, one must know the exact number of injuries and illnesses occurring during the year. (This number can be found in the log of occupational injuries and illnesses.) One must also know the number of hours actually worked by all employees. The hours-worked figures should not include such non-work as vacation, sick leave, or holidays, even though this time may be paid for.

The formula for an accident incidence rate is the number of injuries and illnesses (n) multiplied by 200,000 divided by the number of employee hours worked (EHW).

$$\text{AIR} = \frac{n \times 200{,}000}{\text{EHW}}$$

The 200,000 in the formula represents the equivalent of 100 employees working 40 hours a week, 50 weeks per year. It provides a standard base for accident incidence rates. In other words, the formula is the incidence rate for 100 full-time employees during the year.

A hospitality operation that experiences nine recordable injuries during the year and total hours worked by employees is 290,000 would have the following figures:

$$\text{AIR} = \frac{9 \times 200{,}000}{290{,}000}$$

$$\text{AIR} = 6.2$$

Some Deficiencies Associated with Foodservice Operations

There are, of course, many regulations for which a foodservice operation or a hospitality operation can be liable. Some of the most common deficiencies reported under these regulations have been wet and slippery floors, aisles blocked by obstructions, a lack of railings on stairways, insufficient exits for fires or other emergencies, ungrounded wiring systems, ungrounded equipment, a failure to post danger signs, and untested or uninspected fire extinguishers, no first aid kit, no trained first aid attendant, and unclean or poorly illuminated or poorly ventilated toilets and dressing rooms.

While no one questions the need for safety and the enforcement of safety regulations, many businessmen question the efficiency and effectiveness of OSHA itself. It is, they say, more of a bureaucracy than an effective safety-promoting organization. They question whether compliance officers unfamiliar with the requirements of industries they inspect can use their wide discretionary power fairly to penalize the industries. Since the enforcement of the act, there has been an effort on the part of the government to be somewhat more liberal. But the OSHA compliance officers retain a great deal of discretion, and some businesses feel that they do not have adequate recourse against the occasional unfair OSHA decision.

Fire Safety and Protection

Like sanitation and general safety, fire protection can be crucial to the hospitality manager. The industry bears a strong responsiblity for the protection of its guests, particularly because so many fire dangers are inherent in housing and foodservice operations. Moreover, even if no lives are lost, fire-related injuries and the bad publicity attending them can put an operation out of business. Forty percent of small businesses that experience major fires never reopen.

As you know, fires are all too common in the hospitality industry. We read continual news reports of hospitality fires causing loss of life. One of the most notorious was a Boston nightclub fire in the 1940s in which 460 people died, most from smoke inhalation. The owner and the builder paid heavy fines, and both spent ten years in prison for violating fire safety codes. A 1977 nightclub fire in Kentucky caused a similarly great loss of life.

Most of the many restaurant and hotel fires each year could be prevented. Some of the prevention rests with the original architects, planners, and engineers. But the hospitality manager must undertake continuous responsibility for fire prevention and fire safety on his premises. In addition to curtailed chance of a fire and the resultant tragedy, a conscientious fire safety program can have economic benefits in reduced fire insurance rates.

Types of Fires

It takes three elements to produce combustion or a fire: fuel to burn, oxygen to maintain burning, and sufficient heat to ignite the fuel and oxygen mixture. Fire fighting, therefore, focuses on removing one or more of the three requirements—fuel, oxygen, or heat. Fuel and oxygen, of course, occur all around us, so fire prevention most frequently centers on preventing sufficient heat to cause ignition.

Fires themselves are usually grouped into one of these four classes:

Class A—fires involving ordinary combustibles, such as wood, paper, and textiles. These figures are best extinguished by cooling with water or solutions containing water to wet down the materials and prevent the embers from rekindling. All-purpose dry chemical extinguishers may also be used.

Class B—fires involving flammable liquids and gases, such as gasoline, oil, grease, paint, thinners, hydrogen, and acetylene. These fires can be extinguished by smothering and shutting off their oxygen supply. Carbon-dioxide, dry-chemical, and foam extinguishers are effective on this type of fire.

Class C—fires involving energized electrical equipment. A non-conducting extinguishing agent like carbon dioxide or a dry chemical best extinguishes this kind of fire.

Class D—Fires attributable to combustible metals. A specialized fire classification, this kind of fire is usually not a problem for the hospitality manager and so will not be discussed in this chapter.

As stated, extinguishing a fire involves the removal of one or more of the three combustion elements. This removal can be accomplished by

1. Quenching a fire—removing its heat—usually by applying water
2. Blanketing, or physically separating the fuel from its oxygen supply
3. Smothering, or displacing the atmosphere by a denser gas, usually carbon dioxide (CO_2)

Fire Equipment

Just as there are different types of fires, there are also different types of equipment used to combat them. Some equipment can be dangerous if used on the wrong type of fire. For example, the quenching action of water would extinguish a class A fire but might actually spread a class B fire. Foam, good for class A and B fires, should not be used on class C fires, as it is a conductor.

Equipment commonly used to fight class A fires includes the familiar soda-acid fire extinguisher, which contains water in which bicarbonate of soda is dissolved. A bottle on the top of the extinguisher contains sulfuric acid. When the extinguisher is turned upside down, the chemicals mix, forming a gas which forces the solution up through the hose in 30-foot stream. The soda-acid extinguisher usually has a 2½-gallon capacity.

This type of extinguisher has essentially become obsolete and is being widely replaced by the pressurized-water type.

The air-pressurized-water fire extinguisher can be activated by pulling the pin located on the handle and squeezing the lever-action handle. There is a pressure gauge on top of the extinguisher which indicates the pressure inside the container. The power is derived from stored compressed air in the tank. If the extinguisher is kept in freezing conditions, a specially developed antifreeze solution may be used instead of plain water. The usual capacity is, again, 2½ gallons, and the water can be sprayed from 30 to 40 feet. A pump-type extinguisher is a tank with a hand pump which forces the water out. Either water or antifreeze chemicals dissolved in the water can be used.

A foam fire extinguisher can be used for both class A and class B fires. It is identical in appearance to the soda-acid extinguisher and operates the same way when one inverts the extinguisher. The foam extinguisher consists of two chambers. The outer chamber contains a solution of water, bicarbonate of soda, and a foaming ingredient; the inner chamber contains a solution of water and aluminum sulfate. When the extinguisher is inverted, the chemicals combine and expel a stream of foam. Although the extinguisher contains 2½ gallons of liquid, it generates about eight times that amount of foam.

Carbon-dioxide and dry-chemical extinguishers can be used on class B and class C fires. The carbon-dioxide extinguisher is generally red and has a horn-like nozzle from which carbon dioxide gas, which resembles snow, is expelled. To activate the extinguisher, one either turns a hand wheel or pulls a pin. Then the lever-action handle or trigger is squeezed. Carbon-dioxide extinguishers come in a number of different sizes. Five, ten, or fifteen pounds (the most common models) indicate the weight of the carbon dioxide within the extinguisher. The carbon-dioxide extinguisher defeats fire by displacing oxygen in the air, thereby smothering the fire. It is also a nonconductor of electricity.

A dry-chemical fire extinguisher contains a chemically treated powder, generally potassium bicarbonate or sodium bicarbonate. It resembles the carbon-dioxide extinguisher except that it has a hose instead of a horn-like nozzle. The powder, which is forced out either by a small compressed gas cartridge or a supply of pressurized air, blankets and smothers the fire. It does not conduct electricity. Most dry chemicals have a limited effect on class A fires, although some new powders have been developed that are very effective.

Kitchens invite fires, especially range tops and fryers. Thus, automatic carbon-dioxide or dry-chemical extinguishing systems should be installed in the hoods above these units. Another dangerous kitchen area is in the grease hood and its ducts. A kitchen ventilation system carries grease-laden vapors. As vapors cool, grease can condense in the ducts and can be ignited by wayward sparks. Most dangerous, a duct fire may go unnoticed for a considerable time. Grease filters located at the duct entrance can help prevent these fires. But the filters themselves can become fire hazards if they are not cleaned regularly. The easy way to clean grease filters is to run them through the dishwashing machine. The ducts should be designed so that they are not connected with any other ventilation system, and they should have cleanout covers every twenty feet along their horizontal runs. There should also be clean outs on the vertical risers. If the grease filters are protected by automatic carbon-dioxide or dry-chemical systems, fusible link fire dampers can be installed in the duct. A fire in the duct will cause the fusible link to release and close the damper. Fire protection for ranges and open cooking equipment as well as for ventilation ducts has become a matter of sophisticated and specialized design knowledge. A manager would do well to retain a consultant when addressing these problems.

An automatic sprinkler system is a most effective type of fire control. These systems usually employ fusible link heads which release water to sprinkle over an area the moment heat melts a link. In unheated buildings, the associated system's pipes can be filled with air. This air holds back water until the fusible link melts and releases the air. Although sprinkler systems are extremely effective, they can also cause substantial water damage. Care should be taken to keep the sprinkler shut-off valves from accidentally being closed or inactivated. Large, multistory buildings should have appropriate hose connections on various floors. In fact, local fire ordinances usually stipulate these connections.

Class A extinguishers should be located every 75 feet of travel distance within the operation. There should also be one extinguisher for every 2500 square feet of floor space. Carbon-dioxide and dry-chemical extinguishers should be strategically located wherever quantities of flammable liquids or materials are stored or dispensed, and wherever the possibility of electrical fires exists. A 50-foot travel distance between these extinguishers is the usual practice.

Fire extinguishers cannot be installed and forgotten. Soda-acid extinguishers should be recharged annually and given a hydrostatic test every five years. Pressurized extinguishers should have their pressures checked semi-annually and receive a hydrostatic test every five years. Foam-type extinguishers should be discharged and recharged annually, with a hydrostatic test every five years. Carbon-dioxide extinguishers should be weighed twice a year and be given regular hydrostatic tests. Obviously, too, the extinguisher should be completely recharged after each use, regardless of the amount of extinguishing agent discharged. Outside maintenance firms or local fire companies sometimes do this work. They typically write the date of the last check on the extinguisher.

Those who watch television commercials realize that fire detectors have undergone pronounced improvement lately. In the last few years several companies have developed ionization sensors that detect hydrocarbons and products of combustion in the air. These machines are inexpensive and easy to install. They usually operate on batteries. Other types of sensors include thermal detectors activated by high or rising temperatures. In addition, water from a sprinkler system may trigger an alarm. The detectors sometimes broadcast an alarm to employees with a shrill noise, or they may indicate to the front office a signal that pinpoints the trouble. An alarm system can also be connected with security systems.

Fire Prevention and Protection

A fire-prevention system and fire-fighting system comprise two separate operations. First is fire prevention, which involves good housekeeping, inspection for and correcting of fire hazards, and adequate equipment maintenance, including that of fire-fighting equipment and appropriate alarm systems, which should always be in good working order.

If, in spite of all prevention, a fire occurs, the entire staff should know how to react properly. Everyone should know how and where to report a fire. Should they call the front office, the manager's office, the cashier? Is the fire department to be called immediately? Exactly who makes these decisions? Every staff member should know the answers *before* a fire occurs. The fire department's number should be listed by each telephone. If the premises have to be evacuated, an evacuation plan (including instructions for notifying residents) should be available to all employees. Who will check, for example, that all the hotel guest rooms have actually been vacated? If the fire department is to be called, an operation should have preplanned procedures for directing it to the fire.

Fighting fires is obviously the work of firemen, but fires are much easier to stop in their initial stages. Therefore, personnel should be trained to use the hand-portable extinguishers available. Some hotels have found it useful to load a cart with fire-fighting equipment and dispatch it to the scene of the trouble. Such a cart can contain fire blankets, resuscitators, axes, pry bars, asbestos gloves, lanterns, and extra hose. One such cart we know of has a lock box in which valuables can be placed. The box itself cannot be removed without a key.

The engineering staff would normally be responsible in a fire-fighting situation, but each employee should know what to do and not do. Patrons' safety comes first; their care usually consists of prompt evacuation. Human lives obviously take priority over physical property.

Physical and Structural Factors in Fire Prevention

Certain design factors in a structure can help prevent fires or keep them from spreading. Fire-resistant construction should be mandatory on public premises. The outside of a building may be fully fireproof; but if the inside is of combustible construction, a fire can still spread. Interestingly enough, more live are lost through smoke inhalation than actual flames. Thus, both the exterior and the interior of a building should be as fire resistant as possible. Take steps to include fireproof draperies. Special paints can retard fire. Tall buildings, such as a hotel, should contain fire stops to prevent flames and smoke from moving vertically from one floor to another. Open stairways and elevator shafts should be sealable. Moreover, these vertical openings should be equipped with fire-resistant, self-closing doors. Fire can also spread through air conditioning and ventilating ducts. Therefore, these ducts should be totally constructed of noncombustible material, and fire dampers should be installed at strategic locations. Some hotels retain old-fashioned transom windows for ventilation, but transoms present a real fire and smoke hazard. Fire stopping should surround all unoccupied spaces, such as where a ceiling has been lowered, so that fire cannot spread rapidly through these spaces.

A common cause of hotel fires is smoking, so a hotel should provide noncombustible ashtrays. Unless special precautions are taken, all cooking equipment should be located at least eighteen inches from combustible materials. Finally, appropriate notices or signs, advising occupants of fire-preventing measures and of procedures to follow in event of fire, should be conspicuously posted in each guest room of hotels and motels.

Antichoking Devices and Procedures

It is estimated that as many as four thousand people in this country each year choke to death on food or some foreign object obstructing their windpipe. Naturally enough, many of these deaths occur in restaurants. In the middle 1970s, states began to enact legislation to curtail choking in eating establishments. This legislation typically required restaurants to keep on hand a special device for removing food from the throats of choking patrons.

Meanwhile, restauranteurs began teaching their employees how to administer the Heimlich Maneuver, sometimes called the "hug of life." All people associated with restaurants should be familiar with the Heimlich Maneuver. A choking victim can neither speak nor breathe; he turns blue and then collapses. At this point, about four minutes remain in which to save the victim's life.

Following the Heimlich Maneuver, you wrap your arms around the waist of the choking person (whether he is standing or sitting). Stand behind him letting his head and torso hang forward. Clench your fist and grasp it with your other hand; then place both hands against his stomach just above the navel and under the rib cage. Using a quick, upward thrust, pull your fist into his stomach. Repeat this procedure as many times as necessary. This technique utilizes the residual air at the bottom of the lung to expel the blockage in the windpipe. A plug of food may literally pop out of the victim's mouth, freeing him to speak and breathe. Another helpful technique is to reach into the throat to grasp the obstructing food with your fingers.

Both the American Red Cross and American Heart Association have adopted a modified version of the Heimlich Maneuver as the acceptable procedure to be used on choking victims. Their procedures deal with the obstructed air-way and involve:

1. Four back slaps—striking the choking victim with the heel of your hand sharply four times. If this does not dislodge the foreign obstruction, then it should be immediately followed by:

2. Four abdominal thrusts—the same as in the Heimlich Maneuver.

These procedures should be repeated in both the conscious and unconscious victim until medical or other professional emergency medical services are available at the scene. Naturally, in the unconscious victim there is a slight variation in that the victim will be in the supine position.

Although the Heimlich Maneuver effectively relieves choking, one should be careful in making the diagnosis. Victims of heart attacks sometimes resemble choking victims. Also, convulsions or seizures can mimic choking symptoms. In these cases, the Heimlich Maneuver would probably do more harm than good. The universally accepted signal for a choking victim to notify witnesses that he has an obstructed airway is for the victim to grasp his throat with his own hand.

Assisting a victim with the best of intentions but with superficial knowledge may actually worsen already serious conditions. It can also open the door for civil or criminal liability. Still, fortunately, most people would try to to save someone's life and worry about the lawsuit later. Accordingly, most states have enacted "good samaritan" laws that protect operators and employees to some extent, should attempts at emergency assistance result in injury.

SUMMARY

Union-management relations are becoming an increasingly important part of hospitality management. The modern American labor movement traditionally dates to the Knights of Labor in 1869. In the 1930s, a good deal of legislation favorable to labor was enacted. Foremost was the National Labor Relations Act (Wagner Act) which guaranteed a worker's right to organize and to bargain collectively with employers, or to refrain from all such activity. The Wagner Act, with its five unfair practices, is still our basic labor legislation. The Wagner Act states that:

1. *An employer cannot interfere with, restrain, or coerce employees in the exercise of their rights guaranteed under the Act.*

2. *An employer cannot interfere with or contribute to the administration of a labor organization.*

3. *An employer cannot discriminate in employment on the basis of union activity.*

4. *An employer cannot discriminate against an employee who participated against him in a NLRB proceeding.*

5. *An employer cannot refuse to bargain in good faith.*

The Wagner Act also prohibits unfair labor practices by unions. It has been amended through the years, notably by the Taft-Hartley Act in 1947, and the Labor-Management Reporting and Disclosure Act of 1959.

A union becomes the employees' bargaining agent after being certified by the NLRB. Organizers may associate with employees and ask them to sign cards requesting a union election. If the union receives signed cards from 30 percent of the employees, it may petition the NLRB for an election. If 50 percent of the workers plus one vote for a union, it is certified by the NLRB and the employer by law must bargain with it in good faith.

Collective bargaining is the path this country has taken to try to settle its labor strife. The result of the bargaining is a contract or basic agreement between the workers, through their union, and the employer. Major clauses that may be in the contract typically address conditions of recognition, the employees covered, the duration of the contract, management's rights, union security, working conditions, grievances, and arbitration. Arbitration involves provision for a neutral party to rule on differences that management and labor cannot settle themselves.

Employees join a union both for material and for psychological reasons. Although the great majority of managers would prefer not to have a union, unions do provide some advantages to management. Wages may be kept out of competition; the union can provide standards, common benefits and training programs; and they can supply personnel. The primary disadvantages to management include higher salaries, less managerial discretion, and the fact that unions often work against management's general interests.

The largest unions in the hospitality field are the Hotel and Restaurant Employees and Bartenders International Union and Local 1199 (National Union of Hospital and Nursing Homes Employees). A union may be decertified, but management can only give advice to dissatisfied workers and may not take part in a decertification effort.

Safety is also an increasing part of hospitality management even though the hospitality industry has an unfortunately high accident incidence rate. Every hospitality operation should have a safety program. The steps in a typical program follow:

1. *Establish a definite, written safety program.*
2. *Prepare for emergencies.*
3. *Provide safety instruction.*
4. *Establish safety inspection procedures.*
5. *Develop safe working procedures.*
6. *Reinforce accident investigation and report procedures.*
7. *Comply with state and federal safety codes.*
8. *Audit safety program.*

The Williams-Steiger Occupational Safety and Health Act of 1972 has added many new safety requirements and establishes penalties for noncompliance.

An important aspect of safety is fire protection. Every hospitality operation should have fire plans, adequate extinguishing equipment, and personnel trained in its use.

Fires are often grouped into four classes:

Class A—fires involving wood, textiles and ordinary combustibles

Class B—fires involving flammable liquids

Class C—electrical fires

Class D—fires involving combustible metals

Extinguishing equipment suitable for one class of fires is not necessarily suitable for others and can be even dangerous. All hospitality employees should be able to distinguish between different kinds of fires, know which fire extinguishers to use, and how to use them.

IMPORTANT TERMS

After studying this chapter, you should be able to define or identify these terms:

Knights of Labor

AFL

craft union

ebb and flow theory

CIO

yellow dog contract

National Labor Relations Act (Wagner Act)

Taft-Hartley Act

closed shop

jurisdictional strikes

The Labor-Management Reporting and Disclosure Act of 1959

collective bargaining

iron law of wages

conditions of recognition clause

coverage clause

management rights clause

union security clause

union shop

open shop

right to work laws

agency shop

check off

grievance clause

arbitration

vampire system

workmen's compensation legislation

fellow servant doctrine

OSHA

accident incidence rate formula

the fire triangle

class A fire

class B fire

class C fire

Heimlich Maneuver

REVIEW QUESTIONS

8-1. What are the five "thou shall nots" of the Wagner Act?

8-2. How would a union attempt to organize the workers in a restaurant?

8-3. Briefly discuss the major clauses in a typical hospitality union contract.

8-4. Why would well-treated employees want to join a labor union?

8-5. What possible advantages to management exist in a unionized operation?

8-6. Differentiate between the following union security clauses:

(a) closed shop (b) union shop (c) open shop (d) agency shop.

8-7. Outline the steps in a safety program for a hospitality operation.

8-8. A kitchen employee cuts his finger very badly on a slicing machine. What should you as a manager do?

8-9. List major provisions of the Occupational Safety and Health Act of 1970.

8-10. Explain class A, B, and C fires, indicating a suitable extinguishing device for each.

CASE PROBLEM: The Union

You are the operator of a successful restaurant and have a reputation for treating your employees fairly—perhaps paternally. You also require a fair day's work from them. You know that organizers for a national hospitality union are in your area and that they have approached other operations. But, as far as you know, none of your employees have been contacted.

What actions, if any, should you take?

Some old employees report that two new employees and one who has worked for you for two years are "talking up the union." One of the new employees is satisfactory and the other is marginal. You have been thinking of "separating" the other employee for being a goof-off. They and the organizers are meeting with your employees at the employee entrance and at their homes.

What action, if any, should you take?

One morning, out of the blue, a union organizer comes into your office with a package of cards which he says are requests for a representation election signed by forty five of your eighty employees. He asks if you would like to see them. He also says that if you cooperate now and accept the union, a much better relationship will be established than if a fight for representation, which he claims the union would easily win, ensues.

What actions, if any, should you take?

The NLRB holds an election. A traffic accident keeps two employees you are sure are favorable to you from voting. The union wins by one vote. The new union president turns out to be the employee you were thinking of firing. You find him condescending, irrational, demogogic, and sometimes, very free with the truth.

What action, if any, should you take?

A year has passed. Through the grapevine you hear that a strong majority are "teed off" about the union. The employees feel they are not getting anything for their dues. A small delegation of workers comes to you and asks you to support them in a move to decertify the union before the next contract negotiations.

What, if any, actions should you take?

9 Financial Management

Any **hospitality enterprise,** profit or nonprofit, must acquire initial financing and must, thereafter, maintain a definite pattern of financial management. If the manager has no financial expertise himself, he must make sure it is available. Moreover, he must be able at least to communicate sensibly with his financial advisors and personnel. Consequently, after studying this chapter, you should be able to

- outline briefly the development of financial management in the hospitality industry
- explain briefly the importance of financial understanding to a hospitality manager
- analyze the Income and Balance Sheet Statements of a hospitality enterprise
- discuss two basic sources of financing for a hospitality operation
- explain at least three different methods of calculating interest costs
- explain briefly the difference between ordinary income taxes and capital gains taxes
- explain the three common methods of calculating depreciation
- discuss briefly the role accelerated depreciation plays in the hospitality industry
- provide a short definition for each of the familiar financial terms listed at the conclusion of this chapter

A business is supposed to have three major functions: production, distribution, and finance. Neither production nor distribution can take place without money, and the financial function of the business has the broad responsibility of supplying necessary funds.

The finances in a very small hospitality establishment may be taken care of entirely by the proprietor, perhaps with the periodic assistance of a bookkeeper. A somewhat larger operation may hire a controller interested in accounting, auditing, budgeting, and statistical work. And still larger operations often employ a treasurer who performs the duties of a controller but also assumes such functions as credit, accounts receivable and their collection, and investment management.

In the largest operations, the major financial officer may carry a title like vice president in charge of finance. The controller and treasurer (if there is one) both report to him. One of his main responsibilities may be long-range financial planning. Almost all planning involves money; thus, a financial officer is usually involved.

History and Development of Financial Management

Up until the second quarter of this century financial management was a relatively simple proposition. Its primary concerns were the acquisition of funds and the accounting aspects of a business. The owner or manager could often do much of this work himself. Liquidity (turning assets into cash or having enough money on hand to pay current debts) and solvency (having more assets than liabilities) were both extremely important. Business panics and depressions could greatly affect either. Eighty percent of the nation's hotels, for example, experienced financial difficulty (they had, in other words, liquidity or solvency problems) during the depression years.

Solving liquidity or solvency problems typically required a balance of current debt, long-term debt and equity investment by the owners. The major financial duty of the proprietor or manager was then to raise capital or secure external loans.

After the Second World War, tight money and depressed stock prices made raising outside money considerably more difficult. This led managers to utilize internal cash (money generated by the business rather than from outside sources) more ingeniously. Cash flow analysis, which determines where the money comes from and goes and why, was encouraged. Cash budgeting, or the planning of cash inflow and expenditures to reduce a need to borrow, became popular. Expenditures would be made only when there was enough projected cash on hand to cover them. Conrad Hilton of the Hilton Hotels became a leader in developing new internal cash sources. His "digging for gold" led both to sources of new cash income and more utilization of internal cash in the hospitality field. Financing now included the conservation and utilization of internal funds as well as the raising of funds from outside the operation.

The 1960s increasingly brought forth new management developments. Questions of how large the enterprise should be and how fast should it grow became relevant. Many hospitality operations (as well as operations in other industries) found their profits relatively limited. A single hotel could make only so much profit. But if the hotel company could build several other hotels, profit possibilities might be greatly enhanced with the profits from the additional units. In the food industry, companies that had been operating as conventional, family restaurants decided to expand into such other fields as motor inns, airline feeding, new specialty restaurants, industrial feeding, and fast-food operations.

Stockholders, of course, wanted the best return on investment possible both in terms of current dividends and appreciation or growth in the value of their investment. Questions were asked about what form a company's assets should take. Should it use excess funds to pay off debt? Or use them for further investment and expansion? What should the composition of liabilities (or money owed) be? Long-term or short-term? Should a hotel corporation try to own its hotels, or should it seek only to provide the management for hotels and leave the ownership of them to others? If a company had one million dollars to invest, should it build a one-million-dollar hotel with no debt or should it use the million dollars to provide equity of $200,000 in five different hotels and borrow the rest (or four million dollars assuming each hotel cost one million)? Would this allow greater profit possibilities?

In other words, financial managers now became responsible for the most effective utilization of funds, a job which included investigating new investment opportunities. Therefore, the financial management function changed from merely supplying funds to one involving financial analysis. And accordingly, analytical techniques for evaluating alternative uses of funds have been developed.

In the 1970s, financial management became even more complicated. Capital funds and working capital fund shortages appeared. And, even when these funds were available, the interest costs for them were far higher than recent history had taught us to expect. Planning became increasingly difficult because of risks and uncertainties. Past growth trends were upset by such developments as zero population growth and greatly increasing energy costs.

The government became far more involved in the management of business. An expanding firm had to consider not only financial aspects but the effects on the environment as well. More regulatory bodies appeared on the scene to demand reports of a financial nature. Medicare and Medicaid required health care institutions to arrange their accounting to provide documentary information. Finally, different methods of financing were employed by those businessmen such as in leasing of equipment rather than buying it, franchising expansion, and sale-leaseback, where a hospitality operation raises a new building but sells the real estate to someone else who leases the property back to the original hotel company (keeping only limited funds tied up in real estate).

The sheer physical growth of many enterprises has required financial expertise beyond that of most founders and presidents. Businesses and institutions find that they must diversify their products and services in various ways, and that diversification requires specialized financial decision-making. Heightened competition, too, has led to narrowing profit margins with less room for financial error. Over a short period, a firm can be weak in production or marketing but can be saved by good financial management. But, a hospitality operation may serve the finest food and provide the best service, and still fail with poor financial management. In the world of hospitality one finds accelerated change, and the financial function of its businesses must adapt to it. Many enterprises feel they are at a distinct disadvantage if they remain small, and they decide to grow in volume and activity to remain competitive and increase profits. This has all led to increased reliance on financial management and its increased importance to the enterprise.

Analyzing Financial Statements

Accounting   A hospitality manager should have a knowledge of accounting statements and how to interpret and evaluate the statements of his operation.

Accounting has been defined, quite simply, as a system for keeping financial records. It is essential to any financial enterprise, and it is involved in almost all management functions. It is, in fact, the language of business. When an organization wants to know what its income is, what its expenses are, the value of its assets, and the amount and type of its liabilities, it must resort to accounting. There are a number of different types of accounting:

Financial accounting. This is the preparation of statements that may be used by the enterprise itself and by others to evaluate that enterprise. The primary statements of financial accounting include the *income statement,* or *profit and loss statement* (Exhibit 9-1), which shows income, expenses, and the resulting profits or losses (the difference between income and expenses) over a specified period; and the *balance sheet* (Exhibit 9-2) which shows an operation's assets, liabilities, and equity (the difference between assets and liabilities) as of a certain date. (If liabilities exceed assets, the enterprise is, technically, at least, bankrupt.)

Managerial accounting. This method is used to furnish information to management engaged in the planning, decision-making, and control functions. Its information includes such items as budgets, cost accounting, records, and special accounting studies.

Tax accounting. Tax accounting provides the information to prepare tax returns. There may be several differences in tax accounting and financial accounting. For example, depreciation may be calculated one way on a regular financial statement and calculated another way for tax purposes.

Cash accounting. Income is excluded from consideration (from being entered on the books) until it is actually received. Expenses are not entered on the books until they are actually paid. Cash accounting is used only in very small operations that want to keep their accounting or bookkeeping to a minimum.

Accrual accounting. If a sale is made but cash is yet to be received, the potential income is shown as accounts receivable. Costs or expenses entered into but not paid are entered on the records as accounts payable. This method, called the accrual method of accounting, gives a more accurate picture of the enterprise, since it is not dependent on cash.

The Income Statement

An income statement shows the sales, expenses, and the amount of money an operation makes or loses over a specific period. (See Exhibit 9-1.) A nonprofit operation, for example, would not make a profit, but it could have an overage of income to expenses. Or, if its expenses exceed income, it could show a loss from operations. The three parts of an income statement—sales, expenses and profit or loss—can be analyzed separately. Exhibit 9-1 represents the income statement for a relatively small restaurant and bar. In the exhibit, food and beverage sales are $180,000, and other income is $1800 (candy and cigarette sales are among the possible sources). Total expenses are: food and beverage, $58,800; controllable, $105,000; occupation, $2000; and depreciation, $5000. Subtracting these costs from sales and other income gives a profit of $11,000.

In analyzing its sales of $180,000, we are interested in their makeup. We notice that the bar sales made up about one-third of total sales. In an operation serving beverages, the higher the percentage of beverage sales to food sales the more profitable the operation normally is since beverages produce a higher profit than food.

The $180,000 figure does not tell us whether sales have been increasing or decreasing. Thus, we will want to compare it to past periods or to desired goals. Sales in a foodservice operation are made up of two items: the selling price per meal, and the number of meals sold. Sales may rise in an operation, but this rise may be due simply to inflationary increases in costs that are passed on in higher selling prices. Normally an operation wants to sell as much as possible; so it is interesting to see how its volume, in terms of number of meals served over a period, compares to past periods. The average selling price per meal compared to past averages will indicate whether an operation's meal pricing has kept up with inflation; it may even show that through better merchandising (or some other technique) higher prices are being received.

Expenses are related to sales and are usually analyzed as a percentage of sales. The two major expenses in a foodservice operation are the cost of the food (and beverages) and the cost of labor. These are often called *prime costs*. In this particular operation, since the cost of food was $40,800 and food sales were $120,000, food costs constituted 34 percent

Exhibit 9–1.
Typical Income
Statement for a
Small Restaurant

INCOME STATEMENT
For 19___

	AMOUNT	PERCENT
Sales		
Food	$120,000	66.7%
Beverage	60,000	33.3
Total Food and Beverage Sales	180,000	100.0
Cost of Sales		
Food	40,800	34.0
Beverage	18,000	30.0
Total Cost of Food and Beverage Sales	58,800	32.7
Gross Profit		
Food	79,200	66.0
Beverages	42,000	70.0
Total Gross Profit	121,200	67.3
Other Income	1,800	1.0
TOTAL INCOME	123,000	68.3
Controllable Expenses		
Payroll	60,000	33.3
Employee benefits	66,000	3.3
Employee meals	4,800	2.7
Direct operating expenses	110,800	6.0
Advertising and promotion	5,400	3.0
Utilities	3,600	2.0
Administrative and general	10,800	6.0
Repairs and maintenance	3,600	2.0
Total Controllable Expenses	105,000	58.3
Profit before Occupation Costs	18,000	10.0
Occupation Costs	2,000	1.1
Profit before Depreciation	16,000	8.9
Depreciation	5,000	2.8
PROFIT BEFORE TAXES	$ 11,000	6.1%

of food sales. This percentage can be compared with industry data (prepared by accounting firms specializing in hospitality operations), with past percentages, or with budgeted percentages to see if it is desirable and appropriate. The beverage cost of $18,000 can be compared with the $60,000 beverage sales figure to produce a 30 percent beverage cost. The same comparisons can be repeated. All other controllable expense can be analyzed this way. The term *controllable expenses* indicates those expenses that can be kept under the control of management. Such expenses as depreciation, taxes, fire insurance, and fees are standard in the industry; but management normally has little control over them.

Sometimes the usual, widely published percentages are not appropriate. For example, an operation may decide to spend little on advertising promotion and devote this money, instead, to providing better food. In such a case, food costs would rise above normal and the advertising and promotion decline below normal. And although low cost percentages are normally desirable, there can be danger if certain percentages become too low. For example, repair costs can be held down by curtailing or deferring maintenance. In the short run, this may produce a greater profit, but in the long run it may require considerable additional expense. Or, food costs can be reduced in the short run for greater profit, but the clientele may eventually be driven away.

The profit before occupation cost is sometimes called the *operating profit*. This is the best figure or percentage to use to compare different operations simply because the controllable expenses best reflect management proficiency. Occupation costs or financing costs vary considerably and resist comparisons between different operations.

In our example, a restaurant profit of $11,000 is shown. Is this appropriate? One way to tell is to compare this figure to sales. The $11,000 figure divided by 180,000 gives a percentage of 6.1 percent. This percentage is sometimes called the *operating ratio*. Another way of evaluating the profit is to compare it to the amount of investment (ROI). Exhibit 9-2 shows an investment or owners' equity of $31,000. Dividing this into $11,000 gives a percentage of 35.5. And instead of the owner's equity, the total investment (ROAM) may be used. In this case it would be our profit of $11,000 divided by the total assets of $87,000, or 12.6 percent. If information is available, other figures to be calculated include sales per employee, sales per seat, and average check.

The Balance Sheet

A balance sheet is divided into two main parts (sometimes called sides). The asset side consists of those items owned by the corporation that have value. These are divided into *current assets* which are cash assets and other assets that should be fairly easy to turn into cash such as accounts receivable and inventory; and *fixed assets* which are permanent ones not often sold during the course of business, such as real estate and equipment.

The other side of the balance sheet consists of liabilities or debts or obligations owed by the operation and equity. Liabilities are further divided into *current liabilities*, which are those due and payable within one year, and *fixed* or *long-term liabilities*, which are due and payable after the next year. A debt such as a bank loan would have the part that was due within twelve months classified as current and the remainder classified as long term. Equity is the ownership of the business.

The total assets must equal the total liabilities and equity, to balance the balance sheet. This can be expressed in the fundamental equation, $A = L + E$, or assets equal liabilities plus equity.

Exhibit 9-2 shows the balance sheet for an operation as of December 31. The figures are only for that day; some may change considerably from day to day.

Looking at Exhibit 9-2, we can see the business is owned by a single proprietor because the owner's equity is not expressed in shares of stocks or a partnership's interest. The balance sheet reflects the *liquidity* (or the operation's ability to pay its bills) and the *solvency* (or the operation's excess of assets over liabilities). The most familiar liquidity ratio is the *current ratio*, or current assets over current liabilities. In this case, current assets are $21,000 and current liabilities are $19,000 which yields a current ratio of 1.1:1.0. In many industries a current ratio of 2:1, or two dollars of current assets compared to every dollar of current liabilities, is considered desirable. But, current assets are usually less in the hospitality field because the inventory turns over quickly, because a much lower amount in relation to sales is required than most retail operations, and because accounts receivable are also low. Current assets are defined as cash or those assets readily convertible into cash; current liabilities are those liabilities that must be paid within one year.

Another liquidity ratio is the *acid test ratio*, or cash, accounts receivable, and marketable securities divided by current liabilities. This operation has no accounts receivable or marketable securities, but it does have a cash amount of $16,500. This yields a ratio of 0.7:1.0.

We can see from the statement that such fixed assets, such as equipment, furnishings, air conditioning, and the building, are all reduced by depreciation. Each of these assets normally depreciates over the years, and this depreciation should be considered an expense even though it does not immediately absorb cash. Since the accumulated depreciation amounts are relatively low, one might assume the assets are relatively new. Inventory figures for food and beverages can be analyzed by finding the inventory turnover which is dividing average inventory into costs

Exhibit 9–2.
Typical Balance
Sheet

BALANCE SHEET
As of December 31, 19___
ASSETS

Current Assets

Cash

Cash on Hand	$ 500	
Cash in Bank	16,000	$16,500

Inventory

Food	2,500	
Beverage	1,000	
Supplies	200	3,700

Deposit with Utilities		200
Prepaid Insurance		600
Total Current Assets		$21,000

Fixed Assets

Equipment	15,000	
Less Accumulated Depreciation	1,500	13,500
Furniture	10,000	
Less Accumulated Depreciation	1,000	9,000
Air Conditioning	5,000	
Less Accumulated Depreciation	1,000	4,000
Building	30,000	
Less Accumulated Depreciation	1,500	28,500
Liquor License		3,000
Land		8,000
Total Fixed Assets		$66,000

TOTAL ASSETS	$87,000

(Exhibit 9-2 continued opposite.)

of goods sold. The cost of goods sold for food was $40,800 (as shown on the income statement) and the inventory figure for food was shown as $2500. This would give an inventory turnover figure of 16.3 times per year which is very low.

Ratio Analysis   An income statement provides the profit or loss for a period and a balance sheet shows the financial condition of the enterprise as of a particular date. How are the figures on these statements evaluated? It is usu-

Exhibit 9–2,
Continued

BALANCE SHEET (continued)
As of December 31, 19___
LIABILITIES

Current Liabilities

Trade Accounts Payable	$ 7,000	
Accrued Wages Payable	5,000	
Employee Taxes Payable	1,500	
Mortgage Payable	1,000	
Notes Payable Bank	2,000	
Equipment Contract Payable	2,500	
Total Current Liabilities		$19,000

Long-Term Liabilities

Notes Payable Bank	$ 9,000	
Equipment Contract	10,000	
Mortgage	18,000	
Total Long-Term Liabilities		$37,000
		$56,000

Capital

Owner's Equity 1/1/___	$30,000	
Earnings during 19___	11,000	
Drawings	(10,000)	
Owners Equity 12/31/___		$31,000

TOTAL LIABILITIES $87,000

ally easier to change the amount figures into ratios. These ratios can be compared with past performance, desired performance, other operations, and date supplied by hospitality accounting firms and associations. Some ratios often used in foodservice establishments are in Exhibit 9-3. A foodservice operation may often use other measurements, such as the average selling price per meal served or the sales per seat. Some specialized ratios for hotels without supporting data are given in Exhibit 9-3.

Financing an Enterprise

Probably the most important part of financial management is securing the funds for the establishment and operation of an enterprise (see

RATIOS	EXPRESSIONS/EQUATIONS	COMMENTS
Profitability Operating Ratio	$\dfrac{\text{Profit*}}{\text{Sales}} = \dfrac{\$11,000}{\$180,000} = 6.1\%$	This ratio shows what percentage of each sales dollar is returned in profit.
Return on Investment (ROI)	$\dfrac{\text{Profit*}}{\text{Net worth (or investment)}} = \dfrac{\$11,000}{\$31,000} = 35.4\%$	This ratio shows what return the owners are getting on their own money invested in the business.
Return on Assets Managed (ROAM) (*or* Return on Total Assets)	$\dfrac{\text{Profit*}}{\text{Total Assets}} = \dfrac{\$11,000}{\$87,000} = 12.6\%$	The more assets a manager has available, theoretically the greater the profit should be.
Liquidity Current Ratio	$\dfrac{\text{Current Assets}}{\text{Current Liabilities}} = \dfrac{\$21,000}{\$19,000} = 1.1:1.0$	A measure of short-term solvency indicating how the obligations to short-term creditors are covered by cash assets or assets expected to be converted to cash.
Quick Ratio (*or* Acid Test)	$\dfrac{\text{Current Assets less Inventories and Deposits}}{\text{Current Liabilities}} = \dfrac{\$16,500}{\$19,000} = 0.7:1.0$	Another measure of short-term solvency. This is not as important in the hospitality industries as in most others since the largest inventory is food which is converted into cash much faster than the inventories of other industries.

Activity (Inventory Turnover)

Food Inventory Turnover

$$\frac{\text{Food Cost of Goods Sold}}{\text{Average Food Inventory}} = \frac{\$40,800}{\$2,500} = 16.3 \text{ times}$$

Beverage Inventory Turnover

$$\frac{\text{Beverage Cost of Goods Sold}}{\text{Average Beverage Inventory}} = \frac{\$18,000}{\$1,000} = 15 \text{ times}$$

These ratios indicate how fast the inventories are turned into cash. Normally the higher the ratio, the better. Low turnover can indicate excessive inventories and inventories stocked with items that cannot be readily used.

Activity (Cost Percentage)

Food Cost Percentage

$$\frac{\text{Food Cost}}{\text{Food Sales}} = \frac{\$40,800}{\$120,000} = 34.0\%$$

Beverage Cost Percentage

$$\frac{\text{Beverage Cost}}{\text{Beverage Sales}} = \frac{\$18,000}{\$60,000} = 30.0\%$$

Labor Cost Percentage

$$\frac{\text{Labor Cost (including fringe benefits)}}{\text{Sales (and other income)}} = \frac{\$70,800}{\$181,800} = 39.3\%$$

The lower these cost percentages, the higher the profit percentage can be. They are helpful in indicating if these cost percentages are excessive or appropriate.

Leverage

Debt to Total Asset

$$\frac{\text{Total Debt}}{\text{Total Assets}} = \frac{\$56,000}{\$87,000} = 0.64:1.0$$

Debt to Equity

$$\frac{\text{Total Debt}}{\text{Total Equity}} = \frac{\$56,000}{\$36,000} = 1.8:1.0$$

These ratios indicate how the operation is using debt or new equity money to help finance the operation. This is sometimes referred to as trading on the equity. It also indicates if debt is excessive for the amount of equity.

*N.B.: These are usually expressed as profit after taxes, but in the interest of simplicity we have not considered income taxes.

Exhibit 9-3. Ratios for Analyzing Hospitality Financial Statements
(Using Figures from Exhibits 9–1 and 9–2.)

RATIOS	EXPRESSIONS	COMMENTS
Percentage of Occupancy	$$\dfrac{\text{Number of guest rooms sold}}{\text{Number of guest rooms available}}$$	The higher the percentage of occupancy, the higher the room sales, which should convert into a higher profit.
Percentage of Double Occupancy	$$\dfrac{\text{Number of guests less number of rooms sold}}{\text{Number of rooms available}}$$	Multiple occupancy of guest rooms usually commands a higher rate. Usually additional costs are less than the incurred rate, so double occupancy is more profitable. Thus, a higher rate of double occupancy is desirable.
Average Room Rate	$$\dfrac{\text{Room sales}}{\text{Number of rooms sold}}$$	The higher the amount obtained for each room sale, the more profitable the operation. This figure is also related to the average construction cost for hotel rooms.

Exhibit 9-4. Common Hotel Ratios

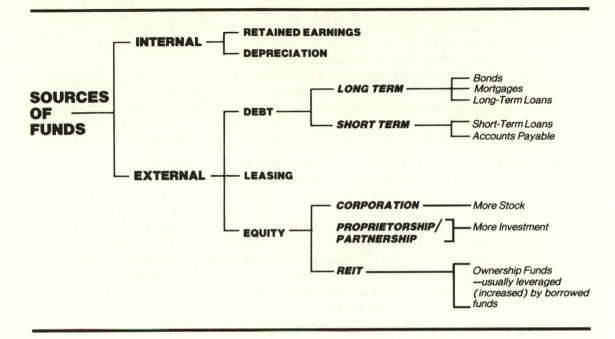

Exhibit 9–5. Sources of Funds

Exhibit 9-5). In considering a new hospitality enterprise one would probably order a feasibility study which, among other things, would show anticipated earnings from the establishment. There should also be a financial plan that would indicate from where capital funds are to be secured, what mix of capital from debt and equity is desirable, and how debt sources of capital will be repaid. Coordinated with the capital financing plan would be a cash flow plan showing inflows and outflows of money; a capital investment plan, which shows when large financing is required; and short-term (a year or less) cash budgets. We are primarily interested here in the capital financing plan.

Debt and Equity Two areas from which an enterprise can receive funds are: *equity sources* or *debt sources.* Equity funds involve ownership in the business. A proprietor or sole owner of a business may increase his equity by putting more of his own money into the business or by not withdrawing as much money out of business as it earns in profits. Partners in a business can do the same thing, and they may either bring in additional money or allow earnings to remain in the business to increase their equity. A corporation is owned by the stockholders. The equity in a corporation is increased by selling more stock (if sold to people other than present stockholders, this additional stock dilutes the interest of the present stockholders in the business.) Or, corporations, like other businesses, can allow profits to remain in the enterprise rather than to be paid out in dividends. This is internal financing.

Debt financing involves borrowing money from a source that does not acquire an equity interest in the business through his loans. Sometimes debt financing can be converted into an equity arrangement, but normally debt financing is the lending of money by nonowners. It is also possible for stockholders to make loans to a corporation.

Equity Sources

As previously mentioned, equity sources can include proprietors, partners, and stockholders. Proprietors and partners simply use their own money for the capital financing. In the financing of those hsopitality establishments that involve some real estate, like hotels, motor inns, or condominiums, specialized arrangements for the stockholders may be followed. For example, a syndicate may be formed. A syndicate often consists of a general partner and several limited partners. Although the arrangements vary widely, the general partner may put in relatively little money of his own but be repaid in stock for his organizing efforts. A limited partner can take little part in the actual operation but supplies funds. His loss in the endeavor is limited to the amount of his investment.

REITs or *Real Estate Investment Trusts* came into prominence in the 1960s. There was increased attention on real estate investment as a hedge against inflation. A primary vehicle for this was the REIT, or a mutual fund of real estate loans. The shareholders had the same tax advantages as mutual funds. As long as an REIT disburses 90 percent of its profits, it is only taxed on its retained earnings and not on earnings paid out to shareholders. The stockholders of course must pay taxes on their dividend income.

Most REITs are mortgage trusts which raise money from the public for an equity base. With this base they can further borrow from banks or other financial sources. A great deal of money was raised this way for the construction of hotels, motels, condominiums, and apartments. For some years a very satisfactory return was provided. However, overbuilding and ill-planned projects were financed. During 1973–1975 the REITs faced other problems such as energy crises, decreased travel, construction cost overruns, increased interests costs, and tighter money supplies. This caused many REIT projects to run into difficulty and many REITs to incur financial distress.

An REIT used as a tax shelter often appeals to people in a high tax bracket. Taxable profits from the enterprise are offset by legitimate tax deductions of depreciation and interest payments. Thus, though they pay limited taxes on current income from the operation, the value of their equity increases. Taxes on the appreciation of the equity can be figured on a capital gains basis, which is normally lower for one in a high tax bracket. It sometimes happens that people involved in building an establishment will take stock for partial or full payment of their services. If an architect or contractor, for example, is willing to do this, the initial cash required for erecting the facilities would, of course, be reduced proportionately.

Debt Financing Debt financing involves the use of someone else's money to start, help, or expand an operation that different people own. Using borrowed funds for expansion is sometimes known as *leverage* or *trading on the equity*. If an operation costs two hundred thousand dollars, and the owners put in fifty thousand of their own and borrow the balance, they are leveraging 80 percent of the cost and supplying 20 percent. In 100 percent leverage projects, all the financing comes from borrowed money, and no equity financing is involved. If the business is profitable and the owners can readily pay off interest and debt amortization (or payment of the principle amounts of the loan), a great deal of money can be made by using leverage. The borrowed money was used to provide resources that produced more profit than the equity resources alone could. On the other hand, in a high leverage project, the debt payments must be made before any return to the owners. Thus, if the cash flow is unsatisfactory, the owners may lose what they have invested in the project.

Sources for the capital structure may be different than sources of funds for short-term or intermediate financing. Capital financing usually involves large amounts of money committed for long periods. Some types of financial institutions avoid this long term commitment. Capital financing in the hospitality industry is generally of a real property nature that may involve land, buildings, and major pieces of equipment with a relatively long life span. A mortgage, or the pledge of a designated property as security for the loan, is often used to secure capital financing in the hospitality industry. Primary sources of these mortgage funds are life insurance companies, pension funds, and REITs. Insurance companies and pension funds generate large amounts of cash as policyholders or members pay premiums in expectation of receiving payments on death or retirement. In the interim, the life insurance companies and pension funds invest the money so that they can get a return on it. Still other possible sources of mortgages may be private investors or, in some cases, savings and loan associations. It is not uncommon for the seller of a hospitality property to give a mortgage loan for the difference between the selling price and the downpayment. Or the seller may give a second or "junior" mortgage to make up the difference between the selling price and the downpayment and any other financing that may have been secured. Having the seller provide mortgage money may be very helpful to both the seller and the buyer. If the seller does not need the money for other purposes, the mortgage can constitute a worthwhile investment with the property as security. From the buyer's standpoint it may be the most satisfactory financing available.

Bonds are another type of long-range debt financing. They constitute long-term promissory notes issued in round amounts like $100 or $1000. Bonds are for a specific denomination or amount, have a definite maturity date or date when they must be repaid, and have a specific interest rate to be paid the bondholders. There may also be provisions for accumulating money to pay off the bonds (this arrangement is called a *sinking fund*) or allowing the bonds to be converted into other securities.

An *indenture* is a formal agreement between the issuer of a bond and the bondholders that spells out the different facets of the particular obligation.

A *mortgage bond* is secured by real property or real estate. If payments are not made according to the terms, the property can be foreclosed and sold for payment of the bonds.

A *debenture* is a long-term debt instrument that is not secured by any mortgage on any specific asset. It is secured, instead, by the general credit of the borrower. In other words, in times of financial distress the bondholders along with any other creditors have access to any assets that have not been specifically pledged.

Types of Mortgages

A *first* mortgage indicates that the holder of the mortgage (or the lenders) have the security of the property in case payments are not made. Theoretically, the property should be worth more than the amount of the mortgaged loan so that the investment is relatively safe. In the 1920s, many hotels were built with the hotel property acting as security for mortgage and bonds. During the Depression, when many hotels experienced financial distress, the mortgages and bonds were worth only a small part of their face value. The hotel properties themselves became worth only a small portion of their cost and represented very little security.

In addition to the security of the assets pledged against the loan, a bondholder will probably want assurance that there will be enough money coming in to pay off the mortgage or the bond's interest and to amortize their principle. One rule of thumb is that operating income should be *twice* the amount of these payments. In other words, even if planned income were cut by 50 percent, enough money for the payments would remain.

A *junior* mortgage is subordinate in security to the first mortgage. It is not paid before the prior mortgage holders, so it is not as safe as a first mortgage. Consequently, junior mortgages usually have higher rates of interest and are written for comparatively short periods.

A *guaranteed* mortgage can be used by a hospitality chain. Money is secured for a new hotel, but no specific mortgage is placed on that property. There is, however, a general mortgage on the real assets of the chain.

Another method of capital financing sometimes employed by hospitality establishments is the *ground lease*. If one is building a hotel and one need not pay for the land, one needs less money. In effect, the owner of the land will be leasing or lending the land to the builder of the hotel. Of course, he will charge a price. The gound lease is not ideal, but it may be utilized when developers are very short of funds. Normally the owner of the land has first priority on payments in the event of financial trouble. Lenders hesitate to give a mortgage on a hotel building when the owner of the land has the first right of payment. To circumvent this reluctance, a *subordinated ground lease* may be employed. In this situation, the owner of the land "subordinates" his normal right to another lender or, in effect, gives up his priority for payment if the property must be sold to pay debts.

Differences between Borrowed and Equity Funds

Not surprisingly, there are both advantages and disadvantages to using borrowed or equity funds in a business, and they should all be analyzed before one or another type of capital financing is chosen.

In a corporation, the directors have no obligation to pay a return on equity funds. They must, of course, have to pay the interest on borrowed money. But stockholders have no legal right to require a return on their investment. (Holders of preferred stock are, however, normally paid before the holders of common stock.)

There is no due date when equity funds must be repaid. Bonds or mortgages, on the other hand, have a definite date when the principle falls due. Equity holders do not, by law, have to have their principle amounts repaid.

By using borrowed funds, equity holders can retain control and management of the enterprise. On the other hand, bringing in new equity money dilutes their equity position. (However, it is not uncommon for lenders to place limitations on an operation as a condition of the loan.)

If borrowed funds are used and profits result, the difference between the profit and the cost of the borrowed money goes to the stockholders. Unless there is some unusual arrangement, the owners do not have to share their profits with debt holders. The debt holders receive only the specified interest and the amortization of the principle. Sometimes, however, lenders require an equity interest as a condition of their loan.

Interest payments to debt holders are a deduction from taxable income and reduce the amount of taxes that must be paid. Dividends to stockholders are paid only after taxes have been deducted from profits. If debt financing is used, the federal government may take less money in

A	B	C	D	E	F	G	H
YEAR ONE	PROJECTED CASH FLOW	FIRST MORTGAGES PAYMENTS	EQUIPMENT CONTRACTS PAYABLE	INTEREST ON DEBENTURES	INCOME TAXES	CAPITAL REPLACEMENTS	NET CASH FLOW
	$320,000	85,000	75,000	40,000	50,000	20,000	50,000
10	$320,000	85,000	—	40,000	60,000	30,000	105,000

Exhibit 9–6. Financing Plan Format

taxes and leave more for the corporation owners than if equity financing is used—assuming the same amount of money is paid to the stockholders as to the debt holders.

Financing Feasibility

To determine the financing feasibility of a project, one should draw up a financing plan to see if the anticipated revenues (from the financial feasibility study) cover the projected capital costs. Exhibit 9-6 shows the format for such a financing plan. Column A represents the years, and year 1 and 10 have been abstracted here. Column B shows the projected cash flow. Since depreciation is not a cash expense it has not been subtracted from the cash flow. Column C shows the payments on the first mortgage bonds, which are $85,000 a year. Column D shows that some of the equipment has been secured with a conditional sales contract, and repayments for year 1 are $75,000. These agreements usually span a relatively short time. Here, the contract has been paid off before Year 10. Column E shows the interest on debentures. In this operation, the financing included a first mortgage, an equipment contract payable, and debenture bonds. This interest will be paid until the maturity of the bonds, and the bonds themselves will be either paid off or refinanced. Column F shows the income taxes. Deducted from profit for the purpose of calculating income tax are depreciation expenses and interest expenses. Column H shows the net cash flow or amount available after all capital expenses and taxes have been paid. This is the "cushion of safety" for the investors. The larger the net cash flow, the greater the chance that all cash outflows can be covered.

Short-Term and Intermediate-Term Financial Help

An operation may, of course, want to borrow money for noncapital purposes. A seasonal resort may want money to finance expenses before the opening of the season. A restaurant may want money to increase its inventory or to make noncapital improvements. A hospital with a large number of slow accounts receivable may want to borrow money until the accounts receivable are paid. An operation may need more money for working capital which is defined as the difference between the current assets (assets readily changed into cash) and current liabilities (liabilities to be paid within one year). *Short-term loans* are those that must be paid back within three years; *intermediate credit* extends from three to ten years; and *long-term credit* extends over at least ten years. Different sources of financial assistance exist for short-term and intermediate loans. Banks which may not be interested in long-term loans may be very interested in making short-term or intermediate loans. Purveyors and suppliers may extend credit when they deliver merchandise, in which case they do not demand that the bills be paid immediately. Assets may be leased rather than purchased, which in effect amounts to credit. Some purveyors also provide credit to hospitality firms by making direct loans. Of course the purveyor who does not demand immediate payment for bills or make loans creates a strong obligation in the operation to buy from him. In such circumstances his prices may not be the lowest.

The government can also provide short and intermediate term credit through its Small Business Administration. It can also provide long-term credit to small firms through the Small Business Administration Investment Corporation. Moreover, some government financing programs are specifically for minority entrepreneurs.

Basis for Lending

Loans are usually made on the basis of the *four C's: character, capital, collateral,* and the *capacity to repay.* Normally one would not want to lend money to a person with a reputation for avoiding payment of his obligations. Thus, lenders often investigate the character of the owners applying for loans. A person of perfectly fine character may because of prior financial difficulties find it difficult to secure new financing.

Capital refers to the general financial position of the firm especially the net worth of the enterprise in relation to debt. The more resources the borrower has in relation to his debt, the more secure that debt will be. (It could always be at least partially paid off through a sale of the resources.)

Collateral refers to specific assets offered as a pledge or security for the debt. If the debt is not paid, the debtor can use the pledged assets to pay off the loan. A car loan, for example, may be secured by the car itself. Loans that are secured by collateral may often carry a lower interest rate than unsecured loans.

Capacity is the apparent ability to pay. Although a lender may make a loan if it is secured by assets with at least the amount of the loan, normally he would rather see the loan repaid by income generated by the loan itself. If a borrower can demonstrate to a lender that he will earn sufficient income to pay off a loan, it makes the loan more feasible.

A fourth "C" might be conditions. Severe economic and money conditions may affect whether a specific loan will or will not be granted at a particular time. If money is tight, a borrower who usually has little trouble securing funds may be unable to so.

Applying for a Loan

Unless you are well-known to a lending institution there are usually definite steps before securing a loan. The lending institution will probably want to see a balance sheet that shows capital and possible collateral for the loan. It may also want past income statement—statements that show past financial results. And it may ask to see pro forma statements (statements that show what you expect to happen in the future of your business). Anticipated inflows and outflows may also be helpful since the money available for the repayment of the loan is not necessarily the same as the anticipated profit. You should indicate any specific collateral available for the loan. And you should specify the exact amount of the loan you want and the exact purposes to which it will be applied. If the income statement and cash budgets do not indicate how the loan can be repaid, calculations should show this. If the business is owned by a proprietor or partnership, financial statements for the proprietor and for each partner may be required. If a business is a corporation with only a few stockholders, financial statements for the major stockholders can be helpful.

A lending institution will probably conduct an investigation of both the company and the principal. They may secure a Dun and Bradstreet report. Dun and Bradstreet provides a history of the operation and of the principals or major participants. The report will include known financing transactions, a history of fires or bankruptcies, and the credit experience of firms selling to the company, among many other possible topics. A bank may have the loan application evaluated either by the loan officer or by a loan committee. A reliable business that borrows often from one bank tends to establish a strong bond with that bank. In this case, the bank (or lending institution) may be able to offer valuable financial advice besides simply lending money.

Small Business Administration Loans

The federal government has established programs that provide funds for small businesses. Some of these programs are of particular interest in hospitality. Government loans are usually made through the Small Business Administration (SBA). The SBA defines a small hospitality business as one that is independently owned and operated, is not dominant in its field, and meets the usual employment and sales standards. The present standard separating a small from a large business is five million dollars per year.

SBA financing does not really compete with private financing. Actually it facilitates private financing by participating with local banks and lending institutions. If no other financing is available, the SBA may advance all the money. In addition, the SBA can guarantee up to 90 percent or up to 350 thousand dollars of a loan made by a bank to a small firm. The SBA may also promote private financing by advancing part of the funds rather than guaranteeing the bank's loan. At the present, the SBAs share of an immediate participation may not exceed one hundred fifty thousand dollars. Through different programs, the SBA can furnish funds for increased working capital, expansion, or even the inauguration of a new business.

The SBA can provide certain specialized loans. Its Surety Bond Program, for example, is designed to make the bonding process more accessible to small contractors who have found funding difficult to obtain. Emergency Energy Shortage Loans (EESL) are available to assist or refinance the existing indebtedness of eligible small businesses seriously affected by a shortage of fuel. (Interstate hotels and motels occasionally fall into this category.) Disaster Loans can help disaster victims repair physical damage or overcome economic injury from storms, floods, earthquakes, and other catastrophes.

Interest Costs
Interest pays for borrowed money. Interest rates vary not only by the interest percentage the lender charges but also by how the rates are calculated. Either can greatly affect the actual amount of interest paid. The interest rate percentage may vary with the size of the loan, the security behind the loan, the length of the loan, and how "good a customer" the borrower is to the lending institution. Most short-term interest rates are based at least partially on the *prime rate* or the rate charged to the largest and most secure borrowers. Therefore, a prime rate is the most desirable rate. As the loan becomes less attractive to the institution, the rate normally increases.

An *add-on interest rate* calculates the amount of interest and adds it to the principal. This amount is divided by the number of payments to determine the amount of each payment, which will include the amortization of the principal, and interest. The interest cost of $1200 at 12 percent is $144, which is added to the twelve hundred to produce a total of $1344. If payments are made in twelve equal installments over a year, each payment is $112. But, the average amount of money the lender has outstanding during the year is not $1200, but only $600. Interest of $144 is paid for this average amount of $600 making an effective interest rate of 24 percent rather than 12 percent.

The *discount method* of calculating interest involves subtracting the amount of the interest from the principal when the loan money is transferred to the borrower. In our previous example, the $144 would be subtracted from the $1200 and the borrower would receive only $1,056. But $1200 would have to be paid back in twelve equal installments during the year. This would represent an installment payment of $100 per month. Notice, however, that the average amount the lending institution lent to the borrower is $528, and for this $144 is paid in interest. Thus, the effective interest cost is more than 27 percent. The fairest and most accurate interest appears when interest is paid on the amount of the unpaid balance—usually every thirty days.

An additional cost of borrowing money may be incurred when a bank requires a compensating balance. In this situation, the bank stipulates that a certain percentage (like 10 or 20 percent) of the loan be kept on deposit. The borrower does not have the use of this money, but the lender does. Thus, the borrower must pay interest on money he cannot use, which effectively raises interest costs.

Leasing Leasing is yet another means of financing for the hospitality industry. By leasing assets, you gain the use of those assets, but you are not required to lay out substantial immediate money for them. In effect, the leasing company finances the purchase. Some types of leasing have been used by the hospitality industry for years. Linen rentals, for example, have been around a long time. A big step in hospitality leasing took place when television sets were first installed in hotels and motels. In many cases the owners did not want immediately to pay large sums for the sets. Nor did they want the bother of servicing them or disposing of worn out sets. Television suppliers began to make leasing arrangements with the hospitality owners so that the TV sets could be installed in a hotel or motel without any of the maintenance problems accruing to the hotel itself. Today, a wide variety of assets are leased, including furniture, kitchen equipment, linens, and vehicles. There can be advantages in leasing rather than buying equipment. A small cash outlay is one. The hospitality operation can use the funds it saves for other purposes. Or perhaps it can borrow only limited funds for the equipment it desires.

If the leased equipment requires service, the leasing may be able to provide better service than the hospitality organization. A car dealer can provide mechanical service comparatively cheaply and may pass some of this savings on to the lessee. Nor does the lessee have to worry about obsolescence or selling problems since the property is owned by the lessor. Some hospitals lease sophisticated equipment simply because they know it will be obsolete in a relatively short time. There can also be tax advantages in leasing since the costs of leasing are deductible expenses in calculating taxes. If the equipment is purchased, the money comes from earnings on which taxes have already been paid or with money that has to be borrowed. The interest charges on money that has to be borrowed and the depreciation costs on assets purchased are also tax deductible items, but leasing the equipment may provide even greater deductions. Although the gross amount of money paid out for leasing may be higher than if you purchased equipment with the cash on hand or borrowed money to buy the equipment, the tax considerations may make the net cost lower.

Leasing does, however, have some disadvantages. Lease costs may still be higher than other means of financing. Also, once a lease is signed it is hard to change, thus you may sacrifice a degree of flexibility. For example, you may desire newer equipment but may have to pay a premium to change the terms on the equipment you presently lease.

Taxation

Taxes are loved by few but are a fact of life. And as Justice Holmes said, "Taxes are what we pay for a civilized society." Taxation is a complex, specialized subject, and the types of taxes and the various tax bases seem limited only by the imagination. In this section we will discuss some of the general aspects of taxation and their effects on a hospitality enterprise.

Taxes in the Form of Business Organization

The chief forms of business organization are a *proprietorship* (in which the business is entirely owned by one person); a *partnership* (in which the business is owned by two or more partners); and a *corporation* (which is an artificial entity created by law and owned by the stockholders). One stockholder could own all the stock but the enterprise would still be a separate corporation. Income taxes are, of course, levied against the profits of an organization.

Assume a person owns a restaurant in a proprietorship form. Profits from the restaurant could be added to any other personal income eligible for taxation, and the proprietor would pay taxes on the total. In this country individual tax rates are progressive, which means the tax rate increases as the amount of taxable income increases. A restauranteur making a great deal of money from his restaurant and from other sources may find himself in a high tax bracket and might desire to have his different money-making ventures taxed separately at lower rates.

If the restaurant were owned by a partnership, the income each partner received from it would be added to all their other taxable income to determine their tax bracket and their tax payment rate. As of 1978 a corporation pays a fixed tax rate of 17 percent on the first $25,000 of income; 20 percent of the next $25,000; 40 percent of the next; and 46 percent on income over $100,000.

The owners of a restaurant who find themselves in high tax brackets might be eager to use the corporate form of organization for tax purposes if they find the corporate rates lower than their ordinary income rates. But, the stockholders or owners of the corporation can suffer from double taxation. The corporation itself pays taxes on its earnings, and when the earnings are transferred to the shareholders in the form of dividends, the shareholders must then again pay taxes on this income.

Subchapter S corporation. To allow small organizations the advantages of a corporate form of organization and also to avoid double taxation on shareholders, Congress has established a *subchapter S corporation.* Most of its income must come from operations and not from such passive investment income sources as rents, royalties, and interest. And all of the stockholders (there can originally be no more than ten) must agree to the election of the subchapter S. With the subchapter S the stockholders can add their dividends to their regular income and have them taxed at their regular income tax rates. No corporation tax rate is involved.

Capital gains and capital losses. An operation is taxed on two types of income. One is *ordinary income,* or profits and losses from operations. The other is *capital gains,* or profits realized from increases in the market value of any assets that are not part of the owner's stock and trade or that he does not regularly offer for sale. A capital loss on the other hand would be the loss realized from a decline in the market value of these assets. Consider capital gains and a restaurant. If it were possible to have no income reported with all excess income over expense being used to improve the restaurant, no taxes would be paid. If no dividends were paid out, no one would pay taxes on dividends. If, however, the restaurant increases in value and the restauranteur sells it to someone else, the profit on the sale is a capital gain. Of course, the restauranteur will pay the taxes at the lower capital gain rates rather than at the operating rate. In calculating capital gains, depreciation which has been used to increase cost and thus decrease taxes must be considered.

Depreciation   Depreciation is a very important factor in calculating taxable income. After an asset is purchased it normally begins to depreciate or reduce in value through wear and tear and obsolescence. This reduction in the value of the asset is a cost of doing business and may be subtracted from operating profit in determining taxable income. Although it is an obvious cost, depreciation is unusual in that it is a noncash cost. You do not have to pay out money as an asset depreciates even though the asset will eventually have to be replaced with a money outflow. For tax purposes, it is desirable to show as much depreciation as possible since it reduces taxes even while the operation retains use of the money until the equipment must be replaced.

Straight-line depreciation, a method of calculating depreciation, is the cost of the asset minus any anticipated salvage value divided by the number of years of anticipated life. If an asset costs $5000, is expected to last four years, and is expected to have a salvage value of $1000 at the end of the four years, the straight-line depreciation would be the original cost of $5000 minus the salvage value of $1000 or $4000. Divided by 4, the $4000 yields an annual straight-line depreciation rate of $1000 per year.

Accelerated depreciation, or faster depreciation, permits more depreciation in the early years (but no more than the total amount of depreciation one would ordinarily be entitled to). One ought to be allowed to depreciate an asset faster whose value may decline rapidly because of advances in technology or those assets that wear out prematurely because of high usage. The time value of money also enters into accelerated depreciation. Most operations would rather receive the more immediate tax benefits of accelerated depreciation than the promised tax benefits later. A dollar saved in taxes today is worth more than the promise of a dollar saved in taxes some years from now.

Accelerated depreciation was partly responsible for the great boom in building motels and motor inns that had its beginnings in the 1950s. At that time a person could build a motor inn and, by taking accelerated depreciation, pay relatively little taxes on the profits. When his depreciation allowance was used up, however, and the profits were liable to be taxed at a heavy rate because of no offsetting depreciation, the owner could sell the facility. Then he could use this money to start another operation and start the cycle over again. (The law has since been changed somewhat to encourage more ownership responsibility.)

The two methods of figuring accelerated depreciation are called *declining balance* and *sum of the digits*. A 150 percent declining balance on the previous example would be one and one-half times the normal depreciation rate. The straight-line depreciation was 25 percent and one and one-half times this would be 37.5 percent; therefore, the depreciation for the first year would be 37.5 percent of $4000, or $1500. Depreciation the second year would be 37.5 percent of the remaining depreciation ($4000 minus $1500 which equals $2500), or $938. Since the double declining balance will not allow the taxpayer to recover the total costs, it is necessary during the lifetime of the asset to switch to the straight-line method. No more than the total depreciated value of the asset, however, can be taken over the life of the asset.

The sum of the digits method involves adding all the digits in the number of the total years of depreciation. For four years, this would be four plus three plus two plus one or ten. The first year's depreciation would be four-tenths of the depreciated amounts of $4000 or $1600. The second year would be three-tenths or $1200; the third year would be two-tenths or $800; and the last year would be one-tenth or $400. Total depreciation would amount to the $4000. In the sum of the digits method, depreciation is higher in the early years compared to the straight-line, but in the later years straight-line depreciation increases.

Investment Tax Credit

A tax incentive first established in 1962 but since amended, suspended, reenacted, repealed, and re-reenacted is the so-called *investment tax credit.* Although its current status should always be investigated (that status varies with the political winds) the investment tax credit can provide significant tax savings. It provides a direct tax credit of up to ten percent of any qualified investment. The investment must be in tangible personal property or certain real property that has application to business activities or operations entered into for profit. Assume an operation has a tax payable of $20,000 and an appropriate tax credit of $5000. It need pay only $15,000 in taxes. Since the tax credit is deducted from taxes liable rather than from gross income it is particularly attractive.

SUMMARY

Finance is one of the major functions of any enterprise. Originally, finance was relatively simple, concerning itself with the acquisition of funds and the accounting aspects of the business. The liquidity or the process of turning assets into cash (having enough money to pay current debts) and solvency (having more assets than liabilities) were crucial.

But financial management has changed considerably since the Second World War. Tight money and depressed stock prices then made raising outside money considerably more difficult. This situation led to cash flow analysis, cash budgeting, and more internal generation of money from the business rather than from external sources. In the 1960s, the internal utilization of funds and the leveraging of them with borrowed additional funds became increasingly important, along with such new ways of financing as franchising, leasing, and sale lease back.

A hospitality manager must be able to interpret and evaluate the financial statements regarding his operation. Financial accounting involves the preparation of statements that may be used by the enterprise itself and by others to evaluate that enterprise. Managerial accounting furnishes information to management for its planning, decision-making, and controlling. The two primary financial statements are the Income Statement, which shows how much money an operation made or lost over a specified period, and the Balance Sheet, which shows the financial status of the operation as of a particular date. These statements can employ percentages or ratios. Profitability ratios include the operating ratio, the Return on Investment, and the Return on Assets Managed. Liquidity ratios include the current ratio and the "acid test." Activity ratios include food and beverage inventory turnovers, food cost percentages, and labor cost percentages. Leverage ratios includes debt to total assets and debt to equity.

The two main sources of financing are debt and equity. Debt financing involves borrowing money from others. Equity financing involves bringing in more ownership money. Debts, of course, must be repaid and interest must be paid on them. There is no such obligation for equity financing, although increased equity financing increases the number that share in the profit and can dilute the ownership of the business. Financing may be long-term, where equity or long-term debt is involved, or it could be short-term, such as a seasonal need to borrow money for noncapital expenses.

Credit is extended on the basis of "the four C's." These are the character of the borrower; the capital the borrower has invested in the business; the collateral, or specific assets, that are used as a pledge or security; and the capacity, or ability of the business to generate funds to repay the debt. A fifth "C" is the prevailing economic conditions—the general availability of credit during that particular time. Money may also be available from the Federal Government through the Small Business Administration.

The cost of borrowing money is called interest, and interest rates vary not only by the interest percentage rate itself, but also by how these rates are calculated. Most short-term interest rates are based on the prime rate or the rate charged the largest and most secure borrowers. An add-on interest rate calculates the amount of interest and adds it to the principal. A discount method of calculating interest subtracts the amount of interest from the principal with the borrower receiving only the net amount while paying back the full amount. Add-on and discount interest calculations are generally higher than interest paid on the unpaid balance each month. An additional interest cost may be incurred in a requirement for compensating balance where the lending institution stipulates that a certain percentage of the loan must be kept on deposit while the borrower pays interest on it even though he does not have the use of it.

Leasing has become popular as a means of hospitality financing. Leasing provides a way of supplying assets when there is no money to purchase them. Service arrangements for equipment that requires servicing may also be incorporated into the lease arrangement. Since lease payments represent a tax deduction, there can be a tax savings in financing compared to purchase for cash or borrowing where the deductions are depreciation and interest costs.

Taxation is also a financial management concern. The two broad types of federal taxation include taxes on ordinary income and capital gain taxes on profits realized from increases in the market value of assets that are not normally part of the owner's stock and trade. For example, an *individual might sell a stock for more than he paid for it. Unless he was in the business of buying and selling stocks, this would be an increase in the value of capital asset of the stock, and the tax rate, unless the individual were in a very low tax rate, would be lower under capital gains than under ordinary income. The form of ownership may also affect taxes. Profits from a proprietorship or partnership are taxed along with other profits and losses of the individual proprietor or partner. A corporation must pay taxes on its profits before they are distributed to its stockholders unless it is a subchapter S corporation.*

A factor that affects taxation is depreciation. Depreciation is a tax-deductible expense, but it is a noncash expense in that unlike most other expenses, no cash actually has to be paid at the time the asset is depreciated. Food cost, for example, is an expense that has to be paid when the food is obtained, but depreciation does not include this direct cash payment. It may be desirable to have accelerated depreciation or heavier depreciation in the early years of the asset's life rather than straight-line or equal depreciation over the lifetime of the asset. With accelerated depreciation, there is more tax deduction in the beginning and less at the end.

To encourage business investment the government has provided for an Investment Tax Credit. This is a direct tax credit of up to 10 percent of qualified investments. A tax credit is more desirable than a tax deduction since the tax credit is subtracted directly from the amount of taxes owed while a tax deduction is subtracted from the taxable income to consider the income upon which taxes must be calculated.

IMPORTANT TERMS

After studying this chapter you should be able to explain or define:

controller

treasurer

liquidity

solvency

cash flow analysis

cash budgeting

internal funds

accounting

financial accounting

income statement

balance sheet

managerial accounting

tax accounting

accrual accounting

prime costs

controllable expenses

operating profit

operating ratio

current ratio

acid test

debt financing

limited partner

embezzlement

profit centers

leasing

proprietorship

partnership

corporation

progressive tax rates

double taxation

subchapter S corporation

REIT

leverage

trading on the equity

capital financing

bond

indenture

mortgage bond

debenture

first mortgage

junior mortgage

guaranteed mortgage

ground lease

subordinated ground lease

working capital

capital

collateral

SBA

prime rate

add-on interest

discount interest

compensating balance

internal control

ordinary income

capital gains

depreciation

noncash cost

straight-line depreciation

accelerated depreciation

declining balance depreciation

sum of digits depreciation

investment tax credit

REVIEW QUESTIONS

9-1. Why has financial management become increasingly important to the hospitality manager?

9-2. Differentiate between financial accounting, managerial accounting, cash accounting, and tax accounting.

9-3. Why did REITs become so popular in the 1960s?

9-4. Discuss the advantages and disadvantages of equity funding.

9-5. On what basis are loans or credit generally extended?

9-6. What are the advantages of leasing as a method of financing?

9-7. Briefly discuss the areas of internal control.

9-8. Why would you want to use accelerated depreciation in your hospitality operation?

9-9. What is the attraction of a subchapter S corporation?

9-10. Discuss the various forms of business organization.

9-11. The City Hospital is a nonprofit voluntary hospital that is nominally owned by the residents of the area with its title vested in a group of trustees who are elected by local residents. For a small membership fee anyone can have voting rights in the "Hospital Corporation." Initial financing for the hospital came through philanthropy and public fund drives. The hospital which has assets of $25 million would like to add a $15 million addition. Donations from the community at this time should bring in only about $3 million. How should the rest be financed? The hospital can adjust its income to meet costs including financing costs.

9-12. Jane Ambitious would like to start a suburban restaurant. She has found an old building that would be suitable and could be bought for $80 thousand. Renovations would cost an estimated $60 thousand, equipment and furnishings $70 thousand, and $10 thousand working capital would be required. Jane can scrape together $30 thousand of her own funds and wants to keep sole ownership. What avenues of financing would you recommend to Jane?

9-13. You have developed an extremely successful foodservice concept featuring unusual food, decor, and service. It is believed the idea would be very successful elsewhere, and you have identified about fifty potential locations. Each unit would cost about $600 thousand. Fifty units could provide considerable advantages by mass advertising, making a commissary feasible and large scale purchasing. Unfortunately, you are in hock up to your neck and can get no direct financing. You desire a chain of fifty units and also to make a great deal of money. Discuss how this might be accomplished.

9-14. A large urban hotel is for sale at a very favorable price of $2 million net of existing loans (totaling $6 million). The hotel is modestly profitable. If an urban renewal program goes through (fifty-fifty possibility) it should be extremely profitable. You realize that your own resources of about $50 thousand are limited. What financial arrangements could be made for you to have an interest in this hotel? to purchase it?

10 Marketing and Sales Management

Every hospitality operation, large or small, profit or nonprofit, should develop and use a marketing strategy. Marketing begins with the earliest planning of an operation and continues through the life of a hospitality enterprise. A hospitality manager should, therefore, understand the principles of marketing and know how to apply those principles. The paramount principle in the marketing strategy is to realize that marketing begins with the customer or patron—not with the product or service a manager happens to have for sale. In other words, a marketing-oriented manager asks first what the customer needs, not what he, the manager, can sell. After studying this chapter on hospitality marketing, you should be able to

- *trace the development of the marketing concept in hospitality*
- *explain in some detail how marketing principles can be applied in hospitality operations*
- *list and explain briefly the components of the marketing mix*
- *describe the organization and operation of a hospitality sales department.*

Why Marketing?

A hospitality operation can serve the finest food and offer the most luxurious rooms and the best service, but these advantages, by themselves, cannot guarantee a successful business. (Their absence can, of course, drive business away.) To be successful an operation must attract customers to its fine products. With few exceptions the best, the most successful, and the most popular establishments must continually promote themselves. This continuous promotion achieves two purposes. It brings former customers back again, (entirely satisfied customers will not return automatically) and it lures new customers from the competing establishments.

Patron loyalty to hospitality establishments seems to be decreasing. Not too long ago, patrons routinely returned to the same establishment time after time. Now, the novelty of the modern establishments attracts these once loyal patrons. Moreover, the mobility of today's population and better transportation facilities have made distant hospitality establishments accessible to those once loyal patrons. Travel can, in turn, work in your favor. Your establishment is accessible to patrons who could not have reached you a few decades ago.

It is necessary to attract new customers constantly. Even the finest places lose some of their customers. The most loyal of customers occasionally move from the area. And rare is the establishment that cannot use an increase in business.

History of Hospitality Sales Promotion

Hospitality establishments have been around for a long time, but hospitality promotion is a rather recent phenomenon. For centuries, promotion consisted largely of an advantageous location and perhaps an identifying sign or symbol. The important thing was that, when the traveler needed food and rest, a hotel was available.

The neighborhood inn or tavern usually attracted local business. Several might compete in one area, but business remained brisk as long as the customer pool was consistent and confined to the local choice. These competing inns usually offered the same quality of service; no one had much of a competitive edge over the others. However, the host of one might be more amiable than the hosts of the others, and a pleasant personality was always most helpful to a hospitality operation.

In this country a new concept of hospitality service and promotion appeared in 1829 with the opening of the Tremont Hotel in Boston. Before the Tremont, customers usually had to accept what was available. Local hospitality people had no real incentive to cater to the individual traveler. They offered only the necessities, and still enjoyed a lively captive trade. The Tremont, however, offered far more than basic necessities. Its dining room employed skillful French chefs—a far cry from the dreary cooking that characterized the period. The Tremont provided individual rooms and even a lock and a key to ensure safety and privacy. (The heavy iron bar on the key reminded customers to return it.) Amenities like soap and gas lighting were provided, along with the first businesslike hotel desk.

Instead of depending on captive customers, the Tremont studied what its customers wanted and provided it. Today, this approach is called *marketing*. The instant success of the Tremont encouraged other hotels to copy its model. Many new establishments began to offer more than the basic essentials of hospitality, and the competing establishments began to engage in promotion. The major contribution of the Tremont, however, was the idea of offering the attractive extra service that would lure new customers.

Other important developments in hospitality promotion came with the era of 1930s. The hotel industry had overbuilt in the 1920s, and the Great Depression of 1929 brought hotels difficult financial problems. Those that survived learned to promote. Hotels began to analyze who their guests were and why they came. Desk clerks were deployed around town to drum up business. Patrons received thank you letters. Fancy touches like imprinted stationary appeared in the rooms. Progressive hotels kept guest history files that listed the pertinent facts about each guest and information on their visits. Thus when a guest arrived, the desk clerk could provide the same room and services he liked before. Catering to the guest to attract business became, in short, a more organized process.

Hotels also established sales departments charged with attracting new business because now business would not come to the hotel just because of the location or service. Hotels that had once ignored conventions or sales meetings, thinking them incompatible with their regular guests, now ardently sought these groups. They added special convention facilities, and some of the larger ones established regional sales offices in other cities to keep in touch with sources of convention business.

The sales efforts of the 1930s were, however, largely forgotten during the war years of the 1940s. In general, the hotel business remained brisk so promotion was not needed. The main problem was finding a staff, the food, and the other resources to run the business. But in the 1950s hotel occupancy began to slip again, so sales departments were revitalized and improved. Also in the 1950s hospitality operations formed chains, which had far greater promotional resources. With multiple units and a chain operation, national advertising became more feasible. A number of hotels could support this kind of promotion whereas even the largest hotel would have difficulty doing it alone. Keeping the patron "in the chain" became extremely important. Many chains started expanding partly because they then could, in effect, pass patrons from one unit in one location to a unit in another location as the patron traveled around the country.

A chain also provided ready identification. People could recognize the huge Holiday Inn sign before they read the letters. Moreover, they could rely on its standardized service. Travelers liked the idea of knowing exactly what they would find. Reservations systems augmented this type of promotion nicely. Units in one city made reservations for units in any other city, and this service increased the sales edge of those units using the system.

In the 1960s, chain business reservation referrals became even more important. In addition, the idea of area promotions gained prominence. Instead of individual establishments in an specific area (like the Poconos or the Catskills) promoting themselves independently, the establishments in an area would cooperate to stage attractions that might bring guests to the area. More business arrived than the operations could have attracted by themselves. Moreover, tie-ins with buses, trains, and airlines began. One result of this joint promotion is the familiar package plan.

And while all this sales promotion took place, the term itself gave way to marketing. Marketing, of course, went far beyond the previous promotion. It bespoke an interest in both serving customers and increasing business. The transportation improvements during the 1960s—better roads, airlines, and bus service transportation means made the traveling guest more mobile. They also led to shorter stays: the guest could reach his stop quickly and no longer felt the need for a long stay to make up for the original traveling effort and expense.

During the 1970s, the emergence of tourism as one of the world's major industries produced many marketing and promotion applications in the hospitality field. With more people traveling and eating out, hospitality business grew. But with this increased business came increased competition. Developments in tourism stimulated interesting mergers. TWA airlines, for example, acquired control of the Hilton hotels and ITT acquired control of the Sheraton chain. Greyhound Bus Lines acquired its own hospitality chains. The large companies, in short, had marketing expertise and resources to apply to their acquisitions. Moreover, new types of competition arose in the hospitality industry. Second homes became more and more popular, and home swimming pools made vacations to the seashore or the lake less important. New vacation facilities abroad, served by jets, forced American establishments to intensify their marketing efforts. On a week's vacation, customers could visit Paris as readily as a nearby tourist spot.

The Marketing Concept

Perhaps the most important development of all was the acceptance of the *marketing concept*—a notion that taught that promotion involved more than just selling. Marketing may be broadly defined as "those business activities involved in the flow of goods and services from the producers to customers." Specifically, marketing involves discovering what your customers want (market research), giving it to them (service), telling them what is available (advertising and promotion) so they will receive value (pricing), and you will make a profit (marketability).

The development of marketing can be illustrated by its evolution in hotel involvement in large functions. Originally, hotels had banquet managers who serviced what function business came to them. This position led to the sales manager, who not only did what the banquet manager did but also tried to attract function business outside of the hotel. This position evolved into the director of sales who coordinated various hospitality areas and tried to improve business. He might train the staff, contact potential business, entertain potential customers, and arrange coordinated campaigns to bring in business. Marketing became an increasingly important and time-consuming aspect of hotel operations. The position of director of marketing evolved, with responsibilities that went far beyond mere selling. In a sense, the director of marketing is the manager of the hotel, since marketing is now tied to all aspects of the hotel operation.

Hospitality Marketing

We have already defined marketing as "those activities involved in the flow of goods and services from producer to consumer." Other definitions might include "the composite of all activities the company engages in or should engage in affecting its relations with its customers;" "matching needs and wants with the appropriate services;" and "studying how people in society go about matching the needs and wants of potential buyers of appropriate goods and services through specialization and exchange." One unusual definition of marketing is "thinking big but with sharpened pencils."

Marketing involves tailoring services to satisfy a specific market. It includes analyses of people, social trends, labor supplies, resources, costs, common markets, and financial considerations. An important aspect of marketing involves the original feasibility study and site selection. But marketing really involves everything that the operating organization does for its patrons. It is not confined to profit-making organizations; it has definite applications in such institutions as nonprofit hospitals and nonprofit nursing homes. In a hotel, marketing people might consider everything that could be done to enhance the enjoyment and comfort of the guest, including special facilities, services, arrangements, and personnel. In a hospital, marketing would require an objective look at what could be done to make a patient more comfortable and at ease. Thus, health care marketing can consider such factors as what is the best way to provide complete service. It is traditional that a hospital serve three meals a day at scheduled times. Is this best for all patients? Should a more selective menu be offered in, perhaps, a regular dining room for ambulatory patients? Should the meals be rigorously scheduled? (Certain patients may be experiencing periods of stress or discomfort during scheduled meals and be unable to eat.) Should the hospital meal resemble more of a commercial restaurant meal than standard hospital fare? Should it include such amenities as wine service?

From the marketing standpoint the hospital operation should also consider the visitors and staff. Few hospitals cater to the relatives of a patient from out of town—where they will stay and how they will manage. Too often hospitals focus only on its medical and nursing responsibilities. Too little thought goes into these other aspects that can have a direct effect on the patient's well-being and recovery.

Service establishments can also do far more in a marketing sense than they have in the past. In fact, one of the reasons for the phenomenal growth of fast-food chains is that they are marketing-oriented. They carefully consider what their target markets want and how to meet these wants. By contrast, the traditional restaurant may tend to rely on its past success or on impressions of what its customers want. Too often things are done for the convenience of the management at the expense of customer convenience.

Consumer Orientation

Marketing is consumer-oriented rather than product- or service-oriented. A hotel built just to sell rooms is product-oriented. A marketing orientation involves more than just supplying a bed for the night. The main reason for the early success of motels was that they provided services to fill the new needs of customers beyond rooms—convenient parking, less formality in the lobby, no tips, cheaper rates, and swimming pools and other recreation. In fact, modern motor inns are constantly changing their services in response to their patrons' changing wants. Thus we see the formal dining room becoming the informal coffee shop or even cafeteria.

Marketing implies, as we said, a total marketplace orientation rather than just a sales orientation. The marketing approach encourages sales by examining the whole "product." More than just tempting people to enter an establishment, it conscientiously seeks to make the establishment as desirable as possible. Moreover, it strives for both an increased volume and a realistic profit derived from that volume. It would be easy for sales personnel to offer unrealistically low prices to attract business and set sales records. But from a marketing standpoint, one is interested, too, in the profitability of this increased business. One does not normally expand volume without trying to increase profits.

A marketing orientation concentrates on the entire organization including design, decor, and services—all part of the product-service mix. Sales are not separate from the operation, and the sales department does not operate apart from the organization. Since sales are an integral part of the organization, improving sales usually means improving the overall product.

Marketing and Demand

In the hospitality industry, as in any other industry, the problem is at least to maintain, and ideally to increase, the demand for the firm's product that produces profitable sales. A nonprofit organization like a hospital, on the other hand, must provide its patrons with the best services possible given the productive resources available. For a commercial operation to flourish, a continuous demand for its product is necessary. For a hospital to flourish, it must provide attractive services while meeting budgetary constraints.

Let us find out what the needs and wants of present and potential buyers are. To begin with, we must make an offer they will choose over competing offers. This offer includes everything about the operation—its image, facilities, promotion, services, and location. This requirement suggests that a market strategy be developed. A market strategy is a plan for solving the market problems and providing a continuous demand for the operation. To determine who the buyers of the products and services are, one must focus on *target markets,* or groups likely to be attracted by the offer. Try as it may, no hospitality operation can satisfy everyone. Thus the operation must limit itself to certain selected groups of people.

A Marketing Systems Framework   The marketing approach to hospitality differs substantially from the strict sales approach traditionally used in the industry. The marketing approach arises out of the realization that a hospitality operation simply cannot pursue every type of potential customer available. Some customer types conflict with others. They may also conflict with the purposes of the operation. (Some customers appreciate fine dining; others prefer fast-food restaurants, to provide one example.) Also, most operations have only limited resources with which to attract patrons. These operations obviously should pursue only those groups suited to the services offered. For example, it may be impossible to devote resources to attracting conventions, vacationers, commercial travelers, and honeymooners all at once.

To determine precisely which markets to pursue, an operation must establish *marketing objectives.* These provide the operation with a clear sense of purpose, a "mission." (The need for definite objectives is, of course, hardly limited to the hospitality industry. It pertains to all facets of business—including the business of acquiring an education!) The objectives we refer to here are more specific than such general objectives as providing a return on investment, being a good neighbor, and supplying worthwhile employment. If these more specific marketing objectives are met, profits should increase as a matter of course.

In determining an operation's objectives, the manager should consider *the product-service mix* and place it in the context of the operation's *external environment.* A hotel's mission is not just to provide food and lodging (products), but to provide hospitality (service) as well. Traditional hotels viewed their objectives in the former light; they suffered, therefore, when the motels arrived. Motel owners had seen their purpose in the latter context and begun to offer the hospitality their patrons desired: swimming pools, abundant parking, baby sitting, reservation service, and general informality. The new recreational facilities now being offered by so many motels further illustrate this general hospitality approach. To cite another familiar industry, railroads have suffered by seeing themselves merely as an agglomeration of trains, track, and stations instead of a system supplying enjoyable transportation.

Once an operation has established its objectives, it can refine these and meld them to the external environment. This narrowing of objectives leads to a concentration on specific markets. It also determines specialized product-service mixes and specific marketing mixes—two terms we will discuss shortly. In addition, the operation can establish reasonable market penetration and return on investment goals. Objectives for a local restaurant might include achieving a certain level of sales to provide an adequate profit or an adequate return on investment. These objectives might be secured by serving predetermined types of food and providing predetermined types of service.

Remember, though, that objectives can be met at the expense of long-term growth—and even survival. Selling at cheap prices can result in market penetration, but can also reduce profits. Meeting social responsibilities by paying high wages or improving the character of the neighborhood can also hurt profits. Once realistic objectives are determined, though, an operation can adopt strategies to achieve the objectives.

Before a strategy can be formulated, an operation must undertake some research. It should prepare a *product analysis,* showing all the services and facilities it has available. This analysis includes the operation's location, the transportation its patrons use, the operation's rates, its size, and the state of its physical plant and inventory. In drawing up this product analysis, management frequently discovers weaknesses or untapped strengths in its business.

A hospitality facility should also consider its present and potential competition. What do competing establishments offer that this operation does not (and possibly should)? What can it offer that the competition can or does not? The answers to these crucial questions often appear in analyses of the competitions' rate structures, locations, facilities, and services. How do we compare, management should ask, with our competition in these and other areas?

To the objectives and the product analysis, an operation should add the *customer profile,* another widely used marketing tool. A lodging operation should examine its reservation requests, its guest registrations, and guest folios. Useful information derived from reservation requests includes who makes the requests, when they are made, how they are made, and who they are made for. The registration card provides names and addresses, the number in a typical party, and dates of arrival. It may also indicate business affiliations and how the guests learned of the establishment. The guest folios can reveal the rates preferred, the length of the average stay, the average total bill, the types of accommodations requested, and how the typical bill was paid. All of this information can be used to develop a customer profile and to direct market strategies.

Once these tools—the objectives, the product analysis, and the customer profile—have been drawn up, an operation can address itself to two marketing concepts used in an overall marketing strategy: *segmentation* and *targeting.*

Market segmentation establishes definite customer groups with definable needs and interests. Since a hospitality operation cannot appeal to everyone, the management should try to identify those market segments it wants to attract. Market segmentation is formally defined as subdividing a market into distinct segments or numerical groups within larger groups of customers.

A market segment must be measurable, accessible, and substantial. Measurable means that the management can determine the approximate number of potential customers in a segment. But even if numerous customers exist in a segment, they are not a reasonable target if they are not accessible. Many millions of people would probably like to stay at the Waldorf Astoria, but, since they cannot afford such luxury, they are not accessible. If a segment is both accessible and measurable, it must also be substantial—it must contain sufficient numbers to warrant a marketing effort. Multi-millionaires might appear to meet all the criteria for the ideal segment, but too few of them exist to make them a practical segment for hospitality targeting. (They might, however, be a sufficiently substantial segment for fashionable jewelers or attorneys specializing in tax shelters.)

Market segments are sometimes considered according to broad geographic, demographic, or psychographic variables. Geographic variables include the region, the climate, and the population density characteristics of a market segment. A hotel would be interested in what areas its customers and potential customers come from. A local restaurant would like to know if its patrons come from nearby or from a distance. The hotel might decide to concentrate its advertising on the "home areas" of its customers, while the restaurant might decide to expand into nonlocal markets.

Demographic segmentation uses the study of such human population variables as age, sex, family size, income level, occupation, interests and hobbies, social class, ethnic background, religion, and family life style. Through these studies, the management tries to determine the size of various segments, their value, and the competition for them. A particular restaurant, having decided that upper-middle-class, professional, middle-aged couples comprise a sizable and an accessible market segment, could use demographics to decide to offer high-priced, rather exotic menus with little concern for the appetites of children. Its furnishings and service, too, would be designed to appeal to the tastes demographics suggest for this market.

A third type of market segmentation is psychographic. This method employs such factors as life styles, buying motives, product knowledge, and intended product use. For the hospitality industry, life style is probably the most important psychographic consideration. For example, wealthy customers were once assumed to follow conservative life styles.

Now we realize that they may as easily be "swingers" or "jet-setters" or they may dislike the ostentation that often accompanies wealth. Segmenting by life styles can reveal unexpected potential markets, because customers' patronization of a particular hospitality establishment can be based on their buying motives. Are customers seeking snob appeal? Are they looking for value? Do they prefer understated luxury? Do they want fast service? Product knowledge is important to these customers. A hospitality manager can increase sales by helping customers acquire that knowledge. It is easier, after all, to sell vacations, resort hotels, and sea cruises to those who already know about vacations, resorts, and cruises.

Once an operation researches its market segments, it must decide which *target markets* to broach. An operation, as we said, cannot pursue all the market segments, only the most profitable ones. Ideally, the target market it focuses on would (a) be of sufficient size to promise a profit, (b) have a potential for growth, (c) not be the target of excessive competition, and (d) exemplify some more or less unsatisfied need that can be supplied by the hospitality operation. All these criteria may not be available for any specific segment, but they may be used to measure one segment against another.

Elements of Marketing

Once the target markets have been determined, the marketing mix to "bring them in" must be defined. The elements of the marketing mix include the merchandising strategy, pricing, brand name, channels of distribution, personal selling, advertising, promotion, packaging, service, personal contact, and display. *Merchandising* a product or service means making it as attractive as possible to the potential customer. *Pricing* means the proper price in relation to the cost of providing the product or service and the appropriate profit. How should prices be fixed? A restaurant may offer a table d'hôte, one price that includes everything in the meal. Or it may go to the other extreme and offer an à la carte menu where everything is priced separately. Or there are a number of variations—for example where the price of the entrée includes vegetables and bread but not dessert and appetizer. What is the best pricing strategy for your facility? Does the price fit into your marketing scheme? Are you going to use low prices to attract a high volume, or high prices to effect a high profit margin? Automobile manufacturers have become pricing experts. They offer a basic price for a car which usually seems rather reasonable. But then they persuade a buyer to order certain options that add considerably to the total price.

Branding involves the image you want the operation to project. A chain operation emphasizes the similiarity of its units so that consumers immediately recognize the golden arches or the orange tile roof even before they see the establishment. The design of the building should, in any case, portray as much as possible the type of operation one finds there. Channels of distribution can include the location or site for the enterprise. (Where you are affects your business.) They can also include how you *sell* your establishment—for example, through direct solicitation, travel agents, mass advertising, or other promotional means.

For nonhospitality operations *packaging* refers to a product's wrapping, but the service industry package can refer to the decor of the establishment. (Is it strictly luxury or determined by no frills?) Packaging may also be used to refer to how services are packaged together and sold to the customers—as in packaged tours. In the hospitality field, display is tied to packaging since the product is part of the establishment itself rather than some small, nicely wrapped gift. The physical premises—both inside and outside—should be display pieces inviting patrons to come in and enjoy the services. Packaging can also refer to how the food or service is provided. The service of a low-cost steakhouse with western atmosphere, for example, is different from that of a luxurious gourmet restaurant. In the hospitality industry the service provided the customers is most important. This service represents a balance between costs and the quality of the offering. From a marketing standpoint, it is essential that the level of service desired by the target markets be determined and that this level be reached.

All of these elements of the marketing mix apply to any enterprise, but their importance varies among industries and with individual situations. The marketing-oriented hospitality executive must be aware of them and be able to use them constructively for his establishment.

Market research should help pinpoint target markets, help determine the proper marketing mix, and help make most effective use of the advertising dollar. Since most hospitality establishments appeal to only a small segment of the general population, and thus cannot use broad outside promotion, market research is most important.

In formulating a marketing mix, one must make sure that the elements are not considered in a vacuum but are, instead, considered as they are affected by changes in consumer attitudes and habits, changes in competition, and changes in government activity. For example, promotion methods that might have been acceptable—even desirable—a few years ago cannot be used now. Some of the hospitality advertising that once displayed attractive bathing beauties is now too sexist to attract modern patrons. Government controls and regulations are, of course, looming even larger for all establishments. For example, a proposed government regulation that all convenience foods be labeled as such on the menu could have implications in packaging, display, branding, and different types of promotion.

**The Marketing
Mix**

As we said, the marketing mix consists of all those strategies that attract the target markets. Elements of the marketing mix include advertising, personal contact, promotion, pricing and branding, distribution channels, packaging, display, servicing, market research, personal selling, and marketing strategy.

Advertising can, of course, be accomplished in many various ways—in newspapers, through direct mail, or on radio and television. Personal contacts may be established among large groups seeking convention facilities. Special promotions can include such inducements as a free bottle of champagne, a free continental breakfast, or a free weekend at a hotel with a low seasonal occupancy rate. Resorts sometimes promote special golf tie-ins.

Pricing strategies in the hospitality industry might include a family plan wherein children room free with their parents. Menu pricing arrangements can range from a strict à la carte policy to the table d'hôte where everything in the meal is included under one price.

Branding has been very effective in chain operations. Instead of stopping at perfectly acceptable but unfamiliar motels or restaurants, patrons may tend to visit establishments they are familiar with due to a chain-fostered national reputation. The inn across the street may be just as good as (or better than) the chain operation but patrons prefer not to take the chance—a fact chain operations stress in their national advertising.

Merchandising denotes the steps taken to set an establishment off from the competition. In a restaurant, merchandising might include original menu items or a house salad dressing or a specialty drink. Lodging establishments may offer such unusual features as individual sauna baths or water beds; or, in a honeymoon resort, heart-shaped bathtubs, vibrating mattresses, or closed-circuit x-rated movies.

**Selling and
Appeals**

One definition of selling is the satisfaction of needs. Another is allowing someone to rationalize what he does. A person's needs may be physiological or psychological—real or imagined. (A psychologist friend of mine insists, however, that psychological needs are "real" needs in the same sense that psychosomatic pain hurts.) The importance of imagined need is demonstrated by the (perhaps shameful) fact that America could survive very well on 40 percent of what it actually consumes. Obviously then, much of our consumption stems from imagined, manufactured, or developed needs.

If someone is hungry and has some money, very little salesmanship is required to get him into the only restaurant around. A different situation arises when a town has fifty restaurants and the individual is not particularly hungry. To survive in this town, a restaurant must have something that appeals to the customer. The appeal may be, in part, food, but it can be other things as well, including the decor, the service, or the advertising. "Selling" the patron may even involve providing other stimulants that make him want to eat—perhaps pictures of food items. If you are not particularly hungry but see a picture of a mouth-watering steak platter, your hunger threshold immediately falls. The popping of a champagne cork may stimulate others to order champagne. And the mere smell of charcoal arouses the taste buds of some people.

Creating an Image

Promotion and advertising no longer consists of just the mention of a product's merit. Today most segments of the hospitality industry (and most other industries as well) engage in brisk competition. The competitors frequently offer equal services and products. How do customers choose one (yours) over the others? Ideally, you want them to develop a strong loyalty to you. Thus you must create some illusion that your product is different from and better than others. We call this *creating an image*. Your image may center on luxury, fast service, or economy—among many possible images. The image cannot be created by advertising alone. It involves the entire enterprise. Thus if an operation places the picture of a colonial gentleman in its advertising, it should follow through with colonial menus, serving uniforms, and decor. Fast-food operations create an image of speed and cleanliness with their relatively small size, large windows, and strong lighting. The strong lighting and small size dramatize the fact that people go in and out quickly. The large windows allow one to observe the fast flow of traffic and much of the food preparation (in modern, clean, sanitary kitchens) as well.

From the psychological standpoint, customer loyalty to various images is immensely interesting. For example, people tend to be intensively loyal to their cigarette brands. But blind-tested, they normally cannot differentiate one brand from the others. The same is true for brands of beer. One inexpensive eastern beer—so its advertising claims—is often confused for an "aristocratic" Rocky Mountain beer, as long as the drinkers are blindfolded. Obviously, the brands of cigarettes and brands of beer have created an image. It might be the "ruggedness" of some cigarette brands, or the boisterous good times suggested by a particular beer. A hospitality operation should consciously work at projecting an image and at strengthening that image once established.

In determining the image desired, it will be necessary again to consider the potential customers and to determine what type of image that they expect from the establishments they frequent. The youth-oriented image, for example, would not be wise in an area where most of the customers are senior citizens. On the other hand, promotion stressing youthfulness often attracts older people to cruises and resort hotels—where they hope to regain some of their youthful feelings. (Resort hotels that advertise with attractive young people in bathing suits may really be aiming for middle aged couples longing to feel a part of the youthful image the ads suggest.)

Motivation and Sales

There are two basic considerations that should be understood about promotion appeals and motivation. First, people are not always logical. Second, we all have certain needs. So if someone can present a product that *seems* to fulfill our needs psychologically or physiologically, the product (or service) will be purchased.

People are not logical. They buy cars they cannot afford, clothes they do not need, and equipment they may never use. Nevertheless, they can almost always rationalize their purchases. Someone purchases a new car when his old car remains in good running order. Why? He rationalizes that the new car fits his needs; it gets better gas mileage; it eliminates the possibility of major repairs in the near future. The real reasons probably have more to do with status, with drawing neighborhood attention, with a desire for novelty, or with advertising that trumpets the joys of owning one of the new models. In promoting a service or product remember that a logical need for something may be immaterial as long as customers can rationalize their purchase.

If a need is created for a product or service it can be sold. As Sigmund Freud said, "Under our simple veneer of rationality, morality, reason, and sanity is the id, which contains lust, passion, and desire." Product and service promotion focuses on the id. As we mentioned before, one definition of selling is "allowing someone to rationalize what he does."

There are a number of appeals that can be used in hospitality promotion. One is pride. In this case, an exclusiveness or even the expensiveness of the establishment can be stressed. The person to whom an appeal is addressed will consider himself superior if he checks into an exclusive and expensive establishment. The opposite of pride is economy, and here one stresses the value of the product or service. Such strategies as family plans or small hotel rates fall into this category. Low rates can be stressed in advertisements, or even in the name, like the Budget Motel.

Closely associated with pride are the appeals of comfort and luxury. The advertisements stressing these appeals could invite a patron to "pamper yourself" and stay at this "most luxurious of hotels." Efficiency can also have an appeal. Perhaps the location is convenient for guests or perhaps the hotel has a drive-in entrance, or maybe it offers a restaurant, and beverage service. Parental love—or status seeking—may be stressed: "Your debutante deserves a reception in a fine hotel."

Novelty can also exert an appeal. People like to experience something new. People are curious, so an advertisement like "see our new cocktail lounge" can be very effective. In fact, the word "new" works like a magnet. Another appeal is the recommendation of others—particularly, it seems, well-known celebrities. The testimony should, of course, come from someone who people have confidence in. But comically absurd testimony sometimes attracts attention. A desire for "social correctness"— the proper thing to do—also sells products and services. This helps account for the growing habit in America of wine with the meal.

The appeal can be negative. For example, hotels used to capitalize on fear by advertising themselves as fireproof. Stressing the pleasures of dining as a social function can sell food, as can display of food in the window of a restaurant.

Hospitality Sales Departments

To illustrate a hospitality organization's sales department, we will consider a large resort hotel using sophisticated selling techniques. Strictly speaking, sales apply to commercial operations, since few nonprofit organizations solicit new business. Although we are considering a larger organization, all commercial hospitality operations, no matter how small, must assign definite responsibility for a sales program. In a small restaurant, the duty may be the owner's or the manager's, but somebody has to be responsible.

Larger operations normally maintain a separate sales department headed by a marketing or sales director. The sales program cannot be separate from the rest of the operation; it must be sensitive to the whole organization. It is futile for the sales department to bring in business if the operation cannot handle it. Word of these mistakes will soon get around, and sales will decline accordingly. A sales program is not only external that it brings in business from the outside, but it is also internal in that it tries to increase the business that has already appeared. And a sales program must motivate the nonsales staff. This staff, in turn, can encourage patrons to use more of the operation's facilities as they quietly go about their jobs competently and well. The best sales efforts and conscientious work by nonsales people can be cancelled by a surly or noncooperative employee. Marketing is *total*, and the hotel sales department is only one part of an organization's total marketing effort. Thus the sales department has not only a customer-relations aspect but also a staff-relations aspect.

The functions of the sales department may vary with the operation, but they typically include advertising; securing group business; servicing these group businesses (sometimes through the banquet department); inside selling efforts (selling the patron already present); and personnel training.

An organization chart (see Exhibit 10-1) of the department shows that it is headed by the director of marketing (or sales), who is responsible to

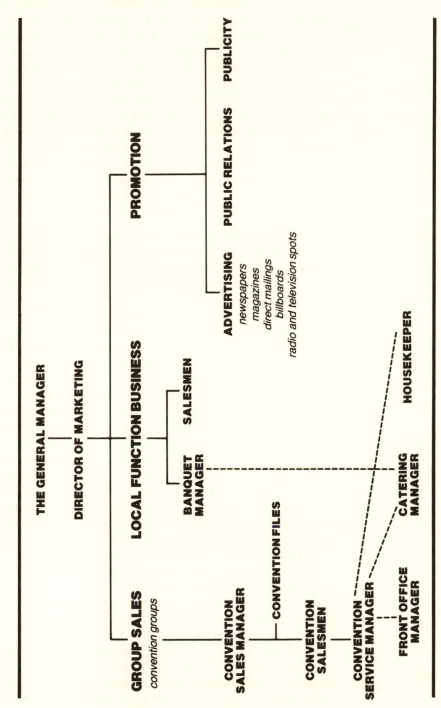

THE GENERAL MANAGER

DIRECTOR OF MARKETING

GROUP SALES
convention groups

LOCAL FUNCTION BUSINESS

PROMOTION

CONVENTION SALES MANAGER

CONVENTION FILES

BANQUET MANAGER

SALESMEN

ADVERTISING
newspapers
magazines
direct mailings
billboards
radio and television spots

PUBLIC RELATIONS

PUBLICITY

CONVENTION SALESMEN

CONVENTION SERVICE MANAGER

FRONT OFFICE MANAGER

CATERING MANAGER

HOUSEKEEPER

Exhibit 10–1. Possible Organization of a Resort Hotel Sales Effort

the general manager. Under him appear a number of divisions: The convention or group business is responsible for bringing in large groups and conventions. The banquet business handles conventions and local functions like weddings, dances, and parties. The promotion department handles advertising defined as purchasing time on radio or television and space in printed matter. There may also be a public relations department, working to put the operation in the best possible public light.

This may involve convincing a reporter to refer blandly to "a downtown hotel" rather than to the specific operation when covering a negative news story. The public relations department also works to get favorable mention for the hotel in the media: stories on guests and conventions currently visiting the hotel, stories about interesting personalities at the hotel, stories of new services available at the hotel, and so on.

Sales Tools A sales department has a number of tools to help it in its work. One of the most helpful are the files on the present and potential patrons. These files depict the history of the operation's relations with its group customers. Some major conventions may take years to attract, and a number of people may have been involved in the convention sales effort.

The guest history, another sales tool, tells as much as possible about the relationship between each individual guest and the operation. Such entries as the number of visits, the rooms occupied, favorite services—even birthdays and anniversaries—can help the operation establish a more personal relationship when it deals with its guests.

It is essential to keep track of sales in the various facilities of the operation, and a *function book* is the proper place for these records (see Exhibit 10-2). Normally each area, the dining room, lounge, or ballroom, has a separate page for each day. The page may be divided according to the type of function or the time of the function—like breakfast, luncheon, dinner, or evening affair. Each of the time slots should have blanks for information about the reserving organizations. Typical information would include the name of the organization, the type of organization, its attendance, the quoted price, any special sales arrangements, and the host. Tentative bookings may be made in pencil; when they are confirmed the bookings can be inked in. Naturally the function book should be kept up-to-date; otherwise the same facility might be sold to two different organizations at the same time.

Flow charts help determine business needs and business trends. A flow chart compares the amount of business of different types to the amount that could be handled over specified periods. It can resemble a graph chart, or it may follow a statistical format where the amount of business generated is listed daily. From the flow chart one can easily determine how many rooms are sold and how many rooms are available. But its special purpose is to pinpoint when business is low so manage-

DATE:	TYPE OF AFFAIR	SIZE	ORGANIZATION NAME	CONTACT NAME/TELEPHONE NO.	SALES-MAN	CONFIR-MATION DATE
MORNING						
East Room						
Ball Room						
Lounge						
Embassy Room						
Penthouse						
NOON						
East Room						
Ball Room						
Lounge						
Embassy Room						
Penthouse						
SUPPER						
East Room						
Ball Room						
Lounge						
Embassy Room						
Penthouse						
EVENING						
East Room						
Ball Room						
Lounge						
Embassy Room						
Penthouse						

Exhibit 10–2. Sample Function Book Page

ment can determine whether extra efforts must be made to erase these low periods.

The sales department may work with a number of associated organizations. For example, if the establishment is a unit of a chain it may be involved with a centralized sales headquarters. The units in various locations may work not only to attract their own sales but also to contact prospects for the units in other localities. Sometimes chain personnel conduct a *sales blitz* congregating in one location to make a concentrated sales effort with the extra manpower.

In larger cities, convention bureaus help attract conventions to their city with the hospitality establishments both participating and benefiting. (Some large conventions may involve most or all the hotels in the city.) An individual hotel may not have the resources to pursue some of these large groups, but a convention bureau can work for all.

Another source of business (or sales tool) for hotels is the travel agent, who sends his clients to the various establishments. Normally a 10 percent commission is sent back to the travel agent by the establishment for whom the guest is referred. This 10 percent must come out of the regular rate, and it is unethical to raise a guest's rates to cover the travel agent's percentage. Travel agents serve a number of functions. Besides acquainting prospective guests with establishments that might appeal to him, they can screen the patron and help to prevent a mismatch in taste and services. The travel agent may also collect an advance deposit, which he forwards to the hospitality establishment. (Having made a deposit a potential guest is less likely to cancel out.) Moreover, it is often easier for an operation to make arrangements through the travel agent than personally with the guest. And of course, travel agents may distribute folders or other advertising which attracts a guest to come to the establishment without actually dealing with the travel agent.

Hospitality establishments may cultivate a relationship with various travel agents by supplying them with literature and current information available. They can dispatch personnel to call on agents, and they may extend hospitality to the employees of the travel agency when they are in the area. Hotels often find that a small proportion of travel agents provide a large proportion of their business; thus it behooves them to cultivate these influential people.

Resort areas may form promotion groups similar to a city convention bureau. These area promoters stress both convention facilities and individual vacation attractions. If all the hospitality establishments in the Poconos or Catskills, for example, were promoted independently, they would spend a lot and profit little. By engaging in area promotion, they increase their resources and share the generous business attracted to the area. Meanwhile, of course, individual operations continue to do some of their own specific promotion on a modest scale.

Referral and reservation systems are traditionally associated with hospitality sales. Referral systems involve hospitality operations in one locality referring their customers to operations in other locales. The reservation systems, of course, go beyond mere referrals. In fact, one of the big attraction advantages of the nationwide lodging chains is that they can make reservations for customers at one of their units for all of the other units. A large part of motor hotel chain business can be attributed directly to this internal reservation system. The future will surely bring more connections between reservation systems, transportation arrangements, and car rental companies.

Independent representatives sometimes serve client hotels. These representatives—freelancers or independent contractors—represent various geographical areas where they take reservations and make sales calls for their clients. The Caribbean resort, for example, may need a representative in New York City but may not be able to afford to employ one by itself. Therefore, it hires a local hotel representative. The hotel representative, of course, extends the work of the individual hotel sales department.

Function Business

Function business includes the hospitality spectrum of banquets service, club luncheons, ladies' groups, bridge clubs, weddings and receptions, (including rehearsal dinners and bachelor breakfasts), dances, coming out parties, fashion shows, and others too numerous to list. It is the responsibility of the hospitality establishment to make all of them memorable affairs.

The function business may be supervised by the catering manager or the banquet manager. This person is responsible for selling, booking, arranging, and serving all these functions. He may also create publicity (if permission is granted by the people holding the reception) which can serve both the customers and the establishment.

The first step is to sell the function. Some business comes in automatically, but most establishments try to bring in more. They regularly check newspaper items involving special functions—promotions, engagements, or retirement announcements, for example. They also keep tabs on organizations that regularly sponsor special functions for one reason or another. Many advertise in local papers. Others use direct mail to promote their facilities.

The selling itself is, of course, important. To the group or person holding the function, it is an important event, even though the establishment may consider it routine. The seller must remember the concern of his clients and try to personalize the function as much as possible.

Perhaps the service can use some originality. Buffets are popular. So are smorgasbords. (Some of these additional touches can mean additional profit.) The sales person must be very conscious of his establish-

Exhibit 10–3.
Sample Sales
Agent's Client
Record

CALL SHEET

File No. _____

☐ Telephone   ☐ Outside   ☐ Inside

ORGANIZATION _____

Executive _____ Title _____

Address — Firm _____ Tel. No. _____

Street Address _____

City _____

Possible Business or Business Booked
Breakfast—Luncheon—Dinner—Reception—Meeting—Dance—Convention

Number Persons Expected _____

Sleeping Rooms—How Many _____

Preferred Dates and Times _____

Tentative ☐   Accepted ☐

Copy To _____ Trace _____

Date _____ Signature _____

---

ment's capabilities and should not promise more than it can fulfill. Moreover, he should usually "sell quality" rather than "price." The sales representative is, after all, more than a salesman; he is the representative and the liaison for the organization. Thus he must feel confident and convey the confidence he has in his organization.

Matters the sales representative and the patron should settle include the menu, the table arrangements and layout, the decorations (including flowers), and such special equipment required as loudspeakers or movie projectors. The sales agent should then make records of these plans, keeping a copy and forwarding another to the hospitality personnel concerned (see Exhibits 10-3 and 10-4).

Once a function is sold, the agent must work closely with others in his organization. The chef must know what is expected; food must be ordered; sufficient serving staff must be on hand; and the room must be set up according to arrangements.

One convenient general procedure to follow is to send out informa-

Exhibit 10–4.
Sample Sales
Agent's Booking
Report

BOOKING REPORT

PHONE_____   DATE OF INQUIRY_____

ORGANIZATION_____

CONTACT_____

ADDRESS_____

DATE_____FUNCTION_____TIME_____

EXPECTED ATTENDANCE_____RENTAL_____ROOM_____

REMARKS:

TENTATIVE   POSTING_____

DEFINITE

PENDING

EQUIPMENT
EASEL_____
PODIUM_____
LECTERN_____
BLACKBOARD_____
PLATFORMS_____
MICROPHONE_____

RENTAL
PROJECTORS_____
SCREENS_____

BILLING INSTRUCTIONS

CREDIT REFERENCE

ROOM ACCOMMODATIONS

SUBMIT ESTIMATE   CC: FILE

SALES REPORT   ARRIVE_____   DEPART_____   BANQUET

CONFIRM   _____SINGLES @   _____TWINS @   RESERVATION
                                                            CHRONO
ISSUE   _____PARLORS @   _____SUITES @   BACKLOG

LEVIS   CREDIT DEPT.

tion sheets about the function to all concerned the week before the function. Two days before, make a last-minute check on the guaranteed number of attendees. On the day of the function, check the arrangements before the host arrives. And when the host does arrive, review the arrangements with him. Be sure to conduct a follow-up after the function to see that the host was satisfied.

Guarantee Policy

A guarantee policy is important in handling functions. The guarantee policy protects the establishment: the agreed-upon number of people will come; the establishment will be compensated if they do not. The policy also reassures the sponsoring organization that sufficient food and service for the planned event will be forthcoming. One guaranteed policy we know of contains the following provisions:

1. A definite guarantee on numbers to be served will be submitted no later than twenty-four hours before the function.
2. Places will be set for 12 percent in excess of that guaranteed number.
3. When attendance falls below the guarantee, full charge will be made for 90 percent of that guarantee and half price for the remainder.
4. When attendance exceeds 100 percent, full price is charged. If attendance is more than 112 percent of the guarantee, every effort will be made to take care of the extra persons but there will be an additional charge of 25 percent for them because of the difficulties in assembling personnel, food, and silverware on short notice.
5. When attendance is over 90 percent, but less than 100 percent, full prices are charged for all meals served and half price for the remaining meals of the guarantee.

This guarantee policy provides that if the agreed number comes, no extra charge is made. Moreover the organization can entertain 12 percent more than the agreed number without any extra charge per person or cover. Only when the number is less than that guaranteed or over 112 percent of the places set, is there an extra charge.

People planning functions sometime question why the per-person price of a function for 100 people comes to more than the price of an equivalent dinner in the dining room. There are a number of reasons. To begin with, a function has no turnover. Only one banquet setting can be used, while the dining room seat can be turned over more than once or twice. Also, a large part of function business often occurs in spurts; the function space tends to remain vacant the rest of the time. Thus the cost of the function must compensate for times when the space is unused. Then too, the equipment used for functions, like special platforms, tables, audio equipment, and decorations, are used only intermittently. Likewise, special waiters or waitresses are used for functions, and these personnel may be more expensive than full-time employees.

Advertising

Advertising involves the purchase of space, time, or printed matter to increase sales. Though we may think of advertising as a comparatively recent innovation, it has been used, more or less as we know it now, since the beginning of recorded time.

Advertising is sometimes considered a three-part business. One part consists of the clients who offer products and services through the advertising media. A second part consists of the agency that prepares and arranges for the advertising. The third part consists of the media that carries the advertising—newspapers, magazines, mailings, brochures, radio, television, skywriting, whatever. Advertising can have various functions. These include:

1. Straight selling—trying to convince potential customers to buy and use a product or services

2. Offering free literature—often used by resorts that expect advertisement to arouse interest among potential patrons

3. Spreading prestige and goodwill—keeping the name of the organization before the public in a positive way

4. Educating the public to use the product—a good way to promote a new product or service coming on the market before any actually selling is undertaken. (Wine producers, for example, spend a lot of advertising money educating people in the social uses of the wine in general before they start to sell specific wines.)

There is some controversy today about the mixed blessings of advertising. Some say advertising is superfluous because we no longer need to expand markets. Thus it increases, instead of lowering the costs of production. Without advertising, these people say, the establishments could charge less. Advertising can also create artificial desires, which can mask the real needs of society. Advertising expensive children's toys, for example, can build a strong demand for these toys even among the children of poor families who need the money for more fundamental things. Moreover, the modus operandi of advertising, which involves playing on a wide range of human impulses (including fear, jealousy, envy, intimidation, snobbery, greed, and lust), can be crass and distasteful. Particularly unpleasant are those ads that equate power, sexual attractiveness, and success with the use of certain products.

Proponents of advertising can, of course, marshal strong arguments for it. It is, they say, necessary to expansion in our capitalistic system. To keep prices low, goods must be sold in large quantities, and advertising helps to distribute these goods widely. Without advertising, in fact, there would be no large markets and little, large-scale economic production. Advertising also subsidizes many worthwhile newspapers, magazines, and television and radio programs. People can buy more intelligently if they learn of the relative merits of various products; they also learn about what is available. Back in 1924, Winston Churchill remarked, "Advertising nourishes the consuming power of men. It creates wants for a better standard of living. It sets up before a man a goal of a better home, better clothing, better food for himself and his family. It inspires individual exertion and greater production.''

Some General Principles of Advertising

Advertising can be very effective, but it is not automatically so. John Wanamaker, the great dry goods merchant, is reported to have said that half of his advertising was wasted; the problem was he did not know which half. Wanamaker should have known that there are general principles that can make advertising more effective. One is repetition. A single mention of a product in an advertising medium may not be enough. The customer may have to see and hear the message again and again—and perhaps in several different media. Advertising should be cumulative. Advertising done in the past should reinforce advertising done today. This investment may not appear on the balance sheet, but past advertising can be a definite asset to an organization.

Advertising cannot be indiscriminate (except for the comparatively few products used by everyone). The hospitality industry has narrow target markets it wants to reach. Thus, its advertising should be directed straight to these target markets with as little waste as possible. People who are not potential patrons must be avoided. Unless something is drastically wrong with an establishment, it will be easier to bring back old customers than to interest new ones, and so its first effort should be directed to former customers. Less money need be spent educating them to what you have available. Of course, a hospitality operation with a doubtful reputation will have to depend on new customers. If they, too, become disenchanted, the prospects for survival are bleak.

SUMMARY

Marketing is necessary for any hospitality establishment. Its usefulness begins with the earliest feasibility study and continues throughout the life of the enterprise. Patrons do not automatically come to an establishment and do not automatically return. An operation must constantly attract new customers. At one time, hospitality marketing constituted just existing in the area, raising some identifying advertising sign, and serving the needs of travelers or other patrons. The next step was to add various aspects of sales promotion. Sales promotions gradually evolved into marketing, a much broader concept that involves all those business activities related to the flow of goods and services from the producers to the customers.

Modern marketing is consumer-oriented rather than product- or service-oriented. Hotels lost business to motels because at one time they saw their function as supplying accommodations to a traveling public that would always come to them. They did not think beyond the accommodations to the other needs of their patrons.

Every hospitality operation should have a market strategy, a plan for solving the market problems and providing a continuous demand for the operation. To do this, a manager must establish marketing objectives or a clear sense of what the operation is striving to accomplish. A hotel does not supply only food and lodging, it also has the mission of supplying hospitality. Once the more specific objectives of the mission have been determined, they can be refined and fitted more precisely to the external environment. At this point, specific market segments can be determined. Research is required to define these segments, and a product analysis showing all the services and facilities available, along with the competition, should be drawn up. An operation should also work with a customer profile,which shows what the typical customer likes and desires. To be valid, a market segment must be measurable, accessible, and substantial. These segments are sometimes arranged according to geographical areas, demographic or human population characteristics, and psychographics, which is concerned with lifestyles of the potential patrons.

From the segment markets, one can develop what marketeers call target markets. Ideally, target markets must:

- *be of a sufficient size to promise a profit*
- *have the potential for growth*
- *not be the target of excessive competition*
- *exemplify some more or less unsatisfied needs that can be met by the hospitality operation*

However, it is very difficult to find target markets that meet all these criteria.

Once the target market has been defined, an operation must develop a marketing mix to attract them. Elements of the marketing mix include a merchandising strategy, pricing, brand names, channels of distribution, personal selling, advertising, promotion, packaging, and service. Part of marketing is selling; selling can be defined as the creation and satisfaction of needs. These needs may be either psychological or physiological. Selling allows the customer to rationalize investment in the product. If needs can be developed, or if the customer is already aware of them, they can easily become a key promotional device.

When two hospitality operations offer similar facilities and services, yet the customers clearly prefer one over the other, the reason may well be that the one operation is projecting the illusion that its product is different and better than the other's. Creating such an image cannot be done by advertising alone; it must involve all aspects of the operation.

Most larger hospitality organizations have sales departments. Hospi-

tality sales departments vary considerably, but typically they take responsibility for advertising, securing group business, selling, and perhaps personnel training. The hospitality sales department must also keep records of precisely what it has sold, which for function business involves the function book. The sales department may work with associate organizations, like the local Convention and Visitor's Bureau. Business may also be attracted to an operation through travel agents, who normally get a ten percent commission. Chain operations have an advantage in that they can refer patrons from one unit of the chain to another and at the same time, enjoy, an immediate recognition factor.

Once a function is sold, there should be some assurance that the specified number of patrons will come. The need for this assurance occasions a guarantee policy. Advertising involves the purchase of space, time, or printed matter to increase sales. It may serve various functions like straight selling, spreading prestige and good will, offering free literature, or educating the public to use the product.

IMPORTANT TERMS

After studying this chapter, you should be able to define or identify the following terms:

marketing

market strategy

target market

market mix

branding

packaging

profit foregone

function book

guarantee policy

product analysis

market segmentation

psychographic variable

demographic variable

geographic variable

advertising

promotion

public relations

REVIEW QUESTIONS

10–1. What promotional advantages do chain hotels enjoy over independents?

10–2. How does marketing differ from promotion?

10–3. Explain the marketing mix.

10–4. "Restaurants are often more restaurant-oriented than customer-oriented." Discuss this statement.

10–5. How does a marketing system framework adapt to both long- and short-range planning?

10–6. What is the relationship between selling and appeals?

10–7. How is image involved in hospitality marketing and promotion?

10–8. What are the functions of a hotel sales department?

10–9. Describe a marketing systems framework.

10–10. What are the functions of a guarantee policy?

10–11. Discuss market segmentation.

10–12. What are the criteria of market targeting?

10–13. Collect six advertisements from hospitality operations. Analyze the advertisements in terms of appeal and effectiveness. What changes might you make?

10–14. Select a hospitality operation with which you are familiar. Describe its present marketing efforts. Your description should include present target markets and appropriate aspects of the marketing mix. Prepare a consultant's report on what changes you would recommend in their marketing approach.

CASE PROBLEM: The Florida Motel

An investment syndicate is considering the purchase of a 200-room motel property located in Florida. Previously the property was a unit of a large national chain, but it was not successful financially and went bankrupt. It has been empty and out of business for the last three years. The property is located four miles from Walt Disney World, Florida's top family attraction, but is twenty miles from any residential area and several miles from high-traffic highways.

Because of its location, the emphasis of the operation should be to serve needs of in-house guests rather than local residents or highway travelers. A preliminary study shows that the property's prime market would be families visiting Disney World and other central Florida attractions. The market profile shows that the typical family stays three to five nights, leaving the property early each morning and returning after the parks and attractions close in the evening. There could, of course, be other fringe markets. It can be assumed that a family visiting the Florida attractions would want a breakfast, but that they would supply only a very limited lunch business. Moreover, the typical family would eat dinner at the motel only on the evening of their arrival and perhaps the night before their departure.

The facilities of the lodging property include two hundred guest rooms, each large enough for two double beds. There is a 90-seat cocktail lounge, 150-seat dining room, a swimming pool with a patio bar and another 1200 square-foot room that was intended for small functions. All furnishings and equipment were sold at bankruptcy proceedings so the new operation will not be hampered by preconceived planning.

The purchase syndicate will contribute a reasonable amount to bring the premises back to a competitive position. The motel enjoys more than the average land and greenbelt areas, and it has the potential of being very attractively landscaped. Although the syndicate will put in enough money to bring the property back to first-class condition, it wants a definite return on investment; any expenditure for new facilities must be carefully justified. With the purchase of new equipment and the renovations you have unusual flexibility in changing the operation.

The previous operation was not successful due to lack of business. The reasons for this included ill-defined markets and, consequently, poor promotion efforts, and higher rates than the clientele seemed willing to pay, as well as an unexpected gasoline shortage.

You are hired as a consultant and have been asked by the chain to make recommendations regarding the feasibility of the operation. As part of your assignment, you are asked to do the following:

Identify possible market segments.

Select target markets and fringe markets.

Develop a pricing strategy for rooms and food operations.

Develop a marketing theme for the operation.

Determine what facilities would be utilized in the new operation.

11 Energy Management

The Energy Problem

Management and Energy Conservation

Water

To say that energy and *water management have become important concerns in American industry would be a monumental understatement. Obviously, managers of hospitality operations (in which customers and employees traditionally use water and electricity liberally) must learn ways to conserve these assets. Consequently, when you finish studying this chapter, you should be able to*

- *explain at some length the importance of water and energy conservation from the viewpoint of a hospitality manager*
- *list and explain briefly the various ways to measure energy and water consumption*
- *plan an actual energy and water conservation program in a hospitality operation*
- *discuss the implications for the hospitality industry of serious electricity, gasoline, and water shortages.*

The Energy Problem

It would have been most unusual, only a few years ago, for a hospitality management textbook to include a discussion of energy management. The cost of energy had traditionally been one of the relatively small business expenses. There was no energy shortage to speak of; in fact, different energy sources actually competed for customers. Moreover, since the New Deal, our government encouraged low-cost energy, which it saw as generating jobs and income.

There appeared to be no reason why this state of affairs would not continue. Consequently, management expressed little concern about energy. The manager of a large operation might, occasionally, look at the reports of the chief engineer on energy consumption, but was concerned only if they deviated from past reports. A manager of a small operation might check his utility and fuel bills, but again, only if they varied from past bills. For a long time, in fact, unit utilities and fuel costs actually decreased, although the total fuel bills increased with an increased energy use.

All this changed in 1973. The Arab oil embargo and the subsequent quadrupling of oil prices drastically altered the energy picture in that year—and ever since. But other forces were also at work; the decline of our own oil production, our steady increase in energy use (in some years by almost 5 percent over the preceding year), and the energy shortages and price hikes of the 1970s, have brought home the realization that some of our current energy sources, especially fossil fuels, are not inexhaustible after all.

Hospitality industries, as you know, consume large quantities of energy. A hotel or housing operation requires considerable energy to maintain its premises, and a foodservice operation requires considerable energy to produce food. The hospitality manager should, therefore, be aware of this energy situation and should actively combat energy waste for a number of good reasons.

One reason appears on the bottomline. No longer can energy costs be disregarded. Fuel costs increased greatly after the winter of 1973–1974, and again during 1979. One forecaster believes natural gas costs will increase 250 percent between 1976 and 1985, and oil costs will increase 125 percent between 1976 and 1985. The present price of energy and such projected costs as these cannot be ignored. To maintain desirable profit margins, an operation must, therefore, keep energy costs as low as possible.

Second, even if the cost of energy were not a problem, its *availability* would be. At one time, electric and gas salesmen competed to persuade hospitality operators to adopt their products. Now some of these same salesmen are trying to discourage use of their products. Some hospitality operations have trouble expanding new units because of the lack of energy availability. A hospitality operation needs the steady source of energy to operate, and if this is not available, the operation is in trouble.

A third concern of energy for the hospitality manager is in planning. Energy shortages can affect the nation's economy and habits. If, for example, an energy shortage is reflected in high gasoline costs or unavailable gasoline, there may be a definite trend toward traveling in mass transit, especially trains and busses. In this case it may not be as desirable to build a highway motel but perhaps more desirable to concentrate on downtown facilities and a prime hotel location may again be across from a midtown depot. During the winter of 1976–1977 and the spring of 1979 many areas experienced fuel shortages and restrictions on hours commercial operations could be opened. Since many hospitality organizations are specifically geared to the traveling public, the hospitality operator should be prepared for the possibility of similar energy shortages in the future.

A fourth concern is that energy conservation has become a major factor in our nation's politics, international relations, and economic well-being. Therefore the hospitality manager, like any good citizen, should be informed about the problem, and he should form knowledgeable opinions on how to proceed to deal with the problem in his own facility.

The basic problem for the nation is that the era of cheap energy has ended. We have left the time when energy was easy to find and easy to exploit. Since we no longer have an assured energy supply, in a severe shortage, activity and jobs would dramatically decrease. We would obviously suffer economic consequences. Such a shortage of energy could also have social consequences. Without enough energy even our physical well-being could be threatened. We are now importing almost 50 percent of our oil; every indication is that this percentage will rise. If the oil-producing and exporting countries (OPEC) threaten to cut off the supply, we would, quite frankly, be susceptible to energy blackmail.

Resources There is, of course, some dispute about how real the energy shortage is. One survey showed 70 percent of the population did not even believe that a shortage existed. By contrast, some experts say they can pinpoint the year when the world's oil supply will run out. For example, by one estimate, proven oil resources will be exhausted by the year 2078. The same estimate predicts that all potential U.S. resources will be exhausted by the year 2096, and that all world resources will be gone by the year 2476.

Other experts dispute such figures as these; they say that energy reserves and resources are largely a matter of definition and price. As the price of energy goes up, it will become economically feasible to develop other energy sources. In 1979 *The Wall Street Journal* printed an article claiming that the country enjoys more than a thousand years of natural gas supplies from all potential sources. On the average, an oil well under the present technology recovers only 40 percent of the oil beneath it. If that technology is improved and oil prices climb high enough to pay for expanded recovery, America might theoretically recover some 300 billion barrels of high-grade oil presently not recovered in drilling. This would equal 40 year's use of energy at present consumption rates. Another possible source is California, where from 35 to 100 billion barrels of "heavy oil" still remain in the ground. Heavy oil is extremely difficult to refine, but if this heavy oil, or "gunk" as it is sometimes called, were included in the country's proven reserves, they would nearly double. Thirty-five billion barrels in California hardly compares to the potential resources in Venezuela, where oil production as yet is too expensive to pursue at current prices. Alaska is another possible contributor of major oil reserves.

Other Factors Even if one takes comfort in the alternative energy supplies apparently available, the problem of lead time refuses to vanish. Lead time is the time it takes to develop a new energy source to the point where it can make a major contribution. Historically, it has taken about fifty years to move from one major energy source to another. In the 1850s we had largely a wood-furnace economy; by 1900 we had converted to largely a coal economy. It took us until almost 1950 to convert to oil and gas. As these resources dwindle, a severe shortage could develop if potential resource development was not accomplished in time to meet continuing energy needs.

Still more factors affect the development of energy sources. Vast amounts of coal can be found in the West, but mining that coal could despoil the land. Possible vast resources of oil occur along the eastern continental Atlantic shelf, but the risk of oil spills along the beaches has forced explorers to proceed with caution, and the first exploratory wells have proven discouraging. A major dam designed for hydroelectric power has been set aside because of concern for the snail darter, a small perch on the endangered species list. Dams also tend to lead to silt and salt buildup. New Western coal resources could possibly be transported in a coal and water slurry. But this procedure would require greater amounts of water than can generally be spared in arid regions where coal deposits are often found.

Government policy, too, may have contributed to the energy problems. Some argue that governmental controls discourage the discovery of new energy sources.

It is almost universally agreed that the price of energy will have to rise. But how shoud the extra money flowing from these increased prices be handled? The government suggests that prices should rise in the form of higher taxes on energy; the government itself would then redistribute the money among the states through various federal programs. Industry spokesmen claim this would promote no new development, instead allowing the vast sums of money necessary for energy development to accumulate in government coffers. The increased price of energy, the industry argues, should go to those in a position to develop new energy sources. Consumer spokesmen say this practice would result in "obscene" windfall profits for industry. They want prices to remain controlled.

Those of the classical school of economics feel that the law of supply and demand will resolve the energy problem. Others say that should an actual crisis develop, methods like rationing and allotment would be fairer. This position is, in turn, rebutted by those who feel that rationing would not increase the amount of energy available. Although such rationing or allotment of available energy might be fairer, this tactic, by itself, would certainly not increase the overall supply as is exemplified by the gasoline shortages of the 1970s and the resultant governmental allotment to various geographical areas. Despite these allocations long lines formed at some gas stations and gas occasionally ran out, even while other areas were well-supplied. Opponents said that the law of supply and demand would have been the better approach. If the price of gas had been allowed to rise, they argued, some people would have stopped driving, and there would, theoretically, have been enough gas for those willing to pay the high prices. (The law of supply and demand applied this simplisticly does, however, discriminate against the poor who cannot afford the higher prices.)

The fact that the United States has 6 percent of the world's population but uses 32 percent of its energy suggests that we are an extremely wasteful country. But even though we use a disproportionate amount of energy, we also produce about one-third of the world's total production—and production requires energy. We Americans, then, tend to use energy to make ourselves far more efficient in production. It has been estimated that a meal in a fast-food operation requires 28,378 Btu's (British thermal units—a Btu is roughly the heat given off by a wooden match). A meal in a hotel might use 43,528 Btu's, and a meal prepared at home might use 36,548 Btu's. These figures include the energy used in preparation, transportation, waste disposal, packaging, and other food production steps. Using these relatively high energy requirements, families and industry can prepare food with relatively low physical labor requirements.

In summary, there appears to be no real consensus on the energy problem. Doomsday people say that we are running out of energy; optimists say that there is plenty of energy if we go ahead and develop it. The statistics are suspect. Exactly how accurate are "proven reserve" estimates? Certainly, we should conserve energy, but conservation has its costs. To increase gasoline mileage in cars, we will need smaller cars. Smaller cars and fewer cars mean less work for our automobile workers. Our efforts to improve the environment strains the energy consumption to the point of inefficiency. Conservation is obviously not the complete answer to our energy problem. Even if we defer the exhaustion of our energy supply by a decade or so, we will still have exhausted it. To keep our economy intact during the next two or three decades, we must use every tool at our disposal: conservation, relaxation of some environmental constraints, incentives for developing new sources of energy, and a coherent national energy program.

Energy's Measurement

It is time now to clarify what energy is and how it is measured. Dictionaries define energy as "an entity rated as the most fundamental of all physical concepts; usually regarded as the capacity to do work." Everything in this universe is either energy or matter, and one can be changed into the other. The relationship between energy and matter is expressed in Einstein's famous equation $E = mc^2$ (energy equals the mass times the square of the speed of light).

A common measurement of energy is the British thermal unit (Btu) defined as the amount of heat required to raise the temperature of one pound of water by one degree Fahrenheit. The value of different energy sources can be expressed in Btu's for example, a gallon of one type of oil contains 142,000 Btu's. A cubic foot of natural gas contains about 1000 Btu's. And a thousand cubic feet of natural gas (MCF) contains one million Btu's.

Another measure of Btu's in natural gas is the therm, which is the equivalent of 100,000 Btu's. The Btu's in a ton of coal would vary according to the texture of the coal, but it could be 13,000 per pound or 26,000,000 per ton. Electric power consumed is measured by the watt, usually expressed in one-thousand-watt units or kilowatts (kW). A kilowatt-hour (kWh) is a measure of electrical energy (power consumed over a specified period). One kWh is equal to the energy consumed at the rate of one kW for one hour. Thus a one-hundred-watt lamp burning for ten hours will consume one kWh of energy. One kWh contains 3,412 Btu's. A one-hundred-watt light bulb burning for one hour will consume 341 Btu's of electrical energy and emit about 95 of these as heat.

The Btu value of fuels does not take into account the efficiency of converting the fuel into energy. If an oil burner is 75 percent efficient, the amount of energy provided by one gallon of oil would be 75 percent of its potential Btu's 142,000. In a gas burner that is 80 percent efficient, the amount of energy from one cubic foot would be 800 Btu's; if a coal burner is 70 percent efficient, the amount of energy from a pound of coal with a Btu content of 13,000 would be 9,100 Btu's. At the site used, electricity is 100 percent efficient, so the full Btu's or kilowatt-hour would be received. (There is, however, a 60 to 70 percent loss in generating and transmitting the electricity to the site where it is used.)

A measurement called the *degree day* is used to calculate heating and cooling. A heating degree day is the difference between the outdoor mean daily temperature and 65 degrees Fahrenheit. If the mean outdoor temperature on a given day is 40 degrees, there would be 25 degree days for that day. Degree days help one calculate how much fuel energy should be used in heating. Moreover, the severity of one winter compared to another can be calculated with degree days. How much fuel one geographical area requires compared to another area can also be determined by degree days. Fairbanks, Alaska, averages 14,279 degree days per year. Fort Myers, Florida, averages only 442 degree days per year. With figures like these one can eliminate "suggesting" how much energy should be required for heating. This is how fuel dealers make their automatic deliveries. Noting the number of degree days that have gone by, they can translate that number into the fuel consumed.

A *cooling degree day* is a measure of the need for air conditioning. It is calculated by subtracting 65 degrees Fahrenheit from the mean daily temperature. If the outdoor mean temperature is 90 degrees, 25 cooling degree days are registered. Humidity also affects the need for cooling, but it is not reflected in a cooling degree day. A measure of cooling (and a measure of air-conditioning capacity) is tons of refrigeration. A ton of refrigeration implies the removal of 12,000 Btu's of heat per hour. A half-ton air conditioner, for example, would have the capacity to remove 6,000 Btu's of heat per hour.

Horsepower (hp) is the effect of pulling 33,000 foot-pounds in one minute. In energy calculation, one horsepower equals 746 watts or 2,545 Btu's per hour. Lighting energy is measured in lumens. The more lumens produced from the same wattage, the more efficient the lamp; different types of lighting give out different lumens-per-watt ratios. For example, an ordinary incandescent lamp gives out 17 to 20 lumens per watt. A fluorescent lamp provides 67 to 83 lumens per watt, and a sodium lamp provides 105 to 130 lumens per watt.

Energy Sources

Between the years 1977 and 2000 this country will probably consume more energy than it has in its entire past. The demand for energy in the year 2000 will probably be double what it was in 1977, and the world demand by then will have tripled. Where will the energy come from to meet these demands? And what are the energy sources already available to us? The following sections consider some of those questions.

Oil. Oil has been formed from marine life, plants, and animals that lived millions of years ago. The amount of oil available is finite, and proven reserves could be exhausted in the first half of the twenty-first century if the demand for energy grows at currently projected rates. Potential and undiscovered reserves could extend that deadline. Since 1950, oil has been the favorite fuel, increasingly supplanting coal. In 1975, for example, oil provided 47 percent of our country's energy. It is obvious, therefore, that we must shift much of our energy consumption to other fuels.

Oil was used at first only as a lubricant. It came into widespread use for energy when the Civil War interrupted whaling expeditions. This, combined with depletion of whale herds, produced a shortage of oil for oil lamps. Besides its use as an energy source, petroleum is also used in the manufacture of many plastics and other products.

Natural gas. Natural gas has been called "the perfect fuel" because it is clean, cheap, and traditionally abundant. But our production of natural gas "topped out" in the early 1970s. Proven reserves will provide only ten to twelve years use at our current rate of consumption; the tapping of potential or undiscovered reserves would probably extend the supply into the twenty-first century. In 1975, natural gas provided some 28 percent of United States energy.

Coal. Coal is easily our most abundant fossil fuel. Some estimates give us supplies sufficient to carry us through hundreds of years. The amount of coal actually available to us is affected by technological constraints, environmental controls, and economic factors. At one time, before being supplanted by oil and natural gas, coal was our primary energy source. Its disadvantages include the fact that it is dirty, bulky, and often dangerous to mine. It also produces sulfur dioxide (SO_2) when burned. But coal could once again become the major energy source, or at the very least, an increasingly important energy source for the foreseeable future. New sources of coal include vast strip mines in the western states, but there are strong environmental objections to extensive mining in these areas.

Shale oil. Oil shale is sedimentary rock from which oil can be extracted with heat. Some geologists estimate that this country has three times as much oil in this form as Saudi Arabia's present proven oil reserves. Although it is technically feasible to extract oil and gas from shale oil, actual procedures are as yet neither environmentally sound nor economical enough for large-scale operations. But oil shale does have great potential as a major energy source, and it may become important when energy from other sources dwindles.

Water power. The energy of water flowing over a dam or waterfall can easily be converted to electrical energy through turbines. But the most desirable sites have already been utilized. Therefore, although this energy is desirable, nonpolluting, and has no direct fuel costs, its potential is limited.

Nuclear power. In the early 1970s nuclear power seemed to offer real hope for abundant energy. Since then, however, nuclear plant construction has slowed down considerably. We have discovered that the spent fuel remains radioactive and dangerous for many generations and that radioactive fuel can be stolen and possibly used by terrorists for bombs. By 1980, nuclear reactors may produce about 13 percent of our country's electricity. Some experts still estimate that by the year 2000 nuclear plants will account for 30 percent of our electrical generating capacity. At this writing it is not possible to evaluate the long-range implications or consequences of the 1979 Three Mile Island nuclear plant failure for the use of nuclear power.

Nuclear fusion, different from the fission process used in nuclear reactors, is a possible energy source and could provide energy for thousands of years. The fusion concept has yet to be proven scientifically, but in the summer of 1978 scientists at Princeton University made some important strides toward making this kind of energy feasible.

Solar energy. The most abundant energy source is the sun. For us it is a renewable and virtually inexhaustible resource. Some hot water heating, space heating, and air conditioning are already accomplished by solar energy. The systems concentrate useful heat from collectors much as water in a garden hose is heated on a sunny day. Currently, solar heating is costly, but as energy costs increase and the cost of solar collectors drops, it will become more economically feasible. The future may well bring the photovoltaic conversion of sunlight into electricity by such sunlight-sensitive materials as silicone. This process is too expensive for widespread commercial use as of this writing.

Biomass. The term *biomass* refers to the use of organic wastes as an energy source. This source could provide a limited amount of energy, but it has the advantage of disposing of undesirable wastes. Municipal solid wastes can be burned directly or be converted to liquids, gases, or solid fuel. Theoretically, certain farm crops could also be converted into energy.

Other sources. Other sources of energy exist but are widely overlooked. The recent energy shortage has brought many of them to the public's attention. Modern, streamlined windmills could be installed at selected spots to generate power. Efficient energy could be provided by the geothermal heat where it comes to the surface of the earth. Numerous hot springs trap heat at or near the earth's crust. This heat could be tapped to produce energy in the dry steam or hot water it releases. Some seacoasts experience powerful tides that could be used to produce energy convertible to electric power. Also, power could be generated from the temperature differences between the warm surface water of the oceans and their cooler, deeper waters.

Management and Energy Conservation

Virtually all hospitality operations could save energy. The National Bureau of Standards (NBS), surveying representative U.S. industries, estimates that approximately 40 percent of the energy used for heating is wasted, that 30 percent of the energy used for cooling could be saved with little sacrifice, and that lighting energy could be reduced by 15 percent by matching lighting to actual needs. In particular, the average hotel or motel could probably cut its energy consumption by from 15 to 30 percent. By instituting an energy conservation program, one fast-food operation saved 70 percent of the gas it used and 18 percent of its kilowatt hours (kWh). By programming equipment automatically to when it was actually required in the kitchen, another operation saved 20 percent of its energy costs. A third fast-food operation saved 10 percent of its energy just by installing an off-on schedule for its equipment. In a good many kitchens about half the cooking energy serves only to heat up the kitchen and "cook" the personnel.

But how, you might ask, should an energy conservation program be organized? The program must begin with a firm commitment by management and be followed with enforcement. Too often management pays lip service to energy conservation but never really follows through. Once its commitment is made and publicized, management must proceed with its program.

Although energy saving is everybody's job, some employees will have more responsibility in this area than others. In fact, some operations organize an energy conservation committee. Typically, this committee is composed of department heads and people immediately involved with energy such as the chief engineer, if he is not already a department head. Sometimes it is helpful to have outside people such as a union representative or somebody with special expertise in the group. Heading the energy conservation group should be an energy conservation official, perhaps the manager or someone else to whom both power and responsibility for acting has been delegated.

The next step is to conduct an energy survey. Discover how much energy the operation has been using by examining past utility bills. How much energy do the various pieces of equipment utilize? Ideally, a meter should be installed on every piece of equipment to measure its energy consumption. But, this practice probably is not feasible. To get approximation, however, determine how many hours the equipment is used and then, by examining the plate on that piece of equipment, determine what its power load or gas requirements are. Multiplying these two figures yields the daily equipment usage. All energy consuming equipment and apparatuses should be included.

At this point, you can probably establish an energy goal. This goal might be to reduce energy consumption by 20 percent. If the goal is too unrealistic, your employees will be unwilling to try to achieve it. If the goal is too low, additional savings may be lost when the employees, having achieved the low, relax.

The next step is to implement energy-saving procedures. Many checklists detailing energy-saving devices and plans are already available. The Hospitality Lodging and Travel Research Foundation, Inc., an affiliate of the American Hotel and Motel Association, supplies a particularly helpful energy conservation manual describing energy conservation opportunities for hospitality operations. In many cases, committee decisions will have to be made on some of the important aspects. (For example, when should air conditioning temperatures be raised or heating temperatures cut back a few degrees?) These decisions obviously can affect other areas of an operation. What, for example, constitutes sufficient lighting level? How much can be spent for automatic energy-saving controls?

The energy committee should meet regularly, hear reports, and check to see how well it is achieving its goals. One hotel chain designates a management official in each hotel for a fourteen-day period to be an energy check officer. He maintains checksheets for various areas of the hotel, and when he finds an area that wastes energy, he reduces the area's score by one. The various areas compete; the highest score wins; and the employees in that area receive a cash bonus.

A crucial part of the energy conservation program is measuring its results. These results should be reported to the committee both formally and informally. A sample form from the energy conservation manual of the Hospitality, Lodging and Travel Research Foundation appears in Exhibit 11-1.

Columns 2 and 3 of the form provide the number of heating and cooling degree days to indicate how much heating and cooling may be required. Column 4 records the number of guest-days for the period: the more guest days, the more energy required. Columns 5, 6, 7, and 8 record the amount of energy consumed. Each entry of energy used is translated in column 9 into Btu's and divided by the number of guest-days to yield the figure in column 11. This form, though used for hotels, could be equally effective when foodservice energy is included. Column 13 is the energy utilization index or Btu's per square foot. The amount of energy divided by the number of square feet in a property provides an indication of how much energy by square feet is needed to maintain a property. Although this figure does not automatically incorporate the severity of weather, one can still use it to compare one month to another or (perhaps more importantly) one year to other years. Exhibit 11-1 is a typical form, but individual operations should make up a chart that reflects their particular needs.

Conservation Techniques

There are many excellent energy saving checklists designed for hospitality operations, and this book does not cover them all. Nevertheless, some general conservation principles can apply to many different areas in the hospitality operation. One is the use of insulation. Insulation in ceilings and walls can reduce space heating requirements. Hot and cold water pipes, steam lines, and such appliances as water heaters, ovens, and steam-jacketed kettles, can all be insulated to save energy. Insulating the various appliances in the kitchen not only saves fuel but can also make the kitchen a cooler, pleasanter place to work.

Another fundamental principle of energy conservation is turning off energy-consuming devices when they are not needed. Many cooks turn on cooking appliances before they really need them. This practice may reflect habits from the days when the recovery time and heat time were slow. Nowadays not only are appliances turned on too soon, but they may also be left on throughout the day when they are not needed. Some

PROPERTY NAME _____   FLOOR AREA _____   YEAR _____

MONTH	HEAT DEG. DAYS	COOL DEG. DAYS	OCCUPANCY HOUSE COUNT	ELECTRICITY KWH	PURCHASED STEAM M (LBS.)	FUEL OIL GALLONS	GAS CU. FT.	TOTAL ENERGY USED MILLIONS OF B.T.U.		ENERGY USED PER GUEST DAY M.B.T.U./GUEST DAY		ENERGY UTILIZATION INDEX BTU/SQ. FT.
								THIS YEAR	PRIOR YEAR	THIS YEAR	PRIOR YEAR	
1	2	3	4	5	6	7	8	9	10	11	12	13
JAN.	935		6,556	200,400		33,059	3,561	5,478		835.6		26,380
FEB.	954		6,442	182,400		33,836	3,468	5,530		858.4		26,631
MAR.	135		6,663	198,000		28,421	3,783	4,798		720.1		23,106
APR.	366	19	7,249	190,800		23,337	3,855	4,036		556.8		19,436
MAY	198	35	7,891	235,200		28,978	4,190	5,006		634.4		24,107
JUNE	27	160	7,918	274,800		43,246	4,100	7,209		910.4		34,707
JULY	3	389	7,975	307,200		52,288	4,237	8,630		1082.1		41,559
AUG.		376	10,802	312,000		48,284	4,693	8,067		746.8		38,848
SEPT.	53	117	7,342	264,000		39,048	3,631	6,563		893.9		31,605
OCT.	346		7,824	200,400		19,082	4,084	3,452		441.2		16,624
NOV.	529		6,606	199,200		20,719	3,711	3,685		557.8		17,746
DEC.	807		4,353	202,800		23,368	3,781	4,082		937.1		19,658
TOTALS	4,953	1,096	87,621	2,767,200		393,666	47,094	66,536				320,402

LEGEND

B.T.U.   —   BRITISH TERMAL UNITS
M.B.T.U. —   THOUSANDS OF B.T.U.
K.W.H.   —   KILOWATT HOURS
M LBS.   —   THOUSANDS OF POUNDS

Exhibit 11–1.   Sample Energy Consumption Form
(Reprinted with permission, American Hotel and Motel Association.)

operations have begun, however, to install automatic timers to start up and shut down their equipment. One example of this practice used by hotels is electronically adjusting the temperature in the rooms when they are occupied and changing the adjustment when they are not. Sizing equipment accurately can also save energy. Generally, too, energy savings result when equipment is used to its full capacity rather than running only partial loads. Normally the smaller a piece of equipment is, the less energy it will use—if it has the capacity to do the job in the first place. Preventive maintenance can also cut down on energy use. Improperly adjusted gas ranges waste gas. Dirty shades require larger lightbulbs.

Equipment purchasers should always consider energy utilization. Room air conditioners have an EER (energy efficiency ratio) that provides a measure of their efficiency in advance. The EER can be calculated by dividing the cooling power (as expressed in Btu's per hour) by the number of watts of power used. A 12,000-Btu air conditioner (a one-ton unit) might use 1900 watts and have an EER of 6.3. Another 12,000-Btu unit might use 1350 watts and have an EER of 8.8. The latter will use 20 percent less energy. In some buildings, 60 percent of the air conditioning load is the heat generated by the lighting. This loss could be reduced by installing lights that radiate less heat, such as fluorescent bulbs, by turning off lights when the area is not being used, and by installing improved ventilation or better insulation. Slight changes in the heating or cooling temperature can produce significant changes in energy consumption. Researchers have found that many foodservice dining rooms are too cool because the temperature is adjusted to accommodate working employees rather than the guests.

Insulation, as we said, conserves heating and cooling energy. But, besides saving this energy, good insulation can also enhance comfort during both summer and winter as it renders an area more uniformly heated or cooled without hot or cold spots. Heating or cooling a poorly insulated building is like pumping air into a leaky tire. If the leak is large, you must pump continuously and vigorously. Likewise, insufficient insulation will make your heating and cooling system work harder. The greatest heat loss in most buildings is through the roof, and the roof is the easiest area to insulate.

The overall effectiveness of insulation can be measured by the R value, which shows insulation's resistance to heat transfer. Insulation in outer walls should have a vapor barrier facing the heated area. Otherwise, vapor in the heat that goes through the wall, will be cooled by cool air from the outside of the wall and the moisture will condense within the wall wetting the insulation and causing such other problems as mildew and rot.

Along with insulation, one should incorporate storm windows and doors and see that all cracks are caulked or weather stripped. Unfortunately, many modern hotel operations have outside wall surfaces consisting largely or entirely of glass. Glass is an excellent conductor. It readily transfers heat from the inside to the outside on cold days; and it lets hot summer heat enter in on hot days.

Peak Loads and Demand Charges

Electrical consumption in an operation is rarely consistent throughout a day; peak and slack periods are the rule. An electrical utility tries to maintain enough generating capacity to provide for these peak periods, even though other times of the day much of this capacity lies idle. To compensate for this inequity, some gererating companies determine an operational peak demand period and charge a premium rate for energy used at these times. To save this higher cost and to help the utility even out its load, a hospitality enterprise can arrange to shut off as many electrical appliances as possible during the peak load or demand periods. For example, hot water may not be heated during a peak period but previously heated reserves used. It may even be possible to shut off air conditioning—if the demand period is only fifteen minutes long there will be only a limited temperature rise. Some types of equipment may not be needed during this peak period.

Water

Although not a form of energy, water is an essential commodity for hospitality operations. Most of us take water for granted, but it may well present severe problems to the hospitality managers of the future. The problem is not just national; it is international in scope. In 1977, a severe drought forced water rationing in the West and withered crops in the South and Midwest. At the same time, a prolonged drought in Africa and Europe caused widespread starvation. The problem will probably get worse. By the year 2000, some experts estimate that only three of the federally designated water regions on the U.S. mainland, New England, the Ohio Basin, and the South Atlantic-Eastern Gulf Area, will be able to live comfortably with their water supplies. But even if they have sufficient water, serious purity problems may arise. The 1977 drought was only a test run of what areas of this country could experience by 1990.

These water problems have definite implications for the hospitality operator. To begin with, the cost of water will steadily rise. And so, too, will the indirect costs connected with water quality. Poor water quality will lead to higher treatment costs. Water shortages will cause hospitality insurance rates to jump. Hard water will increase laundry costs and shorten linen life. Hard water can also increase labor time and plumbing expenses and reduce the efficiency of heating systems.

Moreover, the local water situation can directly influence the economic activities of a region and, consequently, the future of a hospitality enterprise within that area. Arizona, for example, is one of the fastest growing areas of the nation. It depends, however, almost entirely on underground water from an ancient glacier lake that underlies the state. This lake receives no replenishment from the surface, and its level is rapidly dropping. Unless some other water source is found, the economic growth of Arizona could be restricted, a situation that would not help a hospitality operation (or any other operation) there. Other areas in the country have similar problems that could limit their economic progress. Hotels are designed for comparatively long lives. If there is not enough business over their lives to amortize the costs and return profits, financial trouble will follow for the hotel owners.

The Problem Unique to Water

Water is not destroyed. It can be used over and over again. Therefore, our water problem is not that we have used up some finite resource, but that the need for water will increase while the quality of water may decrease as our increasing population uses our water resources. Of the great amount of water in the world, only a small portion of it is available for human needs. Over 97 percent of the water in the world occurs in the oceans and is unfit for drinking. More than three-quarters of the remainder is locked in glaciers. Much of the rest is trapped as *fossil water* in underground aquifers far below the earth's surface. Only about one-third of one percent of all the world's fresh water is available for human consumption, and in some cases, it is nowhere near the larger human populations.

Comparatively speaking, humans actually require for sustenance only a little of the water they actually use. More than 80 percent of the water used by humans serves to irrigate between 30 or 40 percent of the world's food production. Obviously, as the population increases, more food will be needed and more water will be diverted for irrigation. Industry also uses increasingly large amounts of water for manufacturing. Industry and agriculture also pollute many water sources, a practice that makes water unfit for human consumption without expensive treatment.

We Americans have also been much too profligate in our use of water. The physiological minimum for human survival is about one quart of water per day. Some tribesmen in arid Africa survive on no more than eight-tenths of a gallon of water a day. A United Nations report estimates that a person in London now uses 68 gallons a day, a person in Paris 130 gallons, a person in Moscow 160 gallons, and a citizen of New York City 270 gallons a day, and per capita water use in this country continues to rise. For example, flushing a toilet disposes of seven gallons; a shower uses from 20 to 30 gallons; and a tub bath uses from 30 to 40 gallons.

Dishwashing also consumes a great deal of water in hospitality operations. An 8-ounce glass of water, in fact, requires 24 ounces of water to wash and sanitize the glass.

What to Do about Water Shortage

The hospitality establishment uses only a small amount of all the water consumed, but the hospitality operator must take strong measures to guard that water will remain available. He can do this in two basic ways: conservation of current resources and development of new ones. Higher water bills by themselves will bring about some conservation.

In some areas where water consumption is not metered, per capita consumption rates grow exhorbitantly high. But where water is metered and paid for by the amount used, the rates often level off or fall. Large amounts of water are often lost through leaking municipal water mains and dripping faucets, and it is possible, even easy, to stop this loss. New devices on the market can curtail water usage. Flow restrictors in showers and toilet inserts that flush less water are two examples. Two water systems could be installed in a building, one supplying potable water, which would be used only once; the other supplying water for sanitary purposes, which could be used over and over again with only minor treatment.

The other way to increase the water supply is to find new sources. Here, unless he runs a self-contained operation, all the hospitality operator can do is to voice a strong civic interest in the community water supply. The continental United States has a daily stream flow of 1160 billion gallons; we could conceivably divert half of this for human use. But sometimes handling the water supply becomes a problem of finding storage capacity for water that is already available. Water is, in short, becoming an increasingly economic and political subject. A hospitality operator should be involved in the discussions not only out of self-interest but also because of the civic concern.

A part of water management for a hospitality operation can be water softening. *Hard water* is water that contains excessive calcium and magnesium salts. Hard water cleans poorly and must be used in larger amounts. It also leaves the traditional ring around the tub, coating on pots and pans, and scale deposits in pipes which curtail the flow. Hard water, particularly hot hard water, can eventually clog a heating system if it is not controlled. A number of processes can, however, soften hard water, including exchange tanks and commercial water softening systems. Besides saving on water, these systems help an operator save soap, linens, and labor. It may not be feasible to provide soft water for an entire hospitality operation, but it may pay to supply soft water to such areas as the kitchen or the laundry.

Water hardness is expressed in grains of hardness, the number of grains of calcium or magnesium salts in a gallon of water. Three grains hardness, for example, would indicate three grains of mineral salts in a gallon, which is equivalent of 50 parts per million.

Possible Solutions to our Water Problems

A number of proposals have been suggested to increase the supply of water. Saudi Arabia has studied the feasibility of towing icebergs from Antarctica to a Red Sea port where it could be melted for fresh water. Desalinization, taking water from the ocean and removing the salt, has become the chief source of supply in some areas of the world. But the cost of desalination is high. In some areas we can still tap underground water resources. But, many of these resources cannot be replenished or can replenish themselves slowly. Recycling water instead of disposing of used water reduces the need for fresh supplies. Manufacturing plants, for example, have begun to install closed-circuit cooling systems that permit recycling.

SUMMARY

Although other factors would have caused an increasing energy problem, the Arab Oil Embargo of 1973 signaled the end of cheap and easily available energy. The oil crisis of 1979 greatly exacerbated the problem. From a relatively minor concern, energy has become crucially important to the hospitality manager. Not only have energy costs skyrocketed, but by 1979, its very availability has become a problem. Gasoline shortages have even touched would-be customers, curbing their patronage of hospitality establishments.

A considerable dispute continues over how much heating oil and gasoline is available and how to handle the shortages. Should price limit consumption? Or should rationing and controls keep prices down while discouraging the development of energy sources? In any case, the amount of oil is finite; proven reserves will probably run out in the next century. Nuclear power, once a promising replacement, now presents severe environmental problems. Coal could supply hundreds of years of energy but would also mean serious environmental difficulties. Natural gas is an ideal fuel, but conventional sources may run out in the next century. Such other sources as shale oil, solar energy, biomass, and hydro-power may be called upon, but unfortunately, even if these other sources are available, their development will require substantial lead-time before any is as effective or accessible an energy source as oil has accustomed us to need.

In the meantime, almost all hospitality operations can reduce energy consumption. First, there must be a commitment from management. Perhaps this commitment could take the form of an energy conservation committee. Such a committee could conduct an energy survey, and from it establish an energy-saving goal. To achieve this goal, energy-saving procedures must be implemented and results must be evaluated.

One important means of saving electrical energy is to reduce energy use during peak hours. Often facilities that must be available for peak periods are not fully used most of the time. Electrical costs may be lower if a hospitality operation can cut consumption at peak periods by spreading the use of its appliances more evenly throughout the day.

Water supply is a problem in some areas. As with energy, a shortage of water can affect the patronage of a hospitality establishment. Moreover, as the quantity of water decreases, so does its quality. Water cannot really be destroyed, but its excessive use can reduce its quality, require expensive treatment, and cause more wear and tear on equipment and linens. Even though he can usually do little to increase the supply, the hospitality manager should take steps to reduce water consumption.

IMPORTANT TERMS

After studying this chapter, you should be able to define the following terms:

> **Btu**
>
> **therm**
>
> **watt**
>
> **kWh**
>
> **heating degree day**
>
> **cooling degree day**
>
> **ton of refrigeration**
>
> **horsepower**
>
> **lumen**
>
> **biomass**
>
> **EER**
>
> **R value**
>
> **peak demand period (electricity)**
>
> **hard water**
>
> **grains of hardness**

REVIEW QUESTIONS

11-1. Why should a hospitality manager be interested in energy?

11-2. Discuss the energy problem in America.

11-3. It is generally agreed that the price of energy will have to rise. Compare these alternatives: (a) the increase takes the form of government taxes; (b) the increase takes the from of a higher return to producers.

11-4. How can a degree day be used in heating fuel calculations?

11-5. You desire to cut energy consumption in your hotel. What general procedure would you follow to achieve this goal?

11-6. What are some general principles of energy conservation?

11-7. How can a water shortage in a geographical area affect a hotel?

11-8. What are some possible solutions to the water-scarcity problem?

11-9. Some possible energy sources of the future are heavy oil, oil shale, and nuclear power. What do you think are the advantages and disadvantages of using these sources?

11-10. How could you cut the peak demand electrical load in a hotel?

11-11. A hospitality establishment calculates that it requires one million Btu's of heat for every ten heating degree days. The following data on fuels is presented:

FUEL	MEASURE	EFFICIENCY	COST
Oil	Gallon	75%	$ 1.00
Gas	Therm	80%	0.50
Coal	Pound	70%	50.00
			(per ton)
Electricity	kWh	100%	0.10

Using energy values from the text, calculate (a) the amount of each fuel used per one million degree days and (b) the cost of each fuel per one million degree days.

12 Legal Aspects, Insurance, and Risk Management

*A*ll *managerial supervisors* should be alert to the legal climate in which they do business. Ignorance of the law is neither an excuse nor a defense when a manager commits a legal infraction. Moreover, as the saying goes, "a man who serves as his own lawyer has a fool for a client." Thus, the information in this chapter can be no means substitute for professional legal advice. But it will point out particular legal responsibilities a hospitality operator assumes.

The first part of this discussion will cover some basic provisions of business law essential to the transaction of ordinary business affairs. The second section addresses the specific applications of these laws to the hospitality industry. The chapter continues with brief discussions of laws that have particular significance in the hospitality industry. Since protection against legal claims comes with both vigilance and insurance, the last part of the chapter discusses insurance and risk management considerations appropriate for the hospitality industry. When you have finished studying this chapter, you should be able to

- discuss those principles of tort law, contract law, and the law of negotiable instruments useful to hospitality managers
- list four types of hospitality laws that are particularly important to hospitality managers (laws, for example, grouped under such categories as food liability, property loss, and inn-keeping)
- discuss briefly some possible effects of at least six federal laws that pertain to hospitality, including, the Civil Rights Act, the Fair Labor Standards Act, Unemployment Compensation, and the Social Security Act
- discuss briefly four different types of insurance companies and explain briefly the role of their representatives
- list and explain briefly at least eleven types of insurance appropriate for a hospitality manager to consider

Some Principles of Business Law

Familiarity with some of the principles of business law can help a person manage the activities of both a commercial, profit-making organization or an institutional or non-profit-making operation. Law is composed of rules of conduct governing men in their relations with one another. In one form or another, it is essential to civilization as we know it, and all organized society shares some fundamental laws that describe what is right and prohibit what is wrong. Business law in particular consists of rules of conduct that regulate the rights and remedies of people engaged in business.

Laws may be derived from two general sources. One is the *common law* or unwritten law that has developed from rules that have come into being through custom and usage and have ultimately been enunciated in court decisions. Most American common law began in England and was brought to this continent by the earliest settlers. Common law settles cases in accordance with *precedents*, recorded decisions made by other courts in similar cases. In deciding an issue at hand, attorneys and judges draw analogies to similar cases. The English system of common law has been adopted by all states except Louisiana, which follows the civil or Roman law in force when the Louisiana Territory was purchased from France.

By contrast, *statutory law* consists of laws adopted by Congress or by legislatures of various states. On a still lower level, a city or town can enact statutory laws known as *ordinances*. Together with the American constitution and the various state constitutions, these laws make up what is commonly known as the written law. Statutes normally take precedence over common law.

Law of Torts

The application of the law of torts is important in business law. A *tort* is a physical harm done to a person or property and caused by the act, or the failure to act, or the general negligence of another person. Torts can be divided into two general categories: voluntary and involuntary. Involuntary torts are those that occur through an act of negligence or an accident.

Voluntary torts occur through such deliberate action as assault or libel. When a person's rights have been interfered with by another, the injured party may sue for damages and seek relief in the form of money compensation. The injured party sues for damages on the theory that the person who caused his injuries or losses had a duty to exercise reasonable care and was derelict in that duty, and therefore caused the injuries or damages. Typical injuries sustained in hospitality operations, like slipping on ill-kept floors or being scalded by inadequate plumbing fixtures, may be examples of torts—provided, of course, the owner was actually negligent. The voluntary tort of assault means the threatening to harm someone physically by a person with the apparent ability or power to carry out his threat. The actual striking constitutes the tort of battery. The two torts, assault and battery, are usually committed together. Another familiar tort includes the deceit or deliberate misrepresentation of a material fact or by using trickery—to another's damage or loss. The tort of slander consists of false statements transmitted from one person to another by word of mouth and resulting in an injury to the reputation of the slandered person. False statements in written, printed, or electronic form that injure either the social or business reputation of a person are classed as libel. Financial damages are awarded to a person libeled by such false statements.

Law of Contracts

Contracts are essential to business. A contract may be defined as an agreement between two competent parties, based on sufficient legal consideration to do or not to do some particular act. That act must be possible and cannot be illegal. Certain elements must be present in every contract for that contract to be enforceable. For example, the people entering into the contract must be competent. A minor may not make a binding contract, nor can a person of subnormal mentality, nor someone out of control of his normal senses. The subject matter of the contract must be legal. If betting is illegal, a partnership contract in a gambling casino cannot be enforced. Also, *consideration* must be given for the subject matter. If a contract specifies the purchase of goods, the consideration is the price paid for these goods. A consideration must, in short, constitute something of value such as the relinquishing of a certain right or the promise of doing a certain thing or, more frequently, a certain amount of money. (The sum of money need not be equal to the value of the right or promise.) The agreement in the contract must result from an offer and an acceptance of that offer; that is, there must be a meeting of the minds.

To be legally binding the offer must be made in clear language. And the acceptance that follows must be communicated clearly and without condition. Some contracts such as negotiable instruments must be in writing; others can be verbal. Of course contracts in writing are much easier to prove, if a dispute should arise

Contracts occur in the hospitality industry principally when goods are bought and sold. When a guest registers in a hotel, a contract arises between the hotel offering service for the consideration of payment and the guest himself.

Law of Negotiable Instruments

Commercial paper consists of credit instruments that circulate as freely as money and are known as negotiable instruments. The two most pertinent examples for the hospitality industry are checks and credit cards. But some other familiar types include promissory notes, drafts, bonds, and bank checks. All of these can be transferred from one person to another by endorsement and delivery, or by delivery alone. Although a negotiable instrument is a written contract, it differs from other contracts in the way it can be transferred and in the nature of its consideration. Ordinary contracts may be *assigned* which means that the rights held by a person in a simple contract can be transferred to a third party. In such a case, the assignee (the person succeeding to the contract) must give notice to the debtor when he acquires the rights.

Negotiable paper can, by contrast, be transferred by a simple endorsement. When the person named as the payee endorsed the instrument to someone else, the endorsement usually appears on the back of the paper. An endorsed check, that is a check signed on the back by the payee, can be cashed by its bearer, although the words "pay to the order of _____" and then the payee's signature lessen the possibility of theft or forgery. If there is no known payee—only terms like "bearer" or "cash"—the instrument may be negotiated by simple delivery or transfer.

The main negotiable instrument problem in hospitality operations centers on check cashing. In the interest of being a good host, an operation might choose to cash checks; on the other hand, it risks financial loss if the checks are no good. Checks often come back marked "insufficient funds," indicating what might be a temporary situation in the maker's bank account. Hospitality operations will routinely resubmit the check and quite frequently it is then honored by the bank on which it is drawn, since funds have been deposited in the interim. But, of course, many checks are drawn with an intention to deceive, and in such cases a hospitality operation is stuck by the "paperhanger."

Hospitality operators can take a number of steps to prevent bad check losses. First, try to establish the identity of the person offering a check. Identity cards can be forged, but some are better than others. One of the worst is the social security card which can be secured by virtually anyone. The bank on which the check is drawn will verify whether there is enough money in the maker's account to honor the check. But a bank can state only that there is sufficient money at the time of the inquiry; a "paperhanger" could always write an overabundance of checks and then vanish before the checks reach the bank. If the operator is unsure of a check maker, someone reliable who knows the check writer can endorse the check and become liable in case of nonpayment. All endorsers, unless the endorsement is qualified, become liable for nonpayment, but each endorser has a legal claim on endorsers preceding him. Hotels sometimes try to establish identities by inquiring among local people with whom the guest has done business or has been seen.

Checks can, of course, be forged, and checkbooks are often stolen. Certain technical devices can curtail bad checks. One takes the thumbprint of the maker. Another takes his picture and transmits it over phone lines. Incidentally, all states have statutes that make the issuance of bad checks a punishable crime. The credit problem has lessened in recent years with the distribution of national credit cards. If a hospitality operation has an arrangement with one or more of the issuing organizations, it can accept these valid cards and be reimbursed by the organization. The card-issuing company also takes care of billing the customer and accepts liability for cards illegally used. Of course, the hospitality organization pays a fee, often between 4 and 7 percent of the amount charged to the credit card operation.

Liability in the Sale of Food

Foreign matter occasionally enters the food served by the most conscientious of foodservice operators. It can cause choking, damage, or illness. The patron victimized by a piece of glass or a thumbtack in his food may very well sue the establishment. Likewise, he may sue if he can trace his food poisoning or his case of trichinosis to a certain foodservice establishment.

Historically, two concepts have determined the liability attending unwholesome food served to patrons. The older concept saw the providing of food consumed on the premises as a service and the actual food itself as a part of that service rendered. (Other "aspects" include the preparation of food, the serving, the dishes required, and the decor.) Under this concept the foodservice operation became liable only for its negligence "in failing to exercise due care." The foodservice operation did not ensure the quality of the food, so a plaintiff had to prove negligence against the operation to recover damages.

The other and newer concept is that an operation offers an *implied warranty*, that is, an assurance that its products will conform to consumer expectations or, more specifically, that its food is fit for consumption. (*Implied* means understood though not clearly or openly expressed.) This concept has been incorporated in the Uniform Commercial Code and is now the law in almost all the states. Section 2-314 of the code states:

> Under this Section the serving for value of food and drink to be consumed either on the premises or elsewhere is a sale. A warranty that the goods should be merchantable is implied in the contract for their sale if the seller is a merchant with respect to goods of that kind. Goods to be merchantable must be at least such as are fit for the ordinary purposes to which such goods are used.

This means that exchanging food for consideration is a sale of a product, and when the product itself is sold, it carries an implied warranty of fitness for its intended purpose, and a warranty that the food is wholesome. By selling its food, therefore, a restaurant or foodservice operation automatically becomes liable for its fitness and wholesomeness—regardless of whether it has been negligent or is to blame for any unfit or unwholesome food. Although this burden may seem unfair (a foodservice operation is, after all, not always able to determine whether anything is wrong with its food), the guest is even more helpless. Thus, the foodservice operation is in a better position to determine whether the food is fit for consumption.

A question can arise over what is *fit to eat?* In a case involving fish chowder, a patron required several operations because a bone that came from the chowder lodged in his throat. The restaurant successfully argued that fish bones are a reasonable risk associated with fish chowder. The typical case involves the presence of an unexpected foreign object. (A whole series of cases has arisen over foreign objects—many of them quite unexpected—found in soft drink cans and bottles. A common test of whether these foreign objects or substances constitute an actionable situation is their "naturalness," that is, whether the substance is a *natural* part of the food. Chicken bones would be natural to chicken dishes or chicken soup, but a piece of glass would not.

Liquor Liability

Under common law, sellers of intoxicating liquors were not generally liable for any injuries resulting from the intoxication of one of the customers visited upon third parties. But most states have enacted legislation holding a tavern owner responsible for torts committed by their inebriated customers. In fact, damage awards can be quite high in these cases. Typical situations involve people who have been sold too much liquor by a bartender and subsequently cause an automobile accident. A verdict against a bar was won by the estates of eight nurses who were murdered by a man who had previously been drinking to excess at the bar. Another case involved a suit by the estate of someone who was killed while riding in a car driven by an intoxicated patron. The bar that served the driver was held liable for damages.

Specific statutes regulating the sale of liquor are sometimes called Dram Shop Laws, Liquor Control Laws, or Alcoholic Beverage Control Laws. Even though specific statutes may be lacking, an establishment may still be found liable under the common law. A doctrine expressed by a New Jersey Supreme Court holds that when a tavern owner sells to a minor or person who is physically intoxicated, "he ought to recognize and foresee the unreasonable risk to others through the actions of the intoxicated person or minor." Liquor liability is not necessarily covered under general liability insurance, so an establishment should check with its insurance agent or broker to see if it is adequately covered.

Loss of Property

A legal problem confronting some foodservice establishments is apparel loss—the disappearance of a patron's outer clothing. The responsibility for these losses usually depends on whether a *bailment* relationship has been established. A bailment is created when one's personal property is temporarily placed in the charge of another. If an employee, such as a hat-checker, routinely takes charge of the coats and hats, the restaurant probably becomes a bailee and, therefore, responsible for any misdelivery or loss through negligence. This can be true even though the words "Not Responsible for Hats and Coats" are printed on the menu and posted on the walls. If the patron himself hangs his coat on a rack without giving any specific notice to the restaurant keeper, there would probably be no bailment. Thus, the restaurant would not be held responsible unless there was proof that its general supervision was negligent. If a restaurant provides a checkroom for garments, it would naturally create a bailment relationship. But some courts have held that when an overcoat is checked with a restaurant, a restaurant keeper does not become liable for the loss of valuables in the coat pockets about which the restaurant keeper has no actual notice. In other words, unless the restaurant keeper knew of the valuables in the pocket, he would probably not be liable for their loss even though they might be liable for the coat itself.

Hotel Law

Much of our present law specifically affecting hotels has developed from the English common law and *stare decisis* (the practice of deciding cases according to precedents or past decisions). Thus, predicting hotel liability can be difficult, since different courts can come to different conclusions. Statutory law, on the other hand, is quite predictable.

The beginnings of our hotel law reach back to medieval England and to the time when travel became popular even though the roads were poor and the land was sparsely populated. Widespread rural banditry forced the English to travel in groups. But problems arose at night when they sought food, lodging, and all-night protection against brigands and robbers. The rich and the poor could stay in the castles of nobles or monasteries, but the middle-class travelers began to stay in the homes of local people who opened their doors for profit. This situation left much to be desired. The travelers found themselves at the mercy of unscrupulous innkeepers who overcharged, admitted guests capriciously, and sometimes colluded with the local bandits helping them rob the travelers while they slept in the local inn.

These hospitality abuses led King Edward III to promulgate in 1350 a statute to constrain "hostellers and herbergers" to sell vituals at reasonable rates. Subsequent statutes and common law procedures led to the regulation of charges and also the requirement that inns accept all travelers (with certain exceptions). New laws also held the inns responsible for the belongings of travelers while they were *infra hospitium*, or within the walls of the establishment. In turn, to ensure the innkeepers against unscrupulous guests, new laws allowed them to convert the belongings of deadbeats into payment of the bill.

Collectively, these laws led to the Doctrine of Public Callings. This doctrine points out that while innkeeping is a public calling, no one is forced to engage in it. When one does, however, he must be prepared to recognize the public's interest and be controlled by the public for the common good. While an innkeeper does not have to have a legal franchise and does not, like utilities, enjoy monopolistic advantages, he does have (under this doctrine) the obligation to let himself be regulated for the common good. For example, he must:

accept bona fide travelers at all times

offer food and lodging (This was important in early times but not absolutely necessary now.)

charge reasonable prices (In some areas today prices are regulated and even posted in rooms.)

provide protection for goods of the guests while they are on the premises of the hotel

admit the baggage of guests excluding dangerous items like dynamite and obviously inconvenient baggage, like pets

Under the common law, hotels had to accept all bona fide travelers. But some exceptions included the full hotel, which can obviously refuse a guest. If a hotel falsely represents itself as full, it can be held liable for all damages a prospective guest suffers as a result. Usually a hotel need not supply a room if:

a person is drunk, disorderly, filthy, or profane

a person carries a notorious reputation as, for example, a brawler, a thief, a prostitute, or a gangster (The hotel must be sure of the reputation in question or it might open itself to a libel or slander suit.)

a person is ill with a contagious disease, or obviously irrational

the person refuses to pay in advance

a person refuses to conform to general house rules applicable to all (A hotel may, for example, require that coats and ties be worn in its dining room.)

In a court case, the hotel, not the complainant, must prove that one or more of these conditions existed. It would be the responsibility of the hotel to prove the above and the innkeeper could be liable for civil and criminal liability if they cannot prove the reasons for nonadmittance. Not surprisingly then, a trend featuring more lenient admission policies has emerged.

If the hotel finds it necessary to eject a guest, the legal basis for its act can be the same as for refusing admittance. In some cases, in fact, it makes more sense to admit a guest and then eject him for cause rather than to guess that he will become objectionable. The ejection must be done as privately as possible and with no more force than necessary. The most objectionable guest can sue if he is unnecessarily hurt, and even if he is the object of abusive language. It may require some force to rid the premises of a troublesome guest, but a final extra push can very easily invite legal trouble.

A major area of hotel law concerns responsibility for a guest's property. Under the common law the hotel was considered an insurer of the guest's property unless the loss was due to an act of God—a natural event like an earthquake, flood, over which the innkeeper has no control. If, however, the innkeeper might have taken reasonable steps to counteract the damage from an act of God, he cannot use it as a defense.

An innkeeper is not responsible for a casualty caused by the act of a public enemy—most particularly bandits and invading armies. And an innkeeper is not liable for losses attributable to a guest's own negligence. If a guest carelessly leaves a piece of property in a public room, under no logic can the innkeeper be held responsible for its loss.

One approach to innkeeper liability adopted in many jurisdictions is the *prima facie* (on the face of things) approach. In jurisdictions that subscribe to this theory, a hotel is not liable if it can prove it exercised reasonable care. But the burden is on the hotel to show that in fact it did exercise due care, since, *prima facie*, it is guilty.

The handling of guest property sent ahead or left behind presents many legal complications. Some cases hold that the hotel still insures property; other cases hold that the hotel has only a *gratuitous bailment* relationship with the absent guest. A gratuitous bailment requires the hotel to exercise only reasonable care over the property. Even in states that hold to the insurer concept, the dollar amount of the liability may be limited by statute. Even if not required by state law, liability disclaimers (i.e., "the management is not responsible for unattended or unchecked property") should be posted. And of course, the hotel should provide safekeeping facilities.

While a hotel may be the insurer of a guest's property, it is not an insurer of the person. A guest may injure himself on the premises without the hotel becoming liable. To be sure, an innkeeper must exercise reasonable care to protect the safety of its guests. But the negligence of the guest himself can absolve the innkeeper of liability. Assume a guest slips on marble stairs. Who is to blame? If the stairs are slippery because of the hotel's negligence, the hotel would probably be liable. But if slickness occurs through no hotel negligence, the guest himself might be to blame. Some cases are open and shut. A guest sleeping in a room is injured by falling plaster. In this case the maxim *res ipsa loquitur* ("the thing speaks for itself") would probably apply. The hotel either knew or should have known that the ceiling was in poor condition and likely to cause injury; yet it did nothing about the condition. The doctrine of *res ipsa loquitur* is a rule of curcumstantial evidence that carried a presumption of liability or of fault. An innkeeper cannot escape this liability by delegating it to another person or agency. As example, an innkeeper who contracts an outside elevator maintenance service remains liable for injuries caused by faulty elevator maintenance.

What to Do When an Accident Occurs

Guests of even the best managed establishments experience occasional accidents. Although the accident may seem inconsequential at the time, a lawsuit may develop later. A hospitality operation can defend itself against these suits if it takes certain steps beforehand.

For example, whenever anyone is injured in an accident on the premise, the operation should secure immediate medical assistance. In fact, the establishment can precipitate a suit if it tries to provide its own unqualified first aid assistance. In one case, a speck lodged in a patron's eye. The hotel manager who tried to remove it caused serious eye damage and a sizable lawsuit. Of course, if the injury is superficial, the hotel can readily furnish bandaids or routine first aid. Yet, even though the accident appears to have no serious consequences, the establishment should insist on medical treatment.

Of course an operation should always secure the names and addresses of any witnesses to an accident and get statements from them. Those statements should be signed. If possible, photographs should be taken of both the situation and the victim. A thorough report of the accident, including the statements of employees and supervisors, should be prepared—even in those instances where state law does not require these reports.

In some situations (accidental death, for example), public officials like the police or the coroner must, by law, be notified. In fact, it may be illegal to remove a body before permission is received from the coroner. If there is a death, the hotel should be sure the person is pronounced dead by a competent authority.

If a dead guest leaves property at an operation, it should be inventoried and secured. The inventory should be signed by at least two employees. Moreover, the property should not be released except to authorized persons.

When accidents or deaths occur, the person responsible for handling the operation's insurance should be quickly notified—both by telephone and in writing. The letter should include a detailed report of dates, and the names and addresses of the injured people involved.

Significant Legislation

Civil Rights One of the most active areas of legislation and litigation in recent years has been civil rights. So prominent has it been, in fact, that it is hard to believe that the Civil Rights Act was passed only in 1964. Section 201(a) of The Civil Rights Act assures that all persons be entitled to the full and equal enjoyment of the goods, services, facilities, privileges, advantages, and accommodations of any place of public accommodation, without discrimination or segregation on the grounds of race, color, religion, or natural origin.

Prior to 1964 many minority groups had trouble getting served in hospitality establishments. They might be refused outright, or kept waiting, or served substandard food, or placed in remote locations—all, of course, forms of discrimination. Resort motels might advertise the churches nearby as a subtle signal that they did not welcome people of the Jewish faith. Jewish resorts by contrast stressed, and still do stress, the fact that they offer Hebrew services. Few localities actually enacted laws enforcing segregation. Instead, the unwritten separate-but-equal doctrine remained in effect since the Civil War. In practice, especially in the South, the accommodations were separate and almost never equal. Moreover, if no separate facilities were maintained, no accommodations were furnished to minorities.

There had of course, been efforts to end discrimination since the Dred Scott Decision in 1857 when a slave from the slave state of Missouri had been taken to the free states of Illinois and Wisconsin. It was argued, when he was returned to the slave states, that his residency in the free states had made him free. But the Supreme Court ruled that slaves and their descendants were not citizens and thus had no standing in the United States courts.

As early as 1865 Massachusetts enacted a law to abolish discrimination in hotels. And the Fourteenth Amendment of the Constitution, adopted in 1868, said that "no state should make or enforce any law which shall abridge the privileges or immunities of citizens of the United States; nor shall any state deprive any person of life, liberty, or property without due process of law; nor deny to any person within its jurisdiction the equal protection of the law." This amendment was intended to protect Blacks newly freed from slavery and to guarantee them equal treatment by the state. But in 1883 the Supreme Court ruled that the Fourteenth Amendment did not apply to individual hotelkeepers.

In 1942, discrimination was finally outlawed in defense industries, and in 1948 segregation was outlawed in the armed forces. In 1954 the Supreme Court unanimously ruled that segregation was illegal in public schools. This famous *Brown* v. *Topeka* decision struck down the separate-but-equal doctrine by saying segregation meant inequality, per se, and was therefore unconstitutional. The court specificied that school integration must proceed "with all deliberate speed."

Under English common law, discrimination had never been a problem for hotels since an innkeeper had to take in all bona fide travelers. Accordingly, some states in this country enacted legislation prohibiting hospitality discrimination but the provisions were not uniform or uniformly enforced.

The Civil Rights Act of 1964 does two major things that affect the hospitality industry. First, it prevents discrimination on the basis of race, color, religion, sex, or national origin in places of public accommodation—and this covers all inns, hotels, motels, and other establishments serving transient guests except those of less than five rooms with the premises occupied by the proprietor. (This is known as the "Mrs. Murphy's boarding house" clause.) Restaurants are covered if they serve interstate travelers or a substantial portion of their food comes through interstate commerce. Second, the law, being based on the Constitution's commerce clause, gives Congress sweeping powers to regulate any activity that even remotely affects commerce among the states. Local legislation enforcing segregation is specifically prohibited in hotel facilities serving transient travelers and allows no type of discrimination whatsoever. The act is not applicable to local establishments serving only local people—like a barbershop, a private club. Thus, prohibition could lead to a situation where a hotel barbershop cannot discriminate while a local barbershop across the street can. Hospitality establishments could, of course, still exclude undesirable customers for reasons other than those mentioned in the act—for example, if they were disorderly, drunk, or otherwise objectionable. The act also prohibits discrimination by employers, unions, and employment agencies. With all its interpretational problems, the Civil Rights Act has been strikingly successful. Little more than a decade ago, sit-ins were common, as Blacks tried to receive service in hospitality establishments. Now such demonstrations are almost unheard-of, as is the blatant discrimination they opposed.

Enforcement of The Civil Rights Act must be pursued by the person claiming discrimination. Occasionally (for example, when the plaintiff lacks funds or has been intimidated), the courts may permit the Attorney General to intervene. If a state or locality has a public accommodations law, the plaintiff must register his complaint with the appropriate state and local authority and must wait thirty days before bringing suit in federal court. This permits local officials time to try to clear up the matter informally. If no local public accommodations law exists, the person affected may bring suit in federal court immediately. The court may refer the matter to the federal community relations service, which tries to set-, tle the matter by voluntary methods. Many cases can be settled voluntarily, thus permitting state and local officials to retain responsibility and a measure of autonomy. Moreover, the threat of federal intervention sometimes brings the parties together. The Attorney General cannot initiate cases for individuals, but he can take action against those who systematically deny rights. In such cases, the Attorney General can start proceedings directly in federal courts.

Few people realize that many states already had their own human relations or public accommodations laws when the Civil Rights Act of 1964 was passed. In fact, thirty-one states had enacted such laws protecting some 66 percent of the population. To be sure, the laws varied considerably as did their enforcement. Moreover, the Civil Rights Act of 1964 encourages states to form their own commissions to implement the federal law.

Equal Employment Opportunity Title VII of the Civil Rights Act of 1964 prohibits employers, labor organizations, and employment agencies from using discriminatory hiring practices based on a person's race, color, religion, sex, or national origin. The protected people include employees, applicants, trainees, apprentices, and union members. Some of the unlawful employment practices abolished by the act follow:

It is unlawful for an employer intentionally (1) to refuse to hire (or to fire) a person for discriminatory reasons; (2) to discriminate against a person regarding his wages or other terms, conditions, or privileges of employment; (3) to limit, segregate or classify employees in a discriminatory manner so as to deprive or tend to deprive them of employment opportunities or otherwise affect their status as employees; (4) to discriminate against an individual who is opposed to discriminatory practices, or who has testified or participated in any proceeding arising under Title VII; (5) to print or publish any discriminatory advertising relating to the employment; and (6) to discriminate in the operation of an apprenticeship or other training program.

It is unlawful for a labor organization intentionally (1) to exclude or expel an individual from membership for discriminatory reasons; (2) to limit, segregate, or classify its membership in a discriminatory manner so as to deprive or tend to deprive an individual of employment opportunities, or adversely affect his status as an employee, or as an applicant for employment; (3) to cause or attempt to cause an employer to discriminate; (4) to discriminate in the operation of any apprenticeship or other training program; and (5) to discriminate against an individual who is opposed to discriminatory practices or who has testified or participated in any proceeding arising under Title VII.

It is illegal for an employment agency intentionally (1) to refuse to refer to employment, or otherwise, to discriminate against a person for discrim-

inatory reasons, (2) to discriminate against an individual who is opposed to discriminatory practices or who has testified or participated in any proceeding arising under the Title VII; and (3) to print or publish any discriminatory advertisements relating to employment.

To enforce Title VII, a new federal agency, the Equal Employment Opportunity Commission came into being. It is composed of five members appointed by the President for five-year terms. Either an individual aggrieved by alleged discrimination or a member of the commission itself can institute a proceeding before a commission by filing a charge (which is not made public) within ninety days of the alleged discriminatory practice. If a State Fair Employment practice law or similar law within a local political subdivision exists, the time for filing a charge is extended to 210 days after the discrimination occurred, or thirty days after state or local action on the matter concludes. This extra time gives the local and state agencies the first opportunity to resolve the matter.

After the charge is filed, a copy is sent to the accused party and an agent for the commission conducts an investigation. If the commission decides that the charge has merit, it has at least thirty days, but not more than sixty days, in which to seek voluntary settlements of the alleged discriminatory practice through informal conferences, reconciliation, and persuasion. If the informal attempts fail, the commission notifies the aggrieved individual, who will then have thirty days to bring action in federal district court. Jurisdiction of the court depends on:

1. Where the discrimination occurred
2. Where records relevant to the discrimination are maintained
3. Where the individual would have worked except for the discrimination
4. Which district the respondent has his principal office

The court is permitted to appoint an attorney for the plaintiff, and the Attorney General may intervene if the matter is of "general public importance." If the court finds that the respondent—the accused employer, union, or employment agency—has intentionally engaged in an unlawful employment practice, it may order such affirmative action as it considers appropriate. This action can include an order to hire or to reinstate an individual with or without back pay. Other provisions of Title VII include the authorization of the commission to require employers, labor organizations, employment agencies:

1. To make, keep, and preserve records in order to determine whether they are discriminating.
2. To make such reports as the commission shall require.
3. To make special reports on the operation of training programs.

Those reports must contain such information as a list of applicants, the order in which they applied, and the manner in which they were selected. An employer, union, or employment agency believing that the application of any of these requirements will result in undue hardship may request exemption from the commission or from a federal district court.

The Occupational Safety and Health Act of 1970

A piece of legislation which has had a tremendous effect on all American industry including the hospitality industry is the Occupational Safety and Health Act of 1970. The purpose of this act is "to assure so far as possible every man and woman in the nation safe and healthful working conditions and to preserve our human resources." Under the act each employer has a general duty to furnish each of his employees work and a place of employment free from recognized hazards that cause or are likely to cause death or serious physical harm. The employer has a specific duty to comply with the specific safety and health standards promulgated under the act. In turn, each employee must comply with these safety and health standards and with all rules and regulations in the act that apply to the employee's own actions and conduct. This act was discussed in chapter 8.

The Fair Labor Standards Act of 1938

The Fair Labor Standards Act of 1938 (or the Federal Wage and Hour Law, as it is sometimes called) is a piece of Depression legislation originally enacted in 1938 and amended frequently since. It sets a minimum wage, maximum hours, an overtime pay scale, equal pay, and child labor standards for employment, subject to a few narrow exceptions. Originally the Fair Labor Standards Act applied to employees individually engaged in interstate or foreign commerce and to those employees in certain large enterprises. But amendments in 1966 provided broader definitions of the "enterprises" subject to the act. Among other considerations, the amendments extended the act to include more retail and service enterprises. Included under the 1966 amendments are employees engaged in the operation of hospitals (except federally operated hospitals), nursing homes, and all schools, public or private. Certain hotel, motel, and restaurant employees are also covered. There are exemptions from the act and an operator should check the current provisions of the act for them. The standard for coverage is four consecutive quarters having cumulative total revenues of $274,000. The minimum is scheduled to use up to $324,000 on July 1, 1980 and $362,500 on December 31, 1981. Operations with lower volumes are not covered for minimum wages.

Under provisions of the act, employees must be paid a minimum wage. (The 1977 amendment to the act provided for a $3.10 minimum in 1980 and $3.35 in 1981.) One and one-half times the employee's regular pay rate must be paid for all hours worked in excess of a 40-hour work week. A special provision allows hospitals to adopt a 14-day period in lieu of the usual 7-day work week. Employees of nursing homes, rest homes, and bowling alleys may receive one and one-half times the regular rate for hours over 48 in any work week. The act does not cover an enterprise that has as its only regular employees the owner, a spouse, parents, children, or other members of the owner's immediate family. Moreover, executive, administrative, and professional employees are exempt from the minimum wage and overtime provisions of the act.

Tips received by an employee may be counted as part of his wages. The 1978 amendments provide for a tip credit of not more than 45 percent of the applicable minimum rate. A "tipped" employee is a worker engaged in an occupation that customarily returns more than $30 a month in tips. Total compensation including tips must meet the minimum wage. An employer who uses the tip credit deduction must notify employees of this in advance. For example, assume an employee works 160 hours a month and the minimum wage is $3.10. That employee's monthly earnings should total $496. If the employee makes $60 a week in tips or $240 a month, the employer can deduct 45% of this or $108 from the $496 leaving $388 for the 160 hours and payment at the rate of $2.43 per hour. In addition, an employer may deduct a reasonable amount for furnishing his employees with board, lodging, or other facilities as long as they are primarily a benefit to the employee and if they are customarily furnished by the employer to his employees.

The child labor provision of the Fair Labor Standards Act specifically prohibits the employment of *oppressive child labor*. Oppressive child labor includes the employment of a child under 16 in hazardous working occupations as well as the employment of minors between 16 and 18 years of age in nonagricultural occupations found by the Secretary of Labor to be particularly hazardous or detrimental to health. The employment of a child under 14 in any occupation is oppressive child labor, unless the work is specifically exempt (newspaper delivery, for example). Employers can protect themselves from an unintentional violation of the child labor provision by keeping on file an employment or age certificate for each young person they employ. These certificates include those summer "working papers," familiar to so many parents.

The act as amended in 1963 prohibits employers from discriminating on the basis of sex in the payment of wages for equal work. But this equal pay standard applies to only employees subject to the minimum wage requirements of the act. In general, an employer must pay equal wages to men and women doing equal work at jobs requiring equal skill, effort, and responsibility performed under similar working conditions.

Authorized representatives in the wage and hour division may investigate and gather data regarding the wages, hours, and other working conditions. They may enter establishments, inspect the premises and its records, transcribe records, and interview employees. The act also provides guidelines for the recovery of unpaid wages. For example, the division administrator can supervise the payment of back wages. The Secretary of Labor can bring suit for back pay upon the written request of an employee. Or the employee can sue for back wages and additional sums up to the amount of back pay, attorney fees, and court costs. And finally, the Secretary of Labor may obtain a court injunction to restrain any person from violating the law, including the unlawful withholding of proper wages and overtime compensation. A two-year statute of limitation applies to the recovery of back wages except in the case of willful violations, for which a three-year statute of limitations applies.

The act does not require extra pay for Saturday, Sunday, or holiday work; for vacation or holiday "call-backs;" or for severance pay. Nor does it set any limit on the number of hours of work for persons 16 years of age or older.

Hospitality operators, who seem to have been unusually oblivious to the provisions of the act and its amendments, have had trouble when employees sue for back pay and damages. Thus, it behooves employers to keep accurate records on their employees regarding hours worked, compensation paid, deductions made, and payment dates. The law requires all of this information as well as the name, home address, sex, occupation, and hours worked for all employees—and the birthdates of those under 19.

Unemployment Insurance

Provisions for unemployment insurance were enacted under the Social Security Act originally passed in 1935 and its subsequent amendments. Under this act, a nationwide system of insurance has been provided in all the states, the District of Columbia, and Puerto Rico to protect wage earners and their families against income loss due to unemployment. Unemployment insurance provides workers with a weekly income to tide them over between jobs. It does not assure benefits to every unemployed worker, only to those who had been working on jobs covered under their state unemployment insurance law for a specified period, only to those who are willing and able to work, and only to those who are unemployed through no fault of their own. The program operates under joint states and U.S. Department of Labor auspices. As long as a state law and its operations meet the federal requirements, the federal government pays the cost of administering the state unemployment insurance law and permits employers in the state to credit state contributions paid, which excuses them from federal unemployment taxation.

Each state requires employers who come under its employment insurance law to pay taxes based on their payroll. With a few state exceptions, employees make no contributions to the state unemployment insurance funds. The benefits are paid out of a fund built up from these taxes. The funds are deposited to the state's account with the U.S. Treasury, and those funds the state does not use remain in a trust fund, where they earn compound interest. The state legislatures fix the employers' tax rate, and most states have enacted experienced-rating provisions that allow an employer's tax to vary according to the amount of benefits paid to his former workers—or according to some other method for measuring the risk of unemployment.

Each individual state law specifies the conditions under which workers may receive benefits, the amounts they may receive, and the number of weeks they may draw benefits. To be eligible for benefits, every worker must have received a specified minimum amount of pay or have worked a minimum number of weeks in covered employment during a specified period preceding his lay off. All but a few states provide that a worker who has been employed in more than one state, but is not eligible for benefits in any of them, may combine his wage credits and thus meet the wage and employment requirements under a given state law.

The variation in state laws and their interpretation are so great that any generalized statement could be misleading with respect to a particular state. But, in general, the state laws require that a worker must be ready and willing to accept any suitable work for which he does not have good cause to refuse. *Suitable work* generally means work in which the employee is experienced or trained, that matches his skills and usual wages, and is within a reasonable distance of his home. *Good cause* for refusal has been defined as what a reasonable man would do in similar circumstances.

Although unemployment compensation has saved many a family since 1935, there has also been a good deal of criticism regarding its operation. In some states the supervision of the plan has been loose. Dishonest people sometimes collect benefits for which they are not entitled or collect benefits under assumed names. (When they do so, they are, of course, breaking the law and may be prosecuted.) In extreme cases unemployment insurance has even been used to pay for vacations. Also, some people feel that high unemployment insurance discourages people from seeking work. And others feel that unemployment benefits keep workers from moving to where work is available, thus helping to undermine economic productivity. And to be sure, the amount of unemployment benefits can become a political issue to be decided according to political expediency rather than what is best for the country.

The Social Security Act The Social Security Act provides for two nationwide systems of social insurance to protect wage earners and their families against loss of income due to unemployment, old age, disability, and death. One system includes retirement, survivors, and disability insurance; health insurance for persons over 65 (Medicare); and all federal systems operated by the federal government through its Social Security Administration. The other system involves unemployment insurance, the federal-state plan we just discussed.

To supplement these systems, the Social Security Act provides public assistance under a joint federal-state plan making monthly cash payments and offering welfare services to needy old people, needy families with dependent children, the needy blind, and needy persons who are permanently or totally disabled. The act also provides a federal-state program of medical assistance for persons 65 or over whose income and resources are insufficient to meet the cost of necessary medical services.

In addition, the Social Security Act provides grants to the states for maternal and child health services, services for crippled children, and child welfare services to supplement the state and local funds available for such programs.

Benefits under the programs are payable only to persons (and their dependents and survivors) who become insured under the program by working at jobs covered by the law. Nearly all gainful work, however, is now covered. The amount of work required to become insured is measured in terms of quarters of coverage. A quarter of coverage is a calendar quarter in which an individual is paid at least $50 for work covered by the law or for which he is credited with at least $100 of self-employment income.

Benefits for disabled or retired workers, their spouses and their children; for aged widows and widowers; and for aged dependent parents of deceased workers can be paid only if the worker is fully insured. To be fully insured, he must have at least one quarter of coverage (acquired anytime after 1936) for each calendar year elapsing since 1950, since the year when he attained age 21 and prior to the year he attained age 65 (62 for women) or died (whichever came earlier). No person can be fully insured with less than six quarters of coverage, and once he has earned forty quarters of coverage, he is fully insured for life.

Workers under age 65 who are totally disabled and meet specified work requirements can receive monthly benefits under the retirement, survivors, and disability insurance program. To qualify for disability benefits under the law, a worker must be shown to have a medically determinable physical or mental impairment that is expected to last indefinitely, or has lasted at least twelve months, or is expected to result in death. He must also have a record of substantial recent attachment to the labor market. If he becomes disabled before 24, he needs social security credit for one and one-half years of work in the three years before he became disabled. To help disabled persons restore themselves to gainful activity, applicants for disability benefits are referred to state vocational rehabilitation agencies. Disability benefits are not paid to anyone who, without good cause, refuses rehabilitation services.

Social security is a popular and essential part of our contemporary society. But considerable concern has arisen recently about the financing of future benefits. In 1975 collections fell short of payments by about 1.8 billion dollars, with about 15 percent of the entire U.S. population receiving social security checks. Recent changes have helped alleviate this shortfall, but some say potential benefits payable are fifty times the available reserves.

Social security is sometimes compared to an insurance program, but it is not the usual type of insurance in which payments are determined strictly by the size of the premium. Under social security, lower income workers receive greater retirement benefits in proportion to their former earnings than high income workers receive. And retired workers with dependents can collect more benefits than workers without dependents even though both have paid the same amount of taxes into the system. As more people receive benefits in relation to the number of people currently working and contributing, the money shortfall worsens. Moreover, some people today receive more benefits in one year than they have paid in through taxes over their entire working careers.

The effects of lower birth rates and more longevity is illustrated by the fact that in 1900 only one person in twenty-five was over 65. Today one in ten is over 65. It is predicted that the number of people age 65 and over will grow from twenty-two million to thirty million by the year 2000 and to fifty million by the year 2030. If social security is to remain the nation's primary means of providing economic protection against retirement, death, or disability, additional means of financing it must be found quickly. One suggestion is to use general tax revenues for at least some of the benefits, like Medicare. This approach, however, defeats the concept that a working person pays for his retirement. It is also charged that if general tax revenues instead of payroll taxes were used, it would be an invitation simply to enlarge the program.

Another solution might be to increase the payroll tax which, in early 1976, was 5.85 percent paid by the employee and an additional equal amount paid by the employer. There may, however, be a limit to how much people will pay in taxes, and in any case, this approach would be inflationary, adding directly to an employer's costs and thus boosting prices. In short, Americans will soon be faced with the stark question of how much they are willing to pay for Social Security benefits.

*The Age
Discrimination
in Employment
Act of 1967*

This act promotes the employment of the older worker, emphasizing ability rather than age. It prohibits arbitrary age discrimination in employment and helps employers and employees find ways to meet problems arising from the impact of human obsolescence. It specifically protects people who are at least 40 and less than 65 years of age against discriminatory hiring, discharge, compensation, or other occupational conditions. The act applies to most employers of twenty-five or more persons (federal, state, and local governments are themselves excluded). Public and private employment agencies serving such employers are also included, as are labor organizations with twenty-five or more members that refer persons for employment to covered employers or represent employees working for employers covered by the act.

The act does not apply where age is a bona fide occupational qualification reasonably necessary to the normal operations of the particular business. An age limit for airline pilots can be logically imposed, for example. Nor does it apply where the differentiation is based on reasonable factors other than age; where the "discrimination" is caused by observing the terms of a bona fide seniority system or any bona fide employee benefit plan which is not a subterfuge to evade the purposes of the act; or where the discharge is for good cause.

The act is enforced by the Secretary of Labor who can make investigations, issue rules and regulations for administering the law, and enforce its provisions by legal proceedings when voluntary compliance cannot be obtained. Before the Secretary begins court action, the act requires him to attempt to secure voluntary compliance by informal conciliation, conferences, and persuasion. Before an individual brings court action, he must give the Secretary not less than sixty days notice of his intention.

The procedure for recovering penalties arising out of violations of this act follow:

> *The Secretary is authorized to supervise the payment of amounts owed; in certain circumstances the Secretary may bring suit upon written request to the individual; and an individual may sue for payment, plus attorney's fees and court costs.*
>
> *In the case of willful violations, an additional amount up to the total amount owed may be claimed as liquidated damages, or the Secretary may obtain a court injunction to restrain any person from violating the law— including the unlawful withholding of proper compensation.*

Interference with representatives of the Secretary of Labor engaged in duties related to the act may be prosecuted criminally and the violators subjected to a fine of not more than $500 or imprisonment or both. Employers, employment agencies, and labor organizations must post an officially approved notice in a prominent place where employees may see it and maintain the records required by the Secretary.

Insurance and Risk Management

Every business needs various kinds of insurance protection and hospitality is certainly no exception. As a matter of fact, because hospitality is a service industry dealing with so many people, its need for insurance is greater than most. Insurance is secured to reduce the effects of *pure risk* (a situation that can result in loss). Pure risks include fire, wind storms, thievery, or liability suits—all instances that preclude any chance of gain. Insurance trades the uncertainty of these events occurring for certainty of reimbursement in case they do. A large but uncertain loss is traded for a small but certain cost called a *premium*. Insurance, of course, involves a cost, and it may be better not to pay this cost when the odds are against a loss occurring. (A Las Vegas hotel need not buy flood insurance.) But even if the odds are against the loss occurring, there is no guarantee that a major loss that could devastate the enterprise financially will not occur.

Insurance is written and sold by four types of companies:

1. Stock companies
2. Mutual companies
3. Reciprocals
4. Lloyd's groups

Stock companies are profit making corporations chartered in the various states. Mutual companies are owned by the policyholders and are chartered as nonprofit institutions in the various states. *Reciprocals* (sometimes called interinsurance exchanges) are also cooperatively organized insurers and theoretically offer insurance at cost. Lloyd's groups are composed of groups of individual underwriters who write insurance for a profit. Because of their flexibility, they can often write unusual types of insurance.

In selecting one of these types of insurers, one would do well to determine the financial stability of the insurer or the resources it has at its disposal. *Best's Insurance Reports* publishes a financial rating and analysis of major insurance companies and information on their financial stability. Different companies specialize in different types of coverages and it is generally helpful to be involved with a company that has experience in your particular field.

Flexibility involves tailoring a policy to meet the needs of the buyer. If your business has special requirements, flexibility can be an important consideration. Costs of insurance may vary, too; and if financial stability and flexibility are about equal, the cost of the policy should be a determining factor. Another factor in selecting an insurance company may be the availability of the agents or methods of securing the insurance such as payment schedules and extra company services.

Insurance services are distributed in two principal ways: through the independent agency and through the direct routing system. The independent agency has the right from the insurer to represent it in a given territory. An agent is compensated under a commission arrangement for the insurance he sells. The agent may represent one insurance company or a number of them. Theoretically, at least, the agent selects from among different insurance companies to meet the specific needs of his client. The insurance company has no control over the agent except to accept or reject the business he generates.

In the direct routing system, the insurance company sells the insurance directly to the insured through its own employees with no independent middleman involved. Some direct writers operate through the mail or by telephone without personal contact or local representation.

Both the independent agency system and the direct routing system have worked satisfactorily. Proponents of the independent agency system claim that the independent agents can provide: more convenience, since they represent different companies; better service, since they have a greater incentive to serve their own clients and the premium gives them greater motivation; better claims representation, because the agents have leverage with a company (if they are not satisfied they can withdraw other policies); greater expertise, since the independent agents write a greater number of insurance lines and should have more knowledge than the company employee who is involved only with a limited line. The advantages of dealing through direct routers include, theoretically, a lower cost because of the lack of commission that must be paid and the absence of the middleman, and good service because the direct writing system allows an employee to become a specialist without having to spread his time among different insurers.

An insurance broker represents the insured rather than the insuring company and is the insured's legal representative. An independent agency can also be a broker.

An independent insurance consultant can act only as an advisor and receive compensation only from the businesses that use his services. His purpose is to provide an independent viewpoint and an impartial appraisal of insurance coverage and cost.

Types of Insurance   Insurance, as we noted, is very important to the hospitality industry. A discussion of major types of insurance involved in hospitality operations follows in the next paragraphs.

Fire insurance. Fire insurance compensates for a loss due to fire. The fire insurance policy is standardized throughout the country and the basic policy is nearly identical in every state. The standard policy insures against fire, lightning, and losses to goods temporarily removed from premises because of the fire. The policy does not cover theft, actions resulting from war or social dosorders, or losses due to failure by the insured to use all reasonable means to save the property after a fire loss. It is often desirable to supplement the basic fire policy with an extended coverage endorsement for such perils as windstorms, hail, explosion, riots, riots attending a strike, aircraft damage, vehicle damage, and smoke damage.

Co-insurance is a very important fire insurance complement. The majority of fires damage or destroy only a small part of the insured premises. A hotel operator with a million-dollar property might decide that it would be unlikely for any fire to destroy more than say, $100,000 worth of the property. Therefore he might purchase only $100,000 worth of insurance. In such a case, the co-insurance clause would allow him to recover only in proportion of his insurance to the desired amount of co-insurance. If a 90 percent co-insurance clause is in effect, it means that the insurance company wants the premises insured for 90 percent of their value or for a million-dollar property, $900,000. If the owner purchased only $100,000 worth of insurance, he would be paid only one-ninth of any partial loss regardless of the amount of the loss and in any case no more than the face amount of the policy. For a $450,000 loss he would receive $50,000; for a total loss he would receive $100,000. A co-insurance clause discourages underinsuring because it penalizes recovery unless adequate limits are carried out.

Fire insurance rates often can be substantially reduced by installing an automatic sprinkler system. But sprinklers introduce the new hazards of accidental leakage or discharge from the sprinkler heads or rupture of the sprinkler pipes. A sprinkler loss endorsement can be added to the standard fire insurance policy, or special sprinkler leakage insurance can be purchased.

Liability insurance (other than auto). A hospitality business is subject to both common and statutory laws covering injury to customers and employees arising out of the business' negligence. Some examples of negligence characteristic of the hospitality field include ingestion of foreign objects in food, food poisoning, accidental scalding in a hotel shower, and accidents resulting from slippery floors. Contributory negligence may, of course, be involved: the victim may be at least partly responsible for the accident. But in general, accidents on business premises arising out of business operations are presumed to constitute negligence by the business.

Different types of insurance policies can cover different types of negligence, or a comprehensive policy can cover several types of liability at once. Negligence insurance is particularly helpful because a major liability judgment can run into the hundreds of thousands of dollars (multimillion-dollar judgments have been awarded). If not covered by insurance, such a judgment could wipe out many operations. Liability policies usually limit the amount a victim will be paid and per-accident ceiling. For example, an insurance company might pay up to $100,000 per person in a liability case and up to $500,000 for any one accident, regardless of the number of people involved.

Workmen's compensation and employee liability insurance. Under common law (law developed by custom and refined in court through the centuries) an employer must provide his employees a safe place to work, hire competent employees, provide safe tools, and warn employees of any existing danger. If he fails in these duties, he may be liable for damages in lawsuits brought by injured employees. Under Workmen's Compensation the insuring company pays the employee the sum the employer is legally obligated to pay because of its common law liability and pays also for salary compensation and other benefits that the state workmen's compensation law may require. The usual state laws pay for medical care for the injured workman, pay lump sums for dismemberment and death, pay benefits for disabilities attributable to occupational disease, and pay income payments for a disabled worker or his dependents. The disability payments in some cases may last as long as the worker is disabled—even for a lifetime.

Workmen's Compensation Insurance is now required by law, ratifying the moral obligation to prevent or mitigate the effects of on-the-job accidents. The insurance can be secured from private insurance companies, in some states from Workmen's Compensation Funds, and in some areas through self-insurance. Self-insurance is, however, available only to large operations that can set aside enough money to make major payments.

Fidelity bonds. Fidelity bonds are designed to protect against employee theft. A fidelity bond can cover an individual person; or a blanket bond can cover a list of positions or all employees of the organization. A fidelity bond is not, strictly speaking, an insurance policy. It actually goes farther: it covers not only the insured but also the bonded employee. The employee who is bonded is called the *principal,* the person or firm protected is called the *obligee* and the bonding corporation is called the *surety.* If the principal is found guilty of stealing, the surety will pay the obligee but has the right to attempt to recover its losses from the principal.

Surety bonds. Surety bonds can guarantee that the principal will carry out the specific work an obligee has hired him to do. These bonds are frequently used in construction contracts: the contractor is covered by a surety bond to insure that he will carry out the provisions of the contract, without walking away from the work if it becomes unprofitable. The surety bond permits a small businessman to compete with larger more financially sound companies because his performance is guaranteed by the financial resources of the surety companies. A big advantage of both fidelity and surety bonds is the investigation that precedes their issuance. In the case of fidelity bonds, the bonding company can investigate the employees far more effectively than the hiring company and thus provide more assurance of their future honesty. A surety company can also investigate the principal it covers often more efficiently than the buyers of the principal's services.

Crime insurance. Although big city apartment dwellers often do not realize it, crime insurance is widely available for such crimes as burglary and robbery. These losses are not covered by fidelity bonds since the thefts are perpetrated by outsiders. Comprehensive crime policies are also available to cover losses besides burglary and robbery.

All-risk and multiple line coverage. These approaches to insurance improve considerably on the standard fire insurance and related lines. All-risk policies cover all perils except those specifically excluded in the policy. Multiple line policies list a much larger variety of perils than those covered by standard fire insurance policies. With this type of insurance a business is covered for all perils and can avoid any unintentional duplication in coverage. With one policy, only one agent is required; and since a major policy is involved, the service may be better and the total premium might even be less than on the same coverage purchased in separate policies.

Business interruption insurance. The indirect costs of a loss by a peril like fire may be greater than the damage done by the fire itself. The business may be forced to close for an extended period while still paying key employees. And such expenses as taxes and financing costs go right on. Business interruption insurance can be purchased to cover such expenses; it is, in fact, often attached to the standard fire insurance policy.

To collect business interruption insurance, a business must meet certain conditions:

1. A property loss from the insured peril must have occurred.
2. The business must have been totally or partially shut down because of the loss.

3. The loss must be the cause of the shut down. If the business were about to be discontinued or if the owner does not intend to resume it, no payments will be made.

4. It must be shown that if the business had not been damaged it would have continued to earn at least enough to pay its expenses. If the business had not been able to pay its fixed expenses before the peril occurred, it would in all probability not be able to do so afterward.

The business interruption policy normally pays the amount of profits and fixed expenses the business would have been expected to earn. The ordinary payroll may also be insured for a limited period so a business can pay its regular employees even though they are not needed in the business. Business interruption insurance can usually be purchased on a co-insurance basis covering from 50 to 100 percent of the insurable value of the business.

Power plant insurance. Power plant insurance is sometimes called *boiler and machinery insurance*. It protects against losses caused by furnace, steam boiler, and engine explosions and electrical equipment failures. These problems are not usually covered by the standard fire insurance policy. Obviously both the insured and the insurer like to prevent these kinds of accidents, and part of the premium is spent by the insurance company inspecting boilers and other equipment and making recommendations to prevent potential loss. The power plant insurance contract usually stipulates that coverage does not begin to pay until all other applicable insurance has been exhausted.

Employee group life and health insurance. Life and health insurance can be used in several ways but basically it provides benefits to employees when they become ill or die. Some employers have always felt an obligation to provide this type of benefit even if there were no legal necessity. In cases, though, where the employers could not afford it, their employees suffer. This type of insurance provides employees with a desirable benefit and without bankrupting a business when illness or death occurs. These arrangements also have a tax advantage: their cost offers a tax deduction which employers can deduct before tax calculations are made on income. But, if the employee himself provides this coverage, he has to pay for it with after-tax earnings. Thus he must receive more money from an employer to procure equivalent coverage.

A group life insurance policy is usually issued without medical examinations, accumulates no cash surrender value, and is in effect a type of term insurance. There must usually be a minimum number of employees in the insured group—ten being the typical minimum. The employee is not allowed to set the amount of insurance coverage that he wants; he gets the amount established by the term policy. (This requirement keeps sick employees from purchasing larger amounts of protection.) After leaving the firm, the employee can usually retain his coverage and convert it into an individual plan within a certain period.

Group health insurance plans may take a number of different forms. The major ones include (1) basic medical and hospitalization and (2) major medical and disability income. The basic medical and hospitalization plan pays the costs of hospitalization, medication, and medical care on a service or indemnity basis within limits of the policy. The service plan pays for the complete costs for the hospital care covered by the policy. The indemnity plans, which are usually offered by commercial insurers, compensate an employee a certain sum every day he is hospitalized.

Major medical plans represent an attempt to meet the catastrophic costs of some illnesses. They are installed as an addition to a basic medical and hospitalization plan and pay only when the first benefits are exhausted. There is often a deductible amount before major medical plans begin to pay, but they usually pay up to a large maximum benefit. Disability income plans pay an employee a stated portion of his annual salary should the employee suffer a long-term physical disability that prevents him from performing his normal duties. Workmen's compensation covers employees only for time lost because of accidental injuries. But, of course, an employee may be kept from working by causes unrelated to his job. Disability income may also pay more than an employee could expect from Workmen's Compensation.

Business life and health insurance. Insurance can also be arranged to protect a business when key personnel become disabled or die. *Key man coverage* provides insurance for the loss of key personnel. Managerial or specially skilled personnel may be a major asset of the business. If for some reason these people become unavailable, the business might suffer. If, for example, a certain manager is worth forty thousand dollars a year after subtracting his salary and other costs, and if the company decided that it would like to be indemnified for four years of his possible loss, it would purchase $160,000 worth of business life and health insurance. (At the end of four years the company would presumably have trained replacement.) If the key man suffers a disability, a rider attached to the business life insurance policy naming the company as a beneficiary, or separate insurance contracts may be prepared to indemnify the business.

If in a partnership one of the partners dies, the continuation of the business may be a real problem. In this case, the other partner or partners ought to be able to buy out the dead partner's interest. But they may not have the necessary funds on hand. Insurance can be provided that provides these funds, allowing the heirs of the deceased partner to receive payment for the partnership interest. There should, of course, be a prior agreement on the value of the partnership.

SUMMARY

It is desirable—and necessary—that a hospitality manager be familiar with principles of business law and other laws that affect his operation. A law may be derived from two general sources. One is the common or unwritten law. These are laws that evolved through custom and usage, ultimately enunciated in court decisions. Statutory law consists of laws adopted by Congress or other legislative bodies. Statutory law is commonly known as written law and takes precedence over common law. A tort is a physical harm done to a person or property and caused by the failure to act, or the general negligence of another person. It may be intentional or unintentional. Unintentional torts are usually those that occur through acts of negligence or accident. Intentional torts are deliberate actions such as assault or libel. In either case, when a person's rights have been interfered with by another, the injured party may sue for damages and seek compensation.

Contracts are an essential part of any business, including hospitality. A contract may be defined as an agreement between two competent parties, based on sufficient legal consideration to do or not to do some particular act. Some of the elements of a contract include: that the act cannot be illegal; that the people entering into the contract must be competent; that there must be a consideration; that there must be a meeting of the minds; that the contract must be made in clear language; and that the acceptance must be communicated clearly.

Negotiable instruments, or "commercial paper," are credit instruments which circulate fairly freely. The most common negotiable instrument is a check. A negotiable instrument is also a contract, but, it differs from other contracts in that it can be readily transferred by a simple endorsement.

A hospitality operation usually serves food and therefore has liability in the sale of this food. There are two concepts regarding liability of unwholesome food served to patrons. Under the first concept, the food-service operation can be sued for negligence or failing to exercise due care. This considers that the food is only a part of the total service rendered, with other parts being the preparation, the serving, the dishes, and the decor. The newer concept considers the operation to offer an implied warranty that the food is fit for consumption. Thus a customer purchasing the food has an understood warranty that the food will be good. If the food is not good, the food operation can be sued even though it may not have been negligent.

Many hospitality operations serve alcoholic beverages. These come under various state laws. A major concern is the damage or harm that a customer who becomes intoxicated in a hospitality operation might do after leaving the operation. Some courts have held the operation itself liable.

Occasionally, there is trouble with loss of property in a restaurant checkroom. The deciding factor is usually whether a bailment relation has been established. If it has, the operation is probably liable.

There may also be a problem as to whether a hotel is forced to accept anybody as a guest, and when the hotel can legally terminate the relationship with a present guest. These questions cannot be arbitrarily determined; there are specific criteria which must be considered. In ejecting a guest, care must be taken that the eviction is done as privately as possible, with no more force than necessary.

Hotels may also be liable for injuries which occur on the premises. If a hotel is negligent, of course it will be liable. When an accident occurs, therefore, the hotel should be very sure to have a complete report of all information regarding the accident.

In 1964, the Civil Rights Act changed some aspects of hotel operation. The Act assures that all persons are entitled to full and equal enjoyment of the goods, services, facilities, privileges, advantages, and accommodations of any place of public accommodation, without discrimination or segregation on the grounds of race, color, religion, or national origin. Local jurisdictions may also have their own civil rights acts. Relief under the Civil Rights Act may be pursued by the person claiming discrimination, or the courts may permit the Attorney General to intervene.

The Fair Labor Standards Act of 1938 or the Federal Wage and Hour Law is a basic piece of legislation, although it has been amended a number of times. It sets minimum wages, maximum hours, overtime pay, equal pay, and child labor standards for employment. All larger enterprises come under this Act.

Unemployment insurance provides for payments to tide unemployed workers over between jobs. The law is a federal one but is administered by the State which requires employers to pay taxes based on their payrolls. Benefits are paid out of funds built up from these taxes. Because the law is administered by the states, there is a great variation in the various provisions.

The Social Security Act provides for retirement, survivor's and disability insurance, and health insurance for persons over 65. Another aspect of the Act involves unemployment insurance. Benefits under the program are payable only to persons, and their dependents and survivors, who become insured under the program by working at jobs covered by law. The great majority of workers are now covered. There is some concern *now that Social Security in the future will not have the funds to pay back the benefits expected by present-day contributors.*

In 1967, the Age Discrimination Employment Act was passed. This act is designed to promote the employment of the older worker, emphasizing ability rather than age. It prohibits arbitrary age discrimination in employment and is designed to aid employers and employees in finding ways to meet problems arising from the impact of "human obsolescence." It is designed to protect people who are at least 40 and less than 65 years of age against discriminatory hiring, discharge, compensation, or other occupational conditions.

A hospitality enterprise needs various types of insurance protection. Because it deals with so many people, it probably needs more insurance protection than most. Insurance provides protection against the effects of peril risk. It trades the uncertainty of these perils' occurrence for the certainty of reimbursement. Insurance may be written by various types of companies: stock companies, mutual companies, reciprocals, and Lloyd's groups. It is well to know something of the financial stability of the insurance company which you use.

Insurance may be distributed in two principal ways. One is through the independent agency. The other is through a direct routing system. An independent agent has a right to sell insurance from the company and receives a commission for the insurance. He may represent a number of companies. The direct routing system has the insurance company selling only its insurance through its own employees with no independent middleman involved. An insurance broker represents the insured rather than the insurance company and is the insured's legal representative. An insurance agent may also be an insurance broker. An independent insurance consultant acts only as an advisor and is paid directly by the customer he represents.

There are a number of types of insurance applicable to the hospitality industry. Foremost among these are: fire insurance, liability insurance, workmen's compensation, fidelity bonds, surety bonds, crime insurance, all risk, multiple lines, business interruption, power plant, life, and health insurance.

IMPORTANT TERMS

After studying this chapter, you should be able to define or describe the following:

common law

statutory law

tort

contract

consideration

commercial paper

contract assignment

negotiable instrument

paperhanger

implied warranty

bailment

stare decisis

doctrine of public callings

prima facie

gratuitous bailment

res ipsa loquitur

separate but equal doctrine

Mrs. Murphy's clause

Equal Employment Opportunity Commission

Civil Rights Act of 1964

Fair Labor Standards Act of 1938

Age Discrimination in Employment Act

stock insurance companies

mutual insurance companies

reciprocal insurance company

Lloyd's Groups insurance companies

insurance broker

fire co-insurance

fidelity bonds

surety bonds

all-risk and multiple line coverage

business interruption insurance

REVIEW QUESTIONS

12–1. Briefly discuss the elements of a contract.

12–2. You would like to cash your patron's personal checks. What steps can you take to prevent losses?

12–3. What is the difference in liability between an implied warranty and negligence in the service of food?

12–4. On what basis can a hotel eject a guest?

12–5. How do the provisions of the Civil Rights Act of 1964 affect the hospitality industry?

12–6. How do the provisions of the Fair Labor Standards Act of 1938 affect the hospitality industry?

12–7. What should a hospitality enterprise consider in the selection of an insurance representative?

12–8. Explain co-insurance. Why it is needed?

12–9. What provisions must be satisfied to collect on business interruption insurance?

12–10. Discuss common provisions of employee group life and health insurance plans.

12–11. Upon entering the lobby, a hotel guest slips on the stairs. Examination reveals a hole in the carpet that may have contributed to the fall. The guest claims he wrenched a shoulder. What is the hotel's liability?

12–12. The same guest gets to his room and decides to take a shower to ease the pain. The water is cool; he twists the valve to the hottest. A sudden jet of steam comes out, adding a burn to the previous injury. What is the hotel's liability?

12–13. To combat his increasing pain, the guest goes to the cocktail lounge. A waiter takes his jacket, says he "will take care of it," and hangs it on a coat-hook, near a sign disclaiming any responsibility for lost or stolen property. When the patron is ready to leave, he finds his jacket has disappeared. What is the hotel's liability?

13 Feasibility Studies

Do You Need a Feasibility Study?

Analysis of a Feasibility Study

Perhaps the most important decision a hospitality manager can make is whether or not to go into business in the first place. Oddly enough, this decision has often been dictated by vague impressions and educated guesses. But carefully and thoughtfully conducted feasibility studies now provide hospitality managers with a tool for improving their chances for success before they commit themselves to definite locations and definite types of operations. When you complete this chapter, you should be able to

- explain in some detail how the feasibility study can be used to improve the chance for success of a planned hospitality enterprise
- list and explain briefly the various steps involved in drawing up a feasibility study for a hospitality operation
- explain how you would implement these steps

A foodservice operation's success depends upon numerous factors—all of them connected and related. If just one of these factors is missing, an operation may be doomed to fail even before it opens its doors. The feasibility study is a tool a hospitality professional can use to analyze the appropriate factors and determine his chances of success. And that is why the feasibility study is important enough to receive a chapter of its own.

In a *commercial* restaurant, all of the crucial factors considered in a feasibility study take a back seat to two overriding questions: will the profits justify the investment necessary, and (since the investment could be committed in a number of ways) will this operation provide the best return on investment?

On the other hand, an *institutional* foodservice is usually just one part of a larger enterprise, a hospital, for example, or a school. The main enterprise needs a foodservice to carry on its work. But that foodservice is not normally expected to make a profit and cannot, therefore, have a return on investment. Since a foodservice is necessary to the overall operation, no question of feasibility arises. There can, however, be analyses of the necessary cost investment and of the operating costs required to provide the desired quanity and quality of food and services.

Do You Need a Feasibility Study?

We all know that some perfectly successful foodservices have been started without feasibility studies. A restauranteur may have a gut feeling

Note: Our discussion of hospitality feasibility uses a foodservice operation as a model. Hotels can incorporate the same technique.

that a certain type of operation "will go" in a certain locality, and he begins construction with apparently nothing more than that gut feeling to go on. But even in a situation like this, the developer really relies on more than just his gut feeling. He would probably admit that he has at least sized up the situation, which means that he has subjectively and informally weighed factors alluded to above and described in detail in this chapter.

And then, of course, some operations may be started because of other circumstances. Someone may own a parcel of land, want to make use of it, and decide to "try his hand" at a restaurant. Others may start a restaurant as a tax write-off or merely as a pleasant hobby.

But unfortunately, the failure rate for operations begun without a proper feasibility study is quite high. So unless you have the experience to risk trusting your instincts, or unless you have enough wealth to indulge yourself in an extravagant hobby, you should have a feasibility study done. A prominent hospitality leader once remarked that there were three reasons for his success—location, location, and location. A feasibility study tries to determine whether a particular location is economically feasible for a particular type of foodservice—or what the best type of operation would be for the location available.

Before undertaking a complete feasibility study, however, you can do some preliminary investigating that may rule out some proposed options before you spend too much time, effort, and money considering them. If you intend to use outside financing to supplement your own funds (and most operators must), you can easily discover whether that financing is available. You can also find out whether you can buy land in the desired area and whether the local zoning regulations will permit you to build a restaurant there. If you intend to affiliate, you can easily find out whether the desired chain wants a unit in that area or whether a franchise is available to you. And by looking at businesses in the neighborhood, you can roughly judge its overall economic health.

What Does a Feasibility Study Do?

Basically, a feasibility study determines whether or not you should proceed to build a particular business. In businessman's terms, it can "quantify the prospects of financial success." In simpler words, it can project what the profit should be from an operation. By comparing this projected profit with the investment you plan to make, you can see whether the profit justifies the owner's investment. Dividing the anticipated profit by the amount of your investment, you have the percentage known as *return on investment* (ROI).

A feasibility study can do even more: it can help *define* the operation by suggesting what type of food to serve, what style of service to use, what price ranges to impose, and what size operation to build.

If the operation is to be a unit in an existing system (that is, part of a chain or franchise) a feasibility study can show whether a market exists for this type of system at the proposed location. Different types of operations enjoy different levels of success at different locations, and a feasibility study can help determine what the best type of foodservice should be for a particular area.

Moreover, a feasibility study can help you acquire financing. After all, a lender likes to feel that his loan will be repaid; and a feasibility study that indicates a substantial profit or a cash flow adequate to pay off debts will encourage him to lend the money you need.

As you have already seen, feasibility studies concentrate on three foodservice aspects: marketing, profit, and financing. The *marketing aspect* includes the types of business that seems appropriate (including the prospective menu); the size of the business; and the expected volume.

Projected profits are determined by subtracting expected expenses from projected sales. Once you have estimated your volume of activity, it is relatively easy to determine your expenses. For example, some of your major expenses will present a percentage of sales—the amount of food, for instance. Other expenses will be fixed amounts. Entertainment and insurance are two examples here.

Financing the operation can be broken down into:

1. The total cost of opening an establishment
2. The amount of his own money the operator must put up

Usually the restauranteur or owner contributes only a part of the money. The rest comes typically in the form of loans. The greater the profit in relation to the owner's actual investment, the more desirable the investment.

Who Conducts Feasibility Studies?

An operator can perform his own feasibility study—they are really not difficult to do if one can be objective—or he can hire an expert. Accounting firms, particularly those specializing in hospitality operations, conduct a great many feasibility studies. Hospitality consultants also conduct them as part of their service. Large chain or franchise operations sometimes employ an entire staff to do nothing but feasibility studies. And many of the larger lending institutions routinely require feasibility studies to evaluate the prospects of a foodservice client.

Thus it often happens that one prospective business may undergo two or three feasibility studies before it gets going. The operator may do his own or hire someone to do it for him. The chain or franchise may send its staff to doublecheck on him. And the lending institution may conduct a third to reassure itself about the project's financial risks.

How Are Feasibility Studies Conducted? People in the business of conducting these studies often use a standardized format they have developed over the years. It is wiser, really, to tailor a feasibility study to the particular site or type of operation being considered.

Exactly what the feasibility study covers is crucial to the final decision about starting up or not. The number of pages in the feasibility study is, of course, no guide to its thoroughness. Some studies run to many pages but ultimately mislead; some exceedingly brief ones have proven to be highly accurate.

Analysis of a Feasibility Study

Parts of a feasibility study can usually be accomplished away from the projected site. For example, you can make most of your financial calculations in a comfortable armchair or at your desk. On the other hand, you can measure traffic volumes, interview passersby, and consider a building design only at the site.

Part of an actual feasibility study conducted for a commercial food-service operation appears in this chapter as Exhibit 13-1. But the same sort of analysis could be applied to such other hospitality operations as hotels and motels. And much of the information in Exhibit 13-1 can be applied to noncommercial operations like hospital foodservices.

Part I—Market Survey Notice that the pertinent feasibility factors appear in outline form (as a kind of shorthand). The outline is divided into two parts: the *market* for the contemplated operation, and the actual *on-site* considerations. As we look more carefully at this two-part outline, remember that since no single format applies to all operations, Exhibit 13-1 may overlook some points important for some operations and may include other points that are not pertinent to a specific situation. Nevertheless, it does suggest the scope of a typical feasibility study.

The market survey portion begins (at part A) by suggesting that you evaluate the economic level of your locality. Its purpose is to define characteristics of an area to help determine what type of operation will serve it best. If income levels are low, the chances for success of an expensive gourmet operation would be slim. A fast-food restaurant catering to children and young families will have trouble in an area dominated by senior citizens. Banquet and convention businesses usually depend on nearby organizations that regularly use their services. More specifically, it asks you to look at six definite aspects of that locality in this way:

1. You must decide whether the neighborhood is prosperous, stable, or deteriorating.
2. Whatever the present status of the neighborhood, you must look for evidence that it will grow.

Exhibit 13–1.
Outline for
Feasibility Study

FEASIBILITY STUDY

I. MARKET SURVEY
   A. Economic factors of the community
      1. *Status of neighborhood: progressive, stable, deteriorating*
      2. *Potential growth of community*
      3. *Source of community income: number of major industries, stability of income, average income*
      4. *Demographic factors: families, singles, children, young adults, older persons*
      5. *Associations that use foodservice facilities: civic, religious service, fraternal*
      6. *Food preferences: predominant national, ethnic, religious groups*
   B. Completion analysis
      1. *Foodservice establishments in area: types, sizes, markets, prices, profitability*
      2. *Planned additional operations: size, type, location, target market*
   C. Proposed operation
      1. *Type of operation most feasible*
      2. *Menu type*
      3. *Price ranges*
      4. *Size and capacities*
      5. *Facilities necessary: banquet, other function, beverage, parking*
   D. Projected volume
      1. *Expected seat turnovers: by meal, day of week, month of year*
      2. *Anticipated check average per meal*
      3. *Probable beverage volume*
      4. *Function and other revenue*

3. You must decide whether or not the neighborhood enjoys reliable sources of income, you should list these sources (a stable community enjoys a broad economic base rather than depending on a few dominant industries), and you should find out the average income in the area. Statistical data, like the average income of a specific area, is usually available from the local Chamber of Commerce, banks, radio and television stations, or newspapers.

4. You must list the basic *demographics* of the area—the number of families, young children, young adults, older people. These need be only estimates, but the information is helpful when it

Exhibit 13–1,
Continued

II. SITE ANALYSIS

   A. Location
      1. *Area*
      2. *Frontage*
      3. *Depth*
      4. *Topography*
      5. *Soil conditions*
   B. Traffic patterns
      1. *Traffic counts*
      2. *Cease of ingress and egress*
      3. *Peak traffic periods*
      4. *Contemplated changes*
      5. *Traffic destinations*
      6. *Convenience to main arteries*
      7. *Parking facilities*
   C. Other transportation
      1. *Types and amounts*
      2. *Coverages*
   D. Site visibility
      1. *Sign regulations*
      2. *Present and possible future obstructions by other buildings*
   E. Legal
      1. *Zoning regulations*
      2. *Required set-backs*
      3. *Local or state laws of possible concern*
      4. *Assessments and taxes*
   F. Utilities
      1. *Availability of water, electricity, gas, waste disposal, sewers, other*
      2. *Commercial rates*
      3. *Restrictions*

---

comes time to decide whether to cater to teenagers, families, or youngsters.

5. You must list the dominant civic, religious, service, and fraternal organizations in the area (especially if you plan to offer banquet or large dining area service).

6. You must consider the predominant national, ethnic, and religious groups in the area when it comes time to plan a menu that will attract large numbers of customers.

Part B of the market survey half of our feasibility study suggests that you analyze your competition. It is a good idea, for example, to list the types, the sizes, and the locations of all restaurants within a predetermined *competitive area* (perhaps a ten-mile radius). Moreover, you should list their prices (preferably by visiting the premises and copying the menu). Their general profitability can often be estimated by observing the amount of business they are doing and by noting the prices they charge. Do not forget to investigate whether any other restaurants are planned for your locality. Local bankers and real estate people are often aware of these plans. It should be obvious that, just because the present operations appear to be succeeding, an automatic need does not exist for more of the same.

Your analysis of the competition will carry you directly to section C of the market survey half of your feasibility study. Having determined what sort of operation is presently succeeding in your neighborhood, you will have a pretty good idea about what sort of operation you should establish. You can mark down, for example, the types of service, the price ranges, and the seating capacities that seem to be successful. (The seating capacity is particularly important: no matter how good it is, a facility that is too large for its potential business will suffer excess costs; whereas too small a facility will place a firm ceiling on amount of business that can be handled and on resulting profits.)

Mark down, too, which specific installations—banquet halls, gift shops, tavern rooms—are either abundant or in short supply in the area. And, having decided upon an ideal size for your operation, do not fail to make provision for ample parking facilities—particularly if you intend to attract highway travelers.

It is worthwhile to note here that chains and franchises have already developed their type of operation. Thus, they will want to know not what sort of operation will succeed but whether their established operation will succeed.

A feasibility study may show a need for a full-service restaurant with banquet facilities. Despite this need, it would be foolish for a franchise, fast-food chain to open a new unit, if its market is already handled by similar operations. It is not unheard of, though, for a group of similar restaurants to operate side by side. Sometimes they generate more business for the entire area than if they were far apart. The idea of choosing brings people into the area.

Section D of the marketing survey involves projected volume. Forecasting the volume you expect is perhaps the most important part of a feasibility study, and one of the most difficult to accomplish. If you could estimate your volume with some certainty, you could easily project both your expenses and your profit. Unfortunately, there are no certain principles to guide you through that forecast, mainly because so many variables can affect the fortunes of each individual operation. Occasionally textbooks or foodservice magazines publish rules of thumb suggesting that a population of so many thousand will support a particular kind of foodservice or that x number of hotel rooms are needed for every thousand people in town. But these rules of thumb are often disproved, for example, by large hotels that thrive in small towns located near an interstate highway exit.

No one can offer really reliable volume forecast guidelines. But the information in part I of the feasibility study in Exhibit 13-1 is as helpful as anything when it comes time to determine whether there is sufficient potential business for the foodservice you have in mind.

Turnover rates typically change during different days of the week, for different meals, and during different periods of the year. A city cafeteria does its biggest volume on business days during the lunch hour. Northern resort restaurants tend to thrive on late spring, summer, and early fall weekends—unless there is skiing nearby. To be accurate, you may want to calculate volume by estimating your turnover ratios for every week of the year and calculating each week's volume separately. All the weeks can then be added to derive the total. (Remember that holidays and long weekends can alter weekly volumes.) Once you determine an estimate of the number of *covers* (or customers) for each meal, you can calculate your dollar sales for each meal by multiplying the number of covers by the average check.

Determining an average check can be a problem. For example, the selling prices for the various menu items must be fixed. These selling prices are obviously related to food costs, but other factors can influence them as well—like the amount of service you provide and pressure from your competition. Once you have determined selling prices, you can estimate the number of items the average customer will consume and calculate an average check. Another way to determine the average check is to multiply the selling price of each item by the number of items you expect to sell and then divide this figure by the number of customers you expect.

If you plan to serve liquor, you will want to estimate your probable beverage volume along with your expected turnover and your anticipated check average per meal. There are two easy ways to do this. First, you could assume that beverage sales represent a fixed percentage of food sales. Many foodservice professionals pick a figure in the area of 20 percent, but the actual figure varies from one operation to the next. Assume, then, that your projected food sales are $10,000. You can add $2000 for beverage sales to that.

Second, you could assume that a certain number of drinks will be served for every meal served. (One figure used is 1.3 drinks.) Now you merely multiply the average price per drink by the number of meals you expect to serve and multiply that result by 1.3. The mixture of beverages sold can complicate this calculation or if you offer a wide price range. Beer presents a special problem, being so much less expensive then cocktails. An assumption of two beers served for every regular drink may be required in order to account for beer sales. On the other hand, if cocktail prices are fairly standard, the calculation can be quite easy.

*Part II—Site
Analysis*

Part II of our demonstration feasibility study concentrates on the actual site on which you plan to build. This site analysis has been broken down further into six general headings—each with its own specific considerations. For example, section A asks you to examine the actual location you have in mind in terms of its area, its frontage, the depth of the property, the lay of the land, and the local soil conditions.

If one of these factors is unsatisfactory, certain types of operations have to be ruled out. When acres of parking space are required, for example, you must have the acres. On the other hand, excess area increases costs and (worse) imparts a deserted look to what might actually be a potentially active operation.

The frontage and depth of the lot must be sufficient to accommodate the planned building. The topography of the land can also affect construction or aesthetics or even visibility. The type of soil on the site can affect building costs or the feasibility of sewage disposal. A rocky soil inevitably raises building excavation costs.

Section B of part II, which asks you to analyze traffic patterns, is important because traffic patterns affect the amount of business to expect and, in some cases, what sort of foodservice you can provide. (The roadside establishment obviously requires passing motorists.) Moreover, the convenience of your site—how easy it is to park there and to enter and leave—will determine whether travelers will go out of their way to visit you. Many a restaurant has failed simply because motorists had to turn across a busy, dangerous intersection to reach it.

If peak traffic periods coincide with your busy periods, your operation should be fairly successful. The exception would occur if the traffic makes entry or departing very difficult. Before you count on desirable traffic patterns in planning your operation, you would be wise to check on whether they might possibly change. Many a formerly prosperous food and lodging operation has been forced to close when new routes bypassed them. The classic example is, in fact, Colonel Harland Sanders' own Kentucky restaurant. When an interstate route bypassed the Colonel, he was forced to franchise his "Kentucky fried chicken." For him, things worked out well. But, a future restaurant owner cannot count on acquiring the Colonel's luck and incredible energy.

Traffic destinations can be important. Clever professionals have an uncanny knack of spotting logical, convenient stopping places. For example, one very busy restaurant we know of is located exactly between two large towns 100 miles apart. If it were closer to either town, it's clientele would diminish. People in one town would consider it too far, while people in the other might not stop because they were already near home, thus lumping it together with the other restaurants around town and not considering it quite so special.

In addition, it's best to be located quite close to a main thoroughfare. In an age of rising gasoline prices, accessibility by other means of transportation (where they exist) can be a real asset.

As part II, section D implies, some operations depend heavily on the visual impact they project to attract business. The golden arches of McDonald's or the famous (or notorious) orange tiles of Howard Johnson are examples of readily visible symbols. But they are not effective when they are obstructed by trees or hills or buildings. If you plan to rely on large, gaudy signs, you should determine whether the local advertising ordinances permit them. And while you are at it, see if you can find out what the local zoning board has in mind for your site. Look, too, at the taxes you will be paying, and at any special local ordinances governing the sale of alcoholic beverages.

Part II, section F indicates that an operation must install an array of utilities—some of which may not be immediately available. In fact, some utility companies have, in the light of the nation's energy shortage, declined to serve additional customers. Restaurant plans are occasionally abandoned simply because local sewer authorities refuse to extend their systems. In short, it is wise to check on the availability of such services as these in advance. Utility costs are no longer insignificant—and foodservice professionals have become increasingly concerned with correlating available fuels and services with their particular locations.

A Sales Estimate in Tabular Form

Exhibit 13-2 will also interest someone investigating a future in the restaurant business. It is a sales estimate for a proposed downtown foodservice operation. Notice that the analyst who prepared this table made a series of projections for each definable meal period. More specifically, he multiplied the projected number of seats by the anticipated rate of turnover per seat. The result of this multiplication is the number of covers for each meal, or 200 for breakfast.

When multiplied by the average check ($.90 for breakfast) this figure provides an estimated daily sales figure per meal, which turns out to be $180 for breakfast.

The restaurant pictured in Exhibit 13-2 will be open 256 days a year. So the projected breakfast sales for the entire year are $46,080. Using the same analysis for the other meals, you can derive a total restaurant food sales of $634,880. Adding banquet, special function, and beverage sales produces a total volume of approximately one million dollars.

MEAL PERIOD	NUMBER OF SEATS	RATE OF TURNOVER	NUMBER OF COVERS	AVERAGE CHECK	ESTIMATED DAILY SALES	ANNUAL DAYS	PROJECTED ANNUAL SALES
Breakfast	100	2.0	200	$1.80	$360	256	$ 92,160
Luncheon	100	4.0	400	2.50	1000	256	256,000
Dinner	100	1.0	100	6.00	600	256	153,600
Supper	100	0.8	80	5.50	440	256	112,640
Coffee Break (A.M.)	100	1.5	150	.60	90	256	23,040
Coffee Break (P.M.)	100	1.5	150	.60	90	256	23,040
Total Restaurant Food Sales							660,480
Banquet and Function Sales							139,520
Total Food Sales							800,000
Beverage Sales							200,000
TOTAL ESTIMATED SALES							$1,000,000

Exhibit 13–2.   Sample Sales Estimate for a Downtown Restaurant

The sales estimate depends a great deal on forecasts of activity, which by their very nature can be difficult to produce. The factors contained in part I of the feasibility study in Exhibit 13-1 can help determine this forecast of volume. But again, there are no exact rules, because there are so many variables. Instead of multiplying the number of seats by the rate of turnover, you may find it convenient to approach the problem by estimating only the volume—using the data from Exhibit 13-1. Dividing the planned seating capacity by this estimate yields the rate of turnover. (Dividing a volume of 200 covers by a seating capacity of 100 yields a turnover of two.) Too high a turnover figure indicates an operation too small for its projected volume. Too low a turnover figure indicates that the planned seating capacity is too high.

Imperfect as our analysis of volume, planned size, and turnover may be, it is still better than deciding the size of an operation by extracting a figure from mid-air. The physical characteristics of the proposed site, as explored in part II of Exhibit 13-1, may also help determine the size of the planned operation. Determining the rate of turnover can help you analyze whether the size dictated by the site is, in fact, feasible.

The projected volume for the planned operation is most important since many of your expenses will be based on it. Food costs, for example, should be directly related to food sales.

A Pro Forma Income Statement

Armed with an annual sales estimate, an analyst can prepare a pro forma income statement (similar to the one pictured here as Exhibit 13-3). Pro forma refers to projected or anticipated figures rather than to figures that have been determined from actual past operations. (*Pro forma* comes from Latin and means as a matter of, or according to form.) A regular income statement shows the income and expenses that were actually incurred during an actual past period rather than ones for a projected future period covered in a pro forma statement. The pro forma statement provides our best estimates of what our income should be for a projected period and what our expenses and the resulting profit and loss should be for this same projected income period.

The cost figures on the pro forma statement may be calculated in several ways. One is to consider the cost as a percentage of sales. For example, the food costs should be a certain percentage of food sales, which in this case is 34 percent. To arrive at the 34 percent figure one can consider what other, similar operations are spending for food in relation to their sales. It would be more accurate for the operator actually to determine the food cost in advance of his various menu items and divide this cost by the anticipated sales to provide food cost percentages. It is obvious that not all items sold have the same food cost percentage. For example, a certain dessert that cost 25 cents to make may be sold for 75 cents or

Exhibit 13–3.
Typical Pro Forma
Income Statement

INCOME STATEMENT
For 19___

	AMOUNT	PERCENTAGE
Sales		
Food	$ 800,000	80.0%
Beverages	200,000	20.0
Total Sales	$1,000,000	100.0%
Cost of Sales		
Food	$ 272,000	34.0%
Beverages	60,000	30.0
Total Cost of Sales	$ 332,000	33.2%
Gross Profit		
Food	$ 528,000	66.0%
Beverages	140,000	70.0
Total Gross Profit	$ 668,000	66.8%
Expenses		
Payroll	$ 320,000	32.0%
Payroll taxes and employee benefits	32,000	3.2
Employee meals	29,000	2.9
China, glassware, silver, and linen	15,000	1.5
Laundry and uniforms	15,000	1.5
Cleaning supplies	13,000	1.3
Guest and paper supplies	6,000	.6
Utilities	20,000	2.0
Music and entertainment	20,000	2.0
Menu and wine lists	5,000	.5
Licenses and fees	1,000	.1
Rubbish removal	2,000	.2
Flowers and decorations	6,000	.6
Administrative and general	35,000	3.5
Advertising and promotion	20,000	2.0
Repairs and maintenance	16,000	1.6
Total Expenses	$ 555,000	55.5%
Profit before occupation costs, depreciation, and income taxes	$ 113,000	11.3%

a 33.3 percent food cost. An entrée item, though, may cost $2.00, and be sold for $4.00 and have a 50 percent food cost. The selling prices the operation offers the public depend on such factors as the ability of the clientele to pay, the amount of service provided, and the luxury of the decor. A luxurious operation may have a relatively low food cost since the patron pays for the "trappings." Meanwhile, an economy cafeteria may have a higher food cost since the patron is interested primarily in the food value.

Percentages of the cost of different expense items as compared to sales are available from various sources. The national hospitality accounting firms perform annual studies showing the cost percentages for various types of food operations. The larger restaurant associations often have these figures available. A specialized text like *Controlling and Analyzing Cost and Food Service Operations* by Keiser and Kallio also includes these percentages.

Some costs should not be determined strictly as a percentage of sales. Advertising and promotion costs, for example, should be determined by deciding what types of promotion to utilize and then costing out this desired promotion. For example, if the promotion is to consist of billboards and newspaper advertising, it is a simple matter to determine how much this advertising will cost and then determine the advertising and promotion figure. This can then be divided by sales if a percentage figure is desired.

Beverage cost determination is similar to food cost determination. The operator determines at what price he will be selling various beverages and the amount of the beverage he will be providing. Once the quantity is determined, the cost to the operator can be determined and cost can be compared to sales to derive a beverage percentage. Again, it must be recognized that the percentages will differ according to the types of beverages served. The beverage percentage for cocktails will probably differ from the malt beverage percentage. But the operator can derive a weighted average to determine his normal beverage figure.

Labor costs can be determined by deciding how much staff will be required for the anticipated volume of service. If the operator decides that one serving person can handle thirty patrons, dividing the number of expected patrons by thirty will produce the number of serving personnel required for the serving period. The salary and fringe benefit costs for these people can then be determined. Then, adding the cost of serving personnel to the cost of other personnel gives total labor costs. Comparing this anticipated sales gives the labor cost percentage. In our example, labor costs of $320,000 are compared to sales of $1 million giving a labor cost percentage of 32 percent. The labor cost percentage varies with different volumes of business. Some employees are necessary whether there is a great deal of business or comparatively little. Those employees needed regardless of the business volume are considered to be the fixed-cost employees. Serving personnel and preparation personnel, on the other hand, can usually be increased or decreased depending on the volume of activity and so can be variable-cost employees.

Payroll taxes, like social security and workmen's compensation, represent a percentage of payroll and can be calculated rather easily. Other employee benefits can usually be costed out. For example, a two week's vacation is roughly two fifty-seconds of a yearly salary, or about 4 percent. In calculating the value of an employee's meal, some operations consider this as a certain percentage of total food cost, with 5 to 10 percent of total food cost commonly being used as the figure for employee's meals. Other operations determine what the typical employee meal consists of, cost it out, and then multiply it by the number of meals expected to be served. Other operations can use the amount prescribed as a meal credit for social security benefits, but since this is abnormally low they may multiply it by two or three times to get the average cost per employee meal.

The amount spent for china, glassware, silver, and linens of course varies according to the standards of the restaurant. An operation that uses linen tablecloths has much higher linen charges than one that has no tablecloths and uses paper napkins. Glassware quality can differ greatly. Its cost as a percentage of sales from similar operations may be used. Another, and perhaps more accurate, approach is to determine the quantities of these items used and multiply the quantity by the cost of each item to derive a total cost in any one category.

Laundry and uniforms, cleaning supplies, and paper supplies are usually best estimated by using standard percentages for those items compared to sales. Again, more accurate calculations may be made if one determines what the policy for employee's uniforms should be. If they furnish their own and are responsible for washing their own, there would, of course, be very little expense. On the other hand, if the establishment furnishes employee uniforms, it should determine:

1. How many uniforms each employee will require
2. The cost of the uniforms
3. How often they will be cleaned
4. The cost of all this

Uniforms deteriorate in time, and a factor should be included for this cost. Since uniform costs vary considerably, it is best to get help from a uniform supply house regarding the costs. Cost of utilities will depend on the geographical area. Cold areas require considerably more heating and warmer areas require air conditioning. Once the nature of the physical structure of the premises is known, the local energy companies can usually produce rather accurate estimates of heating or cooling costs.

When determining music or entertainment, an operator must determine the amount he desires. If he wants a combo five nights a week, he can easily determine its cost and multiply that amount by the number of days the combo will appear. General percentages are not very helpful here since the music and entertainment vary so considerably. Piped-in music costs can be readily quoted by the supplier.

Menu supply houses are happy to quote menu and wine list costs. And by calculating the number of menus needed and how often they will change, an operator can produce an accurate cost for the service. Licenses and fees can generally be determined accurately in advance. It is necessary only to ask the issuing agency what the costs will be. Rubbish removal charges vary considerably. Some towns provide service in exchange for local taxes. In other places, a flat charge is made. Still others determine the cost by the number of trash cans or garbage bags handled. In any case, a check with municipal authorities should be sufficient to determine this cost. Floral and decoration costs can vary considerably too, and one should determine in advance to what extent they will be used. The costs are available from florists and specialty shops.

The costs of help in the office and office expenses can be readily estimated. Estimates of accounting, legal, and insurance costs are provided in advance by those who want to supply the respective services. Repairs and maintenance costs can vary considerably depending on the state of the premises. Building experts (engineers or architects) can help estimate these costs.

As we have discussed, our proposed costs can be determined in two ways. One is to use standard percentage amounts which, when multiplied by the anticipated sales, yield the amount of the various costs. The other is actually to cost the item out, which sometimes requires outside help. Even though the item is separately costed to derive a figure, its percentage (the calculated cost over anticipated sales) figure can be compared with industry averages to see if it is generally in line. There are good reasons not to depend too much on general industry averages, especially since individual operations may vary considerably from the industry averages.

The bottom item on Exhibit 13-3 represents profit before occupational costs, depreciation, and income taxes—$113,000, or 11.3 percent of sales. The occupation costs refer to the costs of maintaining the premises. This can include rent, mortgage payments, real estate taxes, and property insurance. Depreciation, covered in the chapter "Financial Management," is the charge made against assets that deteriorate through use, time, or obsolescence. Income taxes are the taxes on the profit of the enterprise. They, of course, vary according to the amount of profit.

Primary
Preliminary
Capital Costs
Estimates

As this chapter has already stressed, the feasibility of a commercial operation is determined largely by economic factors usually expressed as the return on the investment—or how much money a person has to invest in an operation compared to the amount of money he earns from it. The investment usually consists of two parts: the entrepreneur's own money invested and the money borrowed from other sources. Before proceeding too far on a proposed operation, the entrepreneur should have some idea of the amount of money he will need. He can then determine how much of his own funds might be available and how much he

LAND	$ 50,000	Selling price or preliminary appraisal can give a basis for land cost consideration. Costs of site development and landscaping should be included.
PAVED PARKING AREAS AND DRIVEWAYS	10,000	Cost per square foot is usually available. Multiply this by total footage to determine a projected figure.
STRUCTURE COSTS	250,000	Architects or builders can usually give an estimated cost based on type of construction and estimated cost per square foot multiplied by total footage.
FURNISHINGS AND FIXTURES	120,000	An interior designer or supply firm can provide an estimate by multiplying the projected cost per seat by the projected number of seats. Similar type operations are usually close enough in cost per seat to allow a general guide figure to be used.
EQUIPMENT	80,000	The type of menu and projected volume allows for a projected equipment list. This can then be priced out.
OTHER COSTS	30,000	This figure should include architectural and consultant fees (usually between 7 to 10 percent), office equipment, employee facilities, reserve for contingencies, and cost overruns or increases.
TOTAL	**$540,000**	

Exhibit 13–4. Preliminary Capital Cost Estimates

will have to seek elsewhere. The term *entrepreneur* does not necessarily refer only to an individual; it can refer, as well, to an investment group or corporation.

Exhibit 13-4 provides preliminary capital costs estimates for an operation. The term *preliminary* is used because this estimate was done during the first stage of a feasibility study. If it appears that capital costs will be too high, the whole project may be abandoned before too much effort is invested in it. If the preliminary estimates (which are mere "ballpark estimates") appear logical, more exact figures can be determined. Exhibit 13-4 depicts some estimates for a particular project. As we already stressed in this chapter, there are no common guidelines for all operations. In Exhibit 13-4, paving for parking and driveways is a relatively minor amount compared to the structure costs of $250,000. Other operations may be able to get by with a comparatively small structure, but require a much larger parking lot and driveway. They would have an entirely different ratio on these two costs. Exhibit 13-4 does this sort of analysis for major capital costs and explains ways to determine their specific amounts.

Analysis and Return on Investment

The usual criterion for a commercial endeavor is, once again, the return on the investment. Exhibit 13-5 provides a way to analyze this. It is the natural follower of the previous exhibits.

In Exhibit 13-1 we discussed possible markets and competition and determined what type of operation would probably be most suitable. We also discussed the appropriateness of the site for a particular function and other practical considerations necessary to complete the structure on the site.

Exhibit 13-2 provided one approach to determine the number of people served and then the projected sales by considering the rate of turnover for the various meal periods.

Exhibit 13-3 took these projected sales and provided the anticipated profit or loss by calculating expenses appropriate for the sales and for the standards of the operation.

Exhibit 13-4 yielded estimates of the amount of money required to bring a project to fruition.

If these preliminary estimates have been favorable they must still be checked with acutal cost prices and bids. All of the previous information is necessary to calculate Exhibit 13-5, an analysis of the return on investment. The profit of $113,000 from Exhibit 13-4 is presented, and after considering taxes, insurance, interest, depreciation, and other deductions are made, an income for paying off debt of $72,500 is left. This is the income before debt service or before paying the interest and the principal amount of loans, or before any withdrawing of profit. Exhibit 13-5 first shows a mortgage on real estate which has principal and inter-

Exhibit 13–5.
Typical Analysis
of Return on
Investment

	AMOUNT	PERCENTAGE
Profit before occupation, depreciation, and income taxes	$113,000	11.3%
Reductions		
Taxes	$ 5,000	0.5
Insurance	4,000	0.4
Interest	5,000	0.5
Depreciation		
Building	12,500	1.3
Furniture	12,000	1.2
Fixtures		
Equipment		
Other	2,000	0.2
Total Reductions	$ 40,500	40.5%
Income before Debt Service	$ 72,500	72.5
First mortgage	18,000	1.8
Chattel mortgage	12,000	1.2
Total Debt Service	$ 30,000	3.0%
Net Income before Income Taxes	42,500	4.3
Depreciation	24,500	2.5
Cash Flow	$ 67,000	6.7%
Cash flow as percent of equity		33.5
Profit as percent of equity		21.3
Profit as percent of total investment		8.0%

N.B.: In this example, the building is owned rather than being rented. Rental payment may be substituted for other occupation costs.

est payments at $18,000. The *chattel mortgage* is a mortgage on movable property (as opposed to real estate or real property). This mortgage is sometimes considered as a conditional sales contract wherein the purchaser acquires the use and possession of the assets but still does not actually own them until all of the purchase cost debts have been paid off. After subtracting the debt service of $30,000 we find we have net income before taxes of $42,500.

Usually in a new operation the *cash flow*, or the amount of cash available, is more important than the profit. Cash flow may be defined as profit plus depreciation. Although depreciation is an expense, it is a non-cash expense—money does not have to be put out directly at the time as one does when he pays personnel salaries or buys food. The depreciation in Exhibit 13-5 is $24,500, and adding this back to the net income before income taxes, but including depreciation, produces a cash flow of $67,-000. It should be noted that the net income before income taxes is not the same as profit. Principal payments on the first mortgage and on the chattel mortgage are included in the income before taxes, but these are not regular operating business expenses that would be included in the profit figure.

The three ratios employed in Exhibit 13-5 include cash flow as a percentage of equity; profit as a percentage of equity; and profit as a percentage of total investment. If we assume that the owner's equity, or the amount that the owner or owners have invested with their own money, is $200,000, the cash flow as the percentage of equity would be $67,000 divided by $200,000 or 33.5 percent.

As we stated earlier, the cash flow may be more important than the profit because it represents the money actually coming in and available. The return on the investment (ROI) is important. When someone has money to invest, he naturally wants to receive the highest possible return. Thus he asks himself whether the investment balances the risk he takes. Exhibit 13-5 shows a net income before income taxes of $42,-500. If this figure is divided by an investment of $200,000 the return on investment would be 21.3 percent. In our example, we have not considered income taxes because of the complexities involved. Tax computations, however, would cause the net income before taxes to be reduced by the amount of the taxes.

Profit as a percentage of total investment in the enterprise is sometimes called the management proficiency ratio or ROAM. (ROAM means return on assets managed or the total value of the enterprise as expressed by the value of its assets.) ROAM indicates how well management is doing with its assets. In comparing profits of various operations, one should know how the amount of the profit compares to the amount of money invested. One hundred thousand dollars may be a large profit for an operation that has five hundred thousand dollars worth of assets, but it would be a very small profit for one with two million dollars worth of assets. The ROAM ratio is not as desirable as the other ratios in considering the feasibility of an operation because it is concerned more with the money-making proficiency of the management given the available assets than relating profits to needed equity investment.

Exhibit 13–6.
Working Capital
Requirements

CURRENT ASSETS *(cash or assets that can be readily turned into cash)*

1. Cash on hand
   Used for cashier banks and petty cash funds.

2. Cash in the bank
   Funds necessary to meet current obligations such as payrolls, purveyors, and utility charges. A beginning operation will have to have sufficient funds to carry the operation till adequate cash revenue starts being generated.

3. Accounts receivable
   Funds owed by customers for services rendered. There is a lag between the time charge sales are made and the time they are collected. Funds must be available to compensate for this lag if charge sales are produced. This is no problem if all sales are cash.

4. Inventories
   a) *Food—Based on volume of business and number of times the food inventory is turned over during a month. If the cost of sales per month is $9000, and it is estimated the inventory would turn over three times, the amount of inventory required would be $3000. Often high-volume operations require less inventory in proportion to sales than lower-volume ones.*
   b) *Supplies—Varied according to availability, storage capacity, delivery frequency, and types and levels of service provided by the purveyor.*

5. Prepaid expenses
   Items such as license fees, insurance premiums, and utilities that are paid in advance.

CURRENT LIABILITIES *(money owed and payable by the operation, usually within one year)*

6. Trade account payable
   Money that is owed to purveyors. This should be about one-twelfth the annual amount of purchases and services secured from purveyors.

7. Accrued expenses
   Expenses that have been incurred by the operation but not yet paid. Usually these are payroll owed to employees and payroll taxes due. Such items as utility bills and other taxes may also be included. One percent of sales is sometimes used as a "ballpark" figure.

8. Current portions of long-term obligations
   The amount payable within one year of long-term loans.

N.B.: *Items 1 to 8 are required for a going operation. A new operation may have additional costs such as initial promotion costs, grand opening costs, salaries for personnel hired in advance, and training costs. These costs must be able to be carried by cash on deposit or loan sources, until operating revenues catch up.*

Working Capital Requirements

In addition to the cost of land, building, furnishings, and equipment, you must keep money on hand to conduct your business. Thus, in planning your restaurant and in planning for the exact amount of money that restaurant will cost you in the beginning, you should include working capital. By definition, *working capital* is the difference between current assets (actual cash or assets readily convertible into cash) and current liabilities (debts of all kinds due within one year).

If you have insufficient working capital, you may find it difficult to pay your bills and, consequently, to stay in business. Thus your feasibility study must show how much working capital you need, and what your capital expenditures will be. Cash requirements are usually offset, at least partially, by current liabilities. In other words, if you buy food but do not pay for it until the following month when you are billed, you may not have to have the money on hand at the time of your actual purchase. When you sell the food, it generates cash which should more than pay the bill when it arrives.

The relative difference between the current-asset total and the current-liability total is a measure of your *liquidity*—or a measure of how readily you can pay off your current obligations. Liquidity is sometimes expressed as a *current ratio* which is calculated by dividing current assets by current liabilities. For most businesses, a ratio of about two to one is considered right, but in the foodservice business, where one typically finds a fast inventory turnover and comparatively few accounts receivable, a ratio of closer to 1.2:1 is more realistic. Another liquidity ratio is the *acid test* or cash, marketable securities, and accounts receivable divided by current liabilities.

Besides your normal working capital requirements, your new operation will involve some atypical, one-time expenses. The need for promotion, training, and other preopening expenses should be planned upon, so that once your business is open, it must be able to pay off these initial expenses in addition to the usual ones. Exhibit 13-6 discusses the main items involved in determining working capital.

SUMMARY

A feasibility study determines whether or not a particular enterprise should proceed by quantifying the prospects of financial success. It is both marketing and financial in nature. Its marketing phase considers the target markets for the proposed operation and the facilities and services necessary to satisfy these target markets. The financial phase determines if the cash flow is adequate for the required investment.

The physical site considerations are obviously important. For example, is the proposed site appropriate for the planned operation? An anal-

ysis of this question would include such issues as physical characteristics, traffic patterns, utility availability, and zoning restrictions.

The first step in the financial phase is determination of dollar sales. Subtracting necessary cash disbursements leaves anticipated profits and cash flow. These figures can be compared with the necessary investment to see if they are appropriate. Consideration must also be given to the availability of financing. The feasibility of a nonprofit institution is usually determined by deciding what products or services the operation will produce and then determining the costs of providing them.

IMPORTANT TERMS

Having studied this chapter, you should be familiar with these terms:

feasibility study

demographics

pro forma statements

average sales

average check

operating costs

site analysis

cash flow

return on investment

REVIEW QUESTIONS

13-1. How is a feasibility study for an institutional foodservice different from one for a commercial foodservice?

13-2. What does a feasibility study do?

13-3. What criteria are used to determine if an operation is financially feasible?

13-4. Discuss market aspects of a feasibility study.

13-5. List the aspects of a particular locality that should be considered.

13-6. Discuss the aspects of the competition that should be considered.

13-7. How can you determine an average check for a feasibility study?

13-8. How can you determine average sales for a feasibility study?

13-9. What is important regarding traffic patterns?

13-10. Which factors are important in determining your selling prices?

13-11. Discuss two different ways that most operating cost amounts can be determined.

13-12. Why may cash flow be more important than profit in determining an investment?

14 Franchising

*F*ranchising, *a relatively recent but important development in both commercial foodservice and lodging, presents opportunities to the hospitality operation as well as some pitfalls. A hospitality manager must be aware of these opportunities and dangers if, on the one hand, he is interested in participating in the franchise movement or, on the other hand, he has to compete with franchises. When you finish studying this chapter on franchising, you should be able to*

- *explain, step by step, how one generally acquires and operates a franchise hospitality unit*
- *state nine advantages and two disadvantages of operating a hospitality franchise*
- *explain briefly how you would evaluate a franchise's prospects for success*
- *discuss the history of the successful franchise pioneers described in this chapter.*

To a generation raised in front of television sets that, hour upon hour, present ingenious, hypnotic, jingling commercials for McDonald's, Burger King, and Pizza Hut, the fast-food franchise must seem to be the most modern of all foodservice marketing techniques. And indeed franchising was the most important development in the commercial foodservice field to occur in the 1960s. But the franchising idea was with us long before then. Automobile manufacturers, for example, have franchised their dealerships since the days of the Model T, and oil companies have franchised their service stations for as long as there have been cars to pump the gas into.

At least one foodservice enterprise, the A & W Rootbeer company, sold franchises in the 1920s. (One of their early franchises was J. Willard Marriott, who later founded the vast hospitality empire that bears his name.) And, to a limited degree, Howard Johnson's offered restaurant franchises in the 1930s.

It was not until the 1960s that the restaurant franchise idea really took off, and foodservice franchising grew some 3600 percent between 1955 and 1970.

Why the sudden growth? To begin with, Americans suddenly had more money to invest. Many of them wanted a small business of their own, and purchasing a franchise seemed like the quickest path to this dream. Moreover, new markets, especially those that catered to the increasingly mobile young, developed as fast as the United States highway system. And the sophisticated marketing techniques of the franchising companies made it easy for them to place their units so as to tap these specific markets.

In addition, franchising relieved the businessman of the bother of "learning the business" and serving an apprenticeship. To a great extent, in fact, franchising allowed a businessman to borrow and subsequently trade on the expertise of the franchising company.

Furthermore, there was strength in numbers. The franchised units, working together, could accomplish a great deal more in the areas of promotion and wholesale food buying than an independent unit. Franchisers could launch expensive advertising campaigns on behalf of their franchisees, and each new franchise reinforced the visibility and respectability of every other unit.

And finally, the astounding success of such early franchising entrepreneurs as Colonel Harland Sanders and his Kentucky Fried Chicken and the McDonald Corporation encouraged others to franchise everything from pancakes to pizza to fish and chips.

But the two greatest factors in the success of franchising were undoubtedly the franchise's appeal to special markets and their compatibility with the automobile-oriented generation.

Advantages of Franchising

Franchising obviously owes its popularity to the advantages it provides both the franchisor and the franchisee. The *franchisee* is the person or organization who acquires the right to sell the franchisor's products, under specific conditions and with certain stipulations. The *franchisor* sells the franchise, consisting, usually, of his products, perhaps his equipment, and the right to use his name. There are at least eight advantages of franchising to the franchisee.

1. The franchisee buys into an established, successful business. He knows the food is popular, and he need determine only whether he can sell it at the location he has in mind. Not only is the food popular, but it also involves none of the traditional start-up uncertainty.

2. The typical franchise operation uses a standardized facility which has long since been streamlined and refined to appeal to the target customers and to achieve the maximum in efficiency. The franchisee need not hire an architect. He may not even need a construction company since franchisors often build, equip, and decorate the franchise outlets.

3. Just as the architectural plans are available to a franchisee, so too are the operational plans. Purchasing, storing, cooking, serving, and cleaning procedures have all been thoroughly worked out.

4. Many franchisors provide training programs for new franchisees and their employees. (Both McDonald's and the Holi-

day Inns boast about their intensive training schools; McDonald's even confers a diploma from its Hamburger University.) Even if they do not provide formal training, almost all franchisors do provide at least a detailed training manual. In short, the typical franchisee is spared all the anguish of opening a new operation and training his employees at the same time.

5. The independent restauranteur earns his reputation slowly and painfully. But the franchisee buys a well-known name and, with it, instant recognition and acceptance. He saves all the time, effort, and money building a reputation would normally cost him. As a franchisor knows, however, a slovenly franchisee can besmear the name of an entire franchise. Consequently, most franchisors maintain strict control over all their franchises.

6. The franchisor assumes the burden of keeping his operation's name before the public. He at least helps pay for the regional and national advertising that a single franchisee could never afford by himself.

7. In most cases, it is easier to finance a franchise than an independent restaurant. Prospective lenders can observe the results of other franchises in the area and can gauge their risk quite realistically. In fact, the franchising company itself often helps finance a new unit.

8. To put it bluntly, franchises often earn a lot of money. In fact, they often tend to show profits well above those of independent operations doing the same volume of business. A franchise ownership does not, of course, guarantee profit, and quite a few franchises have failed or are currently on shaky financial footing. But the fast-food concept tends to generate a much higher volume than many conventional restaurants. And the carefully arranged procedures they follow (market research having taken much of the guesswork out of attracting customers) increase the likelihood of generous profits.

In the lodging field, franchising provides another advantage: a national and international reservation service. Guests at one motor inn or lodge can readily reserve accommodations in the franchisor's other units. The reservation volume also justifies centralized, computerized reservation facilities. And in the future, lodging reservations will increasingly be tied into transportation and car rental reservation systems. The trend has already begun.

In addition to the advantages to the franchisee, there are strong incentives for the franchising organization. To begin with, once the franchisor formulates his product, his design, and his system, he can start selling the franchises at little additional cost to him. The greater the number of franchise operations, the greater his recognition factor—the more his advertising becomes cumulative and self-reinforcing. An independent restaurant cannot normally expand beyond several units. Franchisers, however, spread their units far and wide and reap all the accompanying benefits. Franchising, then, is a way to expand with relatively little in capital funds required on the part of the franchisor.

Disadvantages of Franchising

The list of advantages may be impressive, but franchising is not all a bed of roses. Its disadvantages are summarized as follows:

First, the franchisor is obviously in business to make money. He makes most of it from the initial franchise fees and the continuing royalties from his franchises. Typically, the initial franchise fee must be paid when the franchise is secured, and depending upon the success and reputation of the franchisor, that fee can be quite steep. And the continuing royalty payments are deducted from profits.

Second, in one sense a standardized operation provides reassurance. But an enterprising foodservice manager will be severely limited in what he can place on his menu, in what he can charge for his food, in what cooking procedures to use—in all those areas that imply creativity.

In the lodging industry the standard services that the franchised unit must supply can limit participation by smaller units who cannot afford such amenities as swimming pools, color television, or twenty-four-hour desk service. Exceptions may appear among budget-type chains that purposely try to eliminate such frills.

A franchisor with recognized, successful products faces few disadvantages in franchising except possibly for the need to see that his franchisees maintain the qualities the public has come to associate with his products. Company-owned units may also produce greater profits to the franchisor than franchised ones.

Opening a Franchise

One does not merely pay a franchise fee and begin a lucrative business. Things are never this easy either in foodservice or in most other businesses. Securing a franchise should require a great deal of hard, thoughtful preliminary work. Before investing in a franchise, for example, you should investigate a number of different franchise companies to see which offers the best arrangement for your particular circumstances.

Moreover, it would be wise to ask yourself exactly *why* you want to invest in a franchise arrangement. Perhaps you see franchising as simply a business investment, in which case you probably plan to have little to do with its actual operation, delegating that work to someone else. Or, perhaps you look forward to managing your franchise and being actively involved in all its functions. In this second instance, you will be committing more than just your money, and you should, therefore, try to determine what sorts of franchises would be compatible with your experience and expectations. (Some require active owner involvement.)

Previous foodservice experience may actually be a liability. In fact, some former foodservice operators encounter difficulty when they try to add a touch of individuality to a standardized franchise product. Thus, the person who enjoys preparing and serving creative dishes is bound for disappointment in a repetitive, fast-food, franchise operation. On the other hand, the largest single element of cost and quality control is usually the owner's presence on the scene over long hours of the day and night. Thus, someone who enjoys supervisory work *per se* may derive a good deal of pleasure and profit from owning a franchise.

You can see then that the choice of a particular franchise will depend upon whether you are seeking merely a return on investment (in which case you will probably be delegating most of your authority), or whether you want to involve yourself in a business, in which case you must plan to supervise carefully and refrain from altering the standard product you have contracted to sell.

Financial Aspects

The amounts one can expect to invest in a franchise will vary enormously, and the payments can take several forms. For example, the initial franchise fee is just one typical element of a franchise investment. This fee can be quite modest or, for an operation with a proven record of success, it can run high into the thousands of dollars.

Bear in mind that the franchise fee sometimes buys certain services beyond the mere right to a name. These services can include feasibility studies, a systematic site selection, training programs, the use of standard designs, and the use of the franchisor's systems.

In addition, franchisors usually demand continuing royalties that often represent a certain percentage of the sales. The typical franchising company receives continuing royalties of about 2 to 4 percent of the yearly sales plus an advertising assessment of about 1 percent of sales.

Methods of payment to a franchisor also vary considerably, but they usually amount to an additional cost to the franchisee and invariably eat into his profits. But this profit erosion may well be more than offset by the higher profit potential associated with franchises.

A Franchising Checklist

Now our discussion of the preliminary franchise purchasing considerations and some of the accompanying financial considerations gives way to a list of those specific questions you should ask before plunging into a franchise ownership:

> Reputation. How is the franchisor's track record? How long, for example, has he been in business? What is his reputation for fair dealing? What can you find out about the relations he maintains with his other franchisees?

The Product. What sort of product does he sell? Has this product been market-tested? Does the franchisor use modern marketing and merchandising techniques?

The Service. What sorts of services has the franchisor agreed to supply? Does your franchise fee include training? A feasibility study? A site appraisal? Can he provide a "turn key operation"? (That is, can he erect and equip an operation and then turn the key over to you?)

Agreement Termination and Mobility. What are the provisions for terminating the franchise agreement? Are you fully protected, or can the franchisor terminate arbitrarily? Can he open new units near you? Can you terminate easily or perhaps sell your business to someone else? Can you operate a franchise near your home, or must you accept the first franchise that becomes available regardless of where it may be?

Financial Estimates. Can the franchisor supply you with realistic operating figures? Franchisees sometimes get trapped by "typical" sales, cost, and profit figures that bear little relation to their particular operation or locale.

Backstopping. Does the franchisor provide a backup staff to help when you have problems? A traditional sore spot is the lack of assistance the franchisee finds when he runs into unforeseen trouble. This happens most often when a franchisor is more interested in expansion than in providing services to his established units.

Business practices. Has the franchisor made a thorough investigation of you? Attention to a detail like this suggests an interest in the success of individual units rather than in just sales increases. An organization that would neglect this sort of investigation would probably neglect other important managerial tasks as well.

Your Resources. Do you have, or can you easily obtain, the capital you need to invest in the franchise? Different franchises require different amounts of capital outlay. The very desirable franchise may be too expensive for you, and it is wise to learn this before proceeding too far.

Appropriateness. You must know whether franchising is really for you. This is the crucial question. Knowing what you now know about the franchisor-franchisee relationship, should you sign a franchise agreement? Do you want and need the services they provide? Or would you feel more comfortable running an operation in which you could exercise a little creativity and not pay the royalties?

The Future of Franchising

Franchising in foodservice operations has enjoyed phenomenal growth until recently, and this growth will undoubtedly continue faster than in the foodservice industry generally. Nevertheless, the rate of franchise growth is already beginning to decrease. The success of some franchise operations encouraged others less adequately prepared for the business to enter the field. Consequently, there has been a substantial "shake out" in the industry, and many companies that boomed briefly now face real financial problems. And, a good many more projected franchises never got off the ground. Franchising also depends on the availability of financing. Tight money can stop many potential operations especially in the lodging field. Shortages of energy will also have a definite effect on the hospitality industry and quite possibly franchising patterns.

If franchise food operations are to continue to enjoy their unusual success, the ground rules on which they have been flourishing will have to change. Since the very success of the franchise has glutted the market in many areas with cheap snack shacks, fewer desirable suburban high-wayside locations are left. Thus, the franchises have begun to enter the city—a trend that will surely continue. Of course urban locations present a whole new collection of problems to be overcome—not the least of which is the hostility that can accompany an intrusion into an established neighborhood. Franchise units have also been established in such previously unconsidered sites as hospitals, bus stations, and student unions.

Real estate management has become almost as important as foodservice to many of the more advantageously located operations. The demand for desirable sites has naturally increased the cost of those sites and the value of the existing operations. So the successful franchises have already started to learn how to manage their real estate investments.

Another interesting trend is the growing practice of granting multiple franchises—to grant franchises to people who have already demonstrated a knack for franchise management. The result is a series of subchains within the franchise chain itself. This practice tends, of course, to keep newcomers out of the franchise business.

The success of franchise operations has, from the beginning, been partly based on current fads. Tastes change, and the successful franchise operation of the future may have to supplement its hamburgers and shakes with a variety of other foods. The cost of food used—for example, the rising cost of beef—can also effect what food is served. McDonald's, once thought to be the most staid of the franchisers, has successfully introduced fish sandwiches, hot ham and eggs on muffins, and pancakes. The cooking procedures remain fairly standard, but the illusion of menu variety is attracting more new customers all the time. Of course the basic goals of a food franchise operation—quality, cleanliness, and quick service—will by definition remain paramount.

Laws and Regulations Governing Franchising

The great good fortune of franchising has unfortunately been marred by occasional unfairness and illegality on the part of both franchisors and franchisees. Franchise holders have complained of misrepresentation and too much interference. In turn, franchisors sometimes complain of the slovenly or incompetent franchisee ruining the "company image." The abuses have led to governmental legislation designed to cut down outright fraud, provide rules for the franchise operation, and restore a little leverage to the franchisee, who is, in general, a small, local businessman.

In addition, some franchisees have organized into the National Association of Franchise Businessmen, with offices in Washington, D.C. The NAFB has listed the most common problems of the franchisee (or most common abuses of the franchisor). The problems, according to the association, include:

> *constant pressure and control by the company to impose mandatory working hours and high sales quotas*
> *fear of loss of investment through cancellation or termination for minor contract infringements*
> *exhorbitant fees and royalties that are vastly out of proportion to sales volume*
> *directed company purchases of merchandise, supplies, and equipment that could be obtained elsewhere for less*
> *restrictions on selling price and private offerings, regardless of local competitive situations*

These complaints center on such basic questions as how much freedom of operation a franchisee must surrender when he joins a franchise organization and how the franchising organization's contract with his franchisee should be controlled. After all, most franchisees spend at least some of their time and effort building up their local businesses. But on the other hand, a franchising company could have a perfectly valid reason—violation of a local sanitation code, for instance—for pressuring a franchisee or even withdrawing the franchise.

Franchisees have, however, done by far the most complaining, for they tend to see themselves as powerless over the corporate franchisors. For example, forcing a franchisee to buy overpriced supplies and products amounts to a monopolistic practice regardless of a franchisor's desire to maintain a uniform image and a standardized food product. Recognizing the franchisor's motives in this area, a franchisee may still see the need for fairness (as, perhaps, defined by legislation).

In addition, franchisees have often complained of exorbitant franchise fees and royalties. Franchisors respond by pointing out that, as businessmen, they charge no more than the traffic will bear. Franchisors tend to be old-style entrepreneurs (as the next section illustrates) who much prefer the controls of the marketplace to legislative interference.

Present and proposed legislation may do much to make relations between franchisees and franchisors more cordial, and it may also eliminate some of the abuses that have accompanied the hasty, headlong growth of the fast-food franchising industry.

Three Case Histories of Successful Franchising

The two prototypical (and most famous) leaders in the fast-food franchising industry are McDonald's and Kentucky Fried Chicken. In about a decade, these two companies surpassed many older and more established foodservice organizations—notably Howard Johnson's. In 1970, Kentucky Fried Chicken was the third largest server of food in the country, and McDonald's was fourth. (The United States Army was first; the United States Department of Agriculture, second.)

Dinner with the Colonel

Kentucky Fried Chicken is the brainchild of the extraordinarily colorful Harland Sanders. Colonel Sanders (the rank is strictly honorary) had been, over the course of a long and robust life, a farmhand, soldier, blacksmith, salesman, fireman, and lawyer before he opened a combination restaurant-motel in Kentucky. When a new interstate highway bypassed his establishment, Sanders found himself once again out of business. At 65, the Colonel had nothing left but social security and a recipe for preparing fried chicken that utilized a pressure cooking principle and his own breading formula of "secret herbs and spices." Resourceful as ever, he hit upon the idea of convincing other restaurant owners to prepare their chicken his way under a franchise agreement that included the use of his own courtly persona.

In the early days of his franchise, Sanders would personally instruct the operators while spending the nights (according to legend) in the back seat of his car. He sold his immensely successful business for $2 million in 1964, but he stayed with the company in a highly visible public relations capacity.

No small portion of the Kentucky Fried Chicken success can be attributed to the grandfatherly image of the gracious Southern Colonel, attired in his immaculate white linen suit and the black string tie. But KFC has moved with the times much quicker than the Colonel's ante-bellum image would suggest. From selling chicken recipe franchises, the company went into selling total operation franchises with its chicken only the centerpiece in restaurants offering numerous other quickly prepared foods. In recent years, however, the company has been under different ownership and has experienced problems.

We Do It All for You

Ray Kroc is responsible for the empire now called McDonald's. A high school dropout, Kroc played piano with traveling bands and later sold real estate in Florida and paper products in the Midwest. Then, in 1937, he went into business for himself, as the head of a small Chicago company that distributed machines that mixed milkshakes five at a time.

In 1954, still a malted milk machine distributor, Kroc noted with some surprise that a small restaurant in San Bernadino, California, had ordered eight of his machines—by far his largest single order to date. Intrigued, Kroc visited the restaurant, run by Mac and Dick McDonald, and found people waiting in line, clamoring for the McDonald's fifteen-cent hamburgers. In fact, the two brothers sold only three items: milkshakes, malteds, and fifteen-cent hamburgers.

Kroc hung around observing the McDonald operation for three days. On the fourth, he offered to help them expand. They refused to expand but agreed, for a percentage of the profits, to let Kroc license other operations to use their system and their name. By 1961, the McDonald brothers had received $2,700,000 from Kroc and his associates.

Stressing a severely limited menu, quick service, cleanliness, and uniform quality, the McDonald's chain grew rapidly. Moreover, it assumed a strong orientation toward children because Kroc realized that (at least among his target customers) the children usually decide where a family will go when it eats out. Media researchers report that only Santa Claus is more universally known among American children than McDonald's trademark, the vapid clown Ronald. The American birth-rate is falling, though, and the percentage of children in the American population will probably continue to decrease. In response to these trends, McDonald's is already taking steps to appeal to older markets.

Kroc took other pains. For example, he established his Hamburger University which provides new franchisees with a nineteen-day course leading to a "bachelor of hamburgerology with a minor in french fries." The idea, of course, is to keep the product standardized and to inculcate an esprit de corps among the franchisees. And most of McDonald's franchisees have, indeed, profited handsomely from their investment. The company has been a number of people's vehicle to becoming millionaires.

McDonald's does, however, operate a little differently than most franchisors in that they remain independent of the food, equipment, and suppliers. They sell no products to their franchisees. Rather, more like licensors, they sell only their name and their methods. Moreover, they license a specific address (since they own the premises) rather than allocating regional territories. To keep responsible people in each of their units, McDonald's requires a franchisee to own and be actively involved in his business. This requirement also keeps "absentee" investors from acquiring several units.

Your Home away from Home

The outstanding franchising organization in the hospitality lodging field has been Holiday Inns. Holiday Inns were started in 1952 by Kemmons Wilson who was outraged by the cost of decent hotel accommodations in taking his family of seven on a trip from Memphis to Washington. In less than twenty years Holiday Inns grew to be the biggest hotel and restaurant chain in the world and is so far ahead of competitors it will retain its lead for the foreseeable future. After his trip to Washington, Wilson went back to Memphis and built four Holiday Inns in cooperation with a partner, Wallace Johnson, who, like Wilson, was a home builder. They named their first motel "Holiday Inn Hotel Court," after the old Bing Crosby movie. They charged $4 a night with children under 12 free. In 1954 the first Holiday Inn was franchised in Clarksdale, Mississippi, at an initial charge of $116.50.

The reasons for Holiday Inns success are many. First, Wilson and Johnson carefully analyzed what the current traveler wanted and supplied it. The hotels of the late 1940s were relatively expensive, often stuffy, and too formal for the casual transients. It took a great deal of effort to get from one's car to a room—a trip which usually took one through the lobby, upstairs, and down long corridors. The hotels were simply not oriented to the automobile, which after the Second World War had become the main means of transportation for millions. Holiday Inns solved these problems by providing low cost accommodations where people could carry their own bags from the car without a bellman. They also led in providing reservation systems that could schedule accommodations at any Holiday Inn (and later at a central reservation office for any other Holiday Inn). They early recognized the need for trained personnel at all levels, and their original training program was developed into Holiday Inn University which has some of the finest facilities for hospitality training in the world.

Next Holiday Inns established subsidiaries to supply furnishings and other products to both Holiday Inns and other facilities. They also set up a financing organization to help finance these purchases.

SUMMARY

Perhaps you have noticed several interesting similarities between Harland Sanders and Ray Kroc. Though both men had some foodservice experience, neither enjoyed outstanding success before starting a fran-

chise operation. Both began franchising as older men (the Colonel in his sixties and Kroc in his fifties), and both had very limited financial resources to start. But more important, while both made a good deal of money for themselves, both saw to it from the beginning that their associates also made money.

Their success rested on specialty items prepared under rigorous quality control standards. Both operations stressed cleanliness and a more or less efficient systems approach to service. And to begin with, both offered a severely limited menu.

In both McDonald's and KFC, the limited menu and the specialized equipment originally translated into space economies in both the preparation and service areas. In addition, small seats and only a few booths attract the transient quick-eater more than the sit-down diner. And finally, both systems permit the use of largely untrained help—and a minimum of help, at that, compared to customer volume.

Though a somewhat different type of operation, Holiday Inns is also a prototypical modern hospitality franchise: it is, to begin with, predicated on the automobile and on the casual, time-saving lifestyle associated with it. Too, Holiday Inns features standardization, tight control, and economies that both cut expenses and streamline the business.

And so these descriptions of McDonald's and Kentucky Fried Chicken, and Holiday Inns provide neat summaries of how the ideal franchise operation should work. No doubt, franchising continues to present opportunities for success, especially for people who long to go into business for themselves. But as the franchising business continues to expand, it will get more complicated and more expensive to enter. It will also become increasingly important to join an organization that has a strong public image, proven operating procedures, and the foresight to adapt to changing tastes in food and lodging. Operation has changed considerably in most chains since their conception, and even more change will come in the future.

IMPORTANT TERMS

Having studied this chapter, you should be familiar with the following terms:

franchise

franchisor

franchisee

multiple franchise

turn key operation

REVIEW QUESTIONS

14-1. Why did restaurant franchises dramatically increase in the 1960s?

14-2. Discuss the advantages of franchising to the franchisee.

14-3. Discuss the advantages of franchising to the franchisor.

14-4. What are the outlooks for franchising in the immediate future?

14-5. What problems can arise between the franchisor and the franchisee?

14-6. What elements did McDonalds originally stress? Why?

14-7. How will the typical franchise customers probably change in the future?

14-8. Cite several reasons for the early success of the Holiday Inns.

Glossary

AFL   The American Federation of Labor. An organization founded in 1881 whose main interest was unionization for higher wages and improved working conditions. It has since merged with the CIO.

Accident Incidence Rate

$$\text{AIR} = \frac{(\text{Number of illness or injuries}) \times 200{,}000}{\text{Employee hours worked}}$$

Acid Test   A liquidity ratio determined by dividing the sum of cash, accounts receivable, and marketable securities by current liabilities; also known as the *quick ratio*.

Accounting   A system of keeping financial records.

Accrual Accounting includes income that is yet to be received (*accounts receivable*) and expenses or costs yet to be paid for (*accounts payable*).

Financial Accounting reports financial information about an organization to the outside world. Financial accounting is primarily concerned with financial resources and profits of the enterprise.

Management Accounting produces information specifically to help management conduct the enterprise. Budgets and cost reports are two products of management accounting.

Tax Accounting is a specialized type of accounting that provides information to prepare tax returns.

Add-On Interest Rate   The amount of interest added on to the principal of a loan. This amount is divided by the number of payments to determine the amount of each payment.

Ad Hoc Decision A decision made day-to-day, on the spot; also called an *executive decision.*

Administrative Decision The translation of policies into a general course of action.

Advertising The purchase of space, time, or printed matter to increase sales.

Age Discrimination in Employment Act The federal law promoting the employment of the older worker, emphasizing ability rather than age. It prohibits arbitrary age discrimination in employment.

Agency Shop An arrangement permitting a labor union to compel workers, including non-union workers, to pay the equivalent of union dues.

All-Risk Insurance Coverage Coverage for all perils except those specifically excluded in the policy.

Arbitration In union-management negotiations, the use of a neutral third party to decide issues that labor and management cannot resolve between themselves.

Average Check The average amount of dollars spent by each customer. Average check can be calculated by estimating the number of items each customer will consume, then multiplying that figure by the appropriate selling price of the items, or by dividing sales by number of customers.

Average Sales The amount of dollar sales expected in a specified period. For a restaurant dinner, average sales equals the product of three numbers: the number of seats, the seat turnover, and the average check.

Btu British thermal unit. The amount of heat required to raise the temperature of one pound of water by one degree Fahrenheit.

Bailment The temporary placement of one individual's personal property in the custody of another person; see also *Gratuitous Bailment.*

Balance Sheet An accounting statement showing an operation's assets, liabilities, and equity as of a certain date.

Behaviorist Approach to Organization   In the study of organized groups, emphasis on the individuals and groups involved rather than the work to be done.

Biomass   The use of organic wastes as an energy source.

Bond   Long-term promisory notes issued for a specific denomination, with a definite maturity date when they must be repaid, and a specific interest rate to be paid the bondholder.

Branding   The image an operation wants to project.

Budget   A plan that shows how an operation expects to perform during a specified period.

Business Interruption Insurance   Coverage for expenses such as taxes, financing costs, and payroll of key employees should normal business income be disrupted.

CIO   The Congress of Industrial Organizations. A major American labor organization now merged with the AFL.

Capital   The general financial position of a firm, especially the equity and long-term debt.

Capital Budget   A budget that forecasts asset expenditures to be devoted to long-term equipment and facilities.

Capital Financing   The long-term debt and financing of an enterprise.

Capital Gains   Profits realized from increases in market value of any assets not part of the owner's stock in trade or not regularly offered for sale.

Capitalism   The free enterprise system, involving private property and a free market.

Captive Foodservice Operation   An operation whose patrons have little choice but to eat at the establishment. Schools, hospitals, and prisons are examples of captive foodservice operations.

Cash Budget   A budget that projects the inflow and outflow of cash and the resulting cash position.

Cash Flow   Profit plus depreciation.

Cash Flow Analysis   An analysis that determines where the money comes from and where it goes.

Centralization   The concentration of responsibility, authority, and decision-making power in the upper hierarchy or in one area of the enterprise.

Chain of Command   A principle of traditional organization. According to this principle, every organization should have a top authority together with a clear line of authority from that top to each person in the organization; also called the *scalar principle*.

Check Off   A system that adds to union security by requiring an employer to deduct union dues from the employee's wages and to turn those deductions over to the union.

Civil Rights Act of 1964   A federal law that prohibits discrimination on the basis of race, color, religion, sex, or national origin.

Class A Fire   A fire involving ordinary combustibles such as wood, paper, or textiles.

Class B Fire   A fire involving flammable liquids and gases such as gasoline, oil, grease, or paint.

Class C Fire   A fire involving energized electrical equipment.

Classical Management Science   The management theory of Henri Fayol claiming that common "threads" or principles exist in the management of any endeavor.

Classical Scientific Management   Principles of management and increased productivity developed by Frederick Winslow Taylor.

Classical Theory of Organization   An approach to the study of organization that focuses on enterprise structure and work allocation.

Closed Shop   A hiring policy that requires a worker to be a union member before applying for a job. Closed shops are illegal under the Taft-Hartley Act.

Closed System for Convenience Foods A system that makes and uses its own convenience foods.

Collateral Specific assets offered as a pledge or security for debt.

Collective Bargaining The determination of working conditions by bargaining and agreement between an employer and employees.

Commercial Paper Credit instruments that circulate freely; also known as *negotiable instruments*.

Commodity Departmentation Organization based on the commodity, product, or service produced.

Common Law Law evolved from custom and usage, ultimately enunciated in court decisions.

Compensating Balance A condition of a loan stipulated by the bank that requires a certain percentage of the loan be kept on deposit. A compensating balance is also used to cover expenses involved in a checking account.

Consideration Something of value that must be given for the fulfillment of a contract.

Contract An agreement between two competent parties, over legal subject matter, that has consideration provided, is made in clear language, and results in the acceptance of the offer.

Contract Assignment The transfer by a simple contract of rights held by a person to a third party.

Controllable Expenses Expenses over which the management has a degree of control. Taxes and insurance are examples of noncontrollable expenses.

Controller The financial officer who manages the accounting, auditing, budgeting and statistical work of an enterprise. The controller often manages internal funds.

Corporation A business organization that is an artificial entity, created by law and owned by stockholders.

Cost Center An operation to which costs and profits can be attributed.

Craft Union A union for all workers of the same trade.

Current Ratio A liquidity ratio determined by dividing current liabilities into current assets. This ratio provides a measure of the ability to pay short-term obligations.

Debenture A long-term debt instrument not secured by any mortgage on any specific asset.

Debt Financing The use of borrowed funds as financing.

Decentralization The placement of authority and responsibility at lower levels of an organization.

Deferred Productivity Motivation Plan An employer's incentive tool in which a fund is set up and contributions are credited to an employee's account. Payments from the fund are deferred until retirement, disability, or death.

Degree Days A measurement of energy need in terms of energy use required by outdoor temperature.

Cooling Degree Day measures the need for air conditioning. It is calculated by subtracting 65 degrees Fahrenheit from the outdoor mean daily temperature.

Heating Degree Day measures the need to heat. It is calculated by determining the difference between outdoor mean daily temperature and 65 degrees Fahrenheit.

Delegation The distribution of authority and responsibility downward through an organization.

Delphi Technique The development of a general forecast by individual expert forecasts, revised by participants after reviewing other participant's forecasts.

Demographics The statistical study of human populations, with particular regard to density and distribution.

Depreciation The reduction in value of an asset through wear and tear or obsolescence.

Accelerated Depreciation means increasing the speed of an asset's depreciation cost to effect more depreciation in the early years of its lifetime and less in the later years.

Declining Balance Depreciation calculates depreciation by subtracting the percentage of depreciation from the previous year's depreciation balance.

Straight Line Depreciation calculates depreciation by subtracting any anticipated salvage value from the cost of the asset, then dividing that figure by the anticipated number of years of life.

Sum of the Digits Depreciation is a form of accelerated depreciation that uses the year of depreciation divided by the sum of the digits making up the depreciation life of the asset.

Direct Relationships
Relationships between a supervisor and subordinates that involve no intermediaries.

Discount Interest Rate
The amount of the interest subtracted from the principal when the money is transferred to the borrower.

Doctrine of Public Callings
The principle that no one is forced to engage in innkeeping but that those who choose to do so may be regulated for the public good.

Double Taxation
The payment of two taxes on corporate income, first when the corporation pays taxes on its earnings, and then, after the earnings are transferred to the shareholders in the form of dividends, when the shareholders pay taxes on the dividends received.

EER
The energy efficiency ratio. A measure of energy efficiency.

Ebb and Flow Theory
In the study of unions, the description of early increases and subsequent decreases in union membership due to economic conditions.

Economic Man Concept
A part of the traditional approach to management that stresses material benefits as the prime motivator.

Embezzlement
The fraudulent appropriation of property by a person to whom it has been entrusted.

English System of College Foodservice
The assumption by a college of responsibility for feeding its students as well as providing their academic instruction.

Executive Decision
See *Ad Hoc Decision.*

External Environment Conditions, circumstances, organizations, and individuals with which a system must interact and to which it must react.

External Management Environment Forces outside an operation that affect management. Included are general economic levels, political conditions, and cultural and social changes.

Internal Environment Conditions within an operation that interact with the operation and to which the operation must react. This includes employee morale, informal work groups, and working conditions.

Internal Management Environment Forces within an operation that can affect management, including time available, costs, geographic distance, and personnel.

Equal Employment Opportunity Commission A federal agency established to enforce Title VII of the Civil Rights Act.

Equilibrium A concern of modern management theory, that the effectiveness of an organization depends on its ability to inspire cooperation in employees and avoid conflict.

Exception Principle An aspect of the principle of delegation. According to this principle, recurring decisions are handled in a routine, specified manner, and only unusual ones are referred upward for appropriate action.

External Theft The theft of an operation's property by a customer rather than by employees.

Extrapolation The projection of past trends into the future or the inference of unknown data from known data.

Fair Labor Standards Act of 1938 Legislation that sets a minimum wage, maximum hours, an overtime pay scale, equal pay, and child labor standards for employment.

Fast-Food Operations A noncaptive foodservice operation offering a limited number of menu items which can be prepared, served, and consumed quickly.

Feasibility Study The analysis of potential volume and profitability or feasibility of a proposed operation.

Feedback The element of a system that signals a need for adjustments or exchanges in the input and subsystems.

Fellow Servant Doctrine The principle that, should a worker be injured because of the actions of another worker, any suit would be against the other worker.

Fidelity Bonds A coverage designed to protect against loss by employee theft.

Finger Foods Foods readily carried and consumed anywhere, to be eaten without silverware.

Fire Insurance Insurance coverage for loss due to fire.

Fire Triangle The elements necessary to start and maintain combustion: heat, oxygen, and fuel.

First Mortgage A mortgage whose holder (lender) has first call on the property security in case of default.

Flat Hierarchy An organization with few levels between lower employees and top management; also known as *flat organization*.

Flat Organization See *Flat Hierarchy*.

Franchise A privilege or right granted to another. In hospitality operations, a franchise grants the right to use a name, methods, product, etc., in return for franchise fees.

Franchisee The person or organization acquiring the right to use the franchise obtained from the franchisor.

Franchisor The person or company selling the franchise.

Functional Organization The arrangement of personnel by the nature of their work. The accounting department and the personnel department are two examples of functional organization.

Function Book A record of use for various facilities of an operation by specific days.

Game Playing The attempt to maximize gain and minimize loss through anticipation of possible actions and counteractions of competitors.

Game Theory   A tool of operations research used to determine the maximum-gain or minimum-loss strategy to employ under specified conditions.

Guaranteed Mortgage   Money secured without a specific mortgage placed on one property. This type of mortgage is used by a hospitality chain when a general mortgage exists on various real assets of the chain.

German System of College Foodservice   The assumption of responsibility by a college for only academic instruction, with little or no foodservice provided for students.

Goal Orientation   Knowledge of what is meant to be accomplished; the measurement of performance against predetermined goals. Goal orientation should be a general characteristic of management.

Grains of Hardness   The number of grains of calcium or magnesium salts in a gallon of water.

Gratuitous Bailment   A hotel's limited responsibility to exercise reasonable care over the property of an absent guest; see also *Bailment*.

Ground Lease   The lease of land on which to erect an establishment; an alternate to the purchase of property.

Guarantee Policy   To protect the establishment handling functions, the agreement that a minimum payment for a function will be made if fewer patrons than promised attend.

Hard Water   Water that contains excessive calcium and magnesium salts.

Heimlich Maneuver   Called the "hug of life," a physical maneuver used to unblock the windpipe of a choking person.

Hierarchy of Human Needs   Abraham Maslow's theory that an individual has a scale of needs and that the higher needs do not become pressing until the lower ones have been satisfied.

Homogeneous Assignment   A form of specialization that either assigns an employee to one job or limits the employee to closely related tasks.

Horsepower The effect of horses lifting 33,000 foot-pounds in one minute. One horse-power equals 746 watts or 2545 Btu's per hour.

Implicit Warranty An understood though not openly expressed assurance that products are fit for the purposes intended.

Income Statement An accounting statement showing income, expenses, and the resulting profits or losses over a specified period; also called a *profit and loss statement*.

Indenture A formal agreement between the issuer of a security and the holders that defines the different facets of the particular obligation.

Indirect Relationships Relationships between subordinates rather than between subordinates and supervisors.

Ingredient Room An area where food is prepared for cooking before being sent to the kitchen production area.

Input The resources available to a system. These can include men (personnel), machines, methods, money, markets, and materials.

Insurance Broker A representative of the insurer who helps the client secure insurance.

Lloyd's Groups Insurance Companies are insurance companies composed of groups of individual underwriters who write insurance for a profit. Lloyd's Groups specialize in unusual insurance risks.

Mutual Insurance Companies are insurance companies owned by their policyholders and chartered as nonprofit institutions.

Reciprocal Insurance Companies are insurance companies composed of cooperatively organized insurers that theoretically offer insurance at cost.

Stock Insurance Companies are insurance companies that are also profit-making corporations chartered in various states.

Internal Control A business' plan of organization and the coordinate measures adopted to safeguard its assets, check the accuracy and reliability of its accounting data, promote operational efficiency, and encourage adherence to prescribed management policies.

Internal Funds   Funds or income coming from within the operation, such as depreciation and retained earnings.

Internal Theft   The theft of an operation's property by employees of the operation.

Investment Tax Credit   A tax incentive that provides a direct tax credit of up to ten percent of a qualified investment.

Iron Law of Wages   The belief that wages rise only slightly above subsistence level.

Job Analysis   The description and specifications of a job.

Job Descriptions   A statement of what a job entails: duties, responsibilities, compensation, supervision, uniforms, hours, and any other pertinent information.

Job Rotation   An application of organizational behavior principles in management through the switching of jobs to eliminate monotony and boredom.

Job Specifications   A list of requirements necessary for each job.

Junior Mortgage   A mortgage behind or junior to another in its claim on the collateral assets in case of default.

Jurisdictional Strikes   Strikes that result from disagreement among unions about authority over the workers or prerogative in job assignment.

KWh   Kilowatt-hour. The measure of electrical energy consumed over a specified period.

Knights of Labor   A labor movement that sought to replace a competitive society with one whose workers would share in the wealth they created.

Labor Budget   A budget that shows the amount of personnel required during a certain period. This can be expressed in labor time and in dollars.

Labor Management Reporting and Disclosure Act of 1959   A law that protects the rights of union members, and provides for the filing of reports describing the organizational, financial, and business dealings of labor unions, their officers and employees, certain employers, labor relations consultants, and union trusteeships.

Legitimate Power The power conferred by higher management on a position; also called the *power of authority*.

Leverage See *Trading on Equity*.

Line Organization The arrangement of jobs and personnel to fulfill the functions required by the organization's goals. Compare to *Staff Organization*.

Limited Partner A person who only invests money in a partnership and cannot be active in it or have his name used with it. The limit of loss is the amount of that person's investment.

Linear Programming A tool of operations research, using a mathematical approach, and often computers, to determine the best use of resources.

Liquidity The conversion of assets into cash or the possession of enough money on hand to pay debts as they become due.

Lumen A measure of lighting energy.

Management The accomplishment of an organization's goals using the resources available.

Management Functions Actions common to all management endeavors. These include: planning, organizing, staffing, directing, coordinating, controlling, communicating, budgeting, decision-making, representing, and innovating.

Management Resources The six basic resources that can be used by management to achieve its goals: men (personnel), money, materials, methods, machinery, and markets.

Market Strategy A plan for solving market problems and providing continuous demand for operations, products, or services.

Marketing Those business activities involved in the flow of goods and services from the producers to customers.

Marketing Mix The combination of activities and elements used to bring in customers. These include merchandising strategy, pricing, brand name, channels of distribution, personnel selling, advertising, promotion, and service.

Marketing Segmentation Definite customer groups with definable needs and interests. A market segment must be definable, sizeable, and available.

Marketing Variables

Demographic Variables include population variables such as age, sex, family size, income level, and occupation. They are used to determine the size of the segment, to size up the competition for these segments, and to estimate the value of these segments.

Geographic Variables include region, climate, and population density characteristics of a market segment.

Psychographic Variables refer to such aspects as life style, buying motives, product knowledge, and intended product use.

Mechanistic Approach to Organization

In the study of organizations, the strong reliance on rules, operating regulations, and formal procedures; also called the *traditional approach to organization.*

Mental Revolution

Frederick Winslow Taylor's goal of employees who would voluntarily give their best efforts for the business. Taylor asserted that after management would then share the increased profits with its workers, much industrial strife would be eliminated.

Model Making

A tool of operations research that attempts to represent the real world with a mathematical formula or model.

Mortgage Bond

A bond secured by real property or real estate.

Multiple Line Coverage

A number of different types of coverage on one kind of risk, covered by one policy

Multiple Franchise

More than one unit of a franchise granted to one franchisee.

Mrs. Murphy's Clause

A clause in the Civil Rights Act of 1964 that exempts establishments of less than five rooms, whose premises are occupied by the proprietor, from coverage in the Act.

National Labor Relations Act

A law that guarantees the right of workers to organize and to bargain collectively with their employers, or to refrain from all such activity; also known as the *Wagner Act.*

Negotiable Instruments

See *Commercial Paper.*

Noncash Cost

An expense for which no money is directly paid out. Depreciation is a kind of noncash cost.

OSHA Occupational Safety and Health Administration, whose purpose is to assure safe and healthful working conditions and to preserve our human resources.

Open Shop A working situation in which the worker is not required to be a union member or join a union to keep a job.

Open System for Convenience Foods A system that uses convenience foods purchased outside the system itself.

Operating Budget Revenue and expense projections for an operation or suboperation.

Operating Costs Costs, usually variable, involved in running an enterprise. Operating costs do not normally include fixed or general overhead costs.

Operating Profit The profit from operating before deduction of fixed costs, often the best figure by which to judge a manager's performance.

Operating Ratio A comparison of profit to sales. This ratio shows what percentage of each sales dollar is returned in profit.

Operations Research The use of quantitative and scientific bases for decision-making in management; also called *quantitative common sense, mathematical decision-making,* and *the scientific method approach.*

Organic Approach to Organization An approach that uses a minimum of formal rules and regulations; also called the *modern approach.*

Ordinary Income Income or profit from normal and regular operations of an enterprise (as opposed to capital gains).

Organizational Balance In a business, the relationship of such aspects as sizes of various departments, standardization or flexibility of procedures, and flexibility between centralization and decentralization.

Organization Chart The graphic representation of the relationship between jobs, describing the lines of authority, responsibility, and communication.

Output The end product or goals of a system.

Packaging   A product's wrapping. In the hospitality industry, the appearance, decor, and ambience of the establishment.

Paperhanger   One who passes bad checks or other false negotiable instruments.

Partnership   A form of business organization in which the business is owned by two or more partners.

Peak Demand Period   The time during which the greatest demand is placed on the electrical energy supply.

Policy Decision   A long-run decision in which a manager sets precedents or lays down general principles covering the conduct of the establishment.

Prima Facie   Literally, "at the first view." In legal practices, evidence on which liability is established or a case made.

Prime Costs   The major expenses in an operation. For a foodservice business, prime costs would comprise all food, beverage, and labor costs.

Prime Rate   The interest rate charged the most credit-worthy borrowers.

Product Analysis   An analysis showing all the services and facilities available including location, transportation, rates, size and state of physical premises, and inventory.

Productivity Bargaining   An employer-employee agreement, trading economic benefits from the employer for increased productivity from the employees.

Productivity Motivation   Incentives for increasing employee productivity.

Pro Forma Statements   Statements using anticipated or forecasted figures.

Profit and Loss Statement   See *Income Statement.*

Profit Foregone   The profit that is lost by not using one alternative when another alternative is funded and implemented instead.

Progressive Tax Rates   Tax rates that increase proportional to increases in taxable income.

Promotion   An action to favor or encourage the use of a product.

Proprietorship   A form of business organization in which the business is owned by one person.

Public Relations   The relationship between the public and an operation or the light in which an operation is seen by the public.

Queuing Theory   Service that provides the most with the fewest facilities. Also called the *waiting line theory.*

Quick Ratio   See *Acid Test.*

R Value   A measure of insulation's resistance to heat transfer.

REIT   Real Estate Investment Trusts.

Ratio Analysis   Analyzing performance by using figures in ratio or percentage forms.

Res Ipsa Loquitur   Literally, "the thing speaks for itself." In law, obvious facts or evidence.

Return on Investment   A ratio, found by dividing profit by investment and showing the profitability of an investment.

Right to Work Laws   State laws prohibitting employers from entering into any agreement that requires a worker to join a union in order to hold or get a job.

SBA   Small Business Administration.

SOP   Standard Operating Procedures.

Satisficing   Decision-making based on maintaining equilibrium of an organization or "not rocking the boat."

Scalar Principle   See *Chain of Command.*

Scenario Approach   A forecasting method utilizing available facts to produce possible happenings in scenario form.

Scientific Method   A procedure for logically solving a problem or making a decision; see *operations research.*

Separate-but-Equal Doctrine A doctrine formerly used to enforce racial segregation, allowing separate facilities for different races if the facilities met equivalent standards.

Site Analysis A portion of a feasibility study which concentrates on the actual building site, including such considerations as location in terms of area, frontage, depth of property, lay of the land, local soil conditions, traffic patterns, and potential business.

Solvency Having more assets than liabilities.

Span of Control A principle of organization concerned with the number of subordinates one person can effectively supervise.

Specialization A principle of classical organization whose purpose is to increase productivity, make supervision easier, and produce better control.

Staff Organization See *Line Organization.*

Staff Position A position that provides advice and counsel. A staff position does not normally have direct operations responsibility.

Standard Costs A management accounting procedure that pre-costs items in advance and then compares them with actual costs.

Stare Decisis The practice of deciding legal cases according to precedents or past decisions.

Statutory Law Laws enacted by legislative assemblies.

Strategic Planning Long-term planning concerned with the overall objectives of an operation.

Subchapter S Corporation A provision made by Congress to allow small organizations the advantage of a corporate form of organization while avoiding double taxation on shareholders.

Subordinated Ground Lease An agreement whereby the owner of land gives up priority for payment to another lender.

Subsystems The processes or components in a system necessary to change system resources into system goals or output.

Supervisory Departmentation The placement of employees under the supervision of a specified supervisor regardless of the nature of their duties.

Surety Bonds Insurance to guarantee that an insuree will carry out the specific work he was hired to do.

System A group of components working together toward a goal in the most efficient way possible.

Systems Approach The coordination of a system's components to achieve goals.

Tactical Planning Short-range planning that directs day-to-day operations.

Taft-Hartley Act A 1947 law that bans closed shops, provides procedures for dealing with strikes that imperil the national welfare, and provides for an independent federal conciliation service.

Target Markets Market segments selected for their attraction to the marketing offer.

Theory X A part of the analysis of traditional and modern organizational precepts. Theory X represents the traditional theory.

Theory Y A part of the analysis of traditional and modern organizational precepts. Theory Y represents the modern theory.

Therm A measurement of one hundred thousand Btu's in natural gas.

Ton of Refrigeration A measure of cooling and air conditioning capacity that refers to removal of 12,000 Btu's of heat per hour.

Tort A physical harm done to a person or property, caused by the act, the failure to act, or the general negligence of another person.

Total Incentive Systems See *Productivity Motivation*.

Trading on the Equity Using investment in an enterprise as a basis to borrow money to make more money. Also known as *leverage*.

Treasurer A member of a financial management team, often specifically responsible for the securing of external funds.

Turn Key Operation A unit that is ready to begin operations when it is turned over to the operator.

Type A Lunch A lunch served in elementary and secondary schools that aims at furnishing at least one third of the recommended daily dietary allowances.

Union Contracts— Clauses **Conditions of Recognition Clause** specifies the name of the employer and the name of the union the employer recognizes as the bargaining representative for his employees.

Coverage Clause describes the job categories included in the contract.

Grievance Clause specifies how grievances must be handled.

Management Rights Clause states the rights, responsibilities, and areas of action that management retains free from union questioning and interference.

Union Security Clause recognizes the union as the bargaining representative of the employees.

Union Shop An employment situation in which nonunion employees may be hired but must join the union within a specified time.

Unity of Command A management principle stating that one should take orders from only one supervisor.

Unity of Direction A management principle stating that activities having the same direction should have only one head and one plan.

Vampire System A system forcing foodservice workers to turn a percentage of their tips over to the headwaiter or to management.

Variable See *Marketing Variable*.

Wagner Act See *National Labor Relations Act*.

Waiting Line Theory See *Queuing Theory*.

Watt The unit of measure of electrical power.

Working Capital	The difference between current assets and current liabilities.
Workmen's Compensation Legislation	Laws based on the assumption that accidental injury is a cost of production to be borne by the employer. These benefits are financed through workmen's compensation taxes.
Yellow Dog Contract	Contracts which force an employee to agree not to join a union as a condition of employment.

Index